ILLIBERAL VANGUARD

ILLIBERAL VANGUARD

Populist Elitism in the United States and Russia

Alexandar Mihailovic

THE UNIVERSITY OF WISCONSIN PRESS

The University of Wisconsin Press
728 State Street, Suite 443
Madison, Wisconsin 53706
uwpress.wisc.edu

Gray's Inn House, 127 Clerkenwell Road
London EC1R 5DB, United Kingdom
eurospanbookstore.com

Printed in the United States of America
This book may be available in a digital edition.

Library of Congress Cataloging-in-Publication Data

Names: Mihailovic, Alexandar, author.
Title: Illiberal vanguard : populist elitism in the United States and Russia /
Alexandar Mihailovic.
Description: Madison, Wisconsin : The University of Wisconsin Press, [2023] |
Includes bibliographical references and index.
Identifiers: LCCN 2022018265 | ISBN 9780299340506 (hardcover)
Subjects: LCSH: Right-wing extremists—United States. | Right-wing extremists—
Russia (Federation) | Nationalism—United States. | Nationalism—Russia (Federation)
Classification: LCC HN90.R3 M428 2023 | DDC 320.540973—dc23/eng/20220923
LC record available at https://lccn.loc.gov/2022018265

Earlier versions of some of the material presented here were published in the
chapters "Hijacking Authority: Academic Neo-Aryanism and Internet Expertise"
and "'The Order of the Vanquished Dragon': The Performance of Archaistic
Homophobia by the Union of Orthodox Banner Bearers in Putin's Russia" in the
collection *Digital Media Strategies of the Far Right in Europe and the United States*,
edited by Patricia A. Simpson and Helga Druxes (Lexington Books, 2015), and in
the chapter "Whither the State? Steve Bannon, the Alt-Right, and Lenin's *State
and Revolution*" in the collection *The Future of Lenin: Power, Politics and Revolution
in the Twenty-First Century*, edited by Alla Ivanchikova and Robert R. MacLean
(SUNY Press, 2022).

Dedicated to the memory of Olivera Mihailović (1928–2021)
and Miloš Kontić (1930–2019)

Contents

Illustrations

Preface

Speaking from the Kremlin on 21 February 2022, Vladimir Putin made a series of declarations about elites and political authority that escaped notice amid the shock of his declaration of war against a sovereign Ukraine. The establishment of the Soviet Union in 1922 as a quasi-federalist entity was, in his view, the fruit of liberal democracy's poisoned tree. "Practice showed immediately that it was impossible to preserve or govern such a vast and complex territory on the amorphous principles that amounted to confederation." The result, almost a hundred years later, was that Ukrainians had "overturned monuments" to the Soviet political leader who had officially given them a republic of their own. As Putin described it, this expulsion of Lenin from the Ukrainian public square was done in the name of "de-communization," a process initiated by an ungrateful "progeny" (*potomki*) of Ukrainians. Those descendants of the Ukrainians who survived the bloody conflicts of the Ukrainian-Polish War and the Russian Civil War that followed the Revolution are the beneficiaries of Lenin's misguided largesse to local cultures and their elites, a policy that was regrettably made into law by the 1924 Soviet Constitution.

Putin punctuated his speech with taunts and jibes. "You want de-communization? Very well, this suits us just fine. But why stop halfway? We are ready to show what real de-communization would mean for Ukraine." Who is willing to fight against the nationalist and republic-based "local elites" who undermined the Soviet Union? Who will take up the good, if increasingly dormant, cause of what Putin called the "unitary state"? The only legitimate elite is the one that rises above calls for stewardship of specific "ethnic policies," and opposes "superficial and populist rhetoric [*populistskoi boltovni*: literally, 'populist babbling'] about democracy and a bright future." As he acidly put it: Ukrainians "condemn landmarks of history to oblivion, along with the names of state and military figures of the Russian empire without whose efforts modern Ukraine would not have many big cities or even access to the Black Sea."[1] What we need, he implied, is an elite that defines itself according to the imperial past, rather than a notional future.

How do Putin, his political elite, and their alt-right, "based," Christian, and white nationalist sympathizers in the United States frame this war? As a conflict over competing understandings of Christianity, false versus genuine forms of populism, and fundamental belief systems. If the Russian Federation is the last carrier of Christian values, as they see it, Western secularism and the churches in Ukraine who refuse to align themselves with Moscow have a great deal in common: they claim to be concerned about morality even as they undermine Christianity and the integrity of traditional values in favor of a cosmopolitan sensibility, and act at the behest of foreign organizations. Metropolitan Kirill, in his sermon on Forgiveness Sunday (6 March 2022), asserted that the Russian Orthodox Church opposes philosophical formations that demand quasi-religious oaths of allegiance, such as the "test" of a willingness to permit "Gay [Pride] Parades": "That test is both very simple and deeply horrible."[2] In his sermon the following week, he attributed the resistance of the Ukrainian Orthodox churches to the Russian Orthodox Church's advocacy of the invasion to local clerics' "fear of the Jews" (*radi strakha Iudeska*). This is a reference to the New Testament account of Joseph of Arimathea's concealment of his Christian identity when he petitions Pontius Pilate to let him remove Christ's body from the cross.[3]

As Kirill characterizes the war and the contemporary world in general, we live in a time of crisis and collapse brought about by global elites who represent, in the somewhat opaque formulation he derives from the Church Slavonic bible, neoliberal and globalist interests that advocate for a marketplace of identities and desires. They are not necessarily Jewish. Except that in some cases, as Kirill insinuates about Ukraine and its relations with the larger world at this moment, when they are.

The war in Ukraine has provoked the question of what is, and what isn't, a legitimate elite. The acolytes of populist elitism have always been open about who they are. They are people who possess the gift of bodying forth into language the feelings of the common folk. They are defined by singularity and by a zeal for something we can provisionally call "first-person oneness"—a seamlessly fused "us"—versus a shadowy multitude of "them," comprising unknowable and frightening strangers, usurpers, and trespassers. The editor of the *American Conservative*, Helen Andrews, has taken up a range of provocative causes since 2020, from justifying the territorial expansion of the Russian Federation to mourning the end of legislated racial separatism in South Africa, Zimbabwe, and the Jim Crow South. Her columns and tweets make her preoccupation with unitary identity, at the expense of the plural or multifaceted, quite clear. Posting to Twitter more than two months after the beginning of the Russian invasion, she wrote: "The rainbow LGBTQ flag is more legally protected than the American flag, if you can be prosecuted for disrespecting it, if our embassies fly it overseas, then which one is really the flag of the regime?"[4] The Catholic traditionalist academic Patrick Deneen puts the same concern about the perils of liberal pluralism another way: "The fervency of the left opposition to Russia's invasion is driven by a religious zeal, because Russia is a civilizational opponent to [the] Gnostic universalism" that will discard "Ukraine's blue and yellow for a rainbow flag," betraying "the Ukrainian churches in whose crypts its people are sheltering."[5]

On the face of it, the term "populist elitism" seems self-nullifying, a logical impossibility. It is the purpose of the present book to uncover and grapple with the worldview of populist elitism. It is both a distinct ideology and the legacy of empires—the empire (with its "multipolar" global map) being the sole plurality that populist elitism respects. Populist elitists regard themselves as one, rather than many: as the genuine elite, rather than the various contrived ethnic, sexual, or nonwhite elites, or the diabolically mutating elites of Silicon Valley. The populist elite is leader and follower, whisperer and listener, folded into one. They are anti-elitist critics of expert opinion who, like the Russian Orthodox Church in 2022 and the US evangelical groups that supported Hobby Lobby's suit against Obamacare, provoke into existence an "unstable hierarchy of values" that then necessitates a practice of absolute submission to a single spiritual authority.[6]

Populist elitists see themselves as united even in the face of differences among themselves. For them, it is vital to play the roles of cultural warriors conferring around an Arthurian round table, to sideline their squabbles and minor disagreements for the sake of the cause (sometimes the "lost cause"). Most importantly, as Putin hinted, the adherents to this worldview want to restore a unitary rather than a disaggregated state. The singular state is the only institution that can stand against the nightmare of modernity—what the American neo-Nazi Richard Spencer calls "this multicultural mess."[7] As we see in the war that continues to unfold with frightening unpredictability in Ukraine, political imaginaries of purity and oneness have real-life consequences.

Illiberal Vanguard

Introduction

The Neoglobalism of the American and Russian Far-Right Intelligentsia

For many citizens at various points of the political spectrum in the United States and the Russian Federation, the new year of 2021 seemed to inaugurate a winter of discontent. Among the many incongruously comical moments of the January 6 insurrection in Washington, DC, one stands out for its revelation of a surprising anxiety about the chain of command. At 3:22 p.m. the rioters breached the Senate chamber in the Capitol building. A retired Air Force lieutenant colonel named Larry Rendell Brock Jr. insisted that the premises be treated with respect, yelling "no!" and "do not take anything" to a flak-jacketed man who gleefully called out from an upper level: "Take everything! Take all that shit!" In Luke Mogelson's video and written account, the latter man, a young member of Nicholas Fuentes's America First movement, proceeded to sit in "the leather chair recently occupied by the Vice-President," while an "America Firster filmed him extemporizing a speech: 'Donald Trump is the emperor of the United States.'" In response to his inappropriately Napoleonic statement, another rioter with "a thick Southern drawl" remonstrated, "We're a democracy." The man in Mike Pence's seat shot back: "Bro, we just broke into the Capitol. What are you talking about?"

It seems that breaching the Senate chamber was not the triumphant moment that many of the insurrectionists expected. Ideological divides quickly opened among the rioters, even as they fought for their ill-defined cause. The tension and ambivalence of the moment was broken by the entrance of Jacob Chansley, the animal-pelted and Viking-horned Arizonan who dubbed himself the QAnon Shaman. Chansley portentously read aloud a QAnon-inflected version of the Lord's Prayer that he called a "message" of warning to the "tyrants, communists, and globalists," after which he posed and mugged for photographs on the Senate dais. A Capitol police officer approached and asked Chansley to move along: "Now that you've done that, can I get you guys to walk out of this room, please?" In Mogelson's account, Chansley's immediate response seemed respectful, if not cowed:

> "Yes, sir," Chansley said. He stood up and took a step, but then stopped. Leaning his spear against the Vice-President's desk, he found a pen and wrote something on a sheet of paper.
>
> "I feel like you're pushing the line," the officer said.
>
> Chansley ignored him. After he had set down the pen, I went behind the desk. Over a roll-call list of senators' names, the Q Shaman had scrawled, "ITS ONLY A MATTER OF TIME / JUSTICE IS COMING!"

In the end, the anticipation of an apocalyptic moment seemed to neutralize disagreements among the insurrectionists. As Nicholas Fuentes of America First put it outside the Capitol building: "It is the American people, and our leader, Donald Trump, against everybody else in this country and this world." Standing on the Capitol steps while shrewdly refusing to enter the building itself with the other members of his group, Fuentes railed against the constitutional checks and balances that made the transfer of presidential power possible. He concluded: "Make no mistake about it—the system is our enemy."[1]

By the time Fuentes appeared in front of the Capitol, it was already quite clear that Trump would not be arriving to give the protesters succor and support. Outfitted in a blue blazer and red tie that evoked Trump's favored politically symbolic mode of dress— otherwise stodgy business attire, with a tie flamboyantly signaling identification with the "red" states—Fuentes escalated his emulation of Trump simply by moving no further. Within this world of hierarchical political beliefs, it is understood that leaders issue marching orders, while followers move to the front lines. Throughout that day, one had the sense that a particular set of assumptions about who had the right to commit acts of violent disruption was powerfully at work. The insurrectionists were fixated on roles, ranks, and a mythic—as opposed to stubbornly ambiguous—national history. To a striking degree, they bore out the observation of the French sociologist François Cusset two years earlier that "the festive and fictional generalization of violence at the heart of American pop culture is what finally depoliticized and dehistoricized social violence," through "scopic or fetishistic" acts of "impulsive compensation" that drew on the modal properties of the online gaming experience.[2]

In Russia that month, a different kind of conflict was playing out. On 17 January Alexei Navalny, the opposition political activist and putative presidential candidate for Russia's Future Party, was returning to Moscow from Germany, where he had been recovering from an attempt on his life by poisoning. Navalny was arrested as soon as he set foot on Russian soil. The country that the American neo-Nazi Richard Spencer declared "our friend" at the deadly "Unite the Right" rally on 12 August 2017, in Charlottesville, Virginia, was intent on barring Navalny's participation in the political process. In St. Petersburg on the weekend of 30–31 January, a violent confrontation between the police and pro-Navalny protesters resulted in the arrest of more than seven hundred people: quite a contrast to the intermittent solicitude between the American insurrectionists and some of the Capitol police. An encounter on Pionerskaya Square in St. Petersburg sheds light on the enmity between representatives of authority and their opponents:

> Riot police in helmets and full combat gear arrived at the same time as the first protesters. "What a fuss," one of the officers observed, while climbing out of a truck. The police marched toward the theater and stood opposite the protesters, who [were] between 200 and 300 people at the time. The protesters held signs saying: "Russia will be free because Alyoshka [Navalny] is with you," "I am tired of counting your billions," and "Russia is in the hands of fascists." Protesters holding signs were the first to be detained.
>
> "What, are you going to hit me?" one of the protesters screamed as he was dragged away by his arms and legs.
>
> "Who needs you?" one of the officers retorted.
>
> As more people gathered near the theater, the police response grew harsher. People were dragged from among the demonstrators and journalists were knocked down. Some people fell in the muddy snow and crawled away. Members of the crowd shouted, "We are not afraid!" And they threw snowballs.
>
> At one point, a cluster of protesters stood in front of the police line and called out, "Why are you hitting us? We just want Russia to be better! Your mothers live on 10,000 rubles [about $132] a month, you are satisfied with this?" The riot police didn't reply. Behind their fogged-up visors, you could see their stern young faces.[3]

The mutual hostility and contempt between law enforcement and protesters in Russia—many of them belonging to the same generation of twenty-somethings—was resonant and clear. Typical of the exchanges that day was one between the journalist Oleg Dilimbetov from the newspaper *Kommerant* and a member of OMON, the special branch of the National Guard, which has existed since Soviet times. Dilimbetov pointed to the light blue sleeve of his jacket, which indicated that he was a member of the press, telling the guardsman that he was working, not protesting. The guardsman answered, "I'm the one working here, but you . . . you're just stirring shit."[4] The arrest of the flamboyant rapper Oxxxi-miron at the Pionerskaya Square demonstration threatened to further inflame the demonstrators. A chain of shielded police pushed them in the direction of Hay-market Square, where three metro lines converge, presumably with the goal of encouraging the crowd to ride away.[5]

The situational parallels between these confrontations, separated by three weeks and more than four thousand miles, throw into sharper relief the differ-ences in their communicative dynamics. Like the Russian protesters, the Amer-ican insurrectionists sought to find common ground with law enforcement, even as they were physically grappling with them. In the film report "Day of Rage: How Trump Supporters Took the U.S. Capitol Building," we see one insurrectionist yelling at the police to "stop following orders—you know we're right," just a few minutes before others breached the building. A few minutes later, as rioters pour in through the east entrance, we hear an individual from a group of surging Oath Keepers shout at a policeman: "We are one of you—you can't touch us!"[6]

There is much about these exchanges that is consistent with the Russian anti-Putin demonstrators' expressed sympathy with the police in St. Petersburg. Yet one difference in the beliefs and political assumptions that underlie those appeals stands out clearly. The Russian protesters attempted to coax out of the police an appreciation of human rights, whereas the insurrectionists verbalized what they saw as a shared group consciousness. Many of the January 6 rioters held on to a vision of themselves as fellow combatants with the outnumbered law enforcement officers who were attempting to hold them off. Typical of the protesters' vain rhetorical efforts to appeal to their opponents as members of an entity very much like a professional fraternity were a man who yelled, "Is this honoring your oath? Pushing patriots around?" and a woman dressed in a "Trump 2020" sweatshirt who shouted, "You should be on our side. 'We the peo-ple' means police, too."[7]

On 27 July 2021, Capitol Police officers Aquilino Gonell, Daniel Hodges, Michael Fanone, and Harry Dunn recalled for the House and Senate January 6 Commission various statements made by insurrectionists who considered them potential allies, fellow members of grassroots militias, or, failing that, traitors to their badge and country. "Are you my brother?" one man on the Capitol steps taunted Hodges, who realized that "they were trying to recruit me." Implying that no African American could be a police officer worthy of the badge, another rioter told Dunn to put his gun down, and that "we'll show you what kind of n—— you are." Gonell testified that several people in the crowd called the Capitol Police "traitors," and Fanone recalled that his shout "We have some injured officers here" seemed to "really piss them [the rioters] off": apparently they believed that those officers had betrayed their duty by not joining forces with them.[8]

The demonstrations in Russian cities that same month were less dramatic but ideologically starker, with opposing actors who seamlessly embodied irreconcilable value systems: dour and mouse-gray agents of state power versus a sea of eye-catching and witty picket signs and flags. The young members of the liberal intelligentsia and state security personnel were unambiguously set against each other, an opposition that stands in stark contrast to the confusion of the January 6 rioters about their relationship with the Capitol Police.

The Russian protesters recognized the chasm of beliefs separating them from the police and decided to look for common ground elsewhere, in the superficially depoliticized domain of everyday economics: making ends meet for themselves and their families, and a recognition of the morality of a living wage. In the videographic chronicle of January 6, instead of such bread-and-butter appeals, we hear something more abstract, if not metapolitical: appeals to the police as co-workers in the project of protecting the Republic, as opposed to what the insurrectionists regard as the anti-American ideal of "direct" democracy.[9] The insurrectionists saw themselves and their sympathizers among the police as enforcers and defenders, without the meretricious portfolio of being agents of the state. To them, true law enforcers are morally empowered vigilantes who set themselves against illegitimate institutions and assorted rank pretenders to political leadership. They saw themselves as what the historian Eric Hobsbawm calls "social bandits": figures whom "the lord and state regard as criminals, but who remain within peasant society, and are considered by their people as heroes, as champions," and "men to be admired, helped and supported."[10]

Journalists have taken note of the American right's highly distinctive understanding of law enforcement as autonomous from modern civil society and from state as well as local governmental oversight. The right-wing organization of local law enforcement known as the Constitutional Sheriffs and Peace Officers Association (CSPOA), founded by a former Arizona sheriff, Richard Mack, with the goal of "tak[ing] America back, County by County, State by State" from the anti-American policies of President Barack Obama, had, as one researcher puts it, clear "ideological roots in the Posse Comitatus, an organization founded on the West Coast as a vehicle for white supremacism and antisemitism."[11] The historian Ruth Ben-Ghiat has drawn attention to the peculiar appropriation of organized crime structures by unregulated militias at the local level in Italy during the Fascist period, notwithstanding Mussolini's own policy of suppressing Mafia families.[12] Idealized images of unaccountable enforcement and strongman or *caudillo* authoritarianism make for strange, if strikingly frequent, bedfellows in the statements of the insurrectionists both on and after January 6. In contrast, the roots of oppositional thinking in Russian culture have little to do with this kind of violent libertarianism. Distrustful of physical compulsion and lawlessness, Russian dissident movements, from the reign of Nicholas I (1825–56) to the present, have sought to oppose the tyrannical principles of *proizvol* (arbitrary dictatorial will) and *bespredel* (uncontrolled or unlawful domination of others), regarding them as the bane of democracy. But, by their own admission, the insurrectionists were not interested in democracy.

The similarities between the social-media-conscious and highly theatrical protest styles of the Russian left and the American right are also telling, however. That month both Russian progressives and American radical conservatives were drawing on the earlier aesthetic practices of leftist protest. In Russia, the demonstrations recalled the 2011 anti-Putin "Mink Revolution" activism in Moscow and the elaborately carnivalesque springtime student protests in Novosibirsk, called "monstrations," which continued until the invasion of Ukraine in 2022.[13] Events in Washington echoed the well-funded and AstroTurfed Tea Party protests against Barack Obama, which began shortly after his inauguration in 2009, with their vividly printed posters and picket signs depicting a malevolent Obama in Joker whiteface. In their scrupulous pre-event preparation, those public actions are highly reminiscent of the archly theatrical demonstrations organized by Abby Hoffman, Jerry Rubin, and the Youth International Party, or Yippies, notably during the 1968 Democratic National Convention protests in Chicago. At one street march in downtown Chicago, the Yippies and their supporters announced an actual pig named Pigasus, whom they called a viable alternative candidate for the Democratic presidential nomination. The following year, protesters paraded an enormous papier-mâché effigy of this satirical candidate in front of the courthouse where eight activists were held for conspiring to riot during the convention. Perhaps drawing on a memory of this physical representation of the bloat produced by entrenched power networks, early in 2009 the influential talk-radio pundit Rush Limbaugh referred to President Obama's proposed stimulus package for a national economy still reeling from the 2008 stock market collapse as "Porkulus." The bill, Limbaugh wrote, "stimulates [nothing] but the Democratic Party," and is designed to "repair the Democratic Party's power losses from the 1990s forward, and to cement the party's majority power for decades."[14] When a political vanguard launches a protest or a memorable quip, borrowing from the rhetorical playbook of your enemies may be perceived as scoring the most decisive victory over them.

Compared with the cosplaying (occasionally in Revolutionary-era attire) at the January 6 insurrection and the eye-catching and effervescent Occupy Wall Street protests staged in the heart of New York's financial district in the fall of

2011, recent protests by the loose, centrifugal Black Lives Matter (BLM), Antifa, and other leftist movements seem almost ascetic, exercises in tamping down the aesthetic and playful dimensions of public action. The time for the visually arresting and tactically frivolous poster art and Yippie-like street skits that characterized Occupy Wall Street has passed, perhaps because of a sober awareness of the urgent threat to working-class communities, LGBTQ people, and communities of color posed by emboldened Republican-dominated state legislatures, Trump-appointed lifetime judgeships, and redistricting boards.

When we consider the spectacle-oriented protests in the United States and the Russian Federation, one difference stands out: the inverse developmental trajectories of performative advocacy in the two countries. American protesters who sport that style now generally belong to the political right, whereas the Russian progressives are borrowing from the public action playbook of a native far right that emerged from the ruins of the devastated economy and political order in 1991. As Fabrizio Fenghi notes in *It Will Be Fun and Terrifying: Nationalism and Protest in Post-Soviet Russia* (2020), that style of theatricalized protest was especially characteristic of Eduard Limonov's openly fascist National Bolshevik Party (NBP) in the late nineties.

Drawing on an interview he conducted with a former *natsbol*, or NBP supporter, with (largely notional) street-fighting cred, Fenghi recounts one particular action that humiliated Yegor Gaidar, who at that time was eking out a somewhat sad career as a public speaker and apologist for neoliberal economics six years after ignominiously leaving the post of prime minister. "An important turning point in the political strategy of the NBP, [the interviewee] Dima explained, occurred in 1999, when a group of *natsboly* interrupted a speech by Yegor Gaidar, one of the architects of the controversial 'shock therapy'," which Gaidar helped implement at the urging of the American free-market economist Jeffrey Sachs. With other members of the so-called Washington consensus, Sachs believed that impulses toward a viable capitalism in post-Soviet Russia would emerge only when the country was repeatedly thrown into the bracingly cold waters of a radically deregulated economy. "When Gaidar made a predictable allusion to the united 'communist-fascist' threat looming over Russia, the *natsboly* stood up and started shouting the slogan 'This is how we will implement reforms: Stalin, Beria, Gulag!'" As Fenghi notes, the protest "created a scandal and received wide media coverage," thereby serving as a template for the party's subsequent practice of "attracting the attention of the mainstream media" through stage-stealing antics.[15] With their political theater, a handful of *natsboly* became the precursors of social-media "superusers," whom a recent report on cognitive warfare on the internet defined as "popular individuals who serve as an anchoring point for a lot of other individuals who have a much more limited social circle."[16] As the neo-Nazi Richard Spencer admits in Daniel Lombroso's documentary about the alt-right movement, *White Noise* (2020)—in what seems to have been a reverie about his work in the theater department during his college years—"I'm an artist before I'm a politician."[17]

In Spencer's unguarded statement and Dima's recollection of *natsboly* tactics, we glimpse the convergence between the performative styles and social views of the far right in both countries. For them, winning over an audience means dominating it in ways that reinforce their belief in natural hierarchies and in their right to rule. To be a superuser is to be a conqueror. In this vein of complementing seriousness of purpose with fey public statements about rhetorical strategies and goals, the NBP's own flamboyant Eduard Limonov once answered a Frenchman's question about what he does in Russia by quipping, "I'm getting ready to seize power [there]. I think the time is right."[18]

The Wild Style of the New-Right Elites

The new-right elites in the United States and the Russian Federation are highly preoccupied with the style and performance of their radical imperative. In *The Reactionary Mind: Conservatism from Edmund Burke to Donald Trump* (2018), Corey Robin counterintuitively argues that effective conservative movements have always been sensitive to a need for a certain "wildness and extravagance" in the presentation of their views in the public sphere.[19] "Far from yielding a knee-jerk defense of an unchanging old regime or a thoughtful traditionalism," Robin writes, "the reactionary imperative presses conservatism in two rather different directions: first, to a critique and reconfiguration of the old regime; and second, to an absorption" of not just the tactics, but even the ideas, "of the very revolution or reform it opposes."[20]

One figure of particular interest to Robin is the antirepublican French-Sardinian diplomat and political philosopher Joseph de Maistre (1753–1821). His observation that "if you deprive the world of the executioner all order will disappear with him" was arguably embodied in the gallows that a handful of protesters erected in front of the Capitol on January 6, to shouts of "Hang Mike Pence!"[21] De Maistre was the ambassador to Russia from the kingdom of Sardinia during the pivotal years of the aspirationally liberal reign of Tsar Alexander I and the Napoleonic War. He was a keen critic of Enlightenment values and an observer of what he understood as the catastrophes emerging from attempts to graft democratic principles onto traditional and monarchical forms of government. Among other aspects of the Russian social and political order, de Maistre admired the Table of Ranks instituted by Peter the Great for cementing trust in the state by allowing for meritocratic advancement through a professionalized hierarchy, thereby forestalling calls for systemic reform. Furthermore, in a very modern turn that anticipates the cynical moral calculus of modern totalitarian regimes, he also saw the institution of serfdom and the general mental vassalage encouraged by the system of Russian autocracy as instilling a respect for order and rank, and being fully compatible with a broad-based nationalist zeal.[22]

To a surprising degree, the general substance of de Maistre's positive assessment of the undemocratic practices of the Russian state has been adopted by present-day alt-right activists. More recently, their laudatory impressions have become more targeted than the crowd's "Russia is our friend!" battle cry at the Charlottesville "Unite the Right" rally, which they repeated eight months later at a demonstration in Charlotteville together with the slogan "the South will rise again!"[23] The January 6 insurrection was a call for the restoration of a lost, or tragically undermined, social order. De Maistre, who after 1789 waxed nostalgic for most of the structural features of the *ancien régime* that were destroyed by the French Revolution, would have fully sympathized with a revolutionary movement of that kind.

The ideological convergence with Russian culture that US alt-right figures now endorse—most recently Steve Bannon and Erik Prince, who at the beginning of the invasion of Ukraine lauded Russia for being a military juggernaut and defiantly "unwoke"—is not without its own history.[24] Russian and American understandings of racial identity are inseparable from Russian and American political doctrines of territorial expansion dating from the early nineteenth century. In his landmark *Democracy in America* (1831), Alexis de Tocqueville saw Russians and Anglo-Americans as possessing starkly contrastive systems of political values but argued presciently that both were "great nations of the earth [that] seem to be advancing toward the same destination from different starting points." He goes on to compare them in a way that draws attention to the possible conditions for their confluence of interests:

> Americans struggle against obstacles placed there by nature; Russians are in conflict with men. The former fights the wilderness and barbarity; the latter, civilization with all its weaponry: thus, American victories are achieved with the ploughshare, Russia with the soldier's sword.
>
> To achieve their aim, the former rely upon self-interest and allow free scope to the unguided strength and common sense of individuals.
>
> The latter focus the whole power of society upon a single man.
>
> The former deploy freedom as their main mode of action; the latter, slavish obedience.

> Their point of departure is different, their paths are diverse but each of them seems destined by some secret providential design to hold in their hands the fate of half the world at some date in the future.[25]

What Tocqueville notes as a negative quality of Russian political will, the adherence to "slavish obedience," is for de Maistre an unalloyed virtue. Yet even Tocqueville recognizes that the competing values of freedom and obedience are more ambiguous in their implementation than we might expect. Are there circumstances in which one person's freedom compels the submission of another? We may add that the abolition of servitude in both countries resulted in a mixed legacy of what the African American essayist and novelist James Baldwin scathingly called "quasi-freedom." During the Cold War, patriotic intellectuals in the United States and the Soviet Union often cast one another as adversaries in a fundamentally Manichaean conflict, with Russian traditionalist intellectuals viewing Americans as Protestant mercantile imperialists, and American ethnonationalists regarding Russians (whom they identified as the dominating ethnic identity in the Soviet Union) as a racial Other that was more "Asiatic" than European.

In the century and a half that followed Tocqueville's contemplation of American and Russian mentalities—which shared, in his view, a will to dominate and subdue their environment, be it the natural world or the world of men—the countries' shifting perceptions of each other often took the form of a mutual attraction and repulsion. I would argue that the hostility from the US side has significantly waned, with the result that the Russophobia that often hovered in the background of Cold War–era American critiques of Russian culture has largely faded and been displaced by a robust Russophilia among the alt-right and even mainstream conservatives. Long gone from the US right are the sentiments that General George S. Patton controversially voiced at the end of World War II: "The difficulty in understanding the Russian is that we do not take cognizance of the fact that he is not a European, but an Asiatic, and therefore thinks deviously. . . . In addition to his other Asiatic characteristics, the Russian has no regard for human life and is an all-out son of bitch, barbarian, and chronic drunk."[26] Patton's Russophobia was a variant of the colonialist frame of reference that informs Rudyard Kipling's 1898 poem "The Truce of the Bear," a text that articulates a long-standing loathing of Russia as a competitor in the British empire's attempts at stable territorial expansions into Afghanistan and Manchuria. "When he shows as seeking quarter, with paws like hands in prayer, / *That* is the time of peril—the time of the Truce of the Bear!" Patton himself adhered to a nostalgia for the chivalric ethic that he regarded as foreign to Russians; moreover, as the grandson of a Confederate general, he drew deeply from the political discourse that portrayed the Confederacy as a tragic yet noble lost cause that embodied the hallowed values of the West.[27] This racialist script has now been completely flipped: Russia is praised by US political and religious figures (such as the former Orange County congressman Dana Rohrabacher and the politically influential and pro-Trump evangelical leader Franklin Graham) as a theoretical bulwark against the ravages of political correctness and "woke totalitarianism." As one neo-Confederate alt-right blogger put it in 2020, "Russia may be the only country left on the entire planet that is willing to resist globohomo," possibly the "'last best hope' of mankind, or at least, the last refuge for traditionalists and conservatives [sic] Christians."[28] Far-right American nativists are hardly alone in this positive assessment: as Marine Le Pen, the head of France's Rassemblement National (National Rally Party) put it in 2014, the Russian president is a staunch defender of "the Christian heritage of European civilization."[29]

In this book, I devote particular attention to the mutual influence—the informational ebb and flow—between nationalist popular culture and populist academic writing. For very different reasons, the existence of an intellectual class has never been openly welcomed by radical traditionalists and conservative populists in the United States and Russia. New-right elites in the United States and the Russian Federation seek to correct this ambivalence about the need for a cognitive vanguard by making its interior life dramatically visible to those who support radically conservative causes, and by engaging in public behavior that renders their views almost comically explicit. When Russian feminists criticized the Russian Orthodox Church's antiabortion policies as endorsements of a twenty-first-century serfdom aimed at providing future human fodder for the military, the head of the fascist Liberal Democratic Party, Vladimir Zhirinovsky, suggested at a session of the Duma (the state parliament) on 21 June 2021 that women considering abortion should be paid to carry their pregnancies to term, with the understanding that the children would then be the exclusive property of the state.[30] Zhirinovsky, who died in 2022 but whose style of nationalist media provocation lives on in the broadcasts of Russian state television commentators such as Vladimir Solovyov and Olga Skabeyeva, showed himself to be a close student of the contrarian and puckish tactics of the Soviet and Russian left, as well as a deft appropriator of arguments that would seem to be irreconcilable with his worldview. In this instance, he signaled agreement with the St. Petersburg–based Russian feminist groups who in 2019 protested by wearing gas masks and bloodied maternity-ward smocks that exposed their chests while holding up signs with the slogans "Give Birth to Meat!" and "No to Violence toward Men Who Do Not Want to Serve in the Army!"[31]

The other significant aspect of Zhirinovsky's provocation is its avoidance of euphemisms, which makes it appealing to some and gives him a reputation for a certain kind of transactional or fleeting honesty—for "telling it like it is." This pose is common on the right. As a poster for the far-right National Democratic Party (NPD) in Germany put it, their candidate, running in a regional election in Saxony in 2014, said openly what other people only dare to think to themselves ("Ich sage, was Sie denken!").[32] Certainly, Zhirinovsky's bluff advocacy of modern-day chattel slavery is very much a part of the fascist tradition. As Jason Stanley writes, "In fascist ideology, all institutions, from the family to the business of the state," are run according to the principle that the authoritarian leader is both father and CEO.[33] The rightist elites who occupy the center of media attention in both countries believe in the power of the state as consisting of the abstraction "the people," rather than individuals with rights; they are also thoroughly caught up in an understanding of the state as a macrocosm of the traditional family, whose internal diversity needs to be respected, not as an ensemble of overlapping generations that have something to teach one another, but rather as a vertical chain of strictly demarcated roles.

While the vast majority of the pro-reform protesters in Russia from 2019 to the present are too young to have a living memory of the Soviet Union, their contrarian reflexes follow a through line of oppositional orientations that can be traced to the dissidents of the seventies and the eighties. In an interview with Radio Liberty about the pro-Navalny movement, the Russian political scientist and journalist Aleksei Makarkin notes that during the Soviet era the small number of actual political dissidents was considerably surpassed by the sympathy for their views among the general population. "People [in the Soviet Union] knew what the intelligentsia was saying and thinking in their kitchens," he observes. "Things that have changed now, have changed only in their externals [vneshne]," in the sense that people then could not openly express their support "out on the streets."[34]

Since the first half of the nineteenth century in Russia, the concept of an intellectual class, as well as the term "intelligentsia" itself, has been closely associated with progressive, if not radically leftist, causes, in what can be understood as a historiographic archetype. During the first quarter of the twentieth century, Russian Jewish intellectuals who visited the United States, such as Leo Trotsky, Emma Goldman, and the now less well known Alexander Berkman, were dismissed by nativist Americans as rootless cosmopolitans. At the same time, the unapologetically cerebral character of political discourse across the spectrum of Russian culture has often fascinated Anglo-American conservatives, to the point where they express a grudging respect, if not admiration, for even its more utopian acolytes. During the Cold War, anti-Soviet essayists from Eastern European countries, including Leszek Kołakowski and Vaclav Havel, often engaged in lively polemics with other expatriates who occupied the ideological center (most notably Isaiah Berlin). Kołakowski's own considerable influence upon critical discussions of the actual social orders and ideological inconsistencies of the East Bloc outlasted the Cold War and is explicitly acknowledged in *Koba the Dread: Laughter and the Twenty Million*, Martin Amis's controversial 2002 mediation on the murderous legacy of Joseph Stalin.

In much of the American right, Eastern Europe's contested experience with socialist activism and institutional communism has served as a point of departure for contemplating the creation of a vigorously conservative intelligentsia to push back against the orthodoxies of the left. In "2020 Is Tumbling toward 1917," a 2 October 2020 blog essay for the *American Conservative*, Helen Andrews observes with chagrin that during the late nineteenth century, "the robust tradition of intellectual conservatism that had existed in Russia since the time of Catherine the Great had been slowly eroded until it no longer existed." Nonetheless, Andrews takes note of one exception that testifies to the earlier dynamism of Russian conservative discourse, exemplified by Dostoevsky's "lively correspondence" with the "reactionary bureaucrat" Konstantin Pobedonostsev, in which he solicited the Holy Procurator's advice during the writing of *The Brothers Karamazov*.[35]

A Place at the Table: Intellectual Labor and the New Right

The activities of famous conservative thinkers of an earlier age, as filtered through the perceptions of Andrews and other pro-Trump pundits, are not as far as one might think from the impulses and goals of those who took part in the January 6 storming of the Capitol building. Mogelson describes one man on that day "frantically flipping through a three-ring binder on [Ted] Cruz's desk," muttering to himself as he searched for documentary evidence of malfeasance committed by government actors, while another nearby justified the search of Senate printed records, insisting that "Cruz would *want* us to do this, so I think we're good."[36] These searches for information are based on the premise that there is a place for a certain kind of intellectual inquiry on the right, even as facts are stubbornly wrestled into procrustean beds that will scarcely accommodate them. Such efforts at accommodation and reconciliation of inconsistencies in knowledge may, in fact, serve as a goad rather than an obstacle to intellectual activity, in a manner suggestive of medieval European astronomers' increasingly intricate and mathematically sophisticated schemes for mapping the movements of the stars and planets according to a geocentric understanding of the celestial bodies.

In one uncharacteristically aphoristic and seemingly stand-alone statement from the *Prison Notebooks*, Antonio Gramsci writes that "every individual, ultimately, carries on some form of intellectual activity; that is, he is a 'philosopher,' an artist, a man of taste [who] shares a conception of the world, has a conscious line of moral conduct, and therefore contributes to sustain a conception of the world or to modify it—that is, he helps generate new ways of thinking."[37] While the insurrectionists of January 6 may not have viewed themselves as intellectuals, they did see themselves as involved in a public spectacle of arbitration and in the exercise of critical judgment. Gramsci writes that "*the most widespread platitude* [emphasis in the original] about the Risorgimento is the repetition in various ways of the view that such a historical change was brought about through the merit of the cultural classes alone." And yet, he notes, "it is difficult to understand where the *merit* lies." As Gramsci explains, the sole merit of a "cultural class" is "to lead the popular masses." In the instance of the leadership of the movement for Italian nationhood, we can only speak of cultured class abdicating that responsibility, of "*demerit*, that is, of immaturity and inner weakness" (emphasis in the original).[38]

Many on the US right perceive the link to the mythic beginning of their nation as having been sabotaged by a series of policies that fatally (in their view) undermined the ethnonational identity of the United States, like multiple fractures inflicted over time on the same limb. Gramsci wrote that "all members of a political party should be regarded as intellectuals," by virtue of their dual function as those who "educate and lead."[39] The Capitol insurrection was an attempted reclamation of the Republic, imbued with a notionally Gramscian undertaking of educating the wider American public about a 'stolen' election, as well as leading by the personal example of broadcasting their violent participation through social media. For the rioters, the most notable of the traumas to the American sense of self were the Nationality Act of 1790, the post–Civil War passage of the 13th through 15th Amendments, and—most catastrophically— the Immigration and Nationality Act of 1965. Their sense of aggrievement about the emergence of self-appointed and failed vanguards or "elites" is very much at the center of Gramsci's critique of a political leadership class. In Mogelson's recording and written account, one Trump supporter who entered the building "insisted through a megaphone, 'We will *not* be denied.'" There was an unmistakable subtext as the mob, almost entirely white, shouted, "Whose house? *Our* house!"[40]

Gramsci's attempt to democratize the role of the intellectual by liberating it from the specifics of education and class is highly apt for understanding the impulse toward enhanced acumen and inquisitorial passion that is at the center of the far right's love of conspiracism in general, and QAnon in particular. The followers of QAnon have been extraordinarily deft in their practice of revision, reflecting a hermeneutical zeal in compensating for deflated expectations by reinterpreting the gnomic and obscure 8chan utterances of the online individual who calls themselves "Q," with the goal of shifting or evolving the narrative to adapt to changing informational circumstances. This impulse toward recalibration—arguably as old as the QAnon movement itself—was verbalized by the Comet Pizza shooter upon his arrest on 5 December 2016 in Washington, DC: "The intel on this wasn't 100 percent."[41] Well, if the intel is laced with fool's gold, our job is to extract the real thing from the slurry. For these supporters, intellection is hard work, with all the dignity that in earlier and more pragmatic ages, such as Reconstruction and the New Deal, was readily accorded to manual labor. The sentimentalized understanding of the moral superiority of "working with one's hands," like a farmer, tradesman, artisan, building contractor, or carpenter, is most often voiced by academic defenders of conservative populism, such as Patrick Deneen. It is largely absent from the self-images of most members of the alt-right and the traditional right in the United States. Parsing and synthesizing raw information is akin to writing a poem. The Russian Futurist Vladimir Mayakovsky's poem "A Talk with a Tax Collector"—a prickly engagement with governmental oversight that would be congenial to the more libertarian participants in the January 6 insurrection—likens composition to burrowing through "thousands of tons of verbal ore" [*tysiachi tonn / slovesnoi rudy*] for the sake of extracting the purified radium of the single right word.[42]

As someone who idiosyncratically understood the intoxication wrought by poetry as an access point to rational and even scientific knowledge, Mayakovsky's comparison of himself to Marie Curie is telling. The quest for knowledge—what he describes elsewhere in the poem as a "trip into the unknowable" [*ezda v neznaemoe*]—is as laborious as it is fraught with risk. Not surprisingly, the relentless suspicion that motivates this search for the *mot juste* renders the promise of that discovery into a continuously receding horizon: the border that separates what we know from what we don't know. In his landmark essay "The Paranoid Style in American Politics" (1965), Richard Hofstadter pays particularly close attention to the epistemological panic that underpins so much of what he terms "higher paranoid scholarship." This is evident most palpably in its "quality of pedantry":

> One of the impressive things about paranoid literature is precisely the elaborate concern with demonstration that it almost inevitably shows. One should not be misled by the fantastic conclusions that are so characteristic of this political style into imagining that it is not, so to speak, argued along factual lines. The very fantastic character of its conclusions leads to heroic strivings for "evidence" to prove that the unbelievable is the only thing that can be believed. . . . Respectable paranoid literature not only starts from certain moral commitments that can be justified to many non-paranoids but also carefully and all-too obsessively accumulates "evidence."[43]

The activities of the January 6 insurrectionists were dictated as much by a desire to gather facts and uncover secrets that could serve as ammunition in a war of ideas, as by the anarchistic imperative to proclaim *Carthago delenda est* to the political establishment of Washington elites. Air Force Lieutenant Colonel Larry Rendell Brock scolded others in the Senate chamber on that day: "We can't be disrespectful. You have to understand—it's an I.O. [information operations] war."[44] Hofstadter's observations are useful in clarifying how those who engage in this "work" of ferreting out the truth perceive their role:

> The plausibility the paranoid style has for those who find it plausible lie, in good measure, in this appearance of the most careful, conscientious, and seemingly coherent application to detail, the laborious accumulation of what can be taken as convincing evidence for the most fantastic conclusions, the careful preparation for the big leap from the undeniable to the unbelievable. The singular thing about all this laborious work is that the passion for factual evidence does not, as in most intellectual exchanges, have the effect of putting the paranoid spokesman into effective two-way communication with the world outside his group—least of all with those who doubt his views.[45]

The acolytes of the paranoid style are not interested in dialogue, and listening to others is anathema to them. In a 2019 interview with *The Atlantic*, the ex-neo-Nazi Christopher Picciolini identified close listening as a solvent for the ideological rigidity that characterizes the far right. To facilitate disengagement from such groups, Picciolini says that he listens for "potholes" in his interlocutors' lives, those "things that happen to us in our journey of life that detour us, things like trauma, abuse, mental illness, poverty, joblessness." In a shrewd pivot, Picciolini goes on to say that "even privilege can be a pothole that detours us." The purpose of listening is not to "debate or confront them about their ideology, but creating a rapport with them," and "fill[ing] in those potholes."[46]

Much of Hofstadter's work about what we would now call traditions of political illiberalism in American life has not aged well. With the republication in 2020 of his major writings in the prestigious Library of America series, the journalist Chris Lehmann drew attention to Hofstadter's sympathy for political elites, which among other things was tone-deaf to the collaboration between liberals and populist conservatives that resulted in the disastrous policy decisions of the Vietnam War.[47] Jeet Heer points out how Hofstadter minimized the achievements of African American essayists such as Booker T. Washington and W. E. B. DuBois in rebutting the paranoic style of conservative populism, as well as his historically inaccurate advocacy of establishment liberalism as a principled opponent of that populism. Yet, for all its flaws, his work on American anti-intellectualism, with its authoritarian and religiously inflected style of political discourse, has continued relevance as a body of research that points to the ideological permeability between the fringe and the center of the American conservative tradition.[48]

Hofstadter does not address a hidden reservoir from which much of cultural conservatism draws: a potent national mythology that Arlie Russell Hochschild, in *Strangers in Their Own Land: Anger and Mourning on the American Right* (2017), calls the "deep story" of grievance about the disappearance or mistreatment of white Americans. So powerful is that buried narrative that one need only lift a few distinctive formulations from it—such as the United States as a gleaming "city on a hill," or colonial America as a "new Jerusalem"—to bring the entire story to the surface, as a hoisted anchor caught in the forecastle of a sunken ship may raise the whole vessel from its resting place.

We will return to the ways in which an isolated yet vivid detail or figure in the carpet of radical traditionalism may call forth the larger design of a specific worldview in present-day US and Russian conservative cultures. From the perspective of the present moment, Hofstadter's work resembles an intelligently edited and useful sourcebook of historical material about anti-elitist thinking in American culture, rather than a definitive assessment of it. The patterns of thought he catalogued have continued relevance, and, certainly, his characterization of the intellectual tunnel-vision that characterizes the bookish practitioner of the "paranoid style" helps us to understand both the attitudes that undergird the principled unwillingness to listen and the informational hegemony that the right aspires to. In the same essay, Hofstadter writes that the effort of the political paranoic to amass evidence in support of his cause has "the quality of a defensive act which shuts off his receptive apparatus and protects him from having to attend to disturbing considerations that do not fortify his ideas."[49] Picciolini's observation that "even privilege can be a pothole that detours us" is especially significant in the context of Hofstadter's discussion, which ultimately broaches the seemingly counterintuitive possibility that political paranoiacs aspire to become something like the elite that they criticize. "He has all the evidence he needs," Hofstadter writes, for ultimately he is a "transmitter" rather than a "receiver."[50] The cultural project of the right is informed by the spirit of intrepid mental world-building, a mode of thinking that rejects what *is* in favor of what *ought to be*, which means that knowledge must be manufactured if it cannot readily be found in the stubborn reality of those who are different from you. In *Anti-Intellectualism in American Life*, Hofstadter describes this moralistic fabulism—we might regard it as a version of Mayakovsky's use of poetry as an engine for the attainment of knowledge, but one that has gone seriously awry— as exemplified by the pietistic understanding of literature in the United States of the early nineteenth-century. American literature then "was to be committed to optimism, to the more smiling aspects of life, and must not countenance realism or gloom."[51]

The Sneer of Cold Command: How the New Right Reconciles Liberty with Hierarchy and Submission

The resources of imagination we need to marshal in order to understand the redemptive narratives of the January 6 insurrectionists—the vision of a purifying "storm"—are considerable and should not be underestimated. As with the Millerites in the United States, who anticipated the second coming of Jesus and the fulfilment of other prophecies from the Book of Revelation in 1844, the dashing of expectations about Trump's re-election precipitated an effort to modify, or realign, the eschatological calendar. In the case of the "Stop the Steal" movement, this chronological adjustment was achieved by claiming that electoral victory had already taken place without being properly recognized or ratified as such. Midway through his presidency, Trump's allies in the House and the Senate were darkly speaking of a theft by progressive elites; now they believed that theft had transpired. As the Missouri Republican senator Josh Hawley put it in an op-ed piece for *Christianity Today*, less than two years before he raised his fist in support of the insurrectionists while walking past the Capitol building: "For those who can't build an identity around the things they buy, for those whose life is anchored in family and home and nation, for those who actually want to participate in our democracy," the ideology of complete freedom of lifestyle choice "robs them of the liberty that is rightfully theirs."[52] In his public pronouncements during the two years that preceded the insurrection, Hawley made a distinction between the choice of nontraditional lifestyles and the choice of political behavior. "I don't know which of those protesters, if any of them, those demonstrators, participated in the criminal riot," Hawley said in an interview with the *Washington Post* on 4 May. On other hand, he continued, "I think it's a slur on the thousands and thousands, tens of thousands of people who came to the Capitol that day to demonstrate peacefully to lump them in with the criminal rioters and say, 'Oh, you're all basically the same.'"[53]

Hawley's reasoning here is not as inconsistent as it may seem, and his dissociation of the "right" kind of January 6 protesters from those who opted for violence is more shaded than it appears. The political virtue of "liberty," he says, belongs exclusively to the second category of choice, whereas "lifestyle choice" represents a form of servitude. Thus, violence is one choice of action that the protesters had; in contrast, the struggle for LGBTQ rights represents a mind-forged manacle that falsely claims to provide a key to personal freedom. Although he disapproves of violence as a choice, Hawley pointedly indicates that it is at least a genuine option, albeit a situationally incorrect one, reached by someone who lives according to liberty. At this juncture, Hawley's particular religious understanding of liberty is crucial for understanding his argument, which I contend is highly characteristic of the entire right wing's understanding of itself as a new cognitive elite. Hawley suggests that, living as we do in a state of sin and therefore of total depravity, we should not be surprised by the occasional making of the wrong choice, and the taking of the incorrect path, by those who sincerely endeavor to live according to the principles of liberty. The legal scholar Irina Manta, who knew Hawley from their days at Yale Law School and the Federalist Society, quipped to me that "for Hawley, it was never about free markets."[54]

What is significant here is that Hawley recognizes that the possibility for actual violence lies within the penumbra of the right's understanding of political action. As unfortunate as such as a choice may be, at least it is not caught up in what Hawley identifies in his op-ed as the spirit of theological "Pelagianism," named after the fourth-century English monk Pelagius, who argued (in Hawley's paraphrase) that "individuals could achieve their own salvation" simply by "living up to the perfection of which they were inherently capable."[55] This peculiar opposition between freedom and liberty is not new to American conservative thinking. The economist James McGill Buchanan advised the ruling party of Pinochet's Chile on rebuilding the national economy according to radically free-market principles, so that, as the historian Nancy MacLean points out, "the new Chile was free for some, and perhaps that was enough." Buchanan's new employers in Chile "were the same kind of people who counted in Virginia," where he worked for a conservative think tank at the University of Virginia, developing what he and his colleague Gordon Tullock called "public choice theory." By creating administrative mechanisms for state governments to nullify the decisions of majorities, and stipulating that policies formulated by elected officials could move forward only with the unanimous consent of state senators, this theory arguably continued features of Jim Crow well past the Civil Rights era. Buchanan now "pledged to his new employer that he would work to preserve liberty," with the understanding, in the words of one Chilean supporter of Pinochet, that "the individual freedom to consume, produce, save, and invest" would be fully restored. As MacLean dryly observes, "it was always a particular kind of freedom that libertarians cared most about."[56] Buchanan "valued economic liberty so much more than political freedom that he simply did not care about the invitation to abuse inherent in giving nearly unchecked power to an alliance of capital and the armed forces" in Chile.[57] Hawley's raised fist and his bluff denial of endorsing violence make sense only within the matrix of assumptions about "choice" that have dominated American conservative thinking for over half a century. As Buchanan and Tullock put it in their 1962 book about public choice theory, which had the Gramscian-sounding title *The Calculus of Consent: Logical Foundations of Constitutional Democracy*, a "society of free men" naturally seeks to put "effective limits" on those whose administrative resources would be "more productive if left in the private sector of the economy."[58]

The Rise of the Rightist Elite

The main argument of the present book is that new-right elites in the United States and the Russian Federation envision themselves as taking on the role of communicators—what Yuri Slezkine, in *The Jewish Century* (2004), calls the "Mercurian" cultural mode, a category of people who are maximally multilingual and peripatetic, as befits those named after a Greek god (Hermès) who embodied eloquence, communication, and commerce. They are messengers who "use concepts, money, emotions, and other intangibles as the tools of their trade," as opposed to the adherents of the "Apollonian" way, who have a strong fealty to landed property in general, and to agricultural labor in particular.[59] As Slezkine puts it, the Mercurians are "professional internal strangers dependent on cultural difference and economic interdependence"; as exemplified by the Jewish diaspora, the Parsis in Mubai, Germans in Eastern Europe, and overseas Chinese, they are emissaries for the quicksilver operations of global modernity.[60] These communities comprised office workers, lawyers, and businesspeople, whose services were often used by their Apollonian (landowning and farming) compatriots. In Slezkine's telling, the global connections that Mercurian communities cultivate often produced, within their home countries, an asymmetry of need between them and their Apollonian fellow citizens. "The difference between Apollonians and Mercurians," he writes, "is the all-important difference between those who grow food, and those who create concepts and artifacts."[61] As Cynthia Miller-Idriss, Pippa Norris, and other researchers into the contemporary right have noted, a large swath of the participants in the storming of the Capitol were middle-class to upper-middle-class white Americans who had serious financial troubles and who had been small business owners or employed in the service economy.[62] Almost none of them were the laid-off Rust Belt workers eulogized by J. D. Vance in *Hillbilly Elegy: A Memoir of a Family and Culture in Crisis* (2016), people who had come to believe that "hard work doesn't matter as much as raw talent," nor were they farmers immiserated by what the conservative political scientist Patrick Deneen identifies as the pro-urban and anti-agricultural policies of the bi-coastal left's global neoliberalism.[63] "We just stormed the Capital [*sic*]," tweeted Jenna Ryan, a realtor from Texas, who had flown to Washington on a Lear jet and who was on the verge of personal bankruptcy. "It was one of the best days of my life."[64] No doubt, some of the insurrectionists would object to being categorized as nomadic, let alone cosmopolitan communicators, in the mold of a professional profile that was common within the Jewish diaspora because of the historical prohibitions or limitations that many countries imposed on Jewish ownership of landed property. Yet their Twitter- and selfie-propelled practices of self-advertisement and political advocacy through the avenues of social media place these protesters squarely in the category of aspiring members of an evangelizing cognitive elite of their own.

It is at this juncture that we glimpse a specific understanding of the cognitive elite within the traditionalist intelligentsia. Arguably, the extensive if often informal links between groups as geographically far-flung as the Proud Boys in North America, France's Rassemblement National, Italy's Lega Nord, Hungary's Fidesz party, Poland's Law and Justice party, Narendra Modi's Indian People's Party (Bharatiya Janata), and Putin's United Russia Party point to a cosmopolitan or affectively "nomadic" sensibility. This worldview renders these parties, in Slezkine's terms, into Mercurian workshops, *ateliers* for the refinement of cultural constructs. The often thespian-minded participants in the January 6 insurrection may even aspire to the communicative avatar status that Slezkine sees in figures like the Russian-Jewish fiction writer Isaac Babel, who engaged in the challenging project of speaking for pro-Soviet yet anti-Semitic Cossack soldiers in the Polish-Soviet War (1919–21) while maintaining a studied detachment from their views. But there is one important difference. The January 6 insurrectionists, and the critics on the right in both the United States and the Russian Federation who are animated by a dislike for the liberal or progressive intelligentsia, are too caught up in a concern for hierarchy and the chain of command to completely support the ideal of an autonomous cadre of developers of unorthodox ideas and lifestyles. It is difficult to be independent if you are what Hofstadter calls a "transmitter," a mere node within a larger network of knowledge production.

In the Russian Federation, conservative forces have made a similar effort to articulate an understanding of an antiprogressive intelligentsia. The Russian Orthodox Church has been particularly active in striving to serve as the base for a counter-intelligentsia. The difficulties and paradoxes of cultivating a network of cultural workers who will fight for an institutional cause without necessarily taking direct orders from that institution are acute. The challenge the leadership of the largest religious denomination in the Russian Federation faces is comparable to a US Republican Party project of swaying today's "silent majority" back to an extreme form of neo-Confederate populism that would have given even Richard Nixon pause. Culture warriors and their *crème de la crème* brethren—highly articulate bloggers, well-educated activists, trained informational analysts—will always possess a strong preference for autonomy and a diffuse and informal leadership structure, if they accept any structure at all. In both countries, right-wing elites struggle to navigate between a reflexive contrarianism that scorns the niceties of civil discourse and a reverence for hierarchical orders. As the liberal Eastern Orthodox theologian John Chryssagvis put it in regard to the foreign-policy position of the Russian Orthodox Church (ROC) in 2021: "What is clear is that the tyrannical authorities of Church (Patriarch Kirill) and state (President Putin) still retain the scars of Russia's imperial past, while their underlings in the Church (Metropolitan Alfeyev) and state ([Russian Foreign] Minister [Sergei] Lavrov) faithfully enforce the imperial machine's soulless indoctrination."[65] Andrei Shishkov, the co-founder and currently the executive director of Moscow's Center for Advanced Theological Studies, pointed to what he called the ROC's "mumbling" mode of studied neutrality in regard to the outrages of social privilege and state power in the Russian Federation. While "Orthodox Christians are often proud of their nonconformism—of not being led by the forces of this world," their "nonconformism and otherworldliness is often paradoxically combined with loyalty to the authorities and a shock dose of conspiracy theories." Writing from the perspective of a dissident member of the Orthodox clergy, Shishkov notes that this accommodationist reflex is especially visible in Russia, where "too often Orthodoxy's alleged otherworldliness turns out to be simple hypocrisy." In his capacity as the head of the ROC's Department for External Church Relations, Metropolitan Hilarion Alfeyev stated in a televised interview that aired on 30 January 2021 that "the involvement of children and youngsters in the protest movement was unacceptable because the youth should remain outside politics." Yet, despite such concerns for the delicate and impressionable sensibilities of these young people, Shishkov observes that Alfeyev has "never expressed any objections to the participation of children and youngsters in pro-state activities."[66]

Not commented upon by Shishkov is Alfeyev's allegation in the same interview that the January pro–Alexei Navalny youth protests were the result of undue influence from "foreign agents," whom he coyly does not name.[67] With this unsubstantiated assertion, Alfeyev draws a rhetorically potent parallel between political influence from abroad and the corruption of children by "gay propaganda," prohibited by a law in 2013. Such allegations carry a significant payload of religiously inflected assumptions and beliefs in both countries. Above all, those beliefs are anchored in a moral panic about pedophilia and "gender ideology," prompted by anxiety over real and perceived demographic changes. In the language of the American alt-right, we hear the persistent drumbeat of concern about the national census projection that the United States will become "minority white" in 2045, with whites making up 49.7 percent of the total population, Hispanics 24.6 percent, African Americans 13.1 percent, Asians 7.9 percent, and multiracial groups 3.8 percent.[68] American conservative intellectuals and those on the populist right have consistently pointed to a crisis in white manhood, if not virility, as responsible for this demographic shift. As the evangelical pundit Eric Metaxas put it, people who criticized Trump were guilty of practicing "a new and accepted tribalism and xenophobia" directed at "white European 'Christian' varieties" of value systems. Electing a woman, such as Hillary Clinton, as president would send the country "sliding into oblivion, the tank, the dustbin of history"; better to have a man who embodied the martial virtues that evangelical men have respected and revered for generations. "When you are in a war mentality," Metaxas argued, "you say 'who is going to stand up where we need to stand up.'"[69] Hochschild's *Strangers in Their Own Land* quotes a woman interviewed in an area of Louisiana's bayou country that was devastated by run-offs of industrial waste: "These days, American men are an endangered species too."[70]

Within the Russian Federation, anxieties about population decline have a firmer foothold in legitimate concerns about public health. Between 1992 and 2009, the Russian Federation suffered a loss of nearly seven million people, close to 5 percent of its total population.[71] Complicating matters is the lowered life expectancy of Russian men, which, at the mean age of 55 during the nineties and the aughts, was roughly six years lower than that of Russian women. Yet, as in the United States recently, this general picture of demographic decline has often been framed by traditionalist journalists and bloggers as first and foremost a deficit of robust and unapologetic masculinity, repeating signature phrases from a "deep story" about the West's emasculation of post-Soviet Russia through a punishing and deeply humiliating regimen of shock treatment for an economy that did not readily take to the rigors of an imposed capitalist system. The researcher Alexander Kondakov points out that the law against "gay propaganda" suggests that "information about male homosexuality, lesbianism, bisexuality and transgender issues is harmful to children" because "once exposed to such information, they may contribute to the erosion of the state by refusing to procreate in the future."[72] Within this matrix of ideas, the defense of traditional masculinity is very easily transformed into a defense of Russia itself. As the political scientist Alina Polyakova observes, "to Putin and many Russians who support him," the American-abetted European cultural liberalism that "grants rights to same-sex couples is not only degenerate, but also a threat to Russia's survival as a nation."[73]

Conclusion: Tocqueville's Prediction of
American and Russian Ascendency

Going against the grain of their populist beliefs, new-right elites in the United States and the Russian Federation seek to provide a robust justification for the existence of an intellectual class that mirrors the heady activism of their progressive adversaries. They draw attention to their vigorous efforts to defend native populations from threats both within and without. What do figures of the "Populist International," such as Steve Bannon, Alexander Dugin, France's Marine and Marion Maréchal Le Pen, and Brazil's Jair Bolsonaro, reveal about themselves when they let their guard down in front of the camera? To what extent do they express an awareness of themselves as performers? At the same time, grassroots activists and mainstream organizations—such as #BlackLivesMatter, Antifa, and the Democratic Party in the United States, and youth protest movements, the LGBTQ community, and supporters within Russia of Ukrainian territorial sovereignty—find themselves in fragile coalitions as they attempt to push back against the misinformation and digital strategies of the new far right. What can these antiauthoritarian movements, with their intersectional configurations of class, race, gender, and overall political agency, tell us about the actual points of contact between the American and Russian experiences of disempowerment?

Before answering that question, I would like to clarify what this book is not. Its goal is to draw attention to the confluence of the American and Russian far right's conceptions of gender, race, and performative identity, not to solve the conundrum of possible Kremlin involvement in the presidential campaign of Donald Trump. Rather, I am interested in the styles of thinking among Russian and American supporters of the far right, for whom gender and race function as deliberately makeshift narrative constructions, designed to accommodate a wide range of disparate, if not contradictory, political beliefs. The mercurial inconsistencies of the ethnonationalist views expressed by influential radical conservative figures such as the Trump administration's senior policy advisor Stephen Miller and the Russian populist Alexander Dugin serve to reinforce the far right's rhetorical strategy of reducing politics to a game of social dominance that pushes back against the sanctimonious "'virtue signaling" ascribed to the "social justice warriors" among the left.

In chapter 1 ("A Place at the High Table: Mythologizing the Russian Intelligentsia, Crusading against US Elites"), I discuss the American appropriation of Russian cultural models that posit a notionally virtuous model of cognitive elites. The goal here is to combat elites who are complicit with the misguided or plainly malignant policies of the managerial state. Yet even in the context of well-founded critiques of entrenched elites, American commentators like Patrick

Deneen, Helen Andrews, and Rod Dreher engage in open flights of fancy that reinforce what Jan-Werner Müller describes as a "particular moralistic imagination of politics"—one that can easily dispense with concrete evidence for provocative claims.

In chapter 2 ("Whither the State? Steve Bannon, the Alt-Right, and Lenin's *State and Revolution*"), I examine the ways in which Bannon's selective adoption of Russian revolutionary activism opens the door for a subjectively identitarian—if not wholly metaphorical—understanding of the state. Certainly, there is much in Bannon's demeanor and general outlook that would seem indebted to Lenin's *State and Revolution*. Like Lenin in that work, Bannon sees himself as a tireless agitator for the formation of a molecular and diffuse, as opposed to a rigorously centralized, mode of political movement-building. Bannon also seems to share Lenin's view that the theoretical sketching out of tactics is no less important than the advocacy of state dismantlement.

In *State and Revolution*, Lenin asserts that in the full victory of the proletariat we see a society that "no longer [has] the state in the proper sense." He also paradoxically characterizes the "withering away of the state" as an event that is accompanied by the triumph of a diffuse centralism among the citizens of the revolutionary society.[74] What does Bannon's style of contestation have in common with Lenin's, and how does the libertarian and alt-right's disgust with pluralism—expressed in what Ruth Wodak terms the gossipy "fictionalization of politics"[75]—emerge as a close counterpart to Lenin's self-aware performance of politically sectarian rage in *State and Revolution*? I examine Bannon's arguments about state dismantlement, national autarky, and military agency and trace their origins in the appropriation of aspects of Leninism by earlier American conservative radicals, such as James Burnham and the libertarian nationalist theoretician James McGill Buchanan. Bannon endorses a distinctly American libertarian idealization of the first Soviet leader as a principled advocate of a strong national state that functions without a government. Ultimately, I would argue that Bannon's contempt for the traditional institutions of the state opens the door for an affective identitarianism that sees "traditional" communities as coming to occupy the vacuum created by the voiding of the state.

In chapter 3 ("Hijacking Academic Authority: Racism and the Internet Expertise of Kevin MacDonald and Alexander Dugin"), I examine the parallel career paths of Kevin MacDonald, formerly a tenured professor in the department of psychology at California State University in Long Beach, and Alexander Dugin, a professor of sociology at Moscow State University. Since he achieved tenured status in 1994, MacDonald (now retired) has carefully cultivated the role of mediator between the informational pathways of the academy and anti-Semitic fringe activism. He is the "academic expert" whose work is most often cited by the right-wing website Stormfront. Dugin has shrewdly parceled out his internet presence across a range of websites, each of which appeals to a specific niche in the political marketplace, such Russian Orthodoxy, Eurasianism, fascism, antiglobalism, or occultism. In this chapter I focus on the ways in which both men misappropriate mainstream scholarship. We may think of MacDonald and Dugin as web designers of what the Cultural Studies theorist Barbara M. Kennedy terms "delirious narratives": sites of "discursive power" in which "mythical, aesthetic and even scientific worlds" exist "outside the logical constraints of structural thinking."[76] Both are intent upon the construction of self-validating scholarly subcultures, while also intersecting with larger communities of racialist political action.

In chapter 4, "The Spectacle of God's Will: Performing Homophobia in the Russian Federation," I examine the distinctly Russian far-right understanding of liberalism as a form of Russophobic misogyny directed at feminized symbols of Russian national identity. I devote particular attention to the entry of this understanding into the language of the public actions of homophobic antidemocratic groups. Since the sentencing in May 2012 of the punk art collective Pussy Riot for its protest performance in Moscow's Church of Christ the Savior, certain ideological formulas and terms from Russian skinhead and neo-Nazi movements have become more clearly mainstreamed into the political language of the state-controlled media. The performance was widely characterized as a desecration of sacred space and a defamation of the Orthodox doctrine of Mariology.

In the Russian Federation itself, right-wing protest has long sought to articulate itself in ways that are similar to the theatricality of the January 6 insurrectionists. Several of these groups have staged what can be plausibly understood as their own versions of performance art in which the values and publications of LGBTQ culture are ritualistically defiled, in the public square of the internet as well as actual public squares. Figures such as the traditionalist and nationalist activist and political performance artist Dmitri Tsorionov (known as Dmitri Enteo), the protest group known as the Union of Orthodox Banner Bearers, and the dissident theologian and priest Andrei Kuraev represent a new category of religious intelligentsia whose understandings of faith often defy the traditionalism that they vow to defend. They seek to create a specific online persona as Savonarolas who speak truth to the power of entrenched ecclesiastical and political authorities. While Enteo, the Union of Orthodox Banner Bearers, and Kuraev wield no political clout in themselves, their strong presence on social media and their often spectacle-oriented public statements situate them as potent transmitters of a traditionalist deep story about the national salvific project of Russian Eastern Orthodoxy, which they communicate in terms that are more vivid and explicit than the ones made by official representatives of the Russian Orthodox Church, such as Metropolitan Alfeyev. Analogously, we see that a close examination of fringe ideas as expressed by such disparate figures as Bannon and MacDonald in the United States, and Dugin and in the Russian Federation, can afford us an unusually direct access to the network of beliefs that animate militant traditionalists in both countries. The people named here function like threads hanging from a common fabric: once you pull at them, you see how the pattern of the cloth comes undone.

In chapter 5 ("Statuary Performances: Monuments and Neopaganism in the United States and the Russian Federation"), I compare the understandings of public monuments among conservative and far-right groups. Why are such public markers so important for the worldviews of these groups, and how do their opponents on the left rebut them? Equestrian statues strongly suggest the possibility of violent forward momentum: careful, or we'll get trampled! Commenting on the hidden political aesthetics of the white supremacist demonstrations in Charlottesville, the progressive activist, academic, and eloquent BLM supporter Keeanga-Yamahtta Taylor identifies protests against monuments that glorify white privilege as actions that seek to disrupt the ennobling framing of those objects within public spaces.[77] The Russian writer Vladimir Sorokin considers the phenomenon of "hundreds of statues [of Lenin and Stalin] still stand[ing], not only on Russia's squares and plazas, but in the minds of its citizens."[78] For the far right in both countries, statues express powerful reflexes toward asymmetrical understandings of public performativity. Who has the right to perform, and where? The various demands of "traditional" local and state-level holidays throw these questions into even sharper relief. In this chapter, I examine the cryptocultic worship of monuments among ethnonationalists in both countries.

In my conclusion ("The Fight against Rightist Elites"), I discuss the possibilities and some of the actual efforts in both countries to push back against the media spectacle of friendly relations among populists across borders, with a particular focus on the militantly anti-historical bent of US and Russian alt-right thinking.

My comparison of radical traditionalist elites in the United States and the Russian Federation is motivated by two considerations. One has to do with these elites' understanding of their nations as entities that once bestrode the globe. With the rout of the American- and European Union–supported government in Afghanistan and the continued economic decline of the Russian Federation due to its overreliance on oil and gas resources, one might argue that both countries have already moved beyond Tocqueville's prophecy of their holding "the fate of half the world at some date in the future." That future, the Cold War, has now receded into the past. As Edward Gibbon observes at different points in his *Decline and Fall of the Roman Empire*, we should not be surprised that the cultural projects of patriotic elites take on renewed vigor and inventiveness precisely at the stage of their empire's decline, and when their leaders become the focus of cultic national obsession. This book is the study of a postimperial elitism struggling to reassemble itself from the fragments of multiple national humiliations.

The other reason for engaging in this comparison of American and Russian traditionalist elites is that the American political influencers have a largely unreciprocated fascination with their Russian counterparts, and with Russian culture in general. The political scientist Marlène Laruelle has commented that "many Alt-Right figures [in the United States] are big fans of Putin, whom they see as a beacon of the white world," and that "they are attracted to his rejection of so-called decadent U.S. liberalism and multiculturalism, his hard line against Islamic radicalism, his upholding of Christian values, his criticism of Western political correctness, and his support for the idea that global elites conspire against ordinary people."[79] Traditionalist intellectuals in the United States see in Russia what they think American culture used to be: unashamedly yet benignly territorial in its ambitions, majority white and European in its demographics, and an idyll for a rural and socially conservative way of life. Needless to say, this perception of Russia as a white European monoculture—in the past or present—is a work of fiction. Even given its less ethnically and racially diverse population in comparison with the Soviet period, current statistics from the Ministry of Science and Higher Education indicate that the Russian Federation still has 277 languages and dialects spoken on its territory, of which 105 are used as languages of instruction in the primary and secondary school systems, and 81 are subjects of instruction.[80] Moreover, locating one's understanding of America's future in the hierarchical and culturally homogeneous present and past of a mythologized Russia is in a palpable tension with the American civic culture that Tocqueville describes elsewhere in *Democracy in America*, in which "each person in his own sphere takes an active part in the government of society."[81]

The interest of the American alt-right and traditionalist intelligentsia in that particular construct of Russian culture is more significant than their current infatuation with Viktor Orbán's Hungary. Writing for the pro-Trump *Claremont Review of Books*, the political commentator Christopher Caldwell effusively characterizes Orbán as "blessed with almost every political gift," including a "a memory for parliamentary minutiae reminiscent of Bill Clinton."[82] But a leader who is a vulpine master of proceduralism does not, for the American alt-right, exert a very powerful pull. More characteristic of the American alt-right are the views of the pro-Confederate blogger Michael Sisco, a convert to Russian Orthodoxy, who states that he doesn't vote "because to me voting is affirming democracy [and] I don't really like democracy."[83] Yet we must remind ourselves that this reflex toward Bonapartism, if not open Caesarism, has always been a feature of the American conservative landscape of belief. As Irving Kristol put it in an interview from 2000, "What's the point of being the greatest, most powerful nation in the world and not having an imperial role? It's unheard of in human history. The most powerful nation has always had an imperial role."[84]

During the height of the Cold War, the American conservative political theorist James Burnham forcefully argued that managerial elites in the United States and the Soviet Union functioned in much the same way, as deft practitioners of a Caesarism who claim to represent the Rousseauian "general will" of the people even as they reinforce "bureaucratic rule" and engage in the "destruction of intermediary bodies," such as parliaments and political parties that could stand "between the individual and the state, and [uphold] the law and individual rights against the 'raw will' of the executive."[85] I am interested in how this well-founded critique of the cadres who occupy the corridors of power has gone awry in both countries, tipping over into the rhetorical practices of ethnonationalists who represent their enemies as devious and not fully human. In the Russian Federation of today, for example, there are many who take seriously the existence of the "Dulles Plan," a conspiracy theory that is arguably the Russian equivalent of QAnon. The "plan," attributed to Allen Dulles, outlines a US-led covert campaign to undermine Russian cultural values through policies of economic humiliation and cultural imperialism in the form of the demand for LGBTQ rights.[86]

Contrary to what they often assert, American and Russian rightist elites venerate the hegemony of the administrative state. Far-right apologists like Steve Bannon, the vlogger and blogger Don Bongino, and Fox Television's Tucker Carlson in the United States and Alexander Dugin and the ROSSIYA-1 television hosts Dmitri Kiselyov and Margarita Simonyan in the Russian Federation have played a key role in formulating a new, and fundamentally positive, understanding of cognitive elites. Of no little significance for these provocateurs is the institutional persona of rebarbative imperial will that Tocqueville in the 1830s understood as a component of policy implementation in both countries, exemplified by President Andrew Jackson's full-throated advocacy and implementation of the Indian Removal Act in 1830 and Tsar Nicholas I's violent suppression of the movement for independence in the former territory of Poland that same year. From the nineteenth century to the present, a cult of retaliatory national pride and social dominance has been sporadically evident in both countries' ethnonationalist movements and rightist thinkers. The goal of the present book is to reach an understanding of what that resurgence means for conservative intellectuals and for the political future of the United States and the Russian Federation.

CHAPTER ONE

A Place at the High Table

Mythologizing the Russian Intelligentsia, Crusading against US Elites

We experience such profound differences with some of our contemporaries, that the nearest parallel is the difference between the mentality of one epoch and another. In a society like ours, worm-eaten with Liberalism, the only thing possible for a person with strong convictions is to state a point of view and leave it at that.

—T. S. ELIOT, *After Strange Gods: A Primer of Modern Heresy*

Haughty political intriguing [*nadmennoe politikanstvo*] is a great sin. The longer the intelligentsia is proud and haughty, the more bloody and frightful everything will become.

—ALEXANDER BLOK, "The Intelligentsia and Revolution"

Introduction: The American Afterlife of the Prerevolutionary Russian Intelligentsia

THE BLACK LIVES matter protests against the killing of George Floyd elicited a dizzying range of responses among conservative commentators in the United States and the Russian Federation. From her aerie as a contrarian columnist for the left-of-center Moscow-based newspaper *Novaya gazeta* (New gazette), in a piece dated 30 June 2020, Yulia Latynina argued that the protesters were merely an element in a coalition of "New Reds" who were interested not in the defense of human rights, but in the wholesale destruction of the freedoms and achievements of an open society. "Ladies and gentlemen, this is not a protest against the system," she wrote. "This is a new system, one that we, who have lived in the USSR, are all too familiar with—we were there."[1] On the American side of the Atlantic, the Russian literature specialist Gary Saul Morson, the Lawrence B. Dumas Professor of the Arts and Humanities at Northwestern University, delved deeper into the protests' resonances with the ideologically high-strung political debates in the fifty years leading up to the Russian Revolution. In a *Wall Street Journal* interview published three weeks prior to Latynina's article, Morson argued that the weird spectacle of members of the well-educated class lobbing firebombs at police vehicles was comprehensible only in light of their *ressentiment* at not occupying the highest positions of power. To the interviewer's query "Why do people at the top want to destroy the system that enabled them to get there?" Morson pointed to a pattern of thwarted hubris. "You have it wrong. When you're such a person, you don't feel you're at the top. The people at the top are wealthy businesspeople, and you're an intellectual. You think that people of ideas should be at the top." Likewise, Morson stated, the nineteenth-century liberal and radical branches of the Russian intelligentsia were vulnerable to the vain conceit that their mastery of the "theory" of the historical dialectic naturally made them "morally superior" to everyone else. These self-appointed figures of moral authority thought, in fact, that they "should be in charge, and that there was something fundamentally wrong" with a world in which "practical" people were the ones who turned the levers of power. Transposing this model of overheated ideology from late nineteenth-century Russia to the BLM protests with their demands for social justice, Morson asserted that "what you take from your education would be the ideology that would justify this kind of activity—justify it because the wrong people have the power, and you should have it. You don't feel like you're the establishment."[2]

Morson's interview and his subsequent essay "Suicide of the Liberals" for the conservative Catholic magazine *First Things* became the go-to pieces for traditionalist American conservatives who were keen to draw parallels between the doctrinal inflexibility that contributed to the Bolshevik seizure of power and the scourge of militant political correctness or "wokeness" in the United States.[3] A reading audience unfamiliar with the history of nineteenth-century Russian radicalism would be forgiven for missing the connection between social justice ethics and the will to power that animates a particular class. Wouldn't these two undertakings—collective moral reparations on the one hand, and individual personal ambitions on the other—be at cross-purposes? In part, Morson is drawing on his deep knowledge about the behavioral antinormativity of the Russian radical intelligentsia in the nineteenth century, which often viewed etiquette and plain good manners as so much deadwood blocking the proper drainage of a corrupt and hypocritical society. With its roots in the technical educated class of the mid-nineteenth century and the sons and daughters of Russian Orthodox parish priests—highly literate and in some cases reaching a level of cultural knowledge that rivaled that of the Russian landed gentry and nobility—the populist intelligentsia known as the *Narodniki* (roughly meaning "advocates of the common folk") inherited a combustible mix of straitened material circumstances, if not actual poverty, sublimated evangelical zeal, a high level of literacy in the human and natural sciences, and an antipathy to the stark social inequalities all around them. In his clumsily didactic yet intermittently eloquent novel *What Is to Be Done* (1863), the socialist Nikolai Chernyshevsky—whose father was an Orthodox priest and whose mother was the daughter of his father's predecessor in the same parish—espoused an understanding of individual and group rights that could be viewed as an anticipation of present-day social-justice ethics. At one point in the novel, the protagonist dreams that she is taken by an angelic emissary to a future utopia where absolute equality reigns. "Therefore," the emissary tells Vera Pavlovna, "if you wish to express in one phrase what I am, it's 'equal rights.' Without them the pleasures of the body and delight in beauty are tedious, dull and vile. Without them there's no purity of heart, only the deceptive purity of the body. As a result of this equality in me there is also freedom, without which I cannot exist."[4] Morson perceives the BLM protests as echoes of the moral purity ethics of the first Russian revolutionaries, who in 1881 assassinated the tsar responsible for the abolition of serfdom twenty years earlier.

As evidenced by his tentative and speculative tone, Morson is careful not to claim a direct lineage or ancestry for the present-day protests in the nascent elitist socialism of the nineteenth-century Russian populists. The clearest lineal descendant of those views is the political theory of Vladimir Lenin, who ingeniously attempted to reconcile a thoroughgoing empowerment of the masses with unapologetic support for the continued existence of a revolutionary vanguard or political elite. This latter social category is almost completely absent from the writings of Marx and Engels, where it is assigned a lifespan that is—at best—catalytic and fleeting in the unfolding of the historical dialectic. In his essay "Alienation and the Social Classes" (1845) from *The Holy Family: A Critique of Critical Criticism* (Marx's and Engels' first joint writing project), Marx implicitly characterized the sheer wretchedness of exploited workers as emitting a noxious, methane-like substance, so toxic and foul that it explodes in contact with the slightest spark. There, Marx writes that the working class "cannot liberate itself without destroying its own living condition," and "without destroying all of the inhuman living conditions [that] are concentrated in its own situation."[5] Nor is there a need for a revolutionary elite even in Marx's embittered later works such as *The Eighteenth Brumaire of Louis Napoleon*, which attributes the rollback in 1851 of the meager gains resulting from the Paris workers' revolts three years earlier to the machinations of the coalition between the urban bourgeoisie and the political representatives of the rural gentry, rather than to a failure of will among the workers' leaders. Whether in the twenty-first century United States or the Russian empire of the nineteenth century, Morson understands the radical elite as inorganic. Because it does not emerge from traditional institutions such as the church and the civil service, or from the community of exploited industrial or agricultural workers that it endeavors to educate, such a cognitive elite cannot be said to belong to either the traditional intellectuals or the organic intellectuals whom Gramsci describes in his *Prison Notebooks*. This intelligentsia is untethered, a deracinated middle class of cultural workers that has experienced enough material comfort to stave off anxiety about survival while only sipping at the cup of true political capital. Its character—in terms of both economic status and cultural identity—is indeterminate, a signifier that hovers and floats across the social spectrum. Properly speaking, it is not a class at all.

The purpose of this chapter is to examine understandings of the liberal elite by spokespeople and defenders of conservative and far-right movements in the United States and the Russian Federation. American and Russian cultural critics on the right are keen to pathologize educated liberals as deluded popinjays at best, as sad ghosts and self-loathing Otto Weininger–like figures at worst. Most prominent among these fabulations about the frustrated interior life of cultural elites is the notion of their "queerness" or non-normativity, a trait that is understood to motivate their hostility to what they derisively call, in the American context, "fly-over country" or "Jesus land," and "the provinces" (*provintsii*) in the Russian one.

What the hard-right conservative elites in both countries share is an ambition to become something like a Gramscian organic class of intellectuals, a group of cultural workers who are connected to a constituency that they see as firmly rooted in the nation's soil. In other words, they aspire to genuinely take on the Promethean mantle of their rootless adversaries and redeem the category of intelligentsia from its social-justice legacy. When members of the nineteenth-century Russian intelligentsia attempted to "go among the people" (*idti v liudi*), they often discovered that they and the peasantry did not speak the same language, either politically or literally. In this chapter we will observe how speculative constructs about the cultural or cognitive elite are more often mirrors of the traditionalists who fashioned them than of the reality that they seek to decode. In both countries today, the traditionalist intelligentsia sees itself as an anomaly, as a cluster of conservative revolutionaries in a godless republic replete with militant secularist *sans-culottes*. In the end, they are no more successful in their attempts to "go among the people" than those whom they deride.

The Sublimated Religiosity of the Nineteenth-Century
Russian Intelligentsia

At first glance, the emergence and subsequent robust development of the Russian intelligentsia seem anything but organic in terms of class interests. Lenin's "Pamiati Gertsena" (In memory of Herzen, 1912) is about the Decembrists—the members of the nobility who raised demands for a constitutional monarchy, if not a purely constitutional form of government, on 26 December 1825. Lenin placed them among the progressive members of the noble and land-owning classes who were far ahead of their time yet fatally distant from the common folk on whose behalf they imagined themselves as fighting.[6] For all of these men, the institution of serfdom was a festering sore. In a country where roughly 90 percent of the population was functionally illiterate, literature played a peculiarly disproportionate role in the formulation of a detailed progressive rebuttal to the arguments on behalf of unfettered monarchical power or autocracy (*samoderzhavie*), an Orthodox Church that had been completely absorbed into the state in 1721 at the behest of Peter the Great, and—in what was a distinct ideological innovation during the militantly conservative and counterrevolutionary reign of Nicholas I (1825–55)—an insistence on the importance of "nationality" (*narodnost'*), or a privileging of a distinctly Russian national culture.

The empire had acquired an enormous Jewish population literally overnight with the second partition of Poland in 1791, and it already possessed a sizable non-Russian Slavic population in the south and indigenous non-European populations to the east of the Ural mountain range. Thus, foregrounding a particular ethnic group as the third element in a trinity of an absolutist state and a specific religious denomination (with the Holy Synod functioning as a sort of ministry of official religious affairs) was particularly irksome to members of a landed gentry who had fought in the Napoleonic Wars and had in some cases received their university educations abroad. We served our country well and helped defeat the heir to tyrannical Jacobinism, they reasoned, only to return home and be treated as lackeys and factotums for a blinkered state that uses religion and a glorified version of backwater nationalist monoculture to justify a paralyzing fatalism about the system's moral outrages. Under Nicholas I, disaffected members of the rural gentry and nobility took refuge in *belles lettres* as a way of launching attacks on both the feudalistic character of Russian society and the uncompromising verticality of the country's political system. One of the most eloquent statements of this generation came from the philosopher and political essayist Petr Chaadaev in his "First Philosophical Letter" (1829), published in 1836 in a major literary journal because of an oversight by the state censor:

Our memories do not go back beyond yesterday; we are, in a manner of speaking, strangers to our own selves. We move so peculiarly in time that, as we advance, each preceding moment escapes us irrevocably. This is a natural consequence of a culture based wholly on imitation. With us there is no inner development, no natural progression; new ideas sweep away the old, because they do not proceed from those old ones but come to us out of the blue. Since we only adopt ready-made ideas, the indelible characteristics which a movement of progressive ideas engraves upon men's minds and gives them power, does not even make an impression upon our intellects. We grow but we do not mature; we advance but in an oblique line, i.e., in a line which does not lead to any goal. We resemble children who have not been taught to think for themselves, and who, having become adults, have nothing of their own; all their knowledge lies on the surface of their existence, their whole soul exists outside themselves. That is our precise situation.

Peoples are moral beings just as individuals are. It takes centuries to educate them, just as it takes years to educate a person. In a sense, it can be said that we are an exceptional people. We are one of those nations which does not seem to form an integral part of humanity, but which exists only to provide some great lesson for the world.[7]

In a turn of events that would set the tone for subsequent reprisals against critics of the state, Chaadaev was imprisoned for a time in an insane asylum for his observations about the moral vacuity of the Russian empire's conservative elite.

We will come back to the association of the progressive intelligentsia with mental illness and behavioral non-normativity in both American and Russian political cultures later in this chapter. While Chaadaev may have been indiscreet and naïve in expecting his letter to generate a lively and open-minded discussion among educated Russians about their relations with the larger world, he hardly needed to be hospitalized. For him, an open call to abolish serfdom was a bridge too far in a stylized essay that was written with an eye to public consumption and discussion among a highly-educated audience. The demand for that particular institutional change could only be whispered, or shared in handwritten and clandestinely distributed essays and poems. The literary critic Vissarion Belinsky's scathing 1847 letter to the visionary yet politically reactionary fiction writer Nikolai Gogol circulated, in handwritten copies, within progressive circles. Anxieties about this or that individual's soul and the possibilities for spiritual redemption, Belinsky wrote, are nothing in comparison with the original sin within the political system. "The most vital questions in Russia today are the abolition of serfdom, the repeal of corporal punishment, and the introduction of the strictest application—at the very least—of those laws which are already on the books."[8] Quite famously, it was at an 1849 salon reading and discussion of this letter in St. Petersburg, organized by a few members of the imperial guard who were interested in topic of "scientific socialism," and who came to be known as the Petrashevtsy, that a twenty-eight-year-old Fyodor Dostoevsky was arrested; he would be sentenced to ten years of hard labor and exile for his participation in the meeting. For the educated classes in Russia during most of the nineteenth century, literature was a point of departure for discussions of fraught political issues.

The perceived role of imaginative literature as a catalyst for social justice in nineteenth-century Russia can scarcely be overstated. Up until the assassination of Alexander I in 1881, Russian literature of that period can be envisioned as a groaning library shelf of social-problem fiction and poetry, even from Slavophile writers like Dostoevsky, who positioned themselves as adamantly opposed to the progressive intelligentsia, and "Westerners" like Chernyshevsky, Nikolai Dobroliubov, Aleksandr Herzen (who ended up living out decades of exile in London and Paris), and Dmitri Pisarev. In sheer quantity, this writing dwarfs contemporary American works grappling with the legacy of unfree labor and injustice, represented by landmarks such as Frederick Douglass's *My Bondage and My Freedom* and *Narrative of the Life of Frederick Douglass, American Slave*, and Harriet Beecher Stowe's somewhat tone-deaf antislavery novel, *Uncle Tom's Cabin*. The abolition of serfdom in 1861 was the result of a number of practical considerations, most notably the fiscal hemorrhaging that it caused in a country that was keen to compete more vigorously with Western nations. Nonetheless, social-problem fiction like Ivan Turgenev's short story cycle *A Sportsman's Sketches* (1852) was integral to the emancipation of the serfs in a way that US antislavery fiction was not to the abolition of slavery. Although *Uncle Tom's Cabin* raised awareness, internationally and among educated white Americans, of the immiserating practices of slavery, the book's role as a catalyst for the Civil War has been vastly exaggerated.[9] Certainly, its impact was overshadowed by John Brown's rebellion in 1859 and undercut by a pietistic sentimentality that repelled more discerning readers. Douglass's international activism and outspoken publications were far more important than Stowe's novel in drawing attention to an evil embedded within the legal and social fabric of the nation. Yet, while his autobiography and essays were of the highest literary value, they were screens for the projection of an appalling reality of exploitation, rather than a space for the shrewdly oblique literary forms of expression that belong to the category of fiction. Nor did Douglass and his antislavery contemporaries—white as well as black—consider the elevation of fiction and poetry over expository prose to be necessary in their fight for freedom. The publication of Chaadaev's essay in letter form placed the genre of creative nonfiction under harsh and punitive terms of probation, which lasted well into the relatively liberal reign of Alexander II. Thus, the specific strictures of censorship in Russia up to the end of the nineteenth century made imaginative literature a refuge for a social reality that dared not speak its name.

The decades preceding and following the abolition of serfdom saw frenetic shifts in the class system in Russia. The influence of Republican-minded and autocracy-hating aristocrats like Chaadaev was waning, thanks in part to the ease with which the regime could identify and punish such prominent individuals. In a country where the monarch was considered to be the ultimate landowner, members of the nobility could be readily exiled and dispossessed of their estates. Further under the radar were members of the technical and professional intelligentsia, whose gradual emergence from the 1840s through the 1870s was made possible by ambitious infrastructure and public works projects—most notably, improved roads and the national railway line—undertaken by Nicholas I and Alexander II.[10] This "new" class was actually drawn from segments or remnants of others, such as the families of parish priests, the often well-to-do peasant merchant class (*kupechestvo*), freed serfs, landed gentry in long-term military service or in straitened circumstances because of the departure of the serfs from their estates, and members of the civil service that Peter the Great had established in the 1720s in accordance with Prussian models of chancellery hierarchy. Members of this eclectic new class came to be known as the *raznochintsy*, "those of various [or different] ranks."

This is the real beginning of the Russian intelligentsia that Morson and Latynina refer to. Chaadaev and his privileged generation were merely their hesitant forerunners. Among other things, this new generation zealously pursued the material improvement of social reality. The hero of Chernyshevsky's *What Is to Be Done* represents the religious fervor of these values:

> Yes, however rude Rakhmetov's manners, everyone remained convinced that he acted as he did because it was the most sensible and simplest way to act. He would utter his harshest words and most horrible reproaches in such a way that no reasonable man could take offense. In spite of this phenomenal rudeness, he was basically a very tactful person. He always prefaced his comments in a particular way. He began each and every delicate explanation by saying, "You're aware that I speak without any personal emotion. If my words are unpleasant, I beg you to excuse them. I consider it inappropriate to take offense at anything said in earnest, especially when it's uttered out of necessity, with no intention to offend. Moreover, as soon as you consider it pointless to listen to my words, I'll stop. I have the following rule: I always offer my opinion when I should but never impose it on anyone."[11]

Rakhmetov does not suffer fools gladly. His assessment of the spiritualized, self-indulgent Hegelian idealism of those around him is blunt: "'Now you have some idea of my views on this matter. Would you find it useful to hold such a conversation?' If you said no, he'd turn aside and walk away."[12] One distinct advantage of membership in a class that consists of the flotsam and jetsam of other classes is that you feel no particular allegiance to codes of behavior that you regard as arbitrary and unnatural:

> Outside his circle he made the acquaintance only of those people who had some influence over others. Someone who wasn't an authority for other people couldn't even enter into conversation with Rakhmetov. He would say, "You'll excuse me, but I don't have the time," and would walk away. By the same token, no one could avoid becoming acquainted with Rakhmetov if the latter wanted it to happen. He simply appeared and declared what it was he required with the following prelude: "I wish to become acquainted with you. It's essential. If this isn't a good time, set another." He paid no attention whatever to your petty concerns, even if you were his closest acquaintance and were begging him to become involved in your predicament. "I haven't time," he would say and turn aside. But he did get involved in important matters, when in his own opinion it was necessary, even though no one desired it. "I must," he would say. The things he used to say and do on such occasions are beyond comprehension.[13]

Rakhmetov became a vivid archetype for the public demeanor of the Russian progressive intelligentsia. Like Goethe's novel *The Sorrows of Young Werther* and James Baldwin's essay collection *Notes of a Native Son*, *What Is to Be Done?* was a book that both reflected and amplified a changing sensibility among people whose lives were defined primarily by mental and creative, as opposed to manual, labor, or who were shifting from the latter to the former. As evidenced by many characters in the fiction of Turgenev, Dostoevsky, Chekhov, and Tolstoy—most notably in the almost comically dogmatic, yet ultimately tragic, figure of Levin's brother Nikolai in *Anna Karenina*—these men and women were distinctive for their missionary zeal, which often expressed itself in behavioral aberrations. As the neo-Romantic prose writer Prince Vladimir Odoevsky noted in a diary entry from 1866: "One of the nihilists' rules was not to be presentable [*opriatnym*, "neat" or "tidy"]. How disgusting! [*Chto za gadost'!*], especially if they lived in fornication; their stench must be unbearable."[14]

A prominent and much discussed example of aberrant behavior from a member of the prerevolutionary intelligentsia was the life and work of the populist (*Narodnik*) writer Gleb Uspensky. His nervous breakdown, during a period of intensive political and literary work in 1888, coincided with the extended rout of the populist movement that followed the assassination of the tsar in 1881. Uspensky imagined that he was struggling to free himself from two voices in his head: a morally good one represented by his first name (Gleb), and an evil one represented by his middle name, or patronymic (Ivanovich). In "Two Aspects of Language" (1956), Roman Jakobson points out that Uspensky's "bad" name is associated with the patronymic, and therefore with "sins of the father." "The linguistic aspect of this split personality," Jakobson explains, results from "the patient's inability to use two symbols for the same thing," which is to say that Uspensky suffers from "a similarity disorder."[15]

Uspensky belonged to the lower- to mid-level landed gentry, which was dramatically impoverished by the abolition of serfdom; like small plantation owners in the antebellum American South, he belonged to a class whose nagging sense of guilt about their role in the institution of unfree labor and human bondage—what we may call, in accordance with Jakobson's formulation, the "sins of the fathers"—clashed with their bitterness about being dispossessed and coming down in the world. The larger point here is that Uspensky, to himself as well as to his contemporaries, represented an image of the progressive intelligentsia as alienated from itself and deracinated. To use Chaadaev's memorable formulation, the Russian intelligentsia is "a stranger to itself." It is a class that is unwell, racked with a moralistic fervor that is destructive to itself and possibly to others. In an analogous manner, such otherwise highly dissimilar writers as William Faulkner, Allen Tate, and Carson McCullers relied on a lingering contrarian pride in the fallen the Confederacy as an affective stratagem for offsetting their keen sense of guilt about their family histories and their bitterness and ambivalence about the legacy of their regional identities and the decline in their family fortunes since Reconstruction.

Parallel with the image or stereotype of Chernyshevskian, Rakhmetov-like progressive intellectuals as proud of their social maladjustment and ideological tunnel-vision was the figure of the well-meaning yet hopelessly neurotic and politically conflicted Russian liberal. Unlike the typical member of the Russian progressive intelligentsia, the liberal often came from the nobility. Well-known literary representations are Dostoevsky's "A Nasty Story" (1862) and Tolstoy's story "The Death of Ivan Ilyich" (1886) and his essay "Confession" (1879–84). "A Nasty Story" has as its protagonist a hapless and deluded nobleman named Ivan Pralinsky who lives in the capital city of St. Petersburg and imagines himself to be passionately sympathetic to the plight of the urban poor and the recently freed serfs:

> However, the regeneration of Russia suddenly raised great hopes in him. Attainment of the rank of General only confirmed them. He blossomed forth and held

up his head once more. He suddenly began to speak eloquently and profusely; he spoke on most subjects, which he felt very strongly about and which he had absorbed with astonishing rapidity. He sought out occasions to speak; he went about town and in many places succeeded in becoming known as a desperate liberal [*otchaiannym liberalom*], which flattered him greatly.[16]

Dostoevsky's shrewdly psychological and social portrait of Pralinsky explains much about the character's "desperate" liberalism: the Russian adjective chimes more audibly with "despair" than its counterpart in English. He comes from a good family, but he was orphaned at a young age and ended up in the care of a distant relative, who promptly shipped him off to boarding school. Although he works in a government ministry and lives comfortably, he is utterly alone, with no extended family or life partner. The reader is made to understand that these life circumstances resulted in Pralinsky's perception of himself as "too vain and oversensitive": in spite of his affluence, "at times he had attacks of morbid conscience and even a slight feeling of remorse." At such moments he felt "dejected, especially when his attack of piles was at its worst, and called his life *une existence manquée*," losing faith "even in his debating ability," and referring to himself as an "empty talker and phrasemonger."[17] The story centers on his disastrous attempt to be generous to a poverty-stricken clerk in his office by dropping in uninvited to his wedding party in a working-class neighborhood. In a way that seems prescient of current traditionalist attacks upon the cultural elite from commentators like Patrick Deneen and Rod Dreher, whose work we will examine later in this chapter, Dostoevsky portrays the Russian liberal as a clueless solipsist whose awakening to the reality of his pharisaical engagement with others can only lead to a complete mental breakdown.

Such is the blighted internal life of people who, as Tolstoy puts it in his "Confession," devote themselves to the cult of progress in human affairs while "amusing themselves" and "making use of the labor of others," rather than actually "creating life."[18] Liberals, Tolstoy writes, are caught up in a self-theatricalizing "simulation of life" (*podobie zhizni*), in which the "conditions of excess in which we live deprive us of the possibility of understanding life." In "The Death of Ivan Ilyich," Tolstoy describes a well-to-do servant who finds himself rethinking all of his priorities and values when he is faced with a terminal illness. Up to the point of this moral awakening, the entire life of his Ivan Ilyich was governed by the principle that his existence should proceed in a "pleasant and seemly way" that cultivated an equilibrium between his moral conscience and the requirements of material convenience and personal comfort.[19] As Tolstoy indicates, this balancing act lies at the heart of the Russian liberal's hypocrisy and moral disorder, which are inculcated early in the educational setting and in the upbringing characteristic of his privileged class: "All the passions of childhood and youth went by without leaving much of a trace in him; he gave in both to sensuality and to vanity, and—toward the end, in the senior classes [of his university]— to liberalism, but always within the defined limits that his sense accurately indicated to him as correct."[20] The fact that the protagonist of Tolstoy's story about the shock of seeing one's life in its true colors has the same first name and patronymic as that of Dostoevsky's "A Nasty Story" suggests that the author of "The Death of Ivan Ilyich" was seeking to document a long-standing cognitive blindness among those in the propertied class who, since the emancipation of the serfs, imagined themselves to be progressive.

The Russian liberal constantly strives to compensate for the cocoon of economic privilege that surrounds them. The politically liberal class and the radical intelligentsia are represented as severed from the soil of the people, oddly unreceptive to family networks, untouched by the solace of traditional religious devotion and, in the case of the progressive intelligentsia, stable bourgeois comforts. These negative portrayals are amplified in what is arguably the towering classic of anti-intelligentsia literature, the 1909 essay anthology *Vekhi* (Signposts). The contributors—Petr Struve, Mikhail Gershenzon, and the theologian Sergei Bulgakov, among others—aspired to articulate what could be understood as the position of a politically centrist counter-intelligentsia. They attempted to revalidate the significance of spiritual and religious questions for the parsing of injustice; that is, they sought to reverse-engineer a viable religious morality from the sublimated missionary zeal of their ideological opponents.

We see aspects of this project of de-sublimating or extruding the religious content of leftist discourse, in an endeavor to restore religious authority, in the complex and often surprisingly respectful or appreciative responses of militantly right-wing thinkers in their engagement with the legacy of the French Revolution. In *The Reactionary Mind*, Corey Robin argues that a crypto-religious idolatry in the conservative tradition can be traced to opposition to the ascent of the Jacobins. Like the *Vekhi* essayists, the firebrands of reaction whom Robin examines are willing to borrow their opponents' rebarbative rhetorical weapons for the purpose of bringing about the restoration of forgotten or buried values. From this perspective, Robin argues, Edmund Burke's *Reflections on the Revolution in France* (1790) and his seemingly apolitical *A Philosophical Enquiry into the Origin of Our Ideas of the Sublime and the Beautiful* (1757) are, in fact, of one piece:

> The sublime is most readily found in two political forms: hierarchy and violence.
> But for reasons that shall become clear, the conservative—again, consistent with

Burke's arguments—often favors the latter over the former. Rule may be sublime, but violence is more sublime. Most sublime of all is when the two are fused, when violence is performed for the sake of creating, defending, or recovering a regime of domination and rule.[21]

Like Burke and his French contemporary Joseph de Maistre—identified in the introduction to this book as a perceptive observer of autocracy in Russia in his capacity as the French ambassador during the reign of Alexander I—Konstantin Pobedonostsev expressed a moral panic about the consequences of declawing the punitive arm of political authority. Pobedonostsev, procurator of the Holy Synod of the Russian Orthodox Church under Alexander III and Nicholas II, wrote scathing assessments of moneyed liberals in his famous collection *Moskovskii sbornik* (Moscow miscellany, 1901). In terms that foretell the libertarian economist James McGill Buchanan's books about "public choice," with their scurrilous characterization of liberals as a cluster of "rent-seeking" special interests who fool themselves into thinking that they are motivated by the common good, Pobedonostsev, in the years immediately following emancipation, described deluded people involved in a "marketplace of projects" (*rynok proektov*) that is both political and entertainment-driven, rife with the "noise of cheap and superficial ecstasies" that dangerously obscures and disturbs the natural hierarchy of the well-fed and the led.[22]

In reality, liberals and members of the radical intelligentsia in Russia during the second half of the nineteenth century were no more psychologically disordered or sociopathic than people who belonged to the other classes. From the Napoleonic invasion to the 1905 workers' movements, much of Russian political life sought to reckon with the physical suffering and institutional cruelty that, in different ways, distorted the inner lives of people across the spectrum of class. What is important to understand is that the idea of the intelligentsia as psychically crippled by a missionary pride that results from its ambiguous class standing is first and foremost a narrative myth, and not the material actuality that members of the present-day Russian and American traditionalist intelligentsia retrospectively assert. What we see more often in the self-representations of the intelligentsia, in the stifling and repressive atmosphere after the assassination of Alexander II in 1881, is a stubborn pride in their ascetic lifestyle and materially straitened circumstances, which was frequently offset by a distinctive understanding of the power of the political imagination on the quotidian level as well as on the grand scale of utopian visions. As the poet Tatiana Shchepkina-Kupernik once wrote about the hardscrabble bohemian lives of democratic socialists on the eve of the 1905 workers' revolts in St. Petersburg, even a gray tenement that was indistinguishable from thousands of others in the city "seemed like a glorious palace" ([*kazhetsia*] *chudnym dvortsom*) by virtue of the charismatic consciousnesses that inhabited them.[23]

Yet the narrative myth of psychically unwell or disordered intelligentsia is not without power and influence. As Judith Butler points out, we would be very wrong to underestimate artificial constructs, which are in fact potent engines for the manufacturing of self-images. Butler argues that the "double nature" of behavioral norms is manifest in our sense that while "we cannot do without them," we also recognize that we "do not have to assume that their form is given or fixed."[24] Although Butler speaks here about norms that govern understandings of gender identity, this sketching out of a lived engagement with norms as prescriptive models of behavior tells us a great deal about the ways in which American traditionalist intellectuals attempt to promulgate those norms. Extending Butler's insight, we would do well to consider even the stereotype of antinormativity that American traditionalists associate with the progressive intelligentsia as an oblique expression of a norm, in the sense that it points by negative example to normal ways of being in the world. In their writing, these self-christened public intellectuals often revise or alter those traditionalist norms that they admire, even as they endeavor to express or embody them. Furthermore, their representation of the left as wedded to the goal of undermining "family ties" and "traditional commitments to marriage"[25] contains quite a bit of skewed mirroring of their own affective aspirations, in which a libertarian hostility to the values of civic society occupies pride of place. Martin Duberman and other veteran LGBTQ activists have pointed out that supporters of marriage equality, far from seeking to dismantle the category of family, are far more often caught up in a project of expanding and buttressing understandings of it by inviting LGBTQ people into the tent.[26]

These traditionalist intellectuals advertise themselves as apostles of normativity while acting out as acolytes of disruption. In the manner of Dostoevsky and Tolstoy, their dislike of the missionary zeal of the liberal and progressive intelligentsia only partially conceals a similar impulse of their own in regard to those whom they cast as their ideological adversaries. As Robin has noted, "what the conservative ultimately learns from his opponents, wittingly or unwittingly, is the power of political agency and the potency of the mass."[27] In the case of the commentators whom we examine in the next section, who project themselves as staunch spokespersons for social and religious traditionalism, the evocation of the negative example of the prerevolutionary Russian intelligentsia says far more about them than it does about those whom they point to as its present-day reincarnation.

The Christianity of the American Traditionalist Intelligentsia

Cultural elites have often suffered from an image problem in Russia and the United States. What does it mean to be a member of a "cognitive" or "meritocratic" elite (terms of opprobrium used by American conservative commentators as varied as Ross Douthat, Peggy Noonan, Rod Dreher, and Charles Murray) who never endeavored to use their skills either to enrich themselves or to consolidate and reinforce the privilege into which they were born? Isn't there something deeply stubborn, if not perverse, about self-interest that disdains a clear-cut remunerative reward? Indeed, such a self-sabotaging life choice could hardly be understood as rationally self-interested at all. Following this arc of reasoning, some of us might find ourselves less than surprised by the blurry identity profiles of these often unaffluent, if largely hypothetical, cultural influencers. Although this line of argumentation is particularly characteristic of American libertarianism, with its overflowing contempt for cultural workers and the so-called pointy heads of higher education, some of its elements have recently made their way to the Russian blogosphere. In the run-up to the 1 July 2020 Constitutional Amendment referendum—which, among other things, contained a measure that made it possible for Putin to remain in office until 2036, and another that would officially declare marriage as being between a "man and a woman"—Putin's political ally Yevgeny Prigozhin funded a political video in which actors portray a well-heeled if somewhat bohemian same-sex couple trying to adopt a young boy, who yearns instead for a mother and father.[28]

Prigozhin's media group, Patriot, clearly draws on the formulations of the Defense of Marriage Act (DOMA), initially advanced by the conservative Family Research Council, based in Boulder, Colorado, and signed into law in 1996 by Bill Clinton. The replication points up the global convergence of conservative political action organizations. Patriotism is, it would seem, first and foremost a matter of standing up to the increasing hegemony of the cultural elite's deracinated values, even if that means breaking bread with your counterparts across borders. In his polemical study *From Tolerance to Equality: How Elites Brought America to Same-Sex Marriage* (2018), Darel E. Paul, a professor of political science at Williams College, provocatively argues that "the top 20%–25% of households" in the United States serve as "a broad working definition of the American 'elite.'"[29] And who are these people? As Paul elaborates, "Unlike both capitalists and the traditional middle class," they belonged to a "new" class that that "own[s] no physical means of production," thus seeming "to be workers." And, yet, they belonged to a professional class defined by the practice of generally nonmanual labor, such as engineers, civil servants, and members of the educational, legal, and medical professions. "Unlike the industrial and agricultural working classes, they had significant skills, enjoyed special employment benefits, and exercised real if limited control over their own labor." It is these people who form the "mass base for the cultural projects and political activism of the gay rights movement," and have been the most significant advocates in the movement for marriage equality. Yet, above all, this is a class of seemingly inscrutable shape-shifters. "Whether known as the 'upper middle class,' 'knowledge workers,' 'symbolic analysts,' 'creatives,' or 'bobos,' this is the class that turned the dreams of a very small percentage of the American population into reality."[30] The current American conservative understanding of the term "elite" is deeply anchored in this understanding of the category as comprising the middle and upper-middle class of cultural advocates, rather than people who are defined by wealth. As Paul argues, however, this is not to say that it is a class without economic aspirations.

In the revised, post-2016 edition of *Why Liberalism Failed*, Patrick J. Deneen, the David A. Potenziani Memorial College Chair of Constitutional Studies at Notre Dame, characterizes the cultural elite as a new class that "perceive[s] that power lay no longer in static property but in the manipulation of ideas and production processes." The efforts of this class to alchemize ideas into political, if not actual, capital, enabled it to replace "the propertied (aristocratic) class."[31] The curmudgeonly traditionalist undertones of that last statement of Deneen's (which references both Burke's *Reflections on the Revolution in France* [1790] and James Burnham's *The Managerial* Class [1962]) are unmistakable. Above all, this class is intent upon upending the natural order of things. Looking through Deneen's microscope, we should hardly be surprised by all the strange and grotesque creatures that swim into view, created in the biopolitical laboratory of the new class that he loathes:

> Liberalism's logic seeks to eliminate not only borders as we normally consider them—through political and economic globalization—but also the "boundaries" that exist in nature. Today's emphasis upon issues of identity—especially arising from the sexual revolution—arise equally from the liberal abhorrence of "forms." The *human* form above all that requires elimination is sexual difference, a goal advanced by increasingly aggressive efforts to secure state-funded birth control, abortion, and artificial forms of fertilization and gestation of children. The people most committed to protecting and preserving the environment and the technological manipulation of nature are often the most fervent in support of eliminating every evidence of natural differentiation between men and women, through chemical and technological manipulation.[32]

For Darel Paul, all demonstrations and activism on behalf of the queer community serve the purpose of monetizing the tawdry exhibitionism that disrupts settled communities:

In June 1970, America's first gay pride parades hit the streets. Four U.S. cities—New York, Los Angeles, Chicago, and San Francisco—hosted crowds ranging from several hundred to a few thousand marching with homemade signs declaring "pride," "power," and "liberation." Like the 1969 Stonewall riots that inspired them, early parades began as intentional acts of disruption, combining political protest with cultural defiance. Fifty annual marches later, Pride parades are backed by our most powerful individuals and institutions. Fortune 500 corporations bankroll them.[33]

In Deneen's psychologized and vaguely Lacanian interpretation, this elite consists of people whose anxiety over the indeterminacy of their own identity—the result of their own rootlessness and frenetic casting about for symbolic models of identity—has real-life consequences and repercussions for others. Paul refuses to acknowledge that the Stonewall riots were push-back against police harassment and targeted maltreatment. When he looks at gay people, all he sees are dress rehearsals for the self-entertainment and enrichment of an urban "creative" class—a term of opprobrium for him. It is precisely the indeterminacy of the cultural elite's role, function, and place that infuriates these traditionalist commentators.

Elsewhere in *Why Liberalism Fails*, Deneen retrofits this religiously inflected critique of nontraditional ways of being in the world onto John Stuart Mill's *On Liberty* (1859), claiming, with no evidence, that the forging of "offensive forms of individuality" was one aspect of Mill's utopian vision of a society guided by a cognitive elite.[34] According to Deneen, what stands against this spirit of license and unbridled passion or *thumos* in moral affairs is the fact that "Americans, for much of their history, were not philosophically interested in Burke but were Burkeans in practice."[35] One wonders how such a transfusion of ideals into postrevolutionary American culture would take place: a reverence for the hallowed character of ancient social institutions, piped in from the writings of a political theorist who believed in the divine right of kings, and who drew a red line at independence for the North American colonies. Deneen cites the "Burkean" virtues, such as living "in accordance with custom" and with the "basic moral assumptions concerning the fundamental norms that accompanied the good life." Thus, "you should respect authority, beginning with your parents. . . . stay married. . . . thank and worship the Lord. . . . pay respect to the elderly and remember and acknowledge your debts to the dead."[36] Suffice it to say that these were also the values of the slave-owning class in the United States. As the historian Drew Gilpin Faust notes in *The Creation of Confederate Nationalism: Ideology and Identity in the Civil War South* (1988), "Antebellum southern religion had been characterized by an emphasis on personal morality as the key to salvation," eschewing the advocacy for "fundamental structural or institutional transformations" that was characteristic of its northern Protestant counterpart.[37] The pragmatic yet oddly decontextualized pietism that Deneen admires, and that he claims to be an alternative to "much of what today passes for culture"—a persistent reflex of "mocking sarcasm and irony," a jettisoning of "custom," and a pseudo-religion with "late night television" as "the special sanctuary of this liturgy"[38]—is far too generalized to serve as the roadmap to a better way of positioning yourself in a world populated by people who may be different from you. Certainly, cluttering his discussion with culture-war shibboleths about the evils of digital practices and popular culture does not help Deneen's argument.

Deneen and Paul are culturally conservative tenured professors who aspire to be contrarian public intellectuals, in the mode of Mark Bauerlein (currently the editor in chief of *First Things*) and the literary critic Frederick Crews. Deneen's and Paul's academic publications and Twitter posts are fiercely combative yet for the most part high-toned, intended to draw attention to the infiltration of progressivism into American higher education. In a critique that has become a *locus classicus* in diatribes against a leftist American academy, Crews wrote in 1985 that "influential departments in several fields of study have begun to practice what I will call Left Eclecticism, a welcoming of many styles of anti-establishment analysis—not just orthodox Marxist but also structuralist, deconstructionist, feminist, gay, Lacanian, Foucauldian, and assorted combinations of these." Of particular importance for our discussion is Crews's emphasis on the performative, if not pharisaical, aspect of academic leftism. "The atmosphere of Left Eclecticism," he argues, "constitutes a temptation to wanton posturing," writing that seeks to create its own reality of supportive claques through applications of a hermetic system of "interpretive rules." Using Fredric Jameson's *The Political Unconscious* as an example, Crews charges that these performances in print and in the classroom often seek to gloss over the "the antinomies lying at the heart of Marxism" through a rhetoric that is driven more by "incantation" than reasoning.[39]

To a remarkable extent, Crews's assertion about the abstract quality of American academic leftism—the sense that it turns Marxism's relation between economic base and cultural superstructure on its head—is echoed in early twentieth-century Russian critiques of the revolutionary intelligentsia. Nikolai Berdiaev wrote "Philosophical Verity and the Truth of the Intelligentsia" (1909) for the politically centrist yet anti-intelligentsia anthology *Vekhi*, published in response to the events that followed the 1905 workers' revolts in St. Petersburg and Moscow. "Generally speaking," he wrote, "economic materialism and Marxism were misunderstood among us: they were interpreted 'subjectively' and adapted to the traditional psychology of the intelligentsia." As a result, "on Russian soil, economic materialism lost its objective character: the productive-constructive factor was pushed into the background and the subjective class-oriented aspect of social democracy stepped out into the foreground."[40] Morson has drawn attention to the relevance of the *Vekhi* anthology as a prescient critique of militant utopianism that is now no less relevant to political life outside the Russian context.[41]

Such creaky conceits in the academic culture wars from the eighties to the present are useful for drawing our attention to these commentators' own practices of performative signaling. With its involuted structure of embedded statements and quotations in the form of retweets, Twitter provides a framework for a kind of incantatory and gestural politics that Crews could then only have dreamt about. Among other things, Twitter makes it possible to close the gap between abstruse academic theory and its practical applications. The combination of telegraphic simplification and bridge-building between abstract value systems on the one hand, and the affect-driven present of experienced outrage on the other, is a strong part of its appeal as a social-media platform. With this in mind, we need to conceive of Twitter as a meeting place of three classes of intellectuals: the academics, the popularizers, and the followers. Among the popularizers, no one serves more clearly as a bridge between the traditionalist integralism of academics like Deneen, Paul, Helen Andrews, Adrian Vermeule, Gladden Pappin, and others associated with *First Things* than the blogger Rod Dreher.

The Syncretic Religiosity of Rod Dreher

With a Twitter account that currently lists ninety-one thousand followers and two books that breached the top ten of the *New York Times* bestseller list, Rod Dreher is arguably one of the major figures in the campaign to define and defend a grassroots Christianity against a globalist neoliberal culture of secular elites. He is also increasingly prominent as an apologist for Russian foreign policy. At the beginning of 2022, in a series of blog posts, he justified a possible Russian invasion of Ukraine on the grounds that Kyiv would always be precious to devout Russians as the cradle of "Russian" Christianity.[42] An examination of his views is useful for understanding the arguments of traditionalist activists in both countries, and especially those in which they flesh out and clarify their complex ideal of a global populist intelligentsia.

In his 2017 bestseller *The Benedict Option: A Strategy for Christians in a Post-Christian Nation*, Dreher mounts an articulate case for traditionalist religious believers to retreat from an irreligious world with the goal of reflecting upon their losses and core values. He argues that the Benedictine monastic order, founded in the sixth century, serves as a model for all Christian denominations in creating a communal interiority that can withstand full-frontal assaults on the very idea of religious belief. Readers will have barely navigated through half of chapter 2 ("The Roots of the Crisis") before realizing that Dreher is commingling the beliefs and practices of traditionalist Christians from the Catholic and Eastern Orthodox churches and various evangelical Protestant denominations in a way that would not be possible in reality. As he himself comes close to admitting, Dreher is a nimble warehouse attendant of faith, a writer who fluidly brings together on the page religious traditions that otherwise have little in common.

This commingling, he ultimately argues, is more than simply the product of a rhetorical sleight of hand. As he puts it, we are living in a time of "secular nihilism" that openly sneers at "historical biblical orthodoxy," has abolished the category of gender and therefore what it means to be human, and seeks to replace traditional faith with the grotesque postmodernist congeries of Moralistic Therapeutic Deism.[43] We have reached the "end point of modernity," where the "autonomous, freely choosing individual" finds meaning "in no one but himself," and "each person becomes, in effect, his own Pope." Is it any wonder, then, that "Protestant, Catholic, and Eastern Orthodox" churches have become "nothing more than a loosely bound assembly of individuals committed to finding their own 'truth,'" and have ceased to be "the church in any meaningful sense, because there is no shared belief."[44] Fighting back against the onslaught of a post-Christian culture has compelled people to break bread across denominational lines:

> Times have changed, and so have some of the issues that conservative Evangelicals and Catholics face. But the need for an ecumenism of the trenches is stronger than ever. Metropolitan Hilarion Alfeyev, a senior bishop in the Russian Orthodox Church, has on several occasions appealed to traditionalists in the West to form a "common front" against atheism and secularism. To be sure, the different churches should not compromise their distinctive doctrines, but they should nevertheless seize every opportunity to form friendships and strategic alliances in defense of the faith and the faithful.[45]

Dreher wants to finesse a conclave among these three branches of Christianity. Yet if a person takes their religion seriously—if they view its tenets as nonnegotiable—no level of agreement with other Christian denominations on individual issues such as abortion or same-sex marriage will catalyze a convergence on doctrinal positions, which Dreher apparently regards as secondary in their significance or even trivial. A few examples of these issues are the literal truth of scripture (essential to the beliefs of the Southern Baptist Convention, but peripheral in Catholicism and Eastern Orthodoxy) and the centrality of the end times and the Book of Revelation (true for some charismatic Protestant denominations and the Jehovah's Witnesses, arguably of marginal theological significance in the older Christian traditions), not to mention matters reflected in liturgy and weekly devotion, such as devotion to the Virgin Mary and the Eucharist.

Dreher's keenness to elide these doctrinal differences prompts the question of just how much of a traditionalist he actually is. Are you a traditionalist if you pick and choose what to believe? What else can we do, living as we do in an internet-propelled Sodom and Gomorrah, with the "world collapsing around us"?[46] Crisis and end times, he seems to argue, call for a dilution of distinctions among faiths. As he puts it somewhat defensively in his next book, *Live Not by Lies: A Manual for Christian Dissidents* (2020), "It is not a false ecumenism that claims all religions are the same," but rather "a mutual recognition" of the reality of religious persecution" and the need for "spiritual survival."[47] All too often in *The Benedict Option*, his astute observations about the need to disconnect from the imperious sensorium of social media are drowned out by a slurry of reductive categories and pious phrasemaking. In an otherwise compelling chapter where he describes his visit to the world's oldest continuously operating Benedictine monastery, in Norcia, Umbria, Dreher pauses to deliver a battery of banalities: "The rootlessness of contemporary life has frayed community bonds. It is common now to find people who don't know their neighbors and don't really want to. To be a part of a community is to share in its life. That inevitably makes demands on the individual that limits their freedom."[48] A commonsensical reader would point out that barricading oneself in a self-selecting community is hardly conducive to the forging of connections with neighbors.

Then there is "How (Not) to Think About the Caravan," a 25 October 2018, column in the *American Conservative*. This passage effectively disarticulates the brief for the restoration of human connection that serves as the centerpiece for *The Benedict Option*:

> The Bible tells Christians to love their neighbors as they love themselves. But who is their neighbor? The man next door? Yes. The people who live across town? Surely. Those who live in another part of their country? Okay. People from another country who want to settle in their country? Erm . . .
> If everybody is your neighbor, then nobody is.[49]

Like many religiously inclined conservatives who cannot resist the clarion call of the culture wars, Dreher is fond of casting contrived oppositions or false dichotomies as existing firmly within the realm of natural law. Here, the racialization of strangers combines with an understanding of communities as *given* rather than *chosen*, facilitating rigid barriers against migration.

Given the eclecticism of traditionalist practices that Dreher highlights throughout the book, it would hardly make sense to say that he is slyly arguing for the Eastern Orthodox Church as the one true path to salvation. Rather, it seems that Eastern Orthodoxy, by dint of its hidebound antiquity and stubborn antimodernism, is a first among equals at the round table of Christian warriors that he conjures up. The level of Dreher's thinking about Orthodoxy is best gauged by a joke he posted on his Twitter account on 25 July 2020: "Actually good Orthodox joke: Q: How many Orthodox Christians does it take to change a light bulb? A: Change? Vot is zees 'change'?"[50] Writing about the importance of mortification of the flesh for true belief, he writes that "few modern lay Christians outside Eastern Orthodox circles (and too few within them) undertake regular fasting and other regular tangible forms of asceticism."[51] Later, he elaborates upon the lessons that the Orthodox Jewish communities can offer to those who are Christian in name only: "Orthodox Rabbi Mark Gottlieb says that Christians living apart from mainstream culture need 'raw, roll-up-your-sleeves dedication to create deep structures of community.' If we are to survive, we need to develop a 'laser-like focus and dedication to seeing themselves [*sic*] as the next link of the Christian story.'"[52] This gloss hollows out the ethical and intersubjective teachings of Orthodoxy, reflected in its imperative of self-examination during Lent, whose closest equivalent in other religious traditions is the reflective atonement required for Yom Kippur. For Dreher, old things are good simply because they are old; the capital *O* in "Orthodox" serves as a hot button for releasing the endorphin boost of a heady and obdurate traditionalism.

Who are the villains of Dreher's world? He describes a modernity in which each person narcissistically pursues their own—or, in his against-the-grain non-gender-neutral terminology, "his" own—truth.[53] Yet, according to Dreher's own characterization of the Benedictine Rule, we all need to acknowledge our need for engagement with that which is outside of us, and which will make us more self-aware.[54] It should hardly need explaining that this journey of self-discovery could also be interpreted as inwardly focused. Dreher's sculpture garden of straw-man arguments often prevents him from seeing that the paragons of piety whom he interviews fully recognize the need for self-care, a practice of cognitive scaffolding for morally and spiritually compromised selves that can be traced to conversion narratives as old as those of Paul the Apostle and St. Augustine. At the Norcia retreat, one priest states that "when a man first comes to a monastery, the first thing he notices is everybody else's quirks—that is, what's wrong with everybody else. But the longer you're here, the more you begin to think:

what's wrong with me? You go deeper into yourself to learn your own strengths and weaknesses. And that leads you to acceptance of others."[55] The leader of the monastery that Dreher visits speaks of personal transformation in terms that are scarcely different from the "Moralistic Therapeutic Deism" (MTD) that he decries, with its supposed insistence, in a bowdlerized paraphrase of Freud, that we "stop the fruitless search for a non-existent source of meaning and instead seek self-fulfillment."[56]

Nor does Dreher comprehend how highlighting that monastic community's observance of the virtue of hospitality—what one monk he interviews calls, in a faintly multicultural vein, a bringing together of people "from different blood relations, languages, and ethnicities"[57]—might clash with his vitriolic attack on travelers and migrants, be they privileged North Americans and Europeans frustrated by the vacuity of materialistic late-stage capitalism or people of color from the developing world who have become refugees through the upheavals of climate change, politicized religious violence, or exploitive global labor practices. Offering a partial defense of Donald Trump's reference to "shithole countries" in a 2018 blog column for the *American Conservative*, Dreher enjoins us to be "honest" with ourselves and ask whether we truly want "the people who turned their neighborhood a [*sic*] shithole to bring the shithole to your street."[58] In another column two years prior to his publication of *The Benedict Option*, Dreher opined that Jean Raspail's openly racialist novel *The Camp of Saints* (1971) "is not about race, but about culture, and the West having become too broad-minded and humane to protect itself from an unarmed invasion by people who do not share its culture, and who do not want to adopt its culture, but only want to [*sic*] peace, security, and prosperity of the West." In the same piece, he sounds an alarm about the present-day refugee crisis: "If Europe lets them all in, it will soon no longer be Europe. How do those nations defend themselves against invaders who come unarmed, seeking charity? If one is a Christian, what is the Christian response?"[59] Apparently, the response is to suspend the Benedictine rule of welcoming outsiders. As the *New Republic* religion essayist Sarah Jones accurately wrote: "The Orthodox Christian writer did not specifically refer to people of color, but he didn't need to; he just invoked their ghostly outlines and let the reader fill them in."[60] In this regard, it should be noted that Dreher is so wedded to a romanticized vision of the Eastern Church as first and foremost a sanctuary for harassed European white people that he seems utterly insensible—or perhaps is simply indifferent—to the existence of 45 million Orthodox worshipers in Ethiopia, Kenya, Sudan, and Eritrea who are people of color.

The characterization of the Eastern Orthodox Church as a paladin for the values, traditions, and ethnonationalist identities of Western Europe has become an invasive meme among traditionalist commentators like Dreher and Helen

Andrews. For a wide range of present-day demographic as well as historical reasons, this notion is a very poor fit indeed, although the anthropologist Sarah Riccardi-Swartz has documented the spread of this cultural conceit about the church's "chosen" mission to purge the West, and the United States in particular, of the toxins of political correctness, "woke" religiosity, and cultural decadence among Orthodox communities in the United States over the last twenty years.[61]

The participatory aspect of Dreher's journalism—outlining a picture that his followers will fill in or finish—is evident in his rhetorical performance of aporia, or being at a loss for words, as if the evil he contemplates is so prodigious and obscene that language itself fails before it. It is therefore somehow fitting that the real villains of Raspail's novel, according to Dreher, are not those dehumanized hordes of nonwhites but rather the elites, the "do-gooders in the European establishment—government, academia, media, the church—who have come to hate their own civilization, or at least not love it enough to defend it from a flotilla of a million Third World migrants sailing towards Europe."[62] Like Patrick Deneen and Darel Paul, Dreher is animated by a loathing for an imagined duplicitous First World elite—political leaders, diplomats, higher-level civil servants, creative workers who "don't work with their hands," and damnably modernist, if not postmodernist, clerical authorities, whose cosmopolitanism and protean class identity combine to create a rhetorically convenient gallery of shape-shifting monsters. Employing an opaque formulation that is much beloved by Trump-era traditionalist commentators, Deneen characterizes these people as agents of an "anticulture."[63] "Thanks to the shared interests between intellectuals and investors," Paul argues, "left-modernism has combined with capitalism's 'four freedoms'—the free movement of goods, services, capital, and labor across borders—to become the ruling ideology throughout the West."[64] Reflecting a sharp ideological turn within recent traditionalist writing that recalls the road-to-Damascus moment of his New Testament namesake, Paul voices disenchantment with the unfettered global free market. Yet how serious is this critique of neoliberal globalism, and whom do Paul, Deneen, Andrews, and Dreher identify as guilty of these predatory practices? Having undergone a similarly miraculous awakening to the evils of late-stage capitalism, Deneen expresses anguish about the corporate apologists who are keen to "eviscerate" the "old practices" of "care, patience, humility, reverence, respect, and modesty."[65]

In the end, all four commentators are more enraged by these traitors to their social station and Occidental traditionalism than by the racial and ethnic Others whom they see as impinging on the territories of the West. Without calling the cognitive or coastal or globalist elites "race traitors," their arguments certainly gesture toward such a charge. To paraphrase Sarah Jones, they don't *need* to explicitly invoke the category of race traitor. Yet, within this gallery of ogres, members of the LGBTQ community occupy a prominent place because of the ways in which their activist presence would seem to challenge the supremacy of citizenship as defined by an indissoluble conjunction of belief and blood. In his laudatory review of Eric Kaufmann's *Whiteshift: Populism, Immigration, and the Future of White Majorities* (2017), Paul lingers on the conception, advanced by the French populist commentator Pierre Manent, of the social contract as a "mode of communion":

> Manent uses the religious imagery of communion intentionally. At least through-out the West, for the past two hundred years the nation has been the "sacred community" with which people identify and for which they sacrifice. The nation has been the great horizontal comradeship through which our rights and duties of citizenship are created and realized.[66]

It is not altogether clear if Paul understands that this metaphor is rather specific within the French context, a deliberate evocation of notions of national identity favored by the Catholic Church in France until the institution of state-mandated *laïcité*, or secularism, in 1905—a confluence of majority religion with state affairs that the present-day French alt-right swoons over, and whose termination by legislative fiat they decry. When Secretary of State Anthony Blinken on 22 April 2021 authorized the rainbow flag to be flown on the same flagpole as the American flag at embassy compounds, Paul quipped in a tweet: "Why is the US govt so keen on flying the rainbow banner? Because queerness epitomizes the cultural values that are central to contemporary American therapeutic culture."[67]

The soft-focus sententiousness of Deneen's and Paul's inventories of virtues and Dreher's syncretic traditionalism begs the question of what they believe must supplant liberalism. Some answers to this question emerge in *Live Not by Lies*, Dreher's most recent book. The title comes from Aleksandr Solzhenitsyn's essay "Live Not by Lies!" (1974). Literally the day after he wrote the essay, on 12 February 1974, Solzhenitsyn was arrested by the KGB in his Moscow apartment and exiled to West Germany. It was widely circulated in *samizdat* in the following years. One feature that Dreher and many of the writer's other religious supporters ignore is that the piece is primarily a call for intellectual freedom and empirical rigor and honesty about demonstrable reality. In this essay, and arguably in everything he wrote, Solzhenitsyn is more interested in positioning observable facts as touchstones, offsetting the arid generalities and dubious historical claims of official Soviet discourse, than in advancing a religious sensibility. His background in physics is palpable in statements such as we "will not in painting, sculpture, photograph, technology, or music depict, support, or broadcast a single false thought, a single distortion of the truth" as we discern it, and in the warning that even the "safest technical occupations" are not altogether safe from "spiritual servility."[68]

One continued legacy of the prerevolutionary intelligentsia in contemporary Russia is a tendency to regard humanities and natural sciences as complementary endeavors. Among Russians who have been educated past the secondary-school level, there is little evidence of what C. P. Snow described in his essay "The Two Cultures" (1959) as the mutual incomprehension, if not open hostility, between the practitioners of the arts and sciences, which he saw as intellectually crippling to the British university system after the Second World War. As Solzhenitsyn explains, the political standard we should live by is one of "either truth or falsehood: toward spiritual independence or toward spiritual servitude." Solzhenitsyn's use here of the term "spiritual" (*dukhovnyi*) is not exactly what Dreher thinks it is. The Russian word is not dominated by associations with religious sensibility and personal piety, and often refers to the positive qualities of a person whose character manifests decency and integrity. The adjective can also simply refer to the inner or mental life, or the core values, of a person or a community. In some contexts the word may mean nothing more than "intellectual"—a sense that is very far indeed from the faith-based experiencing of the holy spirit. In this essay, what Solzhenitsyn means by "spiritual" is clearly much closer to this cluster of meanings than to any kind of specifically religious experience.

Dreher could not know about this translation issue, but what about his willful distortion of the entirety of Solzhenitsyn's essay, which does not make a single reference to religious belief, into a manifesto for faith against the "Marxist Mordor"[69] of the secular state? This stands uneasily with his stated goal in *Live Not by Lies* of speaking truth to power. Dreher's simplistic framing of the American and Eastern European historical record complements his insistence on the primacy of spirit and faith over flesh and fact. A great deal of the book is an exercise in fabulism. The problem here is not that Dreher draws on the experience of Eastern European peoples without the benefit of speaking or reading their languages—a person can certainly comment or write about cultures whose languages they cannot read or speak as long as they are mindful of the risk of bowdlerizing and misappropriation. Reading is an attempt at dialogue and coalition-building; it is, as Toni Morrison described it, a "sustained surrender to the company of my own mind while it touches" the mind of another;[70] it is a cognitively healthy and ethically beneficial estrangement from oneself that facilitates, or catalyzes, a conversation with someone else, and which furthermore may result in self-knowledge. Dreher should be applauded for the efforts he takes, in this book and in his blog posts, to understand Polish, Czech, Slovak, Romanian, and Russian cultures, whose folkways and political traditions are very different from the assumptions of white Calvinist Protestantism that continue to undergird so much of Anglo-American life. In his essay "Die Weltliteratur" (2007), the novelist Milan Kundera answers his own rhetorical question "Do I mean by this that to judge a novel one can do without a knowledge of its original language?" with a resounding "Indeed, I do mean exactly that!" After all, Kundera notes, "Gide did not know Russian, Shaw did not know Norwegian, Sartre did not read Dos Passos in the original. If the books of Gombrowicz and Danilo Kis had depended solely on the judgment of people who read Polish and Serbo-Croatian, their radical aesthetic newness would never have been discovered."[71] At several points of his arguments in *Live Not by Lies*, Dreher himself draws on Kundera's *The Unbearable Lightness of Being* in ways that are essentially faithful to the 1984 novel. It is therefore unfortunate that Dreher largely, and tendentiously, misunderstands what he takes to be the "traditionalist" values of Eastern Europe. In light of his lack of empathy for people of color and members of the LGBTQ community, whom he regards as little more than cat's-paws for bicoastal elites, this failure should hardly surprise us.[72]

The fatal weaknesses of Dreher's book, and of the American traditionalist critique of "cultural elites" and the liberal intelligentsia in general, occur in those places where the historical record is discussed—or, more often, ignored or hollowed out. Dreher begins chapter 3 ("Progressivism as Religion") of *Live Not by Lies* with an anecdote about Sergei Diaghilev's speech at a dinner held in his honor at the Hotel Metropol in Moscow in 1905. Drawing on James Billington's account of the event in *The Icon and the Axe: An Interpretive History of Russian Culture* (1966), Dreher lingers on Diaghilev's statement about living on the precipice of something "new and unknown" that is both the product of and the possible instrument of demise for those who helped bring it into being. Raising his glass, Diaghilev toasts "the ruined walls of the beautiful palaces, as well as to the new commandments of the new aesthetic," while also expressing hope that he, "an incorrigible sensualist," would still be able to enjoy "the amenities of life," and that "the death [of the old] should be as beautiful and as illuminating as the resurrection." Billington's account of the event is taken from an English-language secondary source, and frames Diaghilev's comments as resonating with, rather than explicitly referring to, the momentous workers' strikes that took place in St. Petersburg and Moscow that same year.[73]

What lesson does Dreher take from this scrap of somewhat formulaic salon oratory in the cultural history of the Russian avant-garde? "What Russia's young artists, intellectuals, and cultural elite hoped for and expected was the end of autocracy, class division, and religion, and the advent of a world of liberalism, equality, and secularism. What they got instead was dictatorship, gulags, and the extermination of free speech and expression."[74] Dreher conflates this speech with later political events that cannot, in any plausible way, be understood as descendants or evolutionary variations of the sentiments that Diaghilev expressed. As a matter of easily accessible historical fact, Diaghilev was no advocate for revolution. Dreher does not seem to understand that the demand for new forms of art is hardly interchangeable with calls for a radically new social order; nor, in his obstinate expectation to hear contempt for religion in every statement made by a nonheterosexual person (as Diaghilev was), does he catch Diaghilev's obvious and arguably traditionalist reference to the resurrection of Christ. Diaghilev saw himself as a facilitator of new movements in the visual arts and in dance, such as Fauvism and Primitivism. Far from being bent on destroying legacies, the practitioners of those movements understood their work as an effort to reconnect with misunderstood, or forgotten and neglected, traditions like folk choreography and icon painting, which, because of its importance for Eastern Orthodox worship, was at that time not considered to be high art of the type that should be studied and displayed in museums. Perhaps this democratic reflex of connecting to folk traditions is what makes Dreher, an avowed lover of only those "old things" that are associated with religious orthodoxy (and Orthodoxy), uncomfortable and queasy. He put things plainly in a blog post from 2017 devoted to what he imagined would be Europe's imminent capitulation to the twin scourges of modernity and Islam: "I love old things, old buildings, old rites, and old places."[75] His reading of Diaghilev's toast expresses an overflowing contempt for the legacy of a man who was crucial for the development of a modernism in the Russian arts that is now considered absolutely canonical and celebrated in museums, dance stages, and concert halls across the globe.

Later in the same chapter, Dreher attempts to close the gap between the current American and prerevolutionary Russian cultural elites by retrofitting a starry-eyed leftist utopianism onto Diaghilev's speech. "We have to throw away this crippling nostalgia for the future, especially the habit that we Americans, a naturally optimistic people, have of assuming that everything will work out for the best." After all, "Diaghilev and the swells at that 1905 banquet had no idea that the beautiful death to which they raised their glasses was going to mean the murder of millions by the executioner's bullet and the engineered famine."[76] The reference to the "swells," or privileged nabobs, listening to Diaghilev's speech manifests an unwillingness to reckon with the otherness of a particular historical moment. Dreher's evocations of prerevolutionary Russia in *Live Not by Lies* function in much the same way as Allan Bloom's references to the supposedly malign legacy of cabaret culture in Weimar Germany in *The Closing of the*

American Mind (1987), another jeremiad against US progressivism that also saw the sixties almost exclusively through the lens of youthful acts of disruption, without looking at the larger panorama of systemic injustices that provoked them. Both authors misidentify the artistic ferment and political activism that were responses to social malaise as the sources of the malaise itself.

And where will this narrowing of the twain—of twenty-first-century America with prerevolutionary Russia—lead us? "There are people who would welcome the Pink Police State. This is a generation that would embrace soft totalitarianism. These are the young churchgoers who have little capacity to resist, because they have been taught that the good life is a life free from suffering."[77] "Pink Police State" usefully conflates two identitarian configurations that Dreher finds loathsome: socialism, diluted from red to a paler or "softer" shade, and homosexuality. Aspects of this contrived dyad were already evident in his characterization of Diaghilev, the nonheteronormative spokesman for an insouciant, and supposedly proto-totalitarian, nihilism. Yet the statement above raises a question that is perhaps more unsettling for Dreher's glib characterization of the cultural elite. What is actual content of Christianity for traditionalist academics like Deneen and Paul and a blogger like Dreher? Given their scorn for the affective and immediate emotive aspects of religious devotion—which for them are often fatally subsumed into postmodernist therapeutic regimens—this turns out to be an extraordinarily difficult question to answer. Attempting to manage the experience of seemingly unbearable suffering, or make sense of it—the affective point of departure for any number of religious traditions—is framed as an exercise in narcissistic frivolity. Drawing on testimony from religious dissidents from the former East Bloc, Dreher comes to the tautological conclusion that Christianity is a "creed" that is tested "in the face of ubiquitous hatred and cruelty," in which "faith is evidence that the True, the real Reality, is the eternal love of God."[78]

Dreher's interviewees tell a story that is more interesting than his reduction of Christianity to a masonic lodge, fraternity, or professional organization asserting a strict distinction between insiders and everyone else. The family of the Czech Catholic dissident Vaclav Benda tells of arranging screenings of movies like *High Noon* in their Prague apartment for themselves and some friends, with no specific agenda with respect to religious instruction. (The choice of that film for viewing by religious believers is interesting, not least because the character played by Grace Kelly goes against the principles of her pacifist Quaker faith to save her spouse's life.) Although Benda and his wife, Kamila, "held their beliefs uncompromisingly within the family, they showed their children by example the importance of working with good and decent people outside the moral and theological community of the church."[79] The Moscow-based

Russian Orthodox dissident Alexander Ogorodnikov tells of interacting in the GULAG with nonpolitical inmates, members of the organized crime networks that proliferated in the seventies and the eighties thanks to the spread of the black market in the Soviet Union. At the insistence of cellmates who were not Orthodox Christians, Ogorodnikov took the unusual step of hearing their confessions even though he was not an ordained priest—a decision that would have been prohibited by church law.[80] The Polish priest Paweł Kęska underscores to Dreher the importance of "not evangelizing people directly but by developing honest relations with one another—not looking for whether one is good or bad, or judging them by their ideology."[81]

To his credit, Dreher pauses in the midst of these testimonies to reflect that "Christians must act to build bonds of brotherhood not just with one another, across denominational and international lines, but also with people of good will belonging to other religions, and no religion at all." Yet this insight is contradicted by almost every other page in a book that gauges the quality of a person's Christianity according to their willingness to excoriate those who do not conform to its creed. Inveighing against "woke" or progressive capitalism, he writes that "Christians today must understand that, fundamentally, they aren't resisting a different politics but rather what is effectively a rival religion."[82] Yet if we let pass this highly dubious presuppositionalist assumption about corporate co-opting of liberal politics as a variety of sublimated faith, the following question arises: why shouldn't adherents of that rival creed, if indeed that is what it is, deserve the good will and nonevangelizing outreach efforts that the Bendas, Kęska, and Ogorodnikov espouse? Dreher's answer seems to pivot on the idea of "woke" religion as consisting of a clergy with no organic laity: a church whose worshipers are exclusively members of the cultural and educational elite, and therefore not a religion at all. Furthermore, like the religions of the mainline churches such as Episcopalianism and Catholicism and of dynamically innovative movements such as Reform Judaism, it is (Dreher, Paul, and Deneen seem to argue) no more a genuine form of faith than the electronically simulated steak that the traitor Cypher enjoys in the 1999 film *The Matrix* is real food. In Dreher's scurrilous formulation: in the "woke" faith, "a white Pentecostal man living in a trailer park is an oppressor; a black lesbian Ivy League professor is oppressed."[83]

In Dreher's world, the latter person would run roughshod over the concerns of religious Americans, whom he defines as those who hew to strict social conservatism. It escapes his notice that believers who belong to politically progressive denominations also have the right to religious freedom. Those who do not follow his straight and narrow heteronormative elitism he deems to be a "shallow self-help cult whose chief aim is not cultivating discipleship but rooting out personal anxieties."[84] In general, Dreher is extraordinarily insensitive to proportion and scale. There is something frivolous in his equivalence of the persecution of East Bloc dissidents with the robust criticism of himself, Deneen, Paul, and the vocal converts to Catholicism J. D. Vance (author of *Hillbilly Elegy*) and Adrian Vermeule of Harvard Law School. It might surprise Dreher to know that the communities he scorns—people of color such as George Floyd, whom he characterizes in a blog post as not being "the innocent victim of racist police officers" that many took him to be, and the LGBTQ community—have more in common with the experiences of political nonconformists and religious objectors from the East Bloc nations than hard-right religious traditionalists in the United States do.[85] To paraphrase T. S. Eliot—himself an eclectic aggregator of traditions, who also posed as a spokesman for a monumentally unitary, if largely mythic, "Tradition"—Dreher sees himself as coming from an epoch that precedes the decay wrought by relativistic liberal values.

Perhaps most troubling is the clear convergence of Dreher's ideal of "Benedictine" communities that wall themselves off from neighbors of other faiths (or no faith at all) and the contempt he expresses for the figure of the stranger in need who comes from another country, or the tepid and wary tolerance he voices for someone from even another part of the country. This fusion opens the door for the possibility of racially exclusionary communities that may serve as microcosms of, or models for, an ethnostate. Dreher's archaistic mini-utopias occupy a conceptual realm that is not far removed from white ethnonationalism. As the historian Alexandra Minna Stern points out, ethnonationalism is a political orientation that is "built on a 'blood and soil' antipathy to the Enlightenment and the worship of an imagined prelapsarian time of tribal solidarity, before the existence of social contracts, citizen subjects, and human rights."[86] Although Dreher often invokes the work of the émigré Russian theologian Alexander Schmemann, who served for decades as the dean of St. Vladimir's Theological Seminary in Crestwood, New York, Schmemann himself was a person from a country other than the United States and would therefore not have readily reflected the image of what we may call the "proximate stranger," the only category of outsider that Dreher is apparently willing to tolerate. While it is true that Schmemann was troubled by the possibility that postwar "therapeutic" culture in the United States would displace or absorb aspects of religious devotion—which, as we have already discussed, is a topic at the center of Dreher's concerns—at no point did he characterize himself as an enemy of secularism or civil society. In a sermon delivered at St. Vladimir's Seminary on 20 March 1983, a few weeks before his death, Schmemann underscored the importance of relationships with the world at large:

So, we have the essential time, the essential relationship with matter filled with reverence, and last, but not least, the rediscovery of the essential *link among ourselves*: the rediscovery that we belong to each other, the rediscovery, that no one has entered my life or your life without the will of God. And with that rediscovery, there is everywhere an appeal, an offering to do something for God: to help, to comfort, to transform, to take with you, with each one of you, that brother and sister of Christ. This is that *essential relationship*.[87]

Although Schmemann wrote his sermons for services at the seminary, the mere fact that he begins this one by addressing "sisters" as well as "brothers" and "fathers" indicates that he was not speaking exclusively to a congregation of men, fellow clergymen or those studying for the priesthood. While wives and daughters of the students and faculty certainly would have been considered "sisters" within the congregation, attendance at St. Vladimir's Church was in fact not restricted to those who lived and worked at the seminary and often included members of the Russian émigré community in the Westchester area.

Schmemann's statement that nothing enters into people's lives "without the will of God" also points to the possibility of contact between Orthodox believers and others, as does his quoting in the same sermon of Boris Pasternak, a Russian writer of Jewish background who was deeply yet idiosyncratically interested in Eastern Orthodoxy: "It is the discovery that God, as Pasternak once said, was ' . . . a great God of details,' and that nothing in this world is outside of that divine reverence."[88] Together with the physical circumstances of his work at the seminary, Schmemann's foregrounding of a larger world of human intersections opens a window onto the diverse lives of Americans who belong to the Orthodox Church of America, which Schmemann himself was involved in establishing as an ethnically and racially neutral denomination that was distinct from the Russian Orthodox Church Outside of America (ROCOR). Schmemann's sermon is a nuanced evocation of dialogue-driven oscillations within Orthodoxy that are amplified exponentially in its interactions and relations with secular society. In contrast, Dreher's writings for the *American Conservative* are awash in apologies for self-selecting localist communities that scorn not only the values of secularism but also individuals who are perceived to be outsiders in terms of religion and nationality.

Conclusion: Traditionalism as a Great Awakening

Trying to establish a niche of institutional authority for themselves that will be distinct from the cultural elite whom they attack, American conservatives search for a positive image of an intellectual class that is consistent with their values.

What would an intelligentsia that is organically responsive to the hallowed traditions of church, state, and the educational system actually look like? For self-declared militant traditionalists like Deneen, Paul, Andrews, Dreher, and Vermeule, this question turns out to be extraordinarily difficult to answer. The present-day category of intelligentsia has its roots in the technically and professionally educated classes of nineteenth-century Russia and the disillusioned legatees of church and state bureaucracies described by Julien Benda in *La trahison des clercs* (The treason of the clerks, 1927). In his novel *Il conformista* (The conformist, 1951) about the capitulation of the Gramscian traditional intelligentsia in fascist Italy, Alberto Moravia powerfully recreates the thinking class's reckoning with a moral crossroads. Such a class is not easily assimilated into the notion of a social order that is based on the Victorian notion of the "Great Chain of Being," itself an inheritance of medieval European scholasticism. Every occupant within a given link of this chain has their own space of operation, and woe betide both the occupant and the larger social body if they strive to transcend the strictly demarcated subrealm that is allotted to them. Tergiversations lead to disruption, with the body parts of the leviathan rebelling against each other in a grotesque seizure that spells chaos and decay.

It is precisely the indeterminacy of the cultural elite's role, function, and place that infuriates traditionalist American commentators, from T. S. Eliot, with his disdainful japes about "worm-eaten liberalism," to Helen Andrews, characterizing the "liberal elite" in prerevolutionary Russia as people who perversely abdicated the authority that was vouchsafed to them. In the same October 2020 opinion piece for the *American Conservative*, Andrews portentously speculates about a possible threat from the Biden campaign: an attempt to manipulate voter responses that is embarrassingly prophetic of the actual behavior of the Republican presidential candidate whom she and her colleagues supported:

> In August, word was leaked that a group of government officials and political operatives calling itself the Transition Integrity Project had gathered a few weeks earlier to game out possible election scenarios. In one, John Podesta, playing candidate Joe Biden, refused to concede after winning the popular vote but losing narrowly in the Electoral College, citing alleged voter suppression. Congress split, blue states threatened to secede, and the hypothetical outcome was determined by the military. Evidently, serious people on the Democratic side are thinking in very broad terms about what the coming months will bring. Republicans should, too, because scenarios like the ones Podesta and Foer are imagining may be unprecedented in the United States, but they are certainly not unprecedented in modern history.[89]

Such a scenario, Andrews suggests, is the inevitable fruiting flower of the moral decadence and self-loathing of a liberal intelligentsia that refuses to accept the responsibilities of the power and authority that it has been afforded. Andrews clearly does not believe that the establishment of the Transition Integrity Project has anything to do with Trump's well-documented refusal, over a period of more than a year preceding the election, to accept voter results that did not run in his favor; instead, she treats the Democrats' contingency plan as an all-but-inevitable strategy of legalized usurpation, opining that *The Atlantic*, "the house magazine of the Resistance, which had done so much to drive the Russiagate soft coup, was apparently preparing the ground for something harder."[90] When the candidate whom she and her magazine endorsed resorted to precisely this strategy of attempted nullification of electoral results, in concert with his own claque of supporters in the Senate and House of Representatives, Andrews herself had no comment. Her colleague at *Compact* magazine Michael Anton is however less reticent about this subject. A former deputy of strategic communication in the Trump administration, Anton has argued that the insurrection was justified because the election was indeed stolen.[91]

In our next chapter, we address resonances of January 6 with the collapse of tsarist Russia—resonances that Andrews and other right-wing intellectuals carefully avoid in their otherwise extensive mining of the Russian historical record. For the time being, we can point to the details of the Russian historical "tragedy" that they find most compelling. Certainly, the image of a rootless nineteenth-century intelligentsia that is restlessly—and perhaps neurotically—in search of a soil in which to nourish itself is not the only aspect of prerevolutionary Russian life that interests these traditionalists. To get a sense of what academics like Deneen and Paul and bloggers like Dreher and Andrews consider to be positive images of an intelligentsia, we need to look at figures and institutional forces that set themselves against the deluded self-regard of the liberals and the strident, quasi-evangelical progressivism of the intelligentsia. Given the centrality for these commentators of questions regarding religious faith, we inevitably turn to the position occupied by the Russian Orthodox Church prior to the Revolution. From 1721 to 1917, the Orthodox Church of the Russian Empire was seamlessly fused into the operation of the state. That these American traditionalists do not believe in the separation of church and state should, of course, surprise no one; furthermore, notwithstanding their fondness for aspirationally illiberal political parties such as Orbán's Fidesz, Putin's United Russia, and Kaczyński's Law and Justice, none of these writers has proposed the establishment of a state church in the manner of the Hapsburg or Russian empires.

Nonetheless, their writings show a marked preference for a state that pivots upon a single faith, which Hungary, the Russian Federation, and Poland arguably have more recently strived to embody. In a tweet responding to an unexpectedly positive assessment of *Boomers*, Andrews wrote that the reviewer "treated a conservative book more fairly than many other reviewers would have, for which I am grateful—so I won't get on his case for mistaking my religious affiliation. (Hint: onion domes.)"[92] Elsewhere, in an essay that could have come straight from the pen of L. Brent Bozell III and the pages of the William F. Buckley's *National Review*, Dreher wrote—in 2019—that "there is simply no way for Christians to read about what the Left was doing to Spanish Catholics before the civil war, and to believe that the wrong side won that conflict."[93] Both Dreher and Deneen have had well-publicized meetings with Orbán in Budapest, praising the efforts of his Fidesz party to establish "pro-family" policies and, as Dreher puts it, a "public square" that is "open and favorable to the ancestral religious beliefs of the nation" and will do righteous battles with the competing faith of Islam and the quasi-religion of LGBTQ advocacy, so that "religious leaders can step into the space politics creates, and do their work of recovery."[94]

Such statements, pitched to an audience that these commentators regard as largely corrupt and close to irredeemable, maintain a coy distance from illiberal content by avoiding its logical conclusions and by articulating only certain aspects of it. After all, what the American traditionalist intelligentsia desires above everything else is legitimacy, gained through a high-toned dignity of expression that speaks of an authority that does not need to listen to the voices of others. Vulgarity and bigotry are the demotic versions of these Matthew Arnold–like effusions about the sanctity of traditions. In the American conservative context, liberalism is associated with a deracinated and unhealthily cerebral sensibility reflecting what Kristin Kobes Du Mez calls, in *Jesus and John Wayne: How White Evangelicals Corrupted a Faith and Fractured a Nation* (2020),[95] a state of societal "moral decay"; in the present-day Russian context, it seems that dissident intellectuals are understood to be fellow travelers of antinormativity and perhaps even sexual alterity.

The nationalist intelligentsias in both countries find common ground in the othering of the liberal intelligentsia and in their aspirations to displace it. To paraphrase Morson, they believe that they deserve the intellectual authority that their adversaries already possess. The American traditionalists sneeringly refer to the "cosmopolitan" or "cognitive" progressive elite; their Russian counterparts, to the "intelligentsia" or *liberasty*. The latter term is a portmanteau of *liberaly* ("liberals") and *pederasty* ("faggots") that roughly corresponds to "libtard," with homophobia taking the place of hostility to people with a disability. While these American commentators do not descend to this level, they often come close.

In an otherwise densely hermeneutic essay about constitutional originalism (written for that "house magazine of the Resistance" *The Atlantic*), Adrian Vermeule, the Ralph S. Tyler Jr. Professor of Constitutional Law at Harvard Law School, drops his mask and asserts that the proper administrative "state will enjoy authority to curb the social and economic pretensions of the urban-gentry liberals who so often place their own satisfactions (financial and sexual) and the good of their class or social milieu above the common good."[96]

With its 280-character limit and absence of a feature for editing or revising tweets, Twitter is an ideal platform for straw-man slurs. Vermeule's writing on antioriginalism is based on an understanding of American constitutional law as necessarily subordinate to the needs of the administrative state, which he argues is undergirded by a notion of the sovereign's supreme will that predates Hobbes's pragmatic treatment of kingship. Among other things, Vermeule's insistence upon the stubborn monarchical traces in American jurisprudence would prohibit atheists or other unbelievers in the state religion from serving in any of the three branches of government. Aspects of Vermeule's historicist anchoring of American constitutional law have distinct affinities with arguments in prerevolutionary Russian jurisprudence about the privileging of the executive branch over the judiciary, which we see in the program of the state's direct management of the evolution of labor unions that was formulated by the Ukrainian sociologist and legal theorist Maksim Kovalevsky (1851–1916).[97] Many of these views about transforming the state into a strong caretaker are subsumed by blood-and-soil understandings of citizenship, in a rhetorical ecosystem where orotund and bellicose expressions of hate feed off one another. Deneen's concern for the lives of the working class never extends to labor unions, whose role as advocates for the rights of the working class is completely absent from his discussions.[98] Making no distinction between the very different economic ramifications of illegal and legal forms of immigration, he does however express a concern that immigration is a problem that "negatively affects" the lives of the working class.[99]

These traditionalists covet authority, even as they pillory the authority represented by the "cultural elite." Ultimately, they long to identify themselves with a rehabilitated state. As Eliot stated in his 1933 lecture series at the University of Virginia (published the following year as his openly anti-Semitic book, *After Strange Gods*), the chances for "the re-establishment of a native culture are perhaps better here," in the South and specifically in Charlottesville, "than in New England." After all, Eliot states, "You are farther away from New York; you have been less industrialized and less invaded by foreign races; and you have a more opulent soil." What has passed with scant comment in the vast scholarly literature about Eliot is that those lectures reflect a close familiarity with the writings of the University of Virginia–based Southern Agrarians group, particularly their book-length borderline racialist manifesto, *I'll Take My Stand: The South and the Agrarian Tradition* (1930).

For Eliot, an influx of "foreign populations" has "almost effaced" an understanding of tradition in the North, a fate that the South thankfully did not share because of its closeness to an agrarian way of life. Not surprisingly, he passes over in silence the fact that this way of life was made possible by the labor of slaves. "What is still important," he told his Charlottesville audience, is "unity of religious background; and reasons of race and religion combine to make any large number of free-thinking Jews undesirable."[100] A short distance (at most) separates the views of the most canonical of American poets from the ones that motivated the participants in the "Unite the Right" rally in the same city eighty-four years later. The white nationalist Nicholas Fuentes, a participant in the Charlottesville riot, yelled to fellow insurrectionists in Washington on 6 January 2021: "It is *us* and *our* ancestors that created everything good you see in this country. . . . All these people that have taken over this country—we do not need them!"[101] And who are "these people"? They are, as Fuentes put it on that same day, "parasites" who go against "*our* interests."

Uses of the phrase "cultural elite" in recent statements by American traditionalist intellectuals betray a number of features: a recycling of anti-Semitic understandings of the intellectual class in American life, nativist agrarian suspicions of any and all who don't, as Deneen has put it in several tweets, "work with their hands," a hostility to alternative or nontraditional versions of family life, and a thoroughgoing animosity toward those who took part in the protests against the Vietnam War and in support of the struggle for Civil Rights. These are old battles, which the contemporary traditionalist intellectuals—or "integralists," as several of them call themselves, particularly those affiliated with the magazine *First Things*—repackage for the present-day consumer of ideas, like video game designers who provide crisp, experiential verisimilitude for conflicts that precede living memory. Their preoccupation with the Russian historical frame of reference for the progressive intelligentsia is useful for four reasons: it establishes a base for a nativist and organicist critique of the intellectual class, shows sympathy for the particular traditionalist institutionalism of prerevolutionary Russian society, highlights the incompatibility between traditional gender roles and progressive politics, and models a correct and religiously engaged cultural elite. The sublimated religious zeal of the nineteenth-century Russian intelligentsia is an especially useful instance of negative modeling, for these traditionalists will have no truck with what they categorize as the "pseudo-religion" of progressivism, manifest in "woke" corporate culture.

The avowed admiration for the conservatism of Eastern European cultures serves, for these intellectuals, as a tool for burnishing their traditionalist bona fides, whilst imagining a new kind of intellectual class that would consist of themselves. The range and types of religious conversions we see within this cluster of commentators is truly astounding, suggesting an intersectionality of denominational orientation that echoes the submerged evangelical reflexes of the nineteenth-century Russian intelligentsia, and perhaps also the experiential mosaic that the LGBTQ community represents: Andrews and Dreher converted to Eastern Orthodoxy; the pro-Trump blogger Eric Metaxas, from Greek Orthodoxy to the evangelical Protestantism of the Southern Baptist Convention; J. D. Vance, from evangelical Protestantism to Catholicism; and Vermeule, from Lutheranism to Catholicism. These pundits are intent on foregrounding the spectacle of their own conversions to stubbornly archaic or dogmatic forms of religious devotion. Their histrionic public meditations on the conversion experience are, we are told, the real thing, with a Benjaminian "aura of the original" that demonstrates or points up the counterfeit character of the fluid class and sexual identity represented by liberal elites.

Yet all here is not what it seems or claims to be. Morson has argued that well-to-do American progressive activists engage in a process of strategizing that recalls the reasoning of revolutionaries in late imperial Russia: with the support of "wealthy, liberal, educated society," they seek to displace the political establishment that they loathe.[102] I would turn Morson's statement about the envy of the cultural elite for the conservative business elite on its head—and enact the same radical reversal for similar assessments by Morson's fellow *First Things* contributors such as Andrews, Paul, Deneen, and Dreher. I would argue that their antiprogressive (and, more pointedly, anti-LGBTQ) views are animated by a fascination with their ideological opponents' perceived flexibility of identity, whose modal properties they in fact wish to emulate.

In the end, their critique of the cultural elite becomes what Tolstoy identified as the "simulation of life"—a performative reflex that never transcends envy for the traits of the entity that it loathes. They recall the impoverished member of the intelligentsia who is the anguished title character of Chekhov's short story "The Dance Pianist" (*Tapior*, 1885), which appeared the year after the publication of Tolstoy's "Confession." Even their attempts to impart a real-life gravitas of commonsensical practicality to their activity run aground with the realization that they and their friends lack the requisite "fire, bile, and strength" to be anything but spectators with profiles in the art of language, rather than doers.[103]

In their besotted idealization of traditionalist cultural orders, and in their antipathy toward those (such as the prerevolutionary Russian intelligentsia) who were critical of them, these pundits place themselves in the awkward position of decrying human agency in favor of a ritualistic and material rootedness that the mercurial details of their own life choices and spiritual chronicles in no way embody. In *Nobody Knows My Name* (1961), a follow-up to *Notes of a Native Son*, James Baldwin explores resonances between the American and Russian literary experiences that these commentators would find discomfiting:

> The charge has often been made against American writers that they do not describe society, and have no interest in it. They only describe individuals in opposition to it, or isolated from it. Of course, what the American writer is describing is his own situation. But what is *Anna Karenina* describing if not the tragic fate of an isolated individual, at odds with her time and place?
>
> The real difference is that Tolstoy was describing an old and dense society in which everything seemed—to the people in it, though not to Tolstoy—to be fixed forever. And the book is a masterpiece because Tolstoy was able to fathom, and make us see, the hidden laws which really governed this society and made Anna's doom inevitable.
>
> American writers do not have a fixed society to describe. The only society they know is one in which nothing is fixed and in which the individual must fight for his identity. This is a rich confusion, indeed, and it creates for the American writer unprecedented opportunities.[104]

It is precisely this idea of a "rich confusion" that these American traditionalists seek to jettison and reject in favor of a fixed social order that Tolstoy himself would have been critical of. It is, of course, hard to read the phrase "rich confusion" without thinking of Baldwin's characterization, in his fiction and essays, of awakening to his own sexual and creative identity, and to a fuller sense of himself as a Black man living in a state of "quasi-freedom." In "Mass Culture and the Creative Artist" (1959), Baldwin identifies this form of awakening or conversion as an opening up to oneself and to others, with the rather Tolstoyan observation that such a moment requires the rejection of adherence to custom and convention: "We are in the middle of an immense metamorphosis" that will, "it is devoutly to be hoped, rob us of our myths and give us our history, which will destroy our attitudes and give us back our personalities."[105]

These traditionalists are only superficially hostile to the idea of an identity that is achieved—or, as Baldwin puts it, fought for. As T. S. Eliot, one of Dreher's touchstones, put it in "Tradition and the Individual Talent": "Some can absorb knowledge, the more tardy must sweat for it." Furthermore, he wrote, regardless of one's capabilities, the past should never be consumed as "a lump, an indiscriminate bolus," or on the basis of "one or two private admirations," or "wholly upon one preferred period."[106] While these bloggers and academics are in search of traditions to define themselves by, we would be wrong to assume that the idea of sociality and community is the object of their quest. With its strain of unruly libertarianism, American conservatism has often had a contentious relationship with the idea of tradition. As we shall see in our next chapter, about Steve Bannon's understanding of himself as both a right-wing populist and a Leninist, reminiscences about Russian history and culture serve, for the American illiberal populists as forms of cultural capital, and as a ballast for a transatlantic journey whose destination is a renewed assessment of tradition, or perhaps even a first genuine contact with it. As Deneen, a self-declared Burkean, put it in an interview with the *New York Times*'s Ezra Klein, "revolutions aren't just the people picking up pitchforks and overthrowing the elites." Rather, "it's someone like a Lenin, who grew up as an elite, who becomes a kind of class traitor and calls out the deficiencies of his own class."[107]

Whither the State?

Steve Bannon, the Alt-Right, and Lenin's State and Revolution

As i've proudly announced to my friends and family, I am a Leninist of the Right. In elections that count, I vote for the most leftist and the most emphatically anti-white candidates. The crazier the better! Let the majority population groan under the added misery until they react. If they don't, then they fully deserve what they get.

—PAUL GOTTFRIED, "America in 2034"

Without democracy = without management by people.
"The roots of statist attitudes [*gosudarstvennosti*] in the souls of the workers"?
Opportunism and revolutionary social democracy.

—VLADIMIR LENIN, "Outline for the article 'Toward the Question of the Role of the State'"

Introduction: Hate and Revolution

BY ALL ACCOUNTS, Steve Bannon's opinions and organizational input were central to the planning and implementation of the January 6 insurrection. He was present during the meetings of Trump advisors at the Willard Hotel on 5 January, which were devoted to developing a procedural strategy for Mike Pence's decertification of the election results. On Tuesday, July 19 proceedings began on Capitol Hill for Bannon's contempt of Congress charges for failing to respond to a subpoena from the House committee investigating the January 6 insurrection. On the podcast he aired live shortly before the Capitol building was breached by the insurrectionists, Bannon used a sports metaphor to describe what he thought ought to happen at the certification of the vote: "We are right on the cusp of victory. . . . It's quite simple. Play's been called. Mike Pence, run the play. Take the football. Take the handoff from the quarterback. You've got guards in front of you. You've got big, strong people in front of you. Just do your duty."[1] Among the many remarkable things about this chatty description of how to disrupt a constitutionally dictated procedure is the way that Bannon cloaks sedition in a preoccupation with strategy, through scrupulously playing by the rules of a game. Bannon imagines himself as a legalist rebel.

In her *Strangers in Their Own Land*, a study of the views of the "forgotten" white Americans on whose behalf Bannon claims to be speaking, Arlie Russell Hochschild describes what a "deep story" can mean. "A deep story is a *feels-as-if* story—it's the story feelings tell, in the language of symbols. It removes judgment. It removes facts. It tells us how things feel. Such a story permits those on both sides of the political spectrum to stand back and explore the *subjective prism* through which the party on the other side sees the world."[2] What is the experience of gaining access to a deep story that belongs to someone else? While she does not explore this question in detail, Hochschild suggests that exploring a deep story that is not your own makes you aware of what it shuts out, or papers over. Those blind spots are largely invisible to communities that share or periodically reach into a given story.

What is Steve Bannon's deep story? On the surface, his views seem to conform to a well-trod narrative of white American ethnonationalism. Bannon has dipped into this deep story of aggrievement on many occasions, perhaps most vividly at a public forum at the Hudson Institute, a center-right think tank, on 24 October 2017. He spoke for less than half an hour at an event for which the institute paid him $30,000, much to the consternation of an audience that was appalled by the offhand and fact-lean superficiality of his commentary.[3] Bannon opined that "President Trump and his whole candidacy" was, first and foremost, a "repudiation of the elites, the repudiation of the foreign policy establishment, a repudiation of the 'Party of Davos,'" of everything that has dictated "this concept we've had of this rules-based international order," which "the American working class and middle class underwrite with their taxes, and more importantly, with the blood of their children."[4] Bannon's rhetorical attempts to fuse rebellion against the deep state and the global order with a respect for hierarchy and the national state point to another deep story, whose roots go back to the eve of the Russian Revolution. In this chapter we examine Bannon's gadfly views and public self-presentation to help make sense of the fascination of the American alt-right with the populist iconoclasm of Vladimir Lenin. From the standpoint of a non-Marxist appropriation of Leninism, categories and shibboleths like "the real people," the "left behind," and the "silent majority" become shrewd distractions from the main focus in populism, which is the primacy of the populist elite or vanguard in lifting the disempowered from their exploited state.

Steve Bannon and the Deep Story of the Deep State

While no longer regarded as counterintuitive, the pose of the modern conservative as rebel against the status quo continues to raise eyebrows. In his revised and updated edition of *The Reactionary Mind*, Corey Robin takes particular note of the appropriation of leftist antiestablishment beliefs and rhetorical tactics by conservative thinkers and movements, beginning with the French Revolution. Writing in 1796 with grudging respect, if not modulated admiration, for the Jacobin cause as the worker of geopolitical wonders, Edmund Burke asserted that the only way to "destroy that enemy" was to fashion an approach that bore "some analogy" and resemblance to "the force and spirit which that system exerts."[5] As Robin explains, conservative reactionaries are moved first and foremost by the projects of recovering and restoring what was, rather than preserving and protecting what is.[6] Thus, the late Supreme Court Justice Antonin Scalia's rigidity on allowable interpretations of the Constitution—an intransigence that Margot Talbot calls the "jurisprudential equivalent of smashing a guitar on stage"—is not "opposed to his idealism," but rather *is* his idealism.[7] Noting the reactionary love for shattering expectations and norms, the Irish political commentator Fintan O'Toole acidly observes that upper-class Brexiteers like Boris Johnson indulge in a "Tory anarchism" that shares many affinities with the "punk nihilism" of Thatcher-era England. Rebellion becomes the domain of the privately educated scions of a "decadent and dilettante political elite," fully expressed by Johnson's often puerile if not violent demeanor and the deliberately fey yet strangely unembarrassed media maunderings of his pro-Brexit confederate Jacob Rees-Mogg.[8] This is a push for "revolution" that is driven by the resolutely undemocratic impulse of *droit de seigneur* that openly embraces its predatory character.

In the contemporary American context, the former Goldman Sachs trader and erstwhile Trump campaign manager Steve Bannon engages in a similar appropriation of leftist affective paradigms. The journalist Joshua Green writes that during the spring and summer of 2016, Bannon openly acknowledged the pursuit of "something like the old Marxist dialectical concept of 'heightening the contradictions,' only rather than foment revolution among the proletariat, he was trying to disillusion Clinton's natural base of support."[9] While Bannon claims to have read a book or two, conceivably including *The State and Revolution*, the work of Lenin's that is quoted most often in the wider non-Russian and nonspecialist readership, we can safely assume that his contact with Marxism-Leninism is at least as much through other conservatives, such as the American apostates from leftism Whittaker Chambers, Sydney Hook, and James Burnham, who, in the *National Review* and other right-leaning publications, traced their political evolutions during the second half of the twentieth century.

The trajectory of ex-leftists, however, is not the link between Leninism and the alt-right. For ideologues like the self-declared "paleoconservative" Paul Gottfried, quoted in this chapter's epigraph, Leninism is a subvariety of the sport of boxing: the "sweet science" of exhausting your opponent through a series of smaller, debilitating parries that culminate in a victory. In an interview from 2018, published in the white nationalist journal *American Renaissance*, Gottfried stated that he was "still in theory a Leninist of the Right," while also noting that "in order for this strategy to work, one needs something like a majority or significant minority that can be moved to a counterrevolutionary stance," adding: "Leninism of the Right will provide an effective strategy only if the political system and political establishment are overwhelmed by a catastrophe."[10] There is little doubt that Gottfried, the coiner of the term "alt-right" and former mentor to Richard Spencer, is a diligent student of Lenin's life and work. The kinship between Gottfried's cool calculus of victory and Lenin's knowing embrace of catastrophe and tragedy is close indeed. According to Trotsky, Lenin "conducted systematic and outspoken propaganda against the relief committees" that were created to mitigate the famine of 1891–92 in the Volga region. He believed that famine should be allowed to follow its natural course: "It's sentimentality to think that a sea of need could be emptied with the teaspoon of philanthropy." Lenin went on to say that the famine would play "the role of a progressive factor" in the eventual fall of tsarist Russia.[11]

Is the alt-right's appropriation of left activist paradigms merely superficial? Gottfried attended college in the late fifties and early sixties, and his work exhibits the deeper furrows engraved by Marxism-Leninism and Trotskyism during that era. His extensive publications testify to a critical engagement with Marxist legacies that is more suggestive of Jacob's wrestling with the angel than the punch and parry of an actual fight. Indeed, the only branch of Marxism for which Gottfried seems to have no esteem is the work of the Frankfurt School. Unlike Gottfried and prominent neoconservatives like Irving Kristol and David Horowitz, however, Spencer, Bannon, and Dinesh D'Souza were never drawn to any form of Marxism in the first place; for them, "useful" leftism is, to a significant extent, a matter of trading its content for its form, its credo for its tactical methods.

Turning the Marxist legacy inside out has the effect of extruding its affective core, making it easier to detach. Marx and Engels devoted little space to an actual theory of strategy, limiting themselves to commentaries about the failures and short-lived victories of 1848 and, over twenty years later, the events surrounding the calamitous rout of the Paris Commune. For any theory of tactics within the socialist legacy that the alt-right would consider adopting, we need to turn to Lenin's life and work.

Bannon has been variously described as the Beast of Breitbart and the "Falstaff in flip-flops" to the Prince Hal figure of the political novice Donald Trump. In this chapter we focus on Bannon as a highly representative example of the alt-right's engagement with Leninism. As we shall see, the dichotomy of the form and content of Marxism-Leninism ultimately dissolves in Bannon's eccentric lateral burrowing into leftist paradigms. He is powerfully drawn to what he perceives as the negative core of Leninism. For him, Leninism is very much a matter of what the theorist of affect Sara Ahmed characterizes as specific "unhappy affects" in daily life, the deliberate exacerbation of transitions into an unexpected gesture of affirmation: "Unhappiness is not our endpoint. If anything, the experience of being alienated from the affective promise of happy objects gets us somewhere." The unhappy "affect aliens" that Ahmed describes are able to achieve things by "refusing to put bad feelings aside in the hope that we can 'just get along.'"[12] For Bannon, those affect aliens are the "deplorables": members of the white working class who are "left behind" by globalism, which for them is the status quo that they reject. They wear their despair and their exclusion from the "new world order" as badges of honor. As Ahmed might put it, their concern for their "histories of hurt" is "not a backward orientation," because the only possibility for "moving on" from narcissistic injury is to return to an understanding of ourselves as people who have been grievously dispossessed of privilege.[13] Agency, it would seem, may be cultivated from the bitter fruit of disappointment.

Blood and Toil: Constructions of Russian Culture in American Conservatism from the Cold War to the Age of Trump

How are we to understand the recent sunny view of the leadership of the Russian Federation among influential American conservatives and members of alt-right groups such as the Proud Boys, Promise Keepers, the League of the South, and Bannon himself? We begin by shining a light on their understanding of themselves as political agents devoted to tilling the soil of grassroots populism.

Perhaps more than the adherents of any other political or ideology-driven movement, contemporary populists are strikingly unified about the need to create theatrical spectacles on the stage of social media. As Jan-Werner Müller points out in his overview of the increasing affinities among populist movements across the globe, populists view the brash and unmediated behavioral style of their activism as a welcome departure from the ponderous advocacy of their mainstream political competitors on both the left and the right. In 1987, a full thirty years before he became president, Donald Trump wrote in *The Art of the Deal* that "the final key" of his mode of self-promotion is his indefatigable "bravado." According to Trump, this practice involves playing to the "fantasies" of people who, while "not always think[ing] big themselves," are capable of becoming very "excited by those who do."[14] Seen from the perspective of this rather specific cultural imaginary, such disinhibition—from the poised diplomacy of multiculturalism's defenders, and from the anxiously cautious public comportment of institutional traditionalists—seems deeply appealing. In his taxonomy of contemporary nativist populism, Müller draws particular attention to the populist politician's willingness to cleave to an "imperative" mandate of an autocratic statism, rather than to the "free" debate-driven mandates of democratic pluralism. Populism is interested only in exclusive or unitary mandates and therefore sees the messy and occasionally makeshift character of polyvocal governance as highly undesirable.[15] The range of positive responses, among American far-right groups, to Putin's "manly" style of imperative governance mirrors the qualities enumerated by Russians who approved of his performance as president of the Russian Federation. According to a 2017 survey conducted by the Levada Center, a nonpartisan Russian research agency, the set of traits in a leader that the pro-Putin percentile flagged as most distinctive and important were the attributes of a "real man" (*nastoiashchii muzhik*), who possessed a demeanor that was "decisive, masculine, firm, headstrong, powerful, calm, brave, laconic, [and] self-confident."[16]

In this chapter we examine contemporary forms of American populist or nativist Russophilia among American evangelical Protestants, neo-Confederates, neo-Nazi and white nationalist columnists, and American libertarian theorists and political figures. We will return to the obsessive masculinism of American and Russian conservative understandings of desirable leadership, but for the time being it is important for us to understand the perception of such leaders as artisans of imagined concretization, magicians of ideology who strategically retreat the closer an electorate comes to demanding that they materially make good on their promises. As Müller explains, contemporary populists and nativists see politics as a naturally dirty business, a ceaseless trafficking in specular commodities that is opposed to "producerism": "populists pit the poor, the innocent, always hardworking people against a corrupt elite who does not really work," except to "further their self-interest" and to operate, like those at the very "bottom of society," as "parasites on the work of others."[17]

This idiosyncratic formulation of a symmetry or affinity between the underclass and the cultural (as opposed to business) elite is a telling mark of many populist groups worldwide. These groups otherwise seem to have little in common because their campaigns are often anchored in local concerns; thus, the Rassemblement National in France is preoccupied with the plight of overtaxed farmers and Islamification, while a draconian policy against drug traffickers forms the core ideology of Rodrigo Duterte's PDP-Laban (Philippine Democratic Party–People's Power) party in the Philippines. Both during and after his campaign for the presidency of Brazil, Bolsonaro expressed nothing but contempt for members of the liberal press—and women journalists in particular—who were unduly concerned about the treatment of indigenous peoples and the urban underclass; in the place of such concerns, he touted the cultivation of an entrepreneurial and socially conservative business elite as the solution to the country's problems.

In the American context, even prior to the "populist" epiphany of Trump's election, we heard elements of this self-image of entrepreneurial material production as the gold standard for moral agency in the 2012 Mitt Romney campaign motto "We Built It!" To thunderous applause that same year at the Republican National Convention, the Utah congresswoman Mia Love stated that the world of small businesses (as opposed to the "big" government cultivated by Barack Obama) "is the America that we know because we built it!"[18] A statement like this is an expression of a very American or libertarian antipolitics: it imagines the task of governance as at best a necessary evil and at worst a stagnant pond for the pullulation of resourceful spongers, out-of-touch, pointy-headed intellectuals, career bureaucrats, and assorted knaves.

To reach a better understanding of the contemporary populist imaginary in its American manifestation, we would do well to bear in mind certain mainstream conservative rebuttals to nativist classism. David Frum, a journalist and former advisor to the George W. Bush administration, persuasively critiqued the starry-eyed libertarian nostalgia that undergirds Charles Murray's *Coming Apart: The State of White America, 1960–2010* (2012). Focused on the hypocrisy of the cultural elite that he labels "OESs" ("Over-Educated Snobs")—those "detested hybrid-driving, NPR-listening, bottle-recycling, [and] cheeseburger-avoiding professors and screenwriters"—Murray is incapable of seeing the intractable mechanisms of social inequality that represent "the most important changes that have occurred since 1960 in America's distribution of wealth and power."[19] Nevertheless, as we shall see, the perception of Russia as an icebreaker fearlessly plowing through the frozen wastelands and submerged behemoths of the globalist economic and cultural order appeals to many members of the American far right. Russia is a doer, an unapologetic thug and unreconstructed hunter-gatherer in a world that increasingly demands resolute action, while the American political orthodoxy has been—for far too long!—an idealist sicklied oe'r with the pale cast of thought.[20]

What is the relationship between antipolitics and this cult of action? Müller describes antipolitics as, among other things, the glorification of a "direct" communication of representation.[21] Populism often identifies certain people—rather than points of view, or even particular politics—as evil. For populism, the entire world of political belief is relentlessly identitarian yet individualistic, and in some ways appealingly agentive: that values do not exist separately from the people who express them should be a truism, a salutary reminder that political institutions are, as Giambattista Vico argues in *Scienza nuova*, made by people and not literally given by God.[22]

This brings us to the mystical character of right-wing populism, which is perhaps most clearly manifested in the striking circularity of its reasoning about leadership and democratic agency. As Müller explains, populist leaders "know that they are part of the elite, and so do their supporters; what matters is their promise that as a *proper* [emphasis added] elite, they will not betray the people's trust and will in fact faithfully execute the people's unambiguously articulated political agenda."[23] How can we tell who belongs to a natural or proper elite and who belongs to a spurious or artificial one? And how does the leader gauge, hear, or even know about the existence of the people's "agenda"? Müller notes that "populists in power," such as Silvio Berlusconi and Viktor Orbán, "often adopt a kind of 'caretaker' attitude toward an essentially passive people," which we may here understand as an extension of the cult of the producer or maker of things. Such a model is profoundly patriarchal, evoking within the US context the image of Christ as a "Decider" in the Book of Revelation, which the evangelical right relates to Trump's brash and truculent demeanor. As the former evangelical minister and author Zack Hunt puts it, a "part of Trump's appeal to this demographic is his embrace of vengeance toward his enemies" which is a "huge component of end-times theology." Hunt explains that "they're finally seeing all the people who made fun of them for going to church or ridiculed them for being pro-life or told them they were wrong for opposing gay marriage are now getting their just due," a comeuppance that easily plays into "a carnal appeal to end-times theology."[24] The leader becomes a prophet-like diviner of other people and broader historical forces; he is a dowser with a stick who just *knows* where the healing waters flow, deep under the parched *terroir* of the broken and humiliated people.

Here, we should note that the animus against "political correctness" valorizes a certain kind of political speech: irrepressible, stage-stealing, culture-war rhetoric. In a speech from 9 September 2013, that endeared him to American conservative evangelicals, Putin asserted: "We can see how many of the Euro-Atlantic countries are actually rejecting their roots, including the Christian values that constitute the basis of Western civilization." Speaking to the pro-Kremlin Moscow think tank known as the Valdai Discussion Club, Putin alleged that Europeans and North Americans "are denying moral principles and all traditional identities: national, cultural, religious and even sexual," and "are implementing policies that equate large families with same-sex partnerships, belief in God with the belief in Satan."[25]

Putin's willingness to speak the language of a religiously inflected culture war accounts for a great deal of the American far right's affection for him. A carried parliamentary motion earlier that summer won particular praise from a number of prominent anti-LGBTQ American clergymen, including Franklin Graham. The United Russia Party drafted a law "On the protection of children from information liable to be injurious to their health and development," along with other measures aimed at protecting children from information promoting the denial of traditional family values. As Graham mused for his organization's web magazine, "Isn't it sad, though, that America's own morality has fallen so far that on this issue—protecting children from any homosexual agenda or propaganda—Russia's standard is higher than our own?"[26] What is most striking here is the perception that Putin and Russia—fused, with telling inaccuracy, into one actor—acted decisively because of their correct understanding of their role as caretakers of children, the most passive and vulnerable people within their country. Putin's status as a paragon of firm and principled action is also reflected, according to Graham, in his tremendous success and indisputable personal charisma at the January 2014 Olympic games:

> American distaste for Putin and his policies, however, hasn't diminished his global standing. Last October, *Forbes* magazine declared Putin to be the most powerful man in the world. Anyone who watched the recent Winter Olympics from Sochi, Russia, could see why. More than any of the gold medal winners, Putin was the commanding presence.
>
> The Olympics were a $51 billion spectacle, but the days leading up to the Games were overshadowed by a controversial issue—a law Putin signed in 2013 to protect minors (children) in Russia from homosexuals promoting their lifestyle. Specifically, the law bans the "propaganda of nontraditional sexual relations to minors."

Who are we to argue with such unimpeachable celebrity, and against such an exemplar of decisive action? Many American evangelicals have argued—including Jerry Falwell Jr. and Graham himself in regard to Trump's history of demonstrably lewd behavior—that perhaps a leader needs to be a little bit evil or benighted in order to have the gumption to accomplish something that is necessary and good for God's elect. They cite the example of King Cyrus of Persia, from the Book of Ezra, who unaccountably released the Jews from their captivity in the Babylonian empire. As it turns out, in a biblical text beloved by Trump's evangelical defenders, that "something" that was accomplished involved a building project: in this case the authorization of the construction of the Israelites' Second Temple. In Putin, American evangelicals see a figure cut from the same agentive cloth, advancing his own interests while unknowingly serving as an instrument for something—whether deity or the populist will—that is far larger than himself.

In contrast, they see the US political elite as oblivious to its obligation to provide, build for, and protect its citizens. In American evangelical and nonreligious conservative responses to the civil law against "gay propaganda," we see a consistent association of the Russian *state*, rather than the Russian *government*, as the welcome author of change. This distinction is in fact of central importance for American religious conservatives, who are loath to see anything good in the apparatus of government. This is a curious development in American political thinking. Perhaps in response to the negative contemporary examples of England and France, the political category of the *state* can hardly be said to exist in the Federalist Papers of 1787, which instead outline an administrative structure of separated powers that is constituted by a *union* of citizens sharing the same broad moral principles, rather than the corporate institution of the nation, embodied by a monarch. Again we see the applicability of Müller's analysis of populism's "direct" and unmediated communication between the leader and the will of the people: "Populists always want to cut out the middleman, so to speak, and to rely as little as possible on complex party organizations as intermediaries between citizens and politicians."[27] Thus, when local judiciaries resisted Trump's immigration travel bans in February 2017, White House policy advisor and former anti-immigrant activist Stephen Miller declared: "Our opponents [in the judiciary], the media and the whole world will soon see as we begin to take further actions, that the powers of the president to protect our country are very substantial and will not be questioned."[28]

Although Miller's authoritarian conservatism is anything but religious or theocratic, his understanding of presidential power relies on a rhetoric of "divinized realism," to use the term coined by Julien Benda to describe the volatile political debates in France after the First World War.[29] As Miller sees it, separation of powers is of no consequence in the monumental shadow of a strong leader. This fetishized autocratic leadership, fully immanent and requiring no justification, rationale, or accountability, seems like a morally grotesque Moloch or an embodiment of divine will. One almost has to use the Russian term for the state to correctly understand the particular fixation upon authority that American populists and neoconservatives express. In Russian, the state is that which is given, or gifted, by God: *gosudarstvo*, from *Gospod'* (Lord) and *darit'* (to give). As Julia Hell and George Steinmetz note in their article about Steve Bannon's intellectual roots, the "logic [that Bannon and his colleagues] followed [was] that of Carl Schmitt's 'state of exception.' That is, his logic justifies assertions of sovereign control outside the legal constitutional order, in the interest of preserving that order."[30] For Bannon and Miller, the populist is more of a Bourbon royalist than an American republican in his understanding of the relationship between sovereign and state.

All the same, we are struck by the oddness and incongruity, if not glaring internal contradictions, within conservatism's current mélange of populist and classical Anglo-American strains: between the US alt-right's cultivation of a rhetorical style that jettisons the norms of civility and scoffs at the very notion of intellectual consistency, on one hand, and conservatism's ostensible mission of preserving or restoring tradition, on the other. We see the seemingly incommensurable values of the American and Russian political traditions that are reflected (as the controversial Harvard historian Richard Pipes has argued) in the absence of stable laws about property ownership in Russian civil law; and we also see US populists' apparently uncritical acceptance of Putin's invocation of territorial *force majeure*. Evidently, choices have been made. Some might ask about the jeopardy to which the time-tested underpinnings of political institutions and diplomatic practices have been subjected. How can destroying those joisted foundations serve the goal of maintaining that "noble freedom" that Burke, in *Reflections upon the Revolution in France*, argues is vouchsafed by "its gallery of portraits; its monumental inscriptions [and] its records, evidences, and titles"?[31]

Müller draws a comparison between Russian and American traditions of populism and elaborates upon some unexpected confluences between the two in a way that might be helpful in framing an answer to that question.[32] There is an unexpected alliance between nationalist and revolutionary movements, or at least the sense that one can easily segue into the other. Seen from this perspective, the People's Will movement in Russia—responsible for the 1881 assassination of Alexander II, and largely composed of highly educated women and men whose families were connected either to the church or the state service economy—is no less a populist groundswell than the Tea Party and the religiously inflected libertarian organizations that came together as a bulwark of support for Trump's presidential campaign. Müller's observation that populism is a "particular moralistic imagination of politics" is very useful in clarifying populists' frequent gravitation to religious understandings of the world; it also draws our attention to the ways in which populists see their movement as a reinsertion of individual agency only to the extent that the movement coalesces into a single collective actor, manifesting an irascible impatience with the "progress" of modernity.

Neo-Confederate Russophilia

Before we return to Bannon, we need to examine in further detail the paradoxes and unexpected pivots of American conservative opinion about Russia's global power. On 17 July 2018 the pro-Confederate advocacy organization known as the League of the South made an announcement that took many political commentators by surprise. Seeing as its mission a campaign to redress the perceived indignities visited upon white Americans during Reconstruction and the Civil Rights era, the League of the South has rarely commented on international affairs. Its founder, Michael Hill, has a doctorate in history. In 1998 he resigned from the faculty of the historically black Stillman College in Tuscaloosa, Alabama, for what he claimed were his full-time responsibilities as president of the League.[33] The grand oratorical style of Hill's statement is reminiscent of the overwrought mid-nineteenth-century political writing that Edmund Wilson examined in *Patriotic Gore: Studies in the Literature of the American Civil War* (1962). Posted on the League's web page just a day after the spectacle of glib fellowship projected by Trump and Putin at their so-called summit in Helsinki, it gives off the heat and angry spark of an instrument still being hammered out on the anvil of international events:

> We understand that the Russian people and Southerners are natural allies in blood, culture, and religion. As fellow Whites of northern European extraction, we come from the same general gene pool. As inheritors of the European cultural tradition, we share similar values, customs, and ways of life. And as Christians, we worship the same Lord and Savior, Jesus Christ, and our common faith binds us as brothers and sisters.
>
> We Southerners believe in societies based on real, organic factors such as shared blood, culture, and religion, and all that stems naturally from these salient factors in the human experience. As fellow White Christians who are grounded in the sublime traditions of our common European cultural heritage, we believe that the Russian people and the Southern people are natural allies against the destructive and impersonal impulses of globalism. We ought to encourage closer ties between our two peoples and between those who represent our interests in all phases of life, including government, business, education, the arts, and other areas. Moreover, we should seek peace and goodwill between our peoples as the foundation for all our cooperative efforts.

In his conclusion, Hill strikes a note of foreboding about a global future without this "natural" alliance between Russians and white American southerners:

A firm and resolute understanding and commitment to cooperation between the Russian people and the people of the South could indeed be the foundation for a better world in which our peoples thrive and prosper far into the future. But should we fail to take advantage of the climate of increasing trust and friendship between us, there are forces that would like to pit us against one another, ever as far as open war. We must oppose those forces with a combined will and commitment to peace and cooperation between our two peoples. Together, we can assure that the world for our posterity is a bright and secure one. Let us start on that journey of mutual cooperation today.

Hill ends with the announcement that "our Russian language section of this website will be our first step in this direction. We hope to hear from our Russian friends soon. May the God of our Fathers bless our efforts to preserve our peoples and their shared faith and culture."[34]

This was something new! Or so some people thought. In fact, among advocates for American global power during the Cold War, we do find calls for Russian-American solidarity. Donning his "public intellectual" cap in the June 1957 issue of *Harper's*, in an article titled "A Better Way to Deal with China," George Steiner argued for recognizing mainland China as a greater geopolitical threat than the Soviet Union and for pushing "Russia" (as he called it) in the direction of opposing China on a number of international measures. Even a left-of-center essayist like Steiner was not immune to the high-toned Cold Warrior argument—voiced, among others, by the former ambassador to the Soviet Union, George F. Kennan—that the United States and the Soviet Union should break bread with each other in order to head a coalition that would stem the tide of Maoist (and therefore anti-American *and* anti-Soviet) influence among revolutionary movements in the developing world. This view was tainted by a racialist, and racist, understanding of China's growing influence: as Steiner bluntly put it, China is "the leader of the Bandung countries," the attendees of the 1955 conference in Indonesia that drafted a statement for principled non-alignment with western countries. As Steiner saw it, the signatories of that statement represented an "immense alliance of colored peoples united by a dislike of the white man and fierce nationalism."[35] From his perch as a descendant of America's patrician ruling class—and as a wry observer, in 1986, of American decline during the second Reagan administration—Gore Vidal used something of same argument for Russian-American *rapprochement*, seeing the threat in Japan rather than China:

Now the long-feared Asiatic colossus takes its turn as world leader, and we—the white race—have become the yellow man's burden. Let us hope that he will treat us more kindly than we treated him. In any case, if the foreseeable future is not nuclear, it will be Asiatic, some combination of Japan's advanced technology with China's resourceful landmass. Europe and the United States will then be, simply, irrelevant to the world that matters, and so we come full circle. . . . There is now only one way out. The time has come for the United States to make common cause with the Soviet Union. The bringing together of the Soviet landmass (with all its natural resources) and our island empire (with all its technological resources) would be of great benefit to each society, not to mention the world. Also, to recall the wisdom of the Four Horsemen who gave us our empire, the Soviet Union and our section of North America combined would be a match, industrially and technologically, for the Sino-Japanese axis that will dominate the future just as Japan dominates world trade today.[36]

A few weeks later, in *The Nation*, Vidal recapitulated his concerns about declining white global power: "For America to survive economically in the coming Sino-Japanese world, an alliance with the Soviet Union is a necessity. After all, the white race is a minority race with many well-deserved enemies, and if the two great powers of the Northern Hemisphere don't band together, we are going to end up as farmers—or, worse, mere entertainment—for the more than one billion grimly efficient Asiatics."[37] The latter essay also included ripe anti-Semitic remarks ("like most of our Israeli fifth columnists, Midge [Decter] isn't much interested in what the goyim were up to before Ellis Island"). Such comments demonstrate that the more recent statement of the League of the South, while peculiar and salient in terms of post–Cold War discussions of Russian-American relations, has a distinct ideology that is traceable to ethnonationalist understandings of the United States as the scion of an anglophone empire, and of it and Russia as pale-skinned brothers-in-arms against an uncompromising coalition of non-European nations.

Very little of this prehistory was acknowledged in articles about the League's outreach to potential Russian supporters. Five days later, in response to outraged pieces from a wide range of online news outlets (among them, the *Daily Beast*, *The Hill*, and the website of the Southern Poverty Law Center), Hill wrote that "we have been the focus of a campaign by the left to castigate us for daring to state that Southerners look upon Russia and the Russian people as potential friends and allies rather than as enemies." Turning to the sources for this criticism and warming to his theme, Hill continued: "When Russia was in the clutches of the Judeo-Bolsheviks and was responsible for the Holodomor and other atrocities that killed well over 100 million people in the previous century, it was seen as a force for 'progress' by Jews and their goyim allies. . . . Now that Russia has abandoned Communism and re-embraced its Christian and national heritage, it has fallen out of favor" with the "Globalist

Left," which "abhors both Christianity and nationalism."[38] Hill carefully over-looks the fact that the federalism that neo-Confederates see as the point of origin for states' rights finds no ready equivalent in prerevolutionary Russia. After emancipation, local councils such as the *zemstvos* fought for the interests of liberated serfs and their descendants against both the landowners and the imperial state itself. In Russian imaginative literature, not even staunch tradi-tionalists like Nikolai Leskov and Konstantin Leonov offered up understand-ings of "natural-law" social orders that corresponded to the preindustrial nos-talgia that was so important to southern writers like William Faulkner, Allen Tate, and the so-called New Agrarians.

Prior to 2001, there is no evidence of any particular affinity or emergent alliance between white American conservatives and their Russian traditionalist counterparts, whose patriotism was largely sublimated into stances of loyalty to the Soviet Union and, in its first decade after the Soviet collapse, the aggres-sively mercantile Russian Federation. During the Cold War, a great many American conservative commentators foregrounded the impossibility of assim-ilating Russians into the traditions of the West because of what they regarded as the fundamentally Asian—and therefore, anti-individualist and inhumane—character of Russian history and culture. In the Reagan and George H. W. Bush administrations, the free-market evangelism and neoconservatism of the Harvard-based advisors Jeffrey Sachs (from the School of Business) and the historian Richard Pipes did nothing to reverse this perception of Russia's iden-tity, and in fact did much to confirm it by emphasizing the need for the Soviet Union and the nascent Russian Federation to acquiesce and thoroughly assim-ilate into a global *pax Americana*. Seen from this perspective—that is, from a vantage point that was overturned almost overnight in 1991—we can under-stand the facile triumphalism of the Reagan, Clinton, and two Bush adminis-trations as representing, as the historian Anatol Lieven has argued, the projec-tion of a depersonalized or generalized Russophobia through the lens of an American neoliberal ethic.[39] Of primary importance of conservative interpret-ers of Russian culture who come from the South—which included Buckley himself, who was raised in North Carolina and whose deeply conservative and openly racist mother was descended from a slave-owning family—is the treachery and imperialism of Russians, a perception that was first evident dur-ing the Civil War.[40] After two years of observing a policy of studied neutrality, Alexander II gave a clear indication of his country's support of the Union over the Confederacy with his order that Russian war vessels dock in New York City.[41] Furthermore, many Southern political figures and journalists saw anal-ogies between the Confederacy's fight against Northern aggression and the 1863 Polish revolt from the Russian empire, and voiced support for the efforts in Poland to secede from Russia and restore the borders of the former Polish-Lithuanian kingdom.[42] Echoes of this animus against the geopolitical meddling of pre-revolutionary Russia can still be heard from present-day defenders of the Confederacy. Pointing to the close diplomatic and economic between the Union states and Russia, one essayist for the Abbeville Institute suggested in 2017 that an investigation by the 36th Congress into the possibility of the "the 1860 election for the Republican ticket" having been stolen as the result of "collusion between the Russian government and Lincoln's presidential campaign" would have had more merit than the calls for investigation of excessive Russian influence on the 2016 election.[43]

The Russophobia of the intellectual conservative establishment from William F. Buckley's journal *National Review* (founded in 1955) to the Mississippi-based Citizens' Council of America (formerly the White Citizens' Council) drew on this network of associations, and on other sources. In the American South, hostility to Russia and its perceived cultural values was largely a reaction to the Soviet Union's official policy of opposition to South African apartheid and US segregation: many conservative activist organizations below the Mason-Dixon line, like the White Citizens' Council, were founded to resist the 1954 Supreme Court desegregation decision *Brown v. Board of Education*. In the American Northwest and Northeast, Buckley's forthright traditionalist Catholicism—which for a short time even took the militant form of opposing the liberalizing reforms of Vatican II—was the source for another, and perhaps less expected, form of Russophobia. The contributors to Buckley's *National Review* formed alliances with émigré public intellectuals and academics such as Leszek Kołakowski, Thomas Molnar, and even the Democrat-aligned foreign policy advisor Zbigniew Brzezinski, all of whom came from East Bloc countries whose majority-Catholic populations tended to regard anti-Russian sentiment as the *sine qua non* of a politically informed underground religiosity.

Bannon's Rebellion against the New World Order

Knowing about these southern responses to Russian political culture is important for understanding Bannon's particular style of Roman Catholic conservatism. He was born and raised in Norfolk, Virginia, and attended high school at Benedictine Preparatory Academy in Richmond, the former capital of the Confederacy. In *Devil's Bargain: Steve Bannon, Donald Trump, and the Storming of the Presidency* (2017), Joshua Green describes the Benedictine curriculum as "steeped in classics and history," presenting "traditional Western Civilization" in a context of Catholicism. One of Bannon's high school classmates recalls: "We were all taught that Western civilization was saved five hundred years ago in Spain, when Ferdinand and Isabella defeated the Moors. . . . The lesson was, here's where Muslims could have taken over the world. And here was the great stand where they were stopped. We were taught a worldview: This is how Catholicism survived."[44] Here we run into some difficulties in making sense of Bannon's current politics. While his Islamophobia can be traced to his immersion in a particular interpretation of Catholic history, other beliefs, such as his hatred for global capital's dominion over the world's left-behind and forgotten people, would not seem to sit easily with a world-view informed by a vision of salvific imperialism. To be sure, we would be fool-ish to expect consistency from Bannon, who prides himself on being inconsis-tent and cultivates a brawn-over-brains verbal style.

Bannon's self-appreciation as a Catholic outsider within his region's reli-gious culture is an underexamined aspect of his biography. The specific, even peculiar, cultural niche of Catholicism in the states of the former Confederacy is a key to understanding his political orientation. Green takes note of his interest in the concept of "subsidiarity," which Pope Pius XI clarified in the encyclical *Quadragesimo anno* (1931). As Green explains, the encyclical stipu-lated that "political matters should devolve to the lowest, least centralized authority that can reasonably handle them," encouraging a retreat of the church from public affairs that complements a rather American—if not libertarian—understanding of "small-government conservatism."[45] Taking the name of the monastic order that Dreher praises for walling itself off from a fallen or cor-rupt world, the founders of Benedictine Preparatory in 1911 saw it as a haven in a South that was often hostile to Catholics, who were still excluded from certain workplaces and many civic organizations. This sense of separation from the mainstream is palpable in Bannon's appreciation of the "aliens" or refugees from economic globalism. It is in their voices that we hear the ornery voices of the male gamers who served as their ideological forebears. The confluence of the white conservative "forgotten men" and women of a minor-ity religious faith and the "millions of intense young men (most gamers were men) who disappeared for days or even weeks at a time in alternate realities" is important for Bannon. His implicit analogy between these two very differ-ent groups summons forth a disquieting tableau of collapsed time, as if the Russian radical men and women of the 1860s and 1870s became fully contem-poraneous with the Bolsheviks who were recognizably their heirs. "These root-less white guys, who [in the aughts] had enormous power" on message boards for MMORPGs (massive multiplayer online role-playing games) like Wowhead, Allakhazam, and Thottbot, became for Bannon both the historical vanguard and the Praetorian Guard of white nationalism.[46] Lenin too imbibed the heady ramifications of living in a time when all rules and expectations could be broken. In "*Glavnya zadacha nashikh dnei*" (The main task of our days, 11 March 1918), he wrote: "In just a few months, we have passed through the stages of dealing with the bourgeoisie and the wearing-out of petit-bourgeois illusions, which other countries" took "decades" to accomplish.[47]

Bannon's engagement with Leninism is motivated, first and foremost, by his fascination with virtual communities that create their own realities in what they imagine to be a happy contravention of the administrative state. As superficial as his understanding of the Marxist-Leninist legacy is, we shall see that his idiosyncratic appropriation of Lenin's antistatism in regard to bourgeois modernity draws attention to the distinctive affective character of the Soviet leader's watershed programmatic essay *State and Revolution* (1917). Under the influence of Gottfried and others who actually read that book and reflected on its rhetorical and affect-driven lessons, Bannon came to see articulated ideals as placeholders, grooved slots for desired emotive responses, rather than as dynamic analytical principles. Bannon's own response to the idea of "Lenin" is itself a demonstration of his prized virtue of sound-bite triggering. His unabashedly parasitic relation to the thinking of others—in regard to Lenin and also to conservative arguments about the blight of leftism on the Catholic Church and Western "decline"—forces us to repeat Corey Robin's question about the popularity of Ayn Rand, given her reliance on a thoroughly bowdlerized understanding of Nietzsche: "How could such a mediocrity, not just a second-hander but a second-rater," exert such a significant influence "on the culture at large?"[48]

First, we need to step into the Ground Zero of Bannon's quasi-Jacobinism, via a statement he made several years before the arrival of Trump's improbable regime. In the weeks leading up to the 2016 election, historian Ronald Radosh recalled a peculiar conversation he had with Bannon during a Washington, DC, book party for David Horowitz's *The Black Book of the American Left*. The date was 12 November 2013. The party was held in Bannon's Georgetown townhouse, which doubled as the headquarters for the Breitbart news service, which Bannon had recently taken over. Already in an expansive and puckish mood, Bannon bantered with Radosh in the midst of a motley company consisting of neoconservative pundits like Horowitz and Anne Coulter, Republican firebrands like Senator Ron Johnson from Wisconsin and Representative Louie Gohmert from Texas's first congressional district, and reality-TV luminaries like *Duck Dynasty*'s hirsute Phil Robertson. The gathering anticipated the eclectic populism that Bannon would excel in promoting three years later, when Donald Trump chose him to serve as "chief strategist" for his presidential campaign: a mix of obscure and fringe talking heads and crypto-celebrities eager to punch up their street cred within the wider public arena. Two years later, Gohmert would become a fire-breathing purveyor of conspiracy theories about Barack Obama's and Hillary

Clinton's launching of "deep state" military maneuvers in Texas under the code name "Jade Helmet," and Robertson would be cast as the oracular narrator of Bannon's culture-war documentary *The Torchbearer*.

In 2013 and afterward, Bannon appeared to see himself as an Alexander Parvus–like figure, facilitating Trump's transformation from a neophyte in the world of political networking into an accomplished practitioner of populist transactionalism. The wealthy Parvus is memorably described as Lenin's charismatic teacher in Solzhenitsyn's novella *Lenin in Zürich*—a text that occupies a place of prominence in both the American and the Russian canon of conservative anti-Leniniana. In this narrative, which Solzhenitsyn eventually incorporated into his "Red Wheel" cycle of Dos Passos–like novels about Russia's disastrous involvement in the First World War and the ten years that followed it, Parvus is a physically grotesque, barely human figure who spurts "hippopotamus blood."[49] Following this lead, Vladimir Khotinenko's crudely nationalistic miniseries *Demon Revoliutsii* (2017) portrays Parvus as a Mephistopheles without portfolio, who engineers great change while largely working on the periphery. Michael Wolff's sensationalistic *Fire and Fury: Inside the Trump White House* (2018) paints Bannon as a "marginal, invisible, small-time hustler" reminiscent of a character from an Elmore Leonard novel. This is the relatively obscure figure who in August 2016 was placed in charge of a Republican presidential campaign focusing on the white working-class constituencies of Florida, Ohio, Michigan, and Pennsylvania.[50]

We will consider the resonances of Bannon's public persona with both Lenin and his "benefactor" Parvus as portrayed in *Lenin in Zürich*. First, let us return to the book party at Breitbart's Washington aerie, almost three years to the day before Trump's election. Walking among his guests, Bannon made no secret of being drolly conscious of the incongruity of his role as a matchmaker among such dissimilar public actors. An avid follower of internecine squabbles at both ends of the political spectrum, he was well aware of Radosh's reputation as a liberal centrist academic who had undergone a conversion from the radical left of the sixties and early seventies. Declining the labels of "populist" and "American nationalist," Bannon proudly proclaimed himself to Radosh as a "Leninist": "Lenin . . . wanted to destroy the state, and that's my goal too. I want to bring everything crashing down, and destroy all of today's establishment." Attempting to push Radosh's buttons, Bannon referred to the solidly conservative and still identifiably Catholic *National Review* and the libertarian *Weekly Standard* as "left-wing magazines" that he also wanted to destroy, given that "no one reads them or cares what they say."[51]

Although Bannon has said that he does not recall the conversation, much in his demeanor and general outlook echoes the Lenin of *State and Revolution*.

Like Lenin, Bannon portrays himself as a tireless catalyst for a revolt to be carried out by those who otherwise have no voice. He seems to share Lenin's view
that the theoretical adumbration of tactics is no less important than the advocacy for state dismantlement; he also claims an affinity with Lenin's cultivation
of a militantly sectarian activism, one that sees misguided political cousins or
allies in the good fight as greater threats than principled enemies. In a characteristic formulation from *State and Revolution*, Lenin called for a break with
his fellow socialists Karl Kautsky, Phillip Scheidemann, Georgi Plekhanov,
and Emile Vandervelde, "traitors to socialism" who refuse to "fight for the
complete destruction of the old state machine [with the goal that] the armed
proletariat itself *should become the government*."[52]

For Bannon, it would seem that wearing the mask of Leninism is more the
performative expression of a particular life experience than the devout espousal
of an ideal.[53] Yet what is Bannon's personal experience, and what are his beliefs?
As Alison Klayman's 2019 documentary *The Brink* demonstrates, they are
more difficult to tease out than one would expect from someone who seems to
cultivate the persona of a dissolute and aging frat boy, and who speaks on
behalf of an unhip white middle-class dowdiness. His faded and frayed shirts,
one worn on top of another, are his body armor, fitted out for the battlefield
of a "new" crusade. On the face of it, his quip to Radosh seems to be a characteristic provocation. Here is an ultramontane American Catholic who grew
up reciting the Latin Tridentine Mass, a reactionary advocate for untrammeled
American military and economic supremacy on a global scale, an adherent to
the notion that Iraq's oil reserves belong to the United States, in consequence
of "natural law," as the spoils of war. What could he have ideologically in common with an advocate for a rigorously Marxian socialism, a forthright enemy
of bourgeois morality, bourgeois democracy, and the predatory forces of capitalism? Bannon's preoccupations and essential beliefs seem very distant from
what Tony Judt incisively describes as Leninism's "doctrinaire positivism."[54] At
best, we may locate his off-the-cuff statement to Radosh in the area where the
"far-left and the far-right blur and merge," which the Belgian-American critic
Lucy Sante regarded as the position of the novelist William S. Burroughs,
another American eccentric and ideological gadfly who seemed to resist any
conventional political taxonomy.[55]

There are two ways to understand or explain Bannon's reference to Lenin as
a political model. The first is to see it as being of the same cloth as the unexpectedly positive assessments of Leninism by other paleoconservatives and
radical libertarians. In a well-known interview on 25 May 2001, the Republican strategist and libertarian activist Grover Norquist stated: "I don't want to
abolish government; I simply want to reduce it to the size where I can drag it

into the bathroom and drown it in the bathtub."[56] Radosh himself and others who have visited Norquist at home have quizzically taken note of the portrait of Lenin hanging there. Twenty years ago, Radosh recalls, Norquist pointed to the portrait and remarked that he shared Lenin's keen interest in dismantling the administrative state.[57] In his memoir of political apostasy, *Blinded by the Right: The Conscience of an Ex-Conservative*, David Brock made the following observations about his contact with Norquist in the conservative movement of the nineties:

> There was nothing traditionally conservative in Grover's approach. As I conformed myself to the movement, I was being inculcated into a radical cult that bore none of the positive attributes of classical conservatism—a sense of limits, fair play, Tory civility, and respect for individual freedom. On the contrary, Grover admired the iron dedication of Lenin, whose dictum "Probe with bayonets, looking for weakness" he often quoted, and whose majestic portrait hung in Grover's Washington living room. Grover kept a pet boa constrictor, named after the turn-of-the-century anarchist Lysander Spooner. He fed the snake mice, all of them named David Bonior, the outspoken liberal House whip.[58]

Norquist's admiration for Lenin's pugilistic ruthlessness and affective pose as a political Darwinist helps to make sense of Bannon's profession of temperamental, if not ideological, Leninism. Looking at Lenin from this perspective—and applying Bannon's own characterization of the prototypical combative populist and white nationalist in the post-Obama era—we would be entirely justified in regarding the first Soviet leader as the original "honey badger" who "don't give a shit." The phrase about the ferocity of the honey badger has become a well-known meme among the far right. One of the most insightful explanations of this meme comes from an unexpected place: Tamsin Shaw's review of a 2016 production of *Othello* at the New York Theatre Workshop:

> In this reading . . . [Daniel] Craig's Iago calls to mind above all the "honey badger" that has become the mascot for the white-supremacist far right. A popular YouTube video, "The Crazy, Nastyass Honey Badger," shows this small creature display a viciousness, fearlessness, and recklessness unparalleled in the animal kingdom, attacking a huge cobra, diving into a beehive to eat the larvae in spite of being stung all over. The video's narrator coined the phrase that Steve Bannon and Breitbart news have taken for their motto: "Honey badger don't give a shit." This is a choice, this not giving a shit. It is the voluptuous enjoyment that Nietzsche described. It is the freedom and exhilaration of moral insensibility.[59]

The "Honey Badger" meme is all about histrionic bullying and gripping theater as a platform for unfurling a conception of natural law that defines the world as populated exclusively by predators, scavengers, and prey.

The second way of making sense of Bannon's self-declared Leninism is to see it as an expression of his American conservative Catholic ambivalence about the Hayekian free market, which oddly or counterintuitively comes to assume the functions of the administrative state that it claims to loathe. We might regard Bannon's comment about destroying the administrative state as closely aligned to the anarcho-populism of the sailors of the 1921 Kronstadt rebellion, whom Lenin despised as partisans of what the historian Paul Avrich insightfully termed a "libertarian socialism" that was inimical to a socialism that replaces the hated (bourgeois) state with its own beloved one.[60] This variety of libertarianism is qualitatively very different from the Koch brothers' brand of unswervingly individualistic libertarianism, favored by Norquist in his capacity as founder and chief executive officer of the political action group known as Americans for Tax Reform. In his now-famous 2014 Skyped-in speech at the Vatican, Bannon made a distinction—a somewhat unexpected one, coming from a cultural conservative and former trader at Goldman Sachs—between "enlightened" capitalism on the one hand and a counterintuitive pairing of "state capitalism" and the "Objectivist School of libertarian capitalism" on the other:

> But there's a strand of capitalism today—two strands of it, that are very disturbing.
>
> One is state-sponsored capitalism. And that's the capitalism you see in China and Russia. I believe it's what Holy Father [Pope Francis] has seen for most of his life in places like Argentina, where you have this kind of crony capitalism of people that are involved with these military powers-that-be in the government, and it forms a brutal form of capitalism that is really about creating wealth and creating value for a very small subset of people. And it doesn't spread the tremendous value creation throughout broader distribution patterns that were seen really in the 20th century.
>
> The second form of capitalism that I feel is almost as disturbing, is what I call the Ayn Rand or the Objectivist School of libertarian capitalism. And, look, I'm a big believer in a lot of libertarianism. I have many many friends that's [sic] a very big part of the conservative movement—whether it's the UKIP movement in England, it's many of the underpinnings of the populist movement in Europe, and particularly in the United States.[61]

In an interview from 2017 with the conservative author Keith Koffler, Bannon bluntly stated that Ayn Rand's Objectivism was the "thing that turned [him] off," reinforcing his belief in the inherent decency and goodness of "working people." He goes on: "I think Ayn Rand is one of the most dangerous individuals in modern thought" because her glorification of leadership elites is "against human nature, and certainly against all the precepts of the Judeo-Christian West."[62]

If we temporarily set aside Bannon's references to the Judeo-Christian tradition, we are not so far from the buoyant idealism of Lenin's unexpected pronouncement in *State and Revolution* about the goodness that is deeply ingrained in working people's repressed cultural practices. In the wake of the state's withering away, "people will gradually *become accustomed* to observing the elementary rules of social intercourse that have been known for ages and repeated for thousands of years in all copybooks—and to observing them without force, without compulsion, without subordination, *without the special apparatus* for compulsion which is called the state" (emphasis in the original).[63] Later, we will devote particular attention to the deeper contradictions within Lenin's understanding of the withering away of the state, which became more overt as he confronted labor movements that were independent of the Soviet state. Returning to Bannon's 2014 Vatican speech, we hear vivid testimony to his fuzzy and idealistic understanding of grassroots spirituality as a natural democracy:

> However, that form of capitalism is quite different when you really look at it to what I call the "enlightened capitalism" of the Judeo-Christian West. It is a capitalism that really looks to make people commodities, and to objectify people, and to use them almost—as many of the precepts of Marx—and that is a form of capitalism, particularly to a younger generation [that] they're really finding quite attractive. And if they don't see another alternative, it's going to be an alternative that they gravitate to under this kind of rubric of "personal freedom."[64]

Bannon's conflation of state capitalism and the unregulated operation of the global marketplace, though counterintuitive at first glance, makes sense if we regard it from the perspective of the pessimism and apparent antihumanism of his religious upbringing. The members of the Catholic authoritarian intelligentsia who published their views in the resolutely pro-Franco *National Review* of the seventies—particularly under the influence of William F. Buckley Jr.'s colleague and brother-in-law L. Brent Bozell III—frequently expressed a moral fatalism about the state of human affairs and the prospects for any ameliorative or progressive action. Bannon's disdainful dismissal of the *National Review* a "leftist" publication should be taken with a grain of salt. Yet it is important to bear in mind that he gave the Vatican speech less than a year after his conversation with Radosh. In both apparently contradictory instances, Bannon is keen to unmoor Marxism-Leninism from its customary place on the political spectrum. When he spoke of one form of capitalism turning "people [into] commodities" and "objectifying" them according to "many of the precepts of Marx," might Bannon have been wistfully contemplating the possibility of a Roman Catholic socialism or a secularized Catholicism, in the manner of the lapsed Catholics in Graham Greene's novels who search for circuitous returns to their faith?

Clearly, the answer to this question must be no. Passionate advocacy for autarky, and against economic globalism, does not in itself a socialist make. Furthermore, for all his talk about lifting up "the forgotten man," Bannon seemed to have forgotten about the need to sketch out an economic platform for the Trump campaign. Yet a somewhat nuanced understanding of the zealotry that accompanies a moral-political conversion—the ways in which the tenor, if not the content, of earlier beliefs can fold itself almost seamlessly into a new belief system—is certainly palpable in Bannon's Vatican speech. That public statement is the closest that he has come to a manifesto or exposition of his worldview. Here, he pays perfunctory dues to Marxism, both as the coin of the political realm and as a referent with at least residually moral value. As someone who straddled the very different professional domains of business and conservative political advocacy, Bannon seems aware of the schematic character of the free-market moral imagination. As William Kristol once observed to the political scientist Corey Robin, the central problem of American conservatism has always been that it is "so influenced by business culture and by business modes of thinking that it lacks any political imagination, which has always been, I have to say, a property of the left."[65] Bannon also critically points to the forms of capitalism that Lenin, in his extensions of Marxist analysis to colonialism, acknowledged as inimical to the dictatorship of the proletariat: the crony capitalism of the bourgeois national state, and the metastatic global capitalism that is as disrespectful of national borders as it is of personal ones.

Bannon's "State and Revolution"

Bannon, like Lenin, recognizes that the two forms of capitalism converge in the creation of colonial empires. In a statement that would not be out of place in Bannon's speech at the Vatican, Lenin argued in *Imperialism, the Highest Stage of Capitalism* (1916), that "monopolies, oligarchy, the striving for domination and not for freedom, the exploitation of an increasing number of small or weak nations by a handful of the richest or most powerful nations—all these have given birth to those distinctive characteristics of imperialism which compel us to define it as parasitic or decaying capitalism."[66] Bannon seems to argue for a postcolonial nationalism that is not far from a stance in Marx's writing that the political scientist Erica Benner characterizes as an "enlightened patriotism which, although quite compatible with a pluralistic internationalism, located the worker's first interests [firmly] within particular national societies."[67] If we substitute "white working class" for "worker," we come very close indeed to Bannon's stated current endeavor, documented by Klayman and others, to create an international network of white nationalists. It should go without saying that this redefinition of labor blocs utterly evacuates the moral impulse that Bannon claims to honor.

Very much like the conservative Catholic political scientists Patrick Deneen and Darel E. Paul, and the popular traditionalist blogger and author Rod Dreher, who are discussed in the previous chapter, Bannon engages in public displays of a road-to-Damascus epiphany about the evils of late-stage capitalism without questioning the ideologies, labor practices, or forms of ownership that contributed to their emergence. Deneen's tweet of 9 December 2020 could have come from any of Bannon's podcasts or public statements: "The U.S. today is a unique form of liberal oligarchy that was disrupted by a momentary burst of democracy," and "the elite made sure to roll that back—amusingly, in the name of 'democracy.'"[68] The alt-right and its sympathizers and enablers in the American traditionalist intelligentsia are fond of making distinctions between genuine and spurious forms of democratic practice, a practice that Lenin pioneered. (Later, we will examine Lenin's use of the specific accusation of "bourgeois democracy" against his opponents.) In articulating a concept as murky as "liberal oligarchy," Deneen uses Marxism-Leninism as a kind of conceptual boilerplate for anchoring his own fanciful elaborations; in his telling, the overaccumulation of capital in the hands of a few is mostly stripped of materiality, rendering it into a metaphor for a fixation on the values of social justice rather than fulfillment of the principles of the free market. This rhetorical sleight of hand, like Bannon's own millenarian rumblings, is propelled by a fabulist narrative that bears little relation to granular reality.

Yet in what sense might a "Judeo-Christian" or enlightened capitalism serve as a counterweight to these two distinct, yet supposedly interwoven, strands of free-market economics: the twin alienations of state capitalism, on the one hand, and "globalism," on the other? Furthermore, how could such a capitalism with a human face succeed in wresting the information sphere from the iron grip of "political correctness" that agitates Bannon and militantly antisecularist intellectuals like Deneen, whom the political scientist Laura K. Field has recently described as reactionary conservatives or "reocons"?[69] Lenin's own paradoxical understanding of the state—as both burden and boon, as a signifier that fluctuates between the categories of organic communities and dictatorship of the proletariat, reminiscent of the consensus or "general will" from Rousseau's *Social Contract*—helps us to understand the self-contradicting character of the state in the libertarian formulations of both Bannon and the alt-right movement as a whole. Like Lenin, they are more interested in the redefinition and reconfiguration of the state than they are in the wholesale shattering of it. The uplifting calls for abolishing the state are, first and foremost, rhetorically useful, the honey spread along the rim of the goblet containing what Plato, in the *Phaedrus*, characterizes as the bitter draught of truth.

One of the least commented upon aspects of *State and Revolution* is the riddle of its intended audience. The first, pseudonymous edition has a title page that is seldom quoted in its entirety: *Gosudarstvo i revoliutsiia: Marsksistskoe uchenie o zadache proletariata v revoliutsii* (The state and revolution: The Marxist theory of the state, and the task of the proletariat in the revolution). Its unwieldiness would seem to have little in common with the Lenin's style of argumentation, in person as well as on paper, as bitingly characterized by his recent biographer Victor Sebestyen: "He used a battering ram rather than a rapier, but in his finest work he can be powerfully convincing in his reason, logic, and intellectual force, albeit often from a fundamentally flawed premise."[70] The second segment of the title seems to hide behind a mask of dry scholarly assessment that is highly uncharacteristic of Lenin, perhaps even suggesting that this particular essay comes from a pedantic and relatively nonpartisan specialist. Yet, the listing of the author's name as "V. Il'in together with an alternate name in brackets "(N. Lenin)—the latter, perhaps *Neizvestnyi [Unknown] Lenin*—offers a glimpse of playfulness from a ferocious political intellect who was not known for his sense of humor. The first author name alludes to Lenin's patronymic *Ilyich*, while the second has his revolutionary surname that was originally a pseudonym. Rather than conceal his identity, these two names drew attention to it in a way that suggested an author who had become attuned to bated reader anticipation for the appearance of new statements of him. Though the publisher "Life and Knowledge" was known to be Marxist, its catalogue had a political and literary breadth (including children's literature and translations of the works of "bourgeois" socialists such as August Bebel) that would have been inconceivable ten years later. We need to bear in mind how the venue of the essay's publication influenced the possibly heterodox way in which its audience received it.

The full title is, in this regard, highly significant. *The Marxist Theory of the State*, following the phrase *State and Revolution*, opens up a range of possibilities about the essay's goals. *Uchenie* [literally, "teaching"] *Marksizma* could point to a meta-pedagogical intent: as a text that instructs members of the

cadre in the art of teaching others. Nowhere in *State and Revolution* do we get
a sense of the institutional identity of the proletarian dictatorship, or the practical mechanisms that bring about the necessary collapse of the bourgeois
state. Several scholars have concluded that Lenin's brief description of the proletarian dictatorship as operating like a post office is largely a metaphorical
afterthought.[71] Here, in contrast to almost all of his other writings, Lenin
seems unconcerned with the logical consistency of his terms. At one point he
states that the correct meaning of Engels's phrase "withering away of the state"
(in his *Anti-Dühring*) is "not 'wither away' but is '*eradicated*' by the proletariat
in the course of a revolution," for it is the "proletarian revolution or semi-state
[that] withers away after this revolution" (emphasis in original).[72] Elsewhere
he asserts, with a nearly Thomistic opacity, that "a state which is withering
away may be called a non-political state at a certain stage of its withering
away"; later, that as a "special machine for suppression, the 'state' is still necessary," only this is "now a transitional state, and is no longer a state in the
proper sense."[73] While Lenin frames the term "democracy" as a political ideal,
he is also careful to draw a distinction between its full embodiment in socialism and the grotesque mimicry of it in a capitalist society, where it invariably
is a "democracy for an insignificant minority," and only "for the rich." Lenin
partially ventriloquizes his opponents with the goal of bringing to the surface
the lack of rigor within their own political vocabularies. In that vein, he writes
that "the elimination of the state also involves the abolition of democracy,"
and conversely, "the withering away of the state means the withering away of
democracy": "Communism alone is capable of providing a truly complete
democracy, and the more complete it is the more quickly will it become
unnecessary and wither away by itself."[74] In all of these instances, Lenin's audience would readily recognize that he is referring to democracy *as these opponents understood it*—that is, in a jejune and thoroughly incorrect way.

The essay effectively ends, unfinished, at its most important moment, when
Lenin needs to speak about the education of the people after the state withers
away. We can almost see him throwing up his hands, having exhausted his
vocabulary for speaking about the unnameable: "And then the door will be
opened wide for the transition from the first stage of communist society
towards its highest phase, and simultaneously towards the complete withering
away of the state."[75] Among other things *State and Revolution* is a surprisingly intimate statement, a performance of political rhetoric with almost hap-
tic qualities. This is a pamphlet composed for activists who would eagerly
fill in the gaps that Lenin provides, in a vivid and instructive demonstration
of the genuinely democratic collective enterprise that the essay seeks to describe. Lenin's admission in the postscript that he "did not manage to finish

writing a single line" of the projected seventh chapter because of what he drolly calls the "hindrance" of the October Revolution only heightens that sense of connection with his followers, who hold in their hands a first edition of what would later be forged (with their participation) into something even more prodigious.[76]

We can imagine Bannon's attraction to a work like this, which pelts its readers with dramatic narrative subroutines without clarifying their significance in relation to one another, while also foregrounding a mirroring between author and audience. Taking note of the teeming logical inconsistencies within Bannon's own politics, Hell and Steinmetz conclude that his understanding of empire is "driven by a political logic, not an economic one—therefore, in Bannon's view, a non-imperialist empire." They go on to point out that this imagined "scenario" of a new balance of power among nations "seems to exist in a tension with the geopolitics flowing from a more radically nationalist populism."[77] The paucity of clearly defined analytical paradigms for "state" and "dictatorship" in *State and Revolution* forces us to consider the possibility that this, Lenin's best-known longer work, may be his least theoretical, which may explain Bannon's seeming fascination with its pseudoanarchism. Lenin asserts that in the full victory of the proletariat, we will see a society that is "no longer the state in the proper sense" (*chto uzhe ne est' sobstvenno gosudarstvo*). He also bluffly asserts that the "withering away [*otmiranie*] of the state" would be accompanied by the triumph of a diffuse centralism among the citizens of the revolutionary society.[78] In this essay Lenin takes particular pains to underscore that the absence of the state will result in greater centralization, and that Marx himself was opposed to federalist models of government while also being a resolute "centralist." In a highly representative passage, Lenin tautologically argues that "there is no retreat whatever from centralism in [Marx's] quoted observations, and only people suffused with philistine 'superstitious belief' in the state can mistake the destruction of the bourgeois state machine for the elimination of centralism!"[79]

This is not writing that is meant to convince or explain; the readers are already clearly positioned as sharing the author's opinions. As we see here and in many other passages of *State and Revolution*, the author is providing his readers with an inventory of memorably stentorian talking points, rather than a series of devastating analytical rebuttals. How do you spread the word about the new doctrine (*uchenie*) of the vanished state? Just have these formulaic statements at hand, and you'll be fine. *State and Revolution* has a strong scholastic bent, while also manifesting the flavor of a face-to-face demonstration of—or a master class in—evangelizing lectureship. The turns of phrase "properly speaking" (*sobstvenno*) and "in the proper sense" (*v sobstvennom smysle etogo slova*) occur several times, often precisely at moments when theoretical issues need to be clarified and explained, rather than dismissed with a chatty verbal tic. Here, Lenin is not primarily interested in convincing his audience of the sound sense of Bolshevik socialism, of its moral or scientific rightness. Rather, he is saying: let me show you the language that *signals*, rather than actually embodies, a deeper reasoning; once you assimilate that language, you will come to understand tactics.

In *State and Revolution*, the formula "the withering away of the state" functions more as a totemic object than as a concept whose ontology is denoted by the operation of its dynamically moving parts. The proper way to understand its significance is as an affective touchstone, rather than a potent heuristic paradigm. The "affect theory" developed by academics such as Lauren Berlant, Sara Ahmed, and Lee Edelman is helpful in untangling the skein of antici-pated reader responses that *State and Revolution* provokes, and it does much to clarify the seeming paradox that conceptual untidiness does not undercut the pamphlet's rhetorical power. As Ahmed explains:

> Anticipations of what an object gives us are also expectations of what we should be given. How is it that we come to expect so much? After all, expectations can make things seem disappointing. If we arrive at objects with an expectation of how we will be affected by them, then this affects how they affect us, even in the moment that they fail to live up to our expectations. Happiness is an expectation of what follows, where the expectation differentiates between things, whether or not they exist as objects in the present.[80]

Ahmed discusses affective politics as a sequence of responses triggered by dis-parate objects. Berlant characterizes the ostensible failures of Trump's presi-dential overture in 2012 as the "wing-flapping [of the fabled butterfly] that sets off revolutions."[81] These insights help us understand why someone like Ban-non, who "produces" aggregated sound bites rather than expressions of a coher-ent politics, is attracted to the particular treatment of antistatism that we find in Lenin's 1917 work.

Reading during his downtime while serving in the Navy, Bannon may have been struck by the description of Lenin in Solzhenitsyn's *Lenin in Zürich*, which enjoyed considerable popularity among the American conservative intel-ligentsia of the seventies. Solzhenitsyn portrays Lenin in 1916 as hopelessly tongue-tied and ineloquent, vainly struggling to explain dialectical materialism to Fritz Platten, the real-life secretary of the Swiss Socialist Party, who helped organize Lenin's return to Petrograd via the sealed train car from Zürich:

Platten's brow became convulsed, his eyes strained and bewildered. How difficult, how terribly difficult it is to master the lofty science of socialism! These grandiose formulas somehow refuse to fit in with your poor limited experience. War is a fraud, and neutrality is a fraud, so neutrality is just as bad as war?

Platten risks a side glance at his comrades, who are equally confused. Briefly switching to the emphatic voice of Platten's anxious thoughts, the narrator writes: "You are ashamed to admit that you don't [understand], so you pretend [*delaesh' vid*]."[82] In Solzhenitsyn's novel, this is a demonstration of how *not* to reach your audience. Conversion is accomplished through deliberate confusion, not appealing to the audience's sense of logic or even justice. As the nineteenth-century Tory and legal theorist Walter Bagehot explained conservative epistemology, truth is "a succession of perpetual oscillations, like the negative and positive signs of an alternate series, in which you were constantly more or less denying and affirming the same proposition."[83] At this point of Solzhenitsyn's novel, Lenin has yet to learn this hard lesson about the necessarily cruel art of persuasion.

From this perspective, we can hardly be surprised that Bannon is clearly influenced by the various conservative biographical accounts (such as Robert Conquest's short and hostile 1972 biography, which Bannon may have read) in which Lenin appears as a ruthless attack dog and nasty political operator, a "honey badger who don't take no shit," rather than the ineffectual Ciceronian sage that he imagines himself to be early in Solzhenitsyn's novel, prior to his pivotal meeting with Parvus in Bern. In Solzhenitsyn's Cold War text, which was foundational for anticommunists of all stripes, the encounter with Parvus shakes Lenin's customary confidence and breezy disdain for ideological rivals. It also gives him the laser-like focus that lets him abandon internecine squabbles for the larger realm of well-financed political action. As Lenin ruefully reflects during his Faustian conversation with Parvus, he always came up short when it came to getting things done. Everything else, he could manage. "But the one thing he couldn't do was to bring *that* moment [pribliz*it' tot* moment] any closer" (emphasis in the original). Whereas Parvus, "with his millions," connections in port cities, gun-running, and deft assistance in the seizure of the Petrograd Putilov weapons factory, was endowed with precisely that skill.[84]

Three archetypes emerge from this narrative: the young, fiercely polemical yet scholastic Lenin prior to his European exile; Parvus, the well-connected provocateur; and the postexile Lenin, who represents something of a synthesis of the first two archetypes. One highly representative assessment of that contempt of Lenin's for the carefully reasoned mode of political suasion comes from Moishe Olgin, his former comrade-in-arms in Petrograd. "He does not reply to an opponent: he vivisects them. . . . [He] is derisive. He ridicules his opponent. He castigates him. He makes you feel that his victim is an ignoramus, a fool, a presumptuous non-entity. You are swept up by the power of his apparent logic. You are overwhelmed by his intellectual passion."[85] As Olgin ruefully acknowledged, logic is often quite palpably beside the point in such discourse.

Bannon's characterization of his relations with Trump during the presidential campaign suggests a rotation of the three archetypes described above. Like the verbally abusive Lenin, Bannon attempts to squeeze dissimilar and occasionally conflicting observations into what he imagines to be a formula for political victory. Yet a jumbled assemblage of melodramatic views strongly suggests that he sees himself and Trump as *doppelgängers*, very much like Parvus and Lenin in Solzhenitsyn's narrative. One example is his contempt for his fellow fringe agitators, extending both to the *National Review* coterie of "establishment" conservatives, cited earlier, and to the white supremacist and neo-Nazi Richard Spencer, whom Bannon dismissed as a "goober" and a "freak."[86] Other examples are his admiration for plutocratic influencers and his love of the public spectacle of thuggish behavior. Following Lenin's behavioral lead, as imagined in the conservative canon, this posture requires some bluster, much fibbing, and the passing over in silence of obvious inconsistencies, if not blatant lapses, in reasoning—what Hell and Steinametz characterize as a deliberate "politics of chaos and incoherence."[87]

Conservatives like Gottfried, Norquist, and Bannon are fascinated by what they understand to be Lenin's default mode of disinhibited obloquy. Lenin dismissed Kerensky, Kautsky, and Plekhanov as guilty of philistinism (*meshchanstvo*), ignorance, and otiose parliamentarianism, as if their views were more deserving of verbal assault than engaged rebuttal. In *State and Revolution*, this rhetoric of unleashed invective lends itself to a slurry of pejorative nomenclature that is signaled by ellipses and trailing abbreviations, as if Kautsky et al. are simply placeholders for a roiling mass of political cluelessness and all-around foolishness that is unworthy of thorough categorization. The pamphlet was, after all, a call to arms rather than an attempt at suasion. Again, it is useful to remind ourselves of its final sentence as we have it: "It is more pleasant and useful to undertake the 'experience of revolution' than to write about it."[88]

This discovery of the cumulative character of the historical moment during the process of writing informs what we sense about the book's target audience: what Robert Service calls "avid followers" rather than a big-tent coalition of social democrats.[89] Service takes note of the curious expository style of the text, which at times seems almost "languid" in its repeated use of incomplete inventories of the political errors of others. In characterizing his opponents, Lenin often "appends a carefree 'etcetera'"—in the Russian text, *i t. d.,* or, with pointed rhetorical extravagance, *i t. d. i t. p.* ("and so on and so forth")—"for the benefit of his readers."[90] As the Turkish and Berkeley-based sociologist Cihan Tuğal observed in 2018, "American right-wing populism is Leninism under democratic conditions." He writes: "Unlike the Russian Bolsheviks who had to avoid almost all above-ground society and politics, American rightists embrace society."[91] Like Bannon himself, Bannon's journalistic mentor Andrew Breitbart engaged in a quasi-Leninist strategy of rhetorical shorthand that was deceptively chatty and slack. (It also emphasized a return to common sense and bourgeois virtues, which did not feature as a part of the landscape in Lenin's writing.) A few days after the death of Ted Kennedy, Breitbart called the Massachusetts senator "a villain," "a prick," and "a duplicitous bastard," adding: "I'm more than willing to go off decorum to ensure that THIS MAN is not beatified." Like Lenin's style of inflammatory language, these insults serve to highlight a particular node among a network of assumptions, analogous to the identification of a poisonous mushroom. What is such a toxic organism if not the external body of a deeper root system, which consists, in this instance, of the deceased man's cowardly and de facto homicidal behavior at Chappaquiddick, his political corruption, his academic dishonesty in college, etc.?

Taking his lead from Breitbart, Bannon openly admired Trump's thuggish demeanor at a debate with Hillary Clinton: "You have to have a certain psychological construct to harass Hillary Clinton by inviting her husband's accusers to the first presidential debate." Trump was, he said, a "classic honey badger—he crushed her."[92] Breitbart and Bannon evoke Lenin's own expository stratagem of critique through truncated or abbreviated invective, even as they turn his political values on their head. The target audience is already firmly on your side and in your corner—all you need to do is nudge its network of trembling mental associations into a frenetic overdrive.

Clearly Bannon's style of contestation has much in common with Lenin's. How does the libertarian and alt-right disgust with pluralism compare with Lenin's self-aware performance of politically sectarian rage in *State and Revolution*? At the very least, there are affinities with his characterization of "equality" as a diffuse structure that is made gravitationally possible by the equal valences of the citizens who inhabit it. Such an understanding of equality is opposed to the conception of "bourgeois right," in which "a *uniform* standard" is applied to "*different* people" (emphasis in the original) who can never, in such a society, be identical or equal to each other.[93] Müller explains that the "anti-politics" of the populist right stakes a claim at validating "direct" communication, which it claims is irreconcilable with the malign factionalism of pluralist political systems.[94] Lenin would doubtless characterize this assertion as specious, in view of the populist right's fixation on complementarian categories—in this instance, based on traditional gender roles as well as class—that presume an understanding of the body politic as a strictly differentiated, if not hierarchized, chain of being.

Of particular significance in the appropriation of Lenin's antistatism by Bannon and the populist right is what Wodak identifies as the alt-right's gossipy "fictionalization of politics," which renders all politics into a series of theatrical, affective prompts, rather than a vigorous dialogue involving different views.[95] As Wodak explains it, this form of propaganda is composed of scripts, a series of jabs or directorial prompts, rather than moments of dialogic engagement. Bannon seems to imagine that Lenin favored this kind of politicized sociality, in which affect is deliberately and artificially driven by the "drama of decision."[96] What matters most here is, as Berlant explains, the high affective drama of "remaining in attachment" to an object—in this case, in an antagonistic relationship to another person.[97] What does that person "signal"? Or, to put it another way, what is the affect that "they" (or images of them) communicate to us?

Bannon has no interest in the Marxist essence of Lenin's writings. What animates him is an appreciation of Lenin as the philosopher of political contestation. In this regard, Bannon has surprising affinities with Louis Althusser, an idiosyncratic Catholic Marxist who attempted to reinvigorate leftism with a new understanding of Lenin as a rigorous system-builder. Above all, Althusser was interested in Lenin as a theorist of materialist unfolding, rather than Lenin as an appropriator of Hegel's historical idealism. As Althusser explains in his controversial essay "Lenin before Hegel" (1969), for Lenin "it is absolutely essential (as he had learnt simply from a thorough-going reading of *Capital*) *to suppress every origin and every subject, and to say*: what is absolute is *the process without a subject*, both in reality and in scientific knowledge" (emphasis in the original).[98] It is unlikely that Bannon, steeped as he is in the ephemeral culture of the smashmouth sound bite, is aware of Althusser's understanding of Lenin as an apostle of developing socialism, of an unfolding perfectibility that recalls Thomist as well as Marxian categories. Yet Bannon and Althusser share an avowed interest in what Berlant identifies as an understanding of any given historical moment as a "visceral moment" in which "corporeal, intimate, and political performances of adjustment" create a "shared atmosphere." Like the physical environment in the Anthropocene, the presence of multiple human actors inevitably transforms that atmosphere, whose new chemical composition becomes, in Berlant's formulation, an object "theory-in-practice of how a world works."[99] The ephemerality of political culture—of a politics without resolution or end, reveling in its own incoherence—is at the center of Bannon's appropriation of Lenin.

Fired from his position at the White House, Bannon made a series of contemptuous remarks about the Trump family. Then, on the last full day of his presidency, Trump announced that he would issue a pardon for Bannon, who had been charged with fraudulently raising money to build a wall on the border with Mexico. This gesture of clemency—from a thin-skinned chief executive not given to forgiveness for public slights—is oddly depersonalized. The spectacle of clemency contingent upon departure—of bad blood superficially purged for actors who leave the scene that has come to define them—seems completely consistent with Berlant's characterization of an emerging politics in which the "affective structure remains," even after the subject has left the building.[100]

Conclusion: Bannon as a Follower of Leninist Populism

In chapter 1, we examined the views of American conservative intellectuals who have used lessons gleaned from the tragic events of the Russian Revolution as keys for gaining access to the deeper currents of the American present, with the goal of framing the populist groundswell of the 2016 presidential election as a rebuke to the forces that tipped tsarist Russia into a very modern kind of authoritarianism. Helen Andrews, Gary Saul Morson, and other conservative intellectuals have tried to coax historical parallels between the self-immolations of prerevolutionary liberal elites in Russia and their twenty-first-century US counterparts. Unacknowledged by these writers is another parallel: the resonance between the January 6 Capitol insurrection and an event on the same day and month 103 years earlier. In view of her focus on drawing conclusions about the fecklessness and irresponsibility of liberals, perhaps we should not be surprised by Andrews's reluctance to address similarities between violent and antidemocratic populist movements in the two countries.

What happened in Petrograd on 6 January 1918 (n.s.)? On that day Lenin delivered his "Speech on the Dissolution of the Constituent Assembly" to the All-Russia Central Executive Committee, a government body that had displaced the administrative body that ran the first free election in Russian history. When the Bolshevik party won an embarrassing 24 percent of the vote, compared with 39 percent for the Socialist Revolutionaries (with the constitutional monarchists or "Kadets" trailing at 5 percent, and the Mensheviks at 3 percent), Lenin peremptorily ordered the Red Guards—a loose confederation of workers' militias—to shut down the Constituent Assembly. This was a prelude to declaring a nullification of election results and preventing peaceful demonstrators—many of them socialists—from approaching the locked Tauride Palace, where the counting took place.[101] Ten of the demonstrators who protested the dissolution of the assembly were shot dead, and seventy were badly wounded.[102] In his speech the next day, Lenin acknowledged the bad optics of declaring invalid the operations of an administrative body that the Bolsheviks had recognized as legitimate only a few days earlier. He then went on to breezily dismiss the Constituent Assembly as a venue for the "speeches of outmoded politicians." He explained that "the people wanted the Constituent Assembly summoned, and we summoned it." Yet, those same people, represented by the workers' councils, the Soviets,

> sensed immediately what this famous Constituent Assembly really was. And now we have carried out the will of the people, which is—All power to the Soviets. As for the saboteurs, we shall crush them. . . .
>
> . . . And by the will of Soviet power the Constituent Assembly, which has refused to recognize the power of the people, is being dissolved.

Lenin concluded by commenting that those who dominated the old political order have been crushed, and that "their attempts at resistance will only accentuate and provoke a new outbreak of civil war."[103] Privately, he later admitted to Trotsky that while dissolving the assembly was a "big risk," doing so meant "the full and open liquidation of formal democracy in the name of the revolutionary dictatorship," which can only "serve as a good lesson."[104]

Lenin's reasoning about the will of the people as equivalent to the will of the Soviets and his contempt for the mechanisms of electoral democracy is completely consistent with the mode of argumentation and specific beliefs of present-day right-wing populist elites. As Müller explains, right-wing populists engage in a rhetorical sleight of hand that relies on circular reasoning, by "creat[ing] the homogeneous people in whose name they had been speaking all along."[105] Populists, he argues, are indifferent to "the genuine process of will-formation or a common good that anyone with common sense can glean"; rather, what matters for them is "a symbolic representation of the 'real people' from which the correct policy is then deduced." Not surprisingly, such subterfuge "renders the political position of the populist immune to empirical refutation."[106]

Disdain for empirical proof is abundantly evident in Lenin's speech, both in his categorical dismissal of election results and in his blithe assumption of his ability to speak for the Soviets. Contrary to his assertion, most of the Soviets were open to working with whatever party emerged victorious in the election, and none expressed a wish to dissolve the assembly. As the historian Geoffrey Hosking points out, during the October Revolution itself, "most participants in the rising thought that they were fighting for 'All Power to the Soviets,'" with the understanding that the principles underlying the slogan would "be embodied in the form of a coalition socialist government which would endorse the authority of workers', soldiers' and peasants' assemblies throughout the country." Instead, even in districts where they were popular, Bolsheviks insisted that they dictate all policies within the workers' councils; wherever they were less popular, they insisted that the local Soviets be taken over by an "armed militia, usually called a Military Revolutionary Committee, to coerce or replace the soviet and enforce 'All Power to the Soviets'" in strict accordance with Bolshevik aspirations to institutional hegemony.[107]

Contemplating the January 6 events in his more recent *Democracy Rules*, Müller explains the self-validating and circular mechanism through which the invocation of the nebulous category "the will of the people" inevitably leads to contested election results and open challenges on the processes of representative democracy. This is what happens when "populists are the people's only morally legitimate representatives," but they "fail to gain overwhelming majorities in the ballot box." Müller's discussion illuminates Andrews's and Bannon's skepticism about the present-day operations of electoral democracy, and also the parallels between their reasoning about these matters and Lenin's hostility to parliamentarianism. "Populists do not all choose what might seem the easiest way" of reconciling their self-images as spokespersons for the "real people" with unsuccessful bids at the ballot box. Nonetheless, many do so with their invocation of the "silent majority":

> By definition, if the silent majority has spoken, populists will always already be in power. If they're not holding office, that's because we are looking not so much at a silent majority as at a *silenced majority* [emphasis in the original]. Someone or something must have prevented the majority from making its voice heard. Thus, populists often insinuate that they did not really lose an election at all but that corrupt elites must have been manipulating things behind the scenes. . . . In 2020, we witnessed a chronicle of a fraud foretold: Trump had again announced that he might not accept an unfavorable outcome; this time, he actively sought to steal the election by accusing his political opponents of stealing the election. The underlying logic was once more inspired by a core populist claim: only a vote for the people's unique representative is legitimate (and legal); and it could not really come as a surprise that Trump called the January 6 crowd assembled on the Mall "the real people"—professing his "love" for them and then giving them marching orders to overturn the election results.[108]

The January 6 insurrectionists' claim of a "stolen" election has suggestive parallels to Lenin's declaration of the need to disband the Constituent Assembly
and give all power to the Soviets. As Bannon put it on his radio show on the
eve of the counting of the Electoral College votes: "All hell will break loose
tomorrow." Populist American conservatives like Bannon are taken with the
idea that one can have Leninism without socialism. Cerebral provocateurs like
Gottfried and Norquist may be attracted to this conceit because they perceive
the internecine squabbles among Russian socialist parties on the eve of the
October Revolution as similar to the upheavals and realignments within
American conservatism that followed both the 2016 election and the January 6
insurrection.

It is at this point that we catch a glimpse of the specific feature that attracts
Bannon to Lenin's legacy. His tendentious study of human affairs and his impressionistic political views—attacking economic globalism and in the same breath
praising corporate entities like Goldman Sachs, for which he once worked, as
genuine builders and producers—exist downstream of the American populist
appropriations of Leninism that are at the center of Gottfried's and Norquist's
public statements and writing. Lenin's order to disband the Constituent
Assembly was an example of a successful insurrection, and one where, as Bannon might see it, proper hierarchies were restored. The operational traditions
of the church and the military—both ideological touchstones for Bannon—
speak to conservatives as models of how to integrate the practice of submission
into one's life.

In her book about American ethnonationalism and the alt-right, Alexandra
Minna Stern observes that the "primary site for the alt-right's Gramscian 'war
of position,' which revolves around an incessant quest to win the hearts and
minds of the white majority," is undergirded by culture-war talking points
about the white working class's being "left behind" by global capitalism and
betrayed by a vaguely defined network of American "cosmopolitan" elites.[109]
Scorning expertise from established institutions is, for Bannon, Andrews, and
many alt-right figures (Eric Metaxas, Ben Shapiro, and Mike Cernovic, among
others) a stimulant in the struggle to build alternative avenues of knowledge.
This effort is almost completely consistent with Edward Said's warnings against
the "danger of specialization" and "professionalization," and may even be understood as an endorsement of his advocacy for an intellectual "amateurship" as a
bulwark against politically compromised institutional knowledge.[110] "The
proper attitude of the intellectual outside the academy," Said writes, "is some
sort of defiance."[111] This is a view shared by Bannon, and the network of new
rightist elites that he cultivates, with a Palestinian American literary critic
from the left whom they normally would not abide. Perhaps we can explain

these inconsistencies and unexpected fellowships by bearing in mind Robin's observation that "ever since Burke, it has been a point of pride among conservatives that theirs is a contingent mode of thought."[112] Here we see the imprint of a Leninist populism on Bannon and other affective firebrands on the far right. Like many other scholars of Russian history, Hosking has pointed out the inner contradictions of Lenin's populism. He was a Marxist, which is to say that he "believed in the existence of scientific laws of social development and in the primacy of class struggle"; on the other hand, he no less strongly identified himself as a "Russian populist," that is, someone who "believed in the leadership of a small elite over the mass revolutionary movement."[113] Bannon argues for the moral superiority of a "silent majority" while also asserting that such people are given a voice only through the intervention of a charismatic strongman leader. At the end of the day, the most difficult contingency for rightist elites to negotiate is the belief in the existence of a cognitive cadre that is answerable only to itself. In the next chapter, about influential academic figures on the right in the United States and the Russian Federation, we will see how radical traditionalists attempt to finesse, even if they cannot completely reconcile, the contradiction between belief in grassroots values and commitment to an inflexible chain of command.

CHAPTER THREE

Hijacking Academic Authority

Racism and the Internet Expertise of Kevin MacDonald and Alexander Dugin

The Alt-Right is doing society a service by addressing an issue that urgently needs sunlight, and by providing an ecosystem of websites and podcasts where authors can be published and critiqued, and points argued back and forth. Much of the discussion of Jewish influence in the Alt-Right is very scholarly, fair and balanced, i.e. the work of Kevin MacDonald or Michael Hoffman.
—CHARLES BAUSMAN, "It's Time to Drop the Jew Taboo," *Russia Insider* (15 January 2018)

Someone once said that Dugin was not an ideologue of the NBP [National Bolshevik Party], but rather the teller of fairy tales. And indeed, he was able to tell fairy tales with a popularizing brilliance. Right-wing legends came to him in an unforgettable way.
—EDUARD LIMONOV, *Moia politicheskaia biografiia* (My political biography)

Introduction: The Emergence of the Alt-Right Academic

THE IMAGE OF STEVE BANNON posing as a Leninist fellow traveler or sympathizer lingers in our mind, even after we become aware of the gadfly character of his persona. Bannon is an example of someone who aspires to form a cognitive elite while deliberately spurning the gravitas of a public intellectual. Until now, our discussion of American nativist populism and its unexpected Russian roots has only peripherally focused on the recurring theme of anti-Semitism. Influential members of the American populist elite—such as Bannon, Helen Andrews, Rod Dreher, and Patrick Deneen—position themselves as opponents of a cosmopolitan or globalist elite whose amoral free-market values are ennobled by a veneer of progressive principles. We do not find in their statements an explicit ethnic or racial identification of that group which Yuri Slezkine calls the Mercurians. In a variety of ways, the populists mentioned here are militantly opposed to this ideal of a fluid category of people who Yuri Slezkine characterizes as skilled "negotiators, translators, and mystifiers," who speak between nations, rather than for the nation they live in.[1]

We have been contemplating the populists' religiously inflected commitment to nationalism, with its underlying assumption of a "real people" who transcend the dry, legalistic concept of citizenship reputedly embodied by urban populations and the "cosmopolitan" class. It is at this juncture that we enter more directly into the material realities of the Russian context that are so tightly enmeshed with with the ideology of conservative populism. The American and Russian academics who are the focus of this chapter can be regarded as evangelists for rightist elitism, and they fully embrace the role of cerebral paladin that is of little interest to Bannon. Here, the idealized persona of the erudite specialist is no obstacle to appealing to an audience of populist traditionalists. An interest in Russia's historical role as the nation with the largest Jewish community—the "Pale of Settlement," abolished in 1917—plays a significant role in the ideas and beliefs of both men, as they tease out the proper relationship between the native and the cultural stranger. In her *Proud Boys and the White Ethnostate: How the Alt-Right is Warping the American Imagination* (2019), Alexandra Minna Stern writes that "alt-righters want to come home, to the safety and sameness of their tribe."[2] The two academics who are the subjects of this chapter are intent on exploring how things went awry after the pivot from tribe-oriented localism to globalism. For both Kevin MacDonald and Alexander Dugin, the Russian story is a useful object lesson in how things went wrong.

The academic and journalistic careers of MacDonald, a retired professor in the department of psychology at California State University in Long Beach, and Dugin, a former professor of sociology at Moscow State University, would not seem to have much in common. The highly specific language of Dugin's pronouncements about the need for a neo-Bolshevik Russian empire reverberates in Putin's speeches and in the tendentious narratives provided by the Kremlin's media empire. MacDonald, anchored within the fringe of American conservatism, would seem to have little potential for crossing over into a more expansive notoriety and influence. Having left his academic position in 2014, his political activity remains within the narrow ambit of his non-peer-reviewed publications and the white identity journal *Occidental Quarterly*, whose editor he became in 2007. In 2011 he served on the board of directors of the anti-immigrant and white nationalist American Freedom Party, which until 2013 was known as the American Third Position Party. Since that time, he has launched the blog webzine *Occidental Observer* as a high-profile online companion to the faux-scholarly *Occidental Quarterly*. In a 2014 issue of the latter, he strongly criticized Dugin's project of pushing back against "American hegemony and Atlanticism," calling it "an unrelenting attack on the very essence of Western civilization."[3]

That assertion of a principled disagreement notwithstanding, there are clear similarities in MacDonald's and Dugin's styles of engagement with the global alt-right audience. They portray themselves as supporters of nationalist authoritarianism who are also possessors of weighty cultural capital within traditional academic institutions: one of the largest state-funded university systems in the United States and the Russian university that has served as an important engine for replenishing that country's political elite. Since he was awarded tenure in 1994, MacDonald has carefully cultivated the persona of an academic expert who is an organic link between the informational pathways of legitimate scholarship and anti-Semitic Christian identity movements and fringe activism. He is the academic whose work is most often cited by the right-wing website Stormfront.

Catering to the ideological eclecticism of the new right in Russia—which aims to forge a synthesis of pre-Soviet Russian nationalism, neo-Stalinist isolationism, Leninist statism, and the energy-resource agendas of plutocratic constituencies—Alexander Dugin has shrewdly parceled out his internet presence across a range of websites. Each of these is meant to appeal to a specific niche in the political marketplace: Russian Orthodoxy, Eurasianism, fascism, antiglobalism, occultism. MacDonald freely distributes most of his amateur scholarship on Jewish culture from his personal web page and the website of the *Occidental Observer*. Both are intent on constructing self-validating scholarly subcultures with a strong diegetic component and a specific appeal to nonrationalist modes of discourse, while intersecting with larger communities of political action.

Psychologist as Historiographer: The Evolution of Kevin MacDonald

MacDonald's three books on Judaism as an evolutionary strategy were originally published in the late nineties by Praeger, a largely respected academic imprint that specializes in research in the social sciences. MacDonald's monographs fell under the rubric of the Praeger series "Human Evolution, Behavior and Intelligence," which included the works of such racialist social scientists as Richard Lynn, Arthur R. Jensen, Michael E. Levin, and J. Phillipe Rushton. MacDonald's first book about Judaism, *A People That Shall Dwell Alone: Judaism as a Group Evolutionary Strategy*, was published in 1994; the second and third, *Separation and Its Discontents: Toward an Evolutionary Theory of Anti-Semitism* and *The Culture of Critique: An Evolutionary Analysis of Jewish Involve-*

Roundtable session at the National Policy Institute, 18 November 2020, Washington, DC. Seated from left to right: Peter Brimelow, Jared Taylor, Kevin MacDonald, and the blogger "Millennial Woes" (Colin Robertson); standing: Richard Spencer. Photo by Linda Davidson/The Washington Post via Getty Images.

ment in Twentieth-Century Intellectual and Political Movements, in 1998. MacDonald's following among the alt-right is enormous, and his long-term impact upon the movement has been considerable. On 18 November 2020, he spoke at a roundtable event with other luminaries of the far right, including Peter Brimelow, Jared Taylor, and the Scottish vlogger Colin Robertson (also known as "Millennial Woes"), at the National Policy Institute Conference, where the neo-Nazi Richard Spencer made his first widely publicized appearance.[4]

The academic respectability of Praeger's "Human Evolution, Behavior and Intelligence" series had already begun to erode when MacDonald published his second and third volumes. It was starting to be perceived as a cluster of publications that bypassed rigorous peer-review outside its coterie of researchers, a view that was reinforced by the unfolding critical discussion of Charles Murray and Richard J. Herrnstein's *The Bell Curve* (1994). In support of their conclusions about the racial heritability of intelligence and the pointlessness of educational reforms in the American public school system, Murray and Herrnstein cite many of the researchers who had contributed to the Praeger series, singling out Rushton's work (controversial for its assertion of an inverse relation in humans between intelligence and the size of genitalia) for particular praise.

By 2002 Praeger had ceased to print MacDonald's books. MacDonald subsequently undertook to have them published by the nonacademic print-on-demand companies AuthorHouse and iUniverse.

MacDonald's writing about Jewish culture and Judaism attracted greater public attention in 2018, when the refereed scholarly journal *Human Nature* published a rebuttal to his theories. Nathan Cofnas, an American who was then finishing his work at Oxford for a PhD in philosophy, formulated a series of objections to MacDonald's theory of a Jewish war waged against gentile European culture, which included distortions about the level of Freud's commitment to internationally pro-Jewish causes, the supposedly philo-Semitic biases of both Boasian anthropology and the Frankfurt School, and the scale of "Jewish influence" on the formation of American immigration policy in the twentieth century.[5] Since then, Cofnas and MacDonald have engaged in a vigorous polemical exchange, not adding any new arguments, but elaborating and in some cases clarifying their earlier assertions.

As is often the case in scholarly debates that continue over a period of years, this bitter exchange has coughed up revealing admissions of otherwise unspoken assumptions and political beliefs. In 2021 MacDonald escalated his claims about Freud's philo-Semitic views by giving them a vaguely religious coloring, grandiloquently claiming that they had a "messianic" component that advocated for a multicultural society. This article was a rebuttal to one by Cofnas and was incongruously published in the peer-reviewed Israeli philosophy journal *Philosophia*, which eventually issued a retraction of MacDonald's article. In his article, MacDonald comes right out with the outraged question: "Should white advocates ignore the historical and contemporary Jewish role in their dispossession?" His partial answer: "Many Jews will inevitably find an honest discussion of the history of white dispossession threatening because of the prominent role of Jews revealed by any objective account of that history."[6]

In his first response to MacDonald, Cofnas hinted at his own interest in "race realist" views by referring to "evolutionary psychology and biosocial science" as useful frames of reference for understanding racial and ethnic-group identity. "Biosociology" is not a field that is recognized by practitioners of historiography, which is essentially the discipline in which MacDonald and Confas (neither of them a trained historian) have been conducting their polemic.[7] On other occasions, Cofnas has voiced the same opinions that serve as the linchpin of MacDonald's theories about biological determinism in cultural affairs. His odd book *Reptiles with a Conscience: The Coevolution of Religious and Moral Doctrine* (2012), which was published by the racialist think tank Ulster Institute for Social Research Press but subsequently withdrawn from publication, makes a series of provocative and unsubstantiated assertions.

Among them are: conservativism is the belief system of evolutionary winners; liberals attempt to shield themselves from, if not actively impede, the forward march of the human species; and there are biological reasons for the "cult of the engineer," or man of action.[8] The same year he wrote his critique of McDonald's anti-Semitic theories, posts to his Twitter account argued that the mass shooting at the Tree of Life synagogue in Pittsburgh was at least partly understandable as a rational response to Jewish endorsement of progressive causes: "Psychologists can't study this b/c they would have to engage with the ideology of the Jew haters. Pitt[sburgh synagogue] shooter/other alt-righters are angry about the role that Jews play in multiculturalism/immigration. But it's considered anti-Semitic to acknowledge Jews have influence at all."[9] Most recently, in his response to MacDonald's *Philosophia* article, Cofnas has indicated that he and other well-known—and professionally ostracized—racialist researchers, whom he names, are endeavoring to bring a larger audience to the awareness of a disquieting truth: "The long-term success of humanity will depend on our ability to come to terms with reality, including controversial facts about group differences."[10] This controversy makes one thing clear about "differences": the narcissism of small ones often underpin an exchange between researchers who claim to be drawing starkly contrastive conclusions.

MacDonald welcomed the opportunity to engage with a reviewer whose hostility seemed to him to be redeemed or offset by the fact that he felt strongly enough about MacDonald's ideas to give them a detailed response. Posting his first reply to Cofnas on the online alt-right news aggregator *Unz Review*, MacDonald wrote that "after 20 years of silence from academics," he was gratified to see that Nathan Cofnas had written a "comprehensive critical review of *The Culture of Critique* in an academic venue." He ruefully notes, "I have been waiting for this to happen and was beginning to think it never would. Academics want their work to be taken seriously, and honest academics value the rough and tumble of academic debate."[11] MacDonald's yearning for recognition is not informed by an understandable desire for respect within one's profession; rather, it is a gateway for initiation into a world of larger political action. His unspooling fracas with Cofnas was the *cause célèbre* that lifted him from the dull, shuffling priesthood of academia into the role of alt-right internet crusader. As we shall see, Dugin had his own breakout moment, albeit one that was considerably more dramatic and publicly embarrassing.

One of the first things that a reader notices in MacDonald's books about Judaism is the redundancy of their argumentation. Their assumption of a uniform cultural self-image among Jews persisting over thousands of years brings to mind Richard Hofstadter's acute observation about "higher paranoid scholarship" as competing with the culturally destructive forces that it seeks to uncloak: "it believes that it is up against an enemy who is as infallibly rational as he is totally evil, and it seeks to match its imputed total competence with its own, leaving nothing unexplained and comprehending all of reality in one overreaching, consistent theory."[12]

In spite of MacDonald's crude and reductionist writing, the reviews of his books that appeared in mainstream academic journals were surprisingly lenient. Certainly, those publications were not met, as he claims, by radio silence. In a highly critical yet temperate response to *A People Who Shall Dwell Alone* in the *Journal for the Scientific Study of Religion*, Eugen Schoenfeld takes issue with MacDonald's use of the term "evolutionary strategy" to describe Jewish practices of endogamy, cultural separatism, and what MacDonald perceives as an unrelenting chauvinism from the fall of the last temple to the present day: "The author proposes that his study investigates Judaism as a group evolutionary strategy. Strategy implies, at least to me, a rational goal-oriented behavior. If this is the case, then who made the decisions that led to Jewish exclusivist social norms?"[13] It is a pity that Schoenfeld did not further explore the considerable problems (from the multiple disciplinary perspectives of biology, cultural studies, and historiography) that beset MacDonald's use of this odd formulation. Evolution is a process, not a social practice: it unfolds over multiple generations of a species undergoing natural selection and adaptation to changing physical environments. In what sense can an animal—much less a human, a group of humans, or a culture—be said to implement strategies for the survival of their species? MacDonald's handling of this formulation is reminiscent of Ayn Rand's equally meretricious and opaque concept of "rational self-interest," only here it seems to be transferred from the level of an individual's consciousness and experience to that of a group, if not a species.

But there are other problems with this way of thinking about adaptive self-defense in a cultural setting. Very often, MacDonald argues for a subconscious solidarity among Jews across wide spans of time and place, which suggests an adherence to the semimystical and discredited notion of collective racial memory that was most famously propounded by Carl Jung. "Many of the Jews involved in the [progressive] movements . . . may sincerely believe that these movements are really divorced from specifically Jewish interests or are in the best interests of other groups as well as Jews [but] the best deceivers are those who are self-deceived."[14]

MacDonald's conception of racial memory—as both an instinctual reflex for collective self-defense and a cognitive engine that takes into account past victories and mistakes before drawing up a calculus for future actions—has a strong Lamarckian component that makes it incompatible with any branch of evolutionary science. Furthermore, assuming that the concept of evolutionary strategies has integrity as an analytical tool, how can we speak of a person or group of people who lived prior to the 1859 publication of *The Origin of Species* as possessing an awareness of it? MacDonald's writing about Judaism is riddled with logical inconsistencies, anachronisms, and methodological fallacies that speak to the serious difficulty of transplanting paradigms from a subfield of the natural sciences into a historiographical context.

But perhaps the central problem with MacDonald's writing about Judaism is that it has very little to do with any branch of psychology or historiography and is more deeply informed by the anti-Semitism that is specific to American nativism. He is particularly exercised by what he sees as the undue influence of Jewish lobbyists on the escalating generosity of American immigration policy, which culminated in the 1965 Immigration and Nationality Act. What was the purpose behind this push for more liberal immigration laws, promoted by Jewish (as MacDonald is wont to remind us) activists like Senator Jacob Javits of New York? The more or less articulated ideal, according to MacDonald, was to foster an "ethnic and religious pluralism"; the concealed, and more passionately felt, agenda was to disperse "political and cultural influence among the various ethnic and religious groups" in order to make it "difficult or impossible to develop unified, cohesive groups of gentiles united in their opposition to Judaism."[15]

In MacDonald's series of books about Judaism—to call it a trilogy seems ennobling and therefore wrong—the mask of scholarly dispassion tends to fall during his discussion of the cultural forces that facilitated the rise of National Socialism. While an undergraduate at the University of Wisconsin in Madison during the late sixties, MacDonald took one course taught by the historian George L. Mosse. As MacDonald notes in a blog post about his short-lived participation in the antiwar movement on the Madison campus, "I took Mosse's course and later came to read several of Mosse's books as background to my chapter on National Socialism in *Separation and Its Discontents*." MacDonald notes that "in his book *The Crisis of German Ideology*, Mosse stressed that an important ingredient in the rise of Nazism was *völkisch* ideology—the ideology that Germans had a unique folk spirit as a result of their evolutionary past."[16] Strikingly, MacDonald does not acknowledge that his conclusions about German mystical nationalism are diametrically opposed to Mosse's.

In *The Crisis of German Ideology*, Mosse consistently underscores the fabulist character of the ideology that MacDonald sees as the rational response of gentiles to the presence of a Jewish culture in Germany. Among other aberrations, the "fear of racial defilement through intermarriage, with its associations of sex, love, and [distinct] physical features, became an obsession" within the *völkisch* cultural imaginary.[17] MacDonald does not acknowledge the extensive testimony of Jews in Germany who passionately identified with gentile German high culture, a tragic generation whose experience was documented by writers as different as Joachim Fest and Gershom Scholem. More poignant and interesting to MacDonald are the anguish and panic of nineteenth-century German gentiles like the composer Richard Wagner,[18] whose incendiary anti-Semitic statements are quoted as if they were dispassionate observations of material reality. In *Separation and Its Discontents*, MacDonald writes feelingly of the responses in *Mein Kampf* and the publications of Houston Chamberlain to the demographic and institutional threats posed by Jewish culture in Germany.[19] He uses these and other *loci classici* of anti-Semitism (such as the inflammatory publications of Henry Ford) as primary historical texts, *engagé* chronicles of events and circumstances, positioning their authors as biased yet thoughtful witnesses to a time of upheaval and cultural dissolution.

Less obvious to many readers, yet more significant in giving his books a patina of respectability, is MacDonald's lengthy bibliography, which cites a wide range of scholarly studies in the social sciences together with other, less well-known publications. He often cites legitimate sources in close proximity to rabble-rousing political pamphlets and egregious and discredited examples of racialist pseudoscience, such as the work of Fritz Lenz (a geneticist who actively worked within the Third Reich),[20] the Russian anti-Semitic propagandist Igor Shafarevich, and the fringe American anti-immigration agitator Peter Brimelow. MacDonald avoids reference to the primary debates and controversies surrounding particular subject areas by embedding his writing in a bibliographical database that is propped up by a clique of researchers who engage in a practice of logrolling peer review.

Such practices are hardly new or unique to the precincts of the far-right academy in the United States. As early as 1964, Hofstadter argued that "the entire American right wing movement . . . is a parade of experts, study groups, monographs, footnotes and bibliographies."[21] MacDonald and his colleagues at the *Occidental Observer* and his numerous supporters on websites like Stormfront are interested, above all, in constructing an informational hub that mimics the administrative structures of institutions of higher learning, while also relativizing the notion of objective criteria for research. Much of MacDonald's internet presence resembles a virtual university. A place of instruction requires, of course, a library, and he is particularly interested in constructing an archive of knowledge whose authority is bolstered by the intellectual cachet of the scholarly monograph. The distinctive configuration of MacDonald's bibliographies is what lets us know that he wrote his books on Judaism in the style of a large hypertext. Their appeal for his audience is that they simulate the experience of browsing in an extensively cross-referenced library.

On what one researcher called "America's most popular online hate site,"[22] over 1,250 discussion threads referenced MacDonald's arguments about the racial aspects of evolutionary psychology in 2014; although that number was far lower in 2022 (listed on the site's search engine as 383), the views on threads with titles like "Jewish Crime Report" and "Is the [white ethnonationalist] William Pierce Dead Forever" that reference MacDonald clock in at the tens of thousands, and in some cases over a million.[23] In one representative posting from 2014, a "sustaining member" of Stormfront writes: "I grew up a liberal who accepted without question the Jewish (false) history of the Third Reich and Adolf Hitler, but beginning with Kevin MacDonald's *Culture of Critique*, I was gradually led to the truth."[24] The postings about MacDonald on Stormfront are overwhelmingly positive; they often refer to him by his professional title of Doctor or endow him with the vaguely hip-hop-sounding celebrity moniker "Kmac." Prior to the temporary shutdown of Stormfront in August 2017 (in response to the news that over a hundred white supremacists convicted of murder were paying members of the site), references to MacDonald's work occurred over a wide swath of subject matter, including such seemingly unrelated threads as "Russia and Ukraine/Maidan," "Aspergers [*sic*] Test," and "WHY do normal average Americans hate Nazis?"[25] In 2014, 108 threads on Stormfront foregrounded MacDonald, not just with a passing reference, but with a dedicated subject tag.

Since 2017, traffic on Stormfront has somewhat slowed down, possibly as a result of widening options for right-wing advocacy on the internet, including 8chan chat rooms, the Twitter-derivative social-media sites Gab, Parler, and Gettr, and the YouTube-inspired vlogging platform Rumbler. Although MacDonald forfeited much of his academic respectability in 2000, when he volunteered to testify on behalf of the anti-Semitic nonacademic historian David Irving in his libel suit against Emory University professor Deborah Lipstadt, among scholarly "researchers" beloved by the right he is currently second only to Irving himself in terms of the number of threads on Stormfront that reference him and those which refer to him in the titles of threads. The multiple hypertextual points of entry into (and from) MacDonald's work undoubtedly account for much of its appeal to Stormfront users: in 2014, no fewer than 488 discussion threads reposted the address of his virtual library site.

Since the publication of the last of his three books about Jewish identity, MacDonald has become much more blatant about the white nationalist agenda of his research. In his review of Slezkine's *The Jewish Century*, MacDonald expresses a partiality for Slavic gentiles that has taken center stage in his writing and public advocacy: "When Jews achieved power in Russia, it was as a hostile elite with a deep sense of historic grievance," resulting in their "bec[oming] willing executioners of both the people and cultures they came to rule, including the Germans."[26] He also writes: "In his attempt to paint with a very broad brush, Slezkine also ignores other real differences among the Mercurians, most notably, I would argue, the aggressiveness of the Jews [in the Russian empire] compared to the relative passivity of the Overseas Chinese."[27] Such statements ultimately earned MacDonald an invitation to speak on 5 September 2019, at the annual conference of the League of the South, the Russophilic neo-Confederate organization discussed in chapter 2.[28]

MacDonald's consolidation of his roles as an academic and an activist for the far right facilitates, or contributes to, a reconfiguration of the ideological landscape of militant American nativist populism. His anticommunism notwithstanding, MacDonald assesses Stalin as a figure with diminished responsibility for the purges that ravaged the country in the thirties and rendered it catastrophically unprepared for the Nazi invasion. MacDonald opines that Soviet Jews—and not the general secretary of the Communist Party of the Soviet Union—made the executive decisions for the implementation of the purges. Seen from this perspective, Stalin's anti-Jewish ("anticosmopolitan") campaign was, as both Cofnas and MacDonald would put it, a "rational" response to a protracted genocidal campaign directed at non-Jews. Rather than seeing the anti-Semitic purge that Stalin launched in 1948 as a product of his pathology and a consequence of a dangerously vertical governmental structure, MacDonald characterizes it as an understandable attempt to reduce "Jewish predominance as a professional, cultural, and managerial elite."[29]

That dubious historiographic conceit has taken on considerable traction in American alt-right circles, particularly those that seek to create a link between Christian and white European identity formations. Among the influential sites that blend discussions of American and Russian history with an interpretation of current affairs that is shot through with social conservatism and religious traditionalism, the Russia Insider site stands out. It was founded by the American businessman Charles Bausman and is funded by the pro-Putin oligarch Konstantin Malofeev. In "It's Time to Drop the Jew Taboo," a tendentious and rambling op-ed written for the site in 2018, Bausman applauds MacDonald's writing about the "Jewish Question," borrowing a Fox News turn of phrase to call it "very scholarly, fair and balanced." In a tellingly awkward sentence that removes Stalin's responsibility for the purges, Bausman writes that "the terror visited on Russia [*sic*] during the civil war and its aftermath," which "continu[ed] well into the Stalin years, for he could not really control it either, was a Jewish one." Like MacDonald and many other populist American commentators, Bausman—who participated in the January 6 storming of the Capitol and may have breached the building—cannot stop obsessing about irreligious cosmopolitan elites who trample on the god-fearing people of the United States and the Russian Federation.

Links to MacDonald's writings shunt readers from his active Twitter page (over 33 thousand followers, and multiple messages posted and retweeted on a daily basis) to his cluster of essays on *Occidental Quarterly*, to his blog on the white nationalist and anti-immigration site VDare, to his California State University page (shut down only in 2021), and back to his personal web page. In designing this interlocking series of domains, MacDonald has displayed a shrewd awareness of the self-validating possibilities of content redundancy in cyberspace.[30] In the end, however, the design flourishes of this internet archipelago cannot offset the traditional alliances of American far-right thought that inform his work. MacDonald hews faithfully to the platform of the American Freedom Party. Unlike the Rassemblement National and the United Kingdom Independence Party (UKIP), the American Freedom Party is avowedly paleoconservative and makes no attempt to modernize its positions by hybridizing them with antiglobalism and the thinking of classical liberals like Raymond Aron or John Stuart Mill.

Indeed, MacDonald abandoned all pretense to scholarly detachment well before he retired from CSU at Long Beach. In 2012 the former Ku Klux Klan Grand Wizard David Duke interviewed MacDonald on his white supremacist radio program, introducing him as "one of the intellects and academics I respect most in the world." MacDonald quickly got down to business with the assertion that "[Jewish] people hate us [and have] this sense of persecution going back to the Middle Ages, of Christianity as the fount of all evil." This animosity is "absolutely fundamental to Jewish identity," and the prospect of "white people" becoming "a minority, is something that they just can hardly wait to have it happen. It's absolute paradise for them. . . . Jewish identity is hating Christianity."[31] Another publication asserts the existence of a Neolithic-era Northern European phenotype that possessed the genetic behavioral markers for altruism and individualism—absent, he claims, from Semitic and African peoples.[32] MacDonald's scholarly neo-Aryanism is perfectly aligned with the anti-immigrant tradition of American racist populism, first articulated in response to the wave of Irish immigration that followed the mid-nineteenth-century potato famine. Jews and others outside the ancient ambit of the ur-homeland of Northern European identity were descendants of cultures that privileged the clan over the nuclear family, the tribe over the individual. Given such dubious and untested assumptions, it is hardly a surprise that MacDonald perceives Jews and people of color as lacking the faculty for morally autonomous judgment that he claims Nordic Europeans possess as a part of their genetic identity. Certainly, his embrace of Eastern Europe as the domain of people largely uncorrupted by Western capitalism is an expression of the deep story that has become central to the American alt-right.

Academic Discourse as Grand Narrative:
The Eurasianism of Alexander Dugin

In contrast with MacDonald's clear-cut racialist thinking about—or, rather, against—cultural and demographic diversity, the work of Alexander Dugin presents a daunting set of evaluative challenges. The volume of Dugin's publications is prodigious. At the time of this writing, Dugin (born in 1962) has published more books than his sixty years. His expository style—alternating between the scholarly, the lyrical, the pedantic, and the plainspoken incendiary—is as bewildering as the eccentricity of his political philosophy. As for his project of attaining a higher synthesis of intellectual traditions as different as Jungian occultism, racial essentialism, and such nineteenth- and twentieth-century glorifications of the state as Bonapartism, Konstantin Pobedonostev's passionate advocacy for the tsarist empire as a modern bureaucratic institution, and the work of the early Nazi political theorist Carl Schmitt— we must withhold for the moment detailed judgment about its success. We should, however, take note of Andreas Umland's observation about the tactical significance of the wide net Dugin casts to gather those who had become bitter or bruised in the wake of the Soviet collapse.[33]

A turning point in Dugin's career was his 1998 stint as an advisor to Gennady Seleznev, the Speaker of the Duma. Dugin's often absurd postmodern pastiches and millenarian thunderings about the geopolitical end times seemed inappropriate for someone who has positioned himself to be a mentor without portfolio to Kremlin policy-makers. Possibly in an effort to curry favor, in 2001 Dugin applauded Putin's economic policy and "new course of power" as "moving ever more clearly in the direction of a Eurasian policy."[34] In 2008 he was chosen to serve as the director of the newly created Center for Conservative Studies within Moscow State University. This appointment to a high position within the flagship institution of the federal educational system—combined with the modesty of his academic training and the unprofessional character of his publications—draws attention to the fact that his ideological authority within the Russian academy is not commensurate with his achievements as a researcher.[35] But what is the core of Dugin's political philosophy?

The most immediate answer is that it represents an updating of Eurasianism, a movement that conceptualizes Russia as a dynamic cultural and historical synthesis of Europe and Asia. Dugin takes pains to distinguish his Eurasianism

Alexander Dugin in his Tsargrad television studio, 11 August 2016.
Photo by Francesca Ebel/AP.

from its more famous and influential twentieth-century articulations in the works of Lev Gumilev and the expatriate philologist Nikolai Trubetskoy. Dugin is intent on building a system of political interpretation of global events. According to him, the contemporary world is dominated by a Huntingtonian clash of civilizations between maritime powers (which Dugin also calls "Atlanticist" and "thalassocratic") and land-based (or "tellurocratic") ones.[36] A union of Russia and several Asian countries would represent the cultural values of tellurocracy, opposing the movement toward neoliberal globalization that is at the center of the constellation of maritime powers guided by the United States. As Dugin himself acknowledges, his rhetoric of antiglobalization is open to creative amplification, if not revision. He regards his opposition to Atlanticist imperialism as a testing ground for the formation of new or unusual political alliances. Two things come to mind when reading his writing against a backdrop of newly fungible global capital. First, his conception of ideological convergences and coalitions has a strong theoretical—if not dialectical—feel to it, as if he is proceeding less from observed actual alliances and more from theoretical constructs and the projection of archetypes into the future. The sociological category of groupuscules seems tailor-made for his approach. Second, his notion of reshuffling powerful countries into new supranational economic and political "zones" is shrewdly pitched at a politically diverse audience. The history of

Eurasianism as a movement has always included in its practice a dynamic engagement with its audience.[37]

But what is most radically new about Dugin's Eurasianism—what diverges most fundamentally from the work of Gumilev and Trubetskoy, who articulated the values of Eurasian identity as forming only in the Mongol period of Russian history, two hundred and fifty years after the Christianization of the East Slavic lands—is his stated belief in the far older existence of what may be termed a "proto-Eurasian" land and people, of the Siberian Arctic territories as the cradle of an Aryan civilization that represents the spiritual ancestor of Russian culture's more recent synthesis between Europe and Asia. It is noteworthy that he began his career as a political writer at the point where MacDonald, in effect, ended his: with a speculative consideration of the ancestral Aryan homeland. Cross-pollinating early forms of Eurasianism with the fraudulent archeological theories of the Nazi-sponsored philologist Herman Wirth, Dugin names this ancient civilization "Arktogaya." Early in his career as a pamphlet writer (as early as 1989, prior to the Soviet collapse), he dubbed his conception of Asian Aryanism as the "Hyperborean theory."[38] One of the most curious aspects of his idiosyncratic theory is its willingness to entertain the possibility that race is more a cultural construct than (as MacDonald and his supporters would insist) a biogenetic reality.

Dugin's soft focus on race is less an attempt to make his ideas palatable to an educated Russian mainstream (where even the most socially conservative elements remain wary of theories developed in the Third Reich) than a strategy of modulated equivocation, aimed at appealing to supporters of Putin's assertive foreign policy as well as those on the far right and the skinhead fringe within Russia. As he explains, the original Nordic race of Arktogaya had a religious system that was pre-eminently metaphysical. They were the people of the transcendent Subject, followers of an Apollonian cult of the Sun. Opposed to them, both culturally and racially, were the swarthier people of the south, who celebrated the reified or fetishized Object and their kinship with the animal world. Dugin insists that the differences between these ancient religious systems are the direct result of an intractable racial (and therefore genetic) divide in the Neolithic era between the Northern people of the Subject and the Southern people of the Object.[39] Yet he also points out two factors that mitigate the importance of race. First, the Tower of Babel–like mixing of languages and peoples that followed the Neolithic era renders racial identity for most people in the present something of an imponderable. Second, the original Aryans were remarkable more for their cultural practices of embarking upon passionate metaphysical missions than for their specific genetic makeup. In other words, the Aryans represent an ideal, which all of us—racial background notwithstanding—are capable of following. The new Aryans are a class, rather than a race, of people. As Dugin writes in *Russkaia veshch'. Ocherki natsional'noi filosofii* (The Russian thing: Sketches of a national philosophy)—whose design suggests Nazi publications, with the title in gold-colored Fraktur-style Cyrillic letters on a black binding—"We are not a Russian nation; we are a Russian class."[40]

Unlike MacDonald and his cohorts, Dugin assigns only secondary importance to racial identity because he sees no particular connection between it and the maintenance of cultural integrity. His nationalism is distinctive in having only a muted element of anti-Semitism, which has furthermore all but disappeared in his writing over the last ten years. As early as 2001, in *Russkaia veshch'*, he states that "the Semitic socialist, revolutionary, communist, and gnostic are much closer to us than ethnically Russian capitalists."[41] In fact, Dugin is not at all opposed to the idea of a multicultural polity. In a pivotal work from 1995, *Tseli i zadachi nashei revoliutsii* (The goals and tasks of our revolution), he articulates a conception of Russian culture as a multiethnic entity: "The New Nation can become understood both as a general, supraethnic category [and] as a union of all nations and all social strata within the New State."[42] The political scientist Marlène Laruelle, who has studied Dugin seriously, takes particular note of the "doctrinal consistency" of his writing and the persistence of his interest in the concept of "blind and determinist destiny" among geopolitical entities.[43] More often than not, those entities are empires, territories with distinct centers and sprawling conurbations of other cultures. Yet for Dugin such territories are as often states of mind as they are actual nation-states. One can certainly be an advocate for an empire that has long ceased to exist. But Dugin considers projects of political nostalgia—the resurrection of previous forms of governance and specific "lost" traditions—to be often impractical if not deluded. Strictly speaking, he is more interested in the full convergence of Eurasia with the Hyperborean ideal of the "metaphysical" Aryans than in the convergence of Eurasia with contemporary Russia. Dugin is a utopian: he believes that the most significant form of advocacy is for the pure ideal: a quixotic agitation for the empire that has never historically existed. Hence his agitation for a "Eurasian" empire that, although roughly coterminous with the political tergiversations of Russia from the era of Ivan the Terrible to the present, cannot be said to be exclusively east Slavic in its character.

None of this is to deny the prominent place of race in Dugin's thinking. In 2013 he wrote in the flagship journal of the Izborsk Club (the nationalist think tank that lists him as a fellow) that assertions that the average Russian was genetically a mix of Turkic, Asian, and European bloodlines were seriously

misguided. He lists percentages from an uncited source that point to the predominance of Slavic and Aryan haplogroups for Russians, arguing for a new
genomic study that would document the proportions of the Russian DNA
profile more precisely. Whilst no reputable geneticist would use "Aryan" as a
racial category for primordial and "pure" Europeans, Dugin walks back the
racialist insinuations of the term by underscoring that Russians' racial profile
is less important than the historical "nucleus" (*iadro*) of their identity, which
has to do with the symbiosis between the Slavs and the Turkic peoples that
emerged from the interaction between the peoples of the forest and the steppe,
between noble equestrian groups and nomadic ones.[44] Their practices, rather
than their racial profiles, are what makes up Eurasian identity and, ultimately,
the special destiny of the Russian empire.[45] Eurasianism itself, Dugin writes, is
nothing less than a rigorous, even "scientific" patriotism; its goal is the "consolidation, flourishing, glory, and prosperity of Russia" and its civilization
against the forces of globalization. At the same time, Eurasianism possesses a
"universal and ecumenical mission."[46]

What is striking in this statement, which is highly representative of Dugin's
writing and lectures on the internet, is its juxtaposition of idiosyncratic understandings of identity. In one breath we confront a confusing series of mutually
exclusive claims: the centrality of race and also its occlusion by (equestrian and
nomadic) historical practices; Eurasianism as a cultural synthesis of Russian
and Turkic cultures that is also somehow pre-eminently Russian; Russianness
not as a synthesis of East and West but as a remnant of a purer European
identity that is also, in ways that are not clarified here or anywhere else in
Dugin's writing, a "third way" between the modern entities of Europe and
Asia; Eurasianism as a glorification of the local over the global, which also
has a universalizing mandate. A Russian reader would immediately identify
here the blatant, and even somewhat embarrassing, derivative quality of such
thinking, coming from a person who in his early twenties taught himself German in order to to grasp all the nuanced distinctions in Nietzsche and
Heidegger.[47]

The statement about Russia's and Eurasianism's "universal and ecumenical
mission" is also quite clearly a crib from (and not a reference to) Dostoevsky's
statement in an August 1880 entry in *A Writer's Diary* about Russian identity
in its racial as well as moral dimensions. We Russians, Dostoevsky famously
wrote, take in all nations, "making no discrimination by race" among them,
because we know "how to eliminate contradictions [and] to excuse and reconcile differences" while also working to bring about a "general reunification"
among the people "of all the tribes of the great Aryan" family (*rod*). From this
conceit, Dostoevsky deduces that, "yes, the mission of the Russian is unques-

tionably pan-European and universal." Sensing the tentative character of these opinions and the anticipating the skepticism of his elite Russian audience, he goes on to say that "to become truly Russian, to become completely Russian perhaps," means nothing more or less than becoming "a brother to all people, a *panhuman*, if you would like."[48] In Dugin's statements, we hear the same unrigorous blurring and drifting of terms regarding ethnic belonging as the product of both nature and nurture, as the juxtaposition of both an intractable racial determinism and the assimilation of cultural norms, that Dostoevsky develops in rambling and impressionistic columns from the 1870s that may be regarded as a precursor genre to the modern blog. Yet Dugin's recapitulation of these ideas lacks the lightly ironizing tone of Dostoevsky's "diary" essays, which among other things are deliberately self-critical contemplations of the performance, or verbal acting-out, of political ideologies—including his own crypto-colonialist and racially inflected nationalism. By contrast, in Dugin's writing the performative aspect of scholarly or "scientific" patriotism is always exempt from the mode of distanced examination. We should not be surprised by this omission on Dugin's part. Even in his 2002 book *Evoliutsiia parag-dimal'nykh osnovanii nauki* (The evolution of the paradigmatic foundations of science), he wrote that methods of academic discourse would always, by themselves, be insufficient: one needs to bring together the scientific and scholarly dispositions with systems and worldviews that are their diametrical opposites.[49] He is more interested in juxtaposing arguments, fashioning sites for assembling far-right ideas for export, than in achieving the grand syntheses that he claims are central to his project.

The influence of Dugin's peculiar aggregation (as opposed to rigorous distillation) of rightist ideologies—most of them pointedly not Russian in provenance[50]—is sometimes evident in policy statements from the Kremlin. In a 29 August 2014 question-and-answer session with a patriotic youth group on the topic of Russian support for independence in the Donbas region, Putin made a lengthy statement about "our interests concentrated in the Arctic" whose lack of relevance to the Ukrainian crisis was almost baffling: "And of course we should pay more attention to issues of development of the Arctic and the strengthening of our position."[51] Putin's odd linking of disputes about national sovereignty in the south with the uncontested borders of the far north can, of course, be understood primarily in emotive and symbolic terms, as an evocation of Russia's northern military bases and untapped natural resources as points of national pride. Yet his wording here is largely a paraphrase of statements from a chapter of Dugin's textbook on geopolitics, which continues to be used in Russian military academies. In *Osnovy geopolitiki* (The foundations of geopolitics) Dugin asserts that the "Russian [far] North" is nothing less than a "transcription" of the cyclically repeating manifestation of the idea of Eurasia, which in the present day takes the complex form of being strategically important for Russia's military identity, being rich in mineral resources, and being the homeland of autochthonous cultures that "preserve the memory of the cosmic proportions."[52]

The oracular tone of this last statement—seemingly out of place in a political science textbook, yet so characteristic of Dugin's expository style of punctuating the unfolding of timelines with quasi-mystical pronouncements—draws our attention once again to the variegated content of his ideas. While he has largely excluded references to the "Hyperborean theory" from more recent policy-oriented publications such as *Osnovy geopolitiki*, they can still be found in abundance in the texts that he posts on his multiple websites. Furthermore, many of Dugin's more pragmatic essays since 2008 about balancing Eurasianist aspirations with the demands of *realpolitik* are written in a way that invites readers to clarify certain enigmatic concepts by consulting the author's diverse internet resources on www.arcto.ru, www.arctogaia.com, www.katehon.com, and his daily-updated pages on Twitter, Facebook, and VKontakte (a social media platform similar in its design to Facebook). In sharp contrast to MacDonald's strategy of using multiple domains as nodes on a self-certifying feedback loop, virtually no links connect Dugin's various personal websites. The Hyperborean theory continues to be the concealed theater director who organizes most of the interactions and affinities that we see enacted on the main stage of Dugin's writing.

We need not argue for the absurdity of Dugin's views about the existence of a proto-Eurasian Nordic race whose mantle Russia has inherited in the form of specific folkways and ancient linguistic paradigms. Like MacDonald, Dugin ignores what serious and mainstream scholarship has said about many of the subjects that interest him, which of course does not prevent him from borrowing some of their methodologies without proper acknowledgment. In his structural analysis of national mythologies, Dugin draws heavily on the interpretive approaches of the Soviet School of Semiotics, without referencing the pioneering work of scholars such as Eleazar Meletinsky and Yuri Lotman—possibly because they were Jewish. Yet the "scholarly" turn in Dugin's publications, the point at which he began to use footnotes with references to academic publications, can be dated with some precision: it came with the publication of his slim monograph entitled *Misterii Evrazii* (The mysteries of Eurasia, 1996). What motivated him to change the tone of his writing, to assume (like MacDonald) the stance of what he understood to be professorial dispassion, counterbalanced (as we shall see) by the occasional eruption of heated advocacy? And why has Dugin fashioned a disaggregated, rather than centripetal, structure for his internet profile?

To answer these questions, and to understand Dugin's internet strategies in contradistinction to MacDonald's, we need to contemplate a pivotal yet largely unexamined event in his career twenty-seven years ago. In the fall of 1995, the jazz and pop keyboard player Sergei Kurekhin persuaded Dugin (who at that time was, as David Remnick memorably puts it, "as marginal as a Lyndon LaRouche follower with a card table and stack of leaflets"[53]) to establish residency in St. Petersburg in order to run for a local seat in the Duma as a candidate for Eduard Limonov's fascist National Bolshevik Party. Kurekhin was a highly eccentric figure, a notorious lover of media pranks and an impresario of musical and theatrical "happenings" that he named Pop Mechanics. In these performances, mute actors dressed in a dizzying array of period costumes—much like a wordless version of Monty Python, but with the additional *épatage* of donning the garb of Soviet military and law enforcement personnel—shared the stage with sauntering geese and the often punk-dancing, thrashing figure of Kurekhin himself. Each Pop Mechanics performance was accompanied by clamorous music that suggested a fusion of Frank Zappa, King Crimson, and Miles Davis's experimental compositions from the early seventies.

Kurekhin organized a Pop Mechanics concert in support of Dugin's campaign and participated in a series of discussions with prospective voters. Dugin performed dismally in the election, netting less than 1 percent of the vote.[54] One video from that time has the two men sitting awkwardly next to each other on a political talk show, with Kurekhin staring directly at the camera, smirking, and occasionally interrupting Dugin's earnest statements with chortling repetitions of the campaign's pithy (if portentously biblical) slogan "*Tainoe stanet iavnym*" ("That which is secret will be revealed").[55] In more ways than one, Dugin's interaction with Kurekhin was an instructive embarrassment, as Dugin himself acknowledged ruefully yet thoughtfully: "Kurekhin was interested in . . . Eurasianism very ironically, with internal irony, if you will. But that irony was not obvious to those who surrounded him, because in that society the topic was taboo."[56]

I would argue that this abortive and mostly tongue-in-cheek campaign—together with Dugin's stinging humiliation in what quickly became a media-driven theater of cruelty—motivated him to cultivate an aggressive style of intellectual gravitas in his published work and public appearances, rendering them into attention-grabbing spectacles of educational experience. A year later, he would write in a eulogistic vein about Kurekhin (who died in 1996), describing Pop Mechanics' relentlessly cruel—one might say imperialistic—art of vanquishing the self, with performers willingly becoming manikins in a strange, cultish rite organized by the magus figure of the artist. "It's in Kurekhin's work—particularly in his colossal, totalistic, mass-oriented 'Pop Mechanics'—that we

Sergei Kurekhin, at a Pop Mechanics concert in Leningrad, 1988.
Photo by Viktor Nemtinov.

see the impressive striving to bring together *absolutely everything* [emphasis in the original], everything that is seized together."[57] Dugin concludes his discussion of Kurekhin's aesthetics of subjugative violence by asserting that it is only natural that someone who was interested in the British occultist Aleister Crowley's uncompromising binary ethics of submission or destruction would also be drawn to the political doctrine of Eurasianism.[58] In the provocative musical and dramaturgical dissonances of Kurekhin's theatricalized concerts, Dugin came to recognize the principle of an anarchist *Gesamtkunstwerk*, where the barrier between act and word, audience and spectacle, is regularly blasted away by performers who sacrifice their egos to an art of total experience. Of all the grand syntheses that Dugin aspires to, it may be this one, of aesthetics and political content, is the one that he completely achieves. To experience his multimedia empire, in the Borgesian totality of its mazelike convolutions and *cul de sacs*—the hardcover books, digital texts, online video lectures, and seemingly innumerable web domains that call out to each other—is to come into a more direct contact with the core of Dugin's worldview. Edith W. Clowes identifies that core as an "obsessive focus on the grand geopolitical picture" and on "power and empire at the expense of the ordinary person." However one experiences Dugin's work, at the end of the day "his amoral megalomania and his indifference to human suffering speak loud and clear."[59]

Conclusion: Academia as Spectacle

MacDonald's self-advertising as a contrarian scholar is similar in several respects to the public practices of right-wing Russian academics such as Dugin and the mathematician (and later anti-Semitic propagandist) Igor Shafarevich. Mimicking Gramsci's conception of the organic intellectual and Said's ideal of the public intellectual as an uncredentialed amateur, both MacDonald and Dugin present themselves as erudite generalists who write with the goal of giving voice to the concerns of a disenfranchised community. The Americans whom Stern describes in her book about the alt-right are powerfully drawn to what they perceive as the pragmatic core of Gramscian seizure of the mainstream conversation about social problems. This hinges on the advocacy of what they call "metapolitics," a term that actually does not occur in Gramsci's writing.[60] As Stern explains, the more intrepid and unapologetically bookish theorists in the European alt-right and radical traditionalist movements coined this term to denote "a philosophical exploration of principles of rights and of the state" that avoids any parsing of contemporary politics. Metapolitics unabashedly embraces the big ideas and scorns the immediate concerns of political life as annoying midges that live for a day, or as vermin that feed off the corpse of the dysfunctional and cumbersome proceduralism that characterizes the modern liberal state; instead, it embraces "the transcendental and religious dimensions of politics," seeking out the residues of the archetypal, the sacred, and the eschatological.[61]

This preoccupation with archetypes is audible in the work of both MacDonald and Dugin, for whom cultural identity exists largely outside history and time. If such identity is resistant to the passage of time, then surely it can always be accessed in the present—right now! With such a spectacle-oriented realization in mind, no wonder internet-based asynchronous teaching, rather than text-driven polemic, has become the educational model for the traditionalist intelligentsia in North America and the Russian Federation, as exemplified by the hundreds of available videos of lectures and interviews by MacDonald, Dugin, and Jordan Peterson. A notion of the irrelevance of the linearity of history and time lies at the center of many Great Books–oriented think tanks in the United States, such as the Federalist Society, the American Enterprise Institute, and the pro-Trump Claremont Institute and in those think tanks in the Russian Federation that serve as creative workshops for collaging ready-made national self-images over the *longue durée* of Russian intellectual and political history. Laruelle describes the work of the Izborsk Club, with which Dugin is affiliated, as "an example of the progressive structuring of a field of think tanks in Russia, whose function is to occupy different ideological niches and offer a wide range of 'products' that the authorities can sample, make official, or reject." She goes on to say that the conservative avant-garde's "Gramsci-inspired strategies to capture the state by first occupying the intellectual space remains an ongoing process, the results of which are so far unknown."[62] Given Dugin's roots in the late Soviet-era Moscow underground milieu (particularly the quasi-fascist "Yuzhinskii Circle"), his openness to improvisational self-formation is predictable.[63] Upon meeting Steve Bannon for the first time in Rome in 2018, Dugin was struck by the fact that the American "came to traditionalism" as a result of reading Gurdjieff. "An Armenian! Part of the Russian silver age. You found your way not as an American—such a thing is impossible. You did it yourself. And what a radical situation."[64]

This love of nonconformist eccentricity notwithstanding, in the final reckoning we see that the new right is most powerfully drawn to hierarchies. As we noted in the case of Steve Bannon (see chapter 2), the church and the military offer templates for integrating the practice of submission into one's life. They are also drawn to the cult of the "builder," or, as Cofnas phrases it, the "cult of the engineer." We should hardly be surprised that the brain trust of the alt-right—MacDonald, Richard Spencer, Paul Gottfried, and Jordan Peterson in North America, Dugin, Valery Averianov, and Zakhar Prilepin in the Russian Federation, a novelist and actual combatant in Russia's "special operation" (*spetsoperatiia*) in Ukraine[65]—together with the thousands of radical traditionalist bloggers and anonymous tweeters who echo their views, find tremendously appealing the notion that intellectuals can, in their own right, have the status of builders and world-makers. No one can say that the intellectual is a lily-livered non-doer who does not understand the "real world": on the contrary, now that figure can create a world that seems as real as the towers built— and, in one instance, willfully demolished in a principled gesture of sovereign ownership—by the iconoclastic architect Howard Roark in Ayn Rand's libertarian touchstone *The Fountainhead* (1943). In one of his many capsule lectures in that novel, Roark states that "the mind is the attribute of an individual," and that "there is no such thing as a collective brain"; furthermore, "the primary act—the process of reason—must be performed by each man alone," as this "creative faculty cannot be given or received, shared or borrowed."[66] The idea that a builder like Roark (a fictional character, and thus himself a built artifact) can also be a teacher seems to democratically open up the possibility that teachers like MacDonald and Dugin can be builders, in their capacity as populist intellectuals. They achieve this, in the words of the historian Federico Finchelstein, by creating political spaces that bypass "the representational and institutional mediations of traditional politics."[67]

MacDonald's and Dugin's preoccupation with the authority of cultural legacies and the imagined communities of a transnational pan-Aryanism ultimately runs against the grain of Gramsci's and Said's interest in the potentialities of the intellectual as an oppositional rather than hegemonic figure. The alt-right intellectuals have constructed academic identities in order to take on the mantle of conventional authority. Both men have made the bulk of their political writing widely available on the internet, gaining reputations as academic experts that far-right groups in the United States and Russia can refer to as authorities. MacDonald's and Dugin's use of social media as a venue for self-credentialization is the ultimate expression of this circular pathway to the creation of an academic reputation with the capability to cross over into a larger world of political action, with the caveat that such lateral shifts preserve the cachet of authority and status that was already robust in their academic careers. For both men, those shifts were precipitated by a narcissistic injury inflicted by a member of their own political tribe: in MacDonald's case, by Nathan Cofnas; in Dugin's, by Sergei Kurekhin. To compensate for those spectacles of negative attention and humiliation, MacDonald and Dugin sought to build a widely accessible world of affective self-categorization, with exponential possibilities for validation from the world of internet consumers.[68]

Yet there are crucial differences between their personae. In his manifesto *Chetvertaia politicheskaia teoriia* (The fourth political theory, 2009), Dugin emphasizes the ideal of a collaborative relationship between teacher and student: "It is essential to expand the target audience by *simplifying the form of the Eurasian message. . . . The simplification has to come from you*" (emphasis in original).[69] By creating groups and sites for political consumers that he later abandons without actively disavowing, Dugin at the very least projects an internet profile that is more dynamic and participatory than MacDonald's. A prime example of this strategy of identity subterfuge is the Dugin-created group

"Eurasian Artists [*sic*] Association," which he coyly lists on his Facebook page as a place where he once worked.[70] He wants his audience to decode his creations, to lose themselves in a search for connections and generalizations that seem to be emanating from somewhere other than Dugin himself. Among his panoply of websites, there is only one direct link: from his VKontakte page to his Facebook page. At the time of this writing, Dugin's VKontakte page has over 54,200 subscribers, and his Facebook page 55,110. He is vividly aware of both his "audience" and his (virtual) lecture hall, concepts that are felicitously joined together in the same Russian word (*auditoriia*). His lecture hall—the space for the dissemination of what he knows, and what he encourages his subscribers to repost—consists of the various internet domains that he has created.

MacDonald and Dugin ultimately believe that academic authority is a fiction, a status they forge through writing that is an extended meditation on personal and national aggrievement. Such writing is meant to attract a general audience that subsequently testifies to their standing as teachers and scholars, thereby retroactively conferring on each of them the status of virtual professor in fields for which they have no credentials. Both men have created internet profiles as figures of authority that stand at the pinnacle of academic subcultures. Dugin models his conception of the teacher-scholar after Kurekhin's definition of the artist as avant-garde demiurge, rendering the figure of the internet professor into a kind of performance artist without walls. In Dugin's online self-presentation as a professor in the trenches of the current Russian-Ukrainian conflict, we see elements of Kurekhin's glorification of violent performativity, particularly the notion that the artist is someone who is ready to put himself at risk. In the dispatch from Donbas in July 2014 that resulted in his suspension from his academic position, Dugin, a "professor of MGU (Moscow State University)," demanded that the supporters of the Maidan movement for Ukrainian independence be "killed, killed, killed"![71] As he ominously wrote in *Filosofiia traditsionalizma* (The philosophy of traditionalism, 2004), the "New University" needs to teach us an "eschatological humanism."[72]

As the title of professor becomes, for both MacDonald and Dugin, the equivalent of a military rank, it is Dugin who has more substantially undertaken the task of constructing an alternate system of learning as the training ground for a real war. In the next chapter, we will meet conservative and far-right activists in Russia who would be, from Dugin's point of view, too caught up for their own good in the heady experience of creating arresting spectacles for the exposure of their values.

CHAPTER FOUR

The Spectacle of God's Will

Performing Homophobia in the Russian Federation

Experiencing some homosexual attraction doesn't mean that you have to choose to behave effeminately. Sexuality is a poor axis for primary identity. Men are men regardless, and I believe that they should strive to earn the respect and honor of other men.

—JACK DONOVAN, alt-right American activist

Is our symbol of the Motherland a relic reminding us of [pre-Christian Slavic] matriarchy? Does our symbol of a society originate in prison? Is our society built on carceral notions? The answer to all these questions is yes. This is an unhealthy symbol, but we have no other. With its mindset proceeding from prison life, the country deifies the old crone Motherland. In other words: "Don't forget your native mother!" "The Motherland calls you!" are two lines from the same melodrama.

I already hear the sound of cast stones whistling their way to me.

—EDUARD LIMONOV, "Matushka," in *Kontrol'nyi vystrel*

Introduction: Homophobic Subcultures as Microcosms

IN CHAPTER 3 we saw how figures on the political fringe in both the United States and the Russian Federation selectively mirror, and in some cases amplify, ideologies that represent the unspoken assumptions of the political mainstream. Assumptions are difficult to critique simply because they are often invisible to the person who adheres to them. Combating nativist populism becomes a project of excavation, exposing the foundations that make a particular edifice of ideas possible. The fact that unearthing the base may bring down the entire structure would seem to be an acceptable risk if criticizing belief systems is meant to be a first step toward undermining and dismantling them. The Russian Jewish literary critic Yuri Lotman once wrote that a detailed description of a cultural artifact may demystify it by exposing the root system that nourishes it: "One and the same system can find itself in a state of both ossification and plasticity. Moreover, the very act of description can switch the second of these two back into the first."[1] Yet demonstrating logical inconsistencies within a belief system and drawing attention to its absurdities are practices that rarely persuade its adherents.

Kevin MacDonald and Alexander Dugin are situated on fringes that are nothing more than extensions of dominant belief systems about territorial sovereignty, cultural exclusivity, and national exceptionalism. In a controversial interview with MacDonald that appeared in the Jewish online magazine *Tablet*, the interviewer explained in a preamble that it was important to understand MacDonald's political language if only to facilitate a recognition of its code terms and euphemisms for audiences who are otherwise not attuned to hearing them. Visiting MacDonald at his home in Medford, Oregon, and seeing the city's "floating population of Oxycontin and methamphetamine addicts," the interviewer wrote, "it is not hard to see why Kevin MacDonald's obsessions appear to be gaining traction among both white supremacists and some elements of the progressive left, among privileged urban whites as well as the urban poor."[2] MacDonald's views about those who are not of "Northern European" heritage, and specifically about Asians—reflected in comments about the temperamental passivity of the overseas Chinese—are deeply resonant with the grassroots efforts among some communities in Oregon to secede and join a majority-white confederation of states in the Pacific Northwest that would be known as Cascadia.[3]

Similarly, while some commentators may have exaggerated Dugin's influence on the foreign policy of Putin's United Russia Party, there is little doubt that his views are simply brasher expressions of those shared by many commentators and citizens on the conservative end of the Russian political spectrum. At the beginning of 2022, as official Russian state narratives reviled Ukraine as a loyal lapdog of the neoliberal West (i.e., the United States, the European Union, and their arm of geopolitical enforcement, NATO), the political scientist Kseniya Kirillova pointed out that Dugin's calls for invading Eastern Ukraine were nothing more than an open expression of what the United Russia brain trust was hinting at: namely, that "the entire Left Bank Ukraine" should be seized, the Baltic countries should be offered a choice of "neutralization or war," and the countries of the former Soviet space should be reincorporated into the borders of what had been the Soviet Union.[4] Quite aside from any direct influence that they have had on militant traditionalist activism, MacDonald's and Dugin's writing and internet profiles bring together many prominent trends of nationalist populism in their respective countries. Like forgotten copies of master keys, they give us access to a disordered warehouse of received wisdom.

In this chapter, we examine the provocative views about LGBTQ identity expressed by fringe groups and individuals in Russia. These ideas and attitudes are firmly part of the conservative "patriotic" mainstream in the country. Taken individually, each of these individuals or groups is an eccentrically painted miniature portrait of larger anxieties. The specifically religious character of their language and rhetoric is especially revealing, as are their scathing attacks on the Russian liberal intelligentsia as unpatriotic and weak. In chapter 1, we broached the topic of the homophobic characterization of that intelligentsia as *liberasty*, a contraction of the words for liberal and pederast. In this chapter, we examine the grim fascination with which conservative activists in the Russian Federation regard homosexuality, with a particular focus on the group that calls itself the Union of Orthodox Banner Bearers, the activist Dmitri Tsorionov or "Enteo," and the priest Andrei Kuraev. Tsorionov and the Union of Orthodox Banner Bearers share an understanding of themselves as actors who emulate aspects of the performativity of the queer culture that they attack. While Kuraev's blog posts and public statements do not manifest the same grim obsession with queer culture, his carefully curated internet persona reflects an interest in asserting a new and vivid performativity for the religious intelligentsia in Russia.

Tsorionov, Kuraev, and the Union of Banner Bearers all draw our attention to the anomalous status of an intelligentsia that prizes traditionalism whilst acknowledging its own alienation from it. Yet, revival of neglected traditions is not what interests these religious activists, all of whom acknowledge the need for creative reconstruction rather than absolute theological correctness. In the end, the "special rights" that some of these individuals seek to oppose or dismantle are mirror images of the expressive possibilities that they explore for themselves. Their struggles to redeem the profile of the intelligentsia from its associations with effeminizing weakness never entirely erase the sense of the uselessness of a cultured and autonomous intelligentsia in a country where efforts are afoot to close the gap between the interests of church and state. In *Strangers in Their Own Land: Anger and Mourning on the American Right*, Arlie Russell Hochschild notes that for many of the Tea Party–affiliated conservatives she interviewed in Louisiana, southern history is "a series of emotional grooves that are carved in the minds and hearts of people."[5] We will examine the analogous ways in which an overflowing reservoir of assumptions about religious belonging and sexual orientation shape a larger political landscape of what it means to be a citizen of the Russian Federation, and how the best aspects of the Russian intelligentsia's historic role as an oppositional voice may be recovered.

The Legal Battle against Same-Sex Love in Russia

On 7 March 2012 the LGBTQ community in Russia found itself in a peculiar situation. On that day, the city council of St. Petersburg ratified an ambiguously worded law against "homosexual propaganda." The law defines such

propaganda as any "uncontrolled promulgation" of discourse about homosexuality that might suggest to underage Russians any equivalence between
traditional and nontraditional marital relations.[6] Thus, it criminalizes speech
about acts that have been decriminalized in Russia since 1993. That law was
adopted by the cities of Ryazan, Arkhangelsk, and the sixth-largest city in the
country, Nizhny Novgorod. The independent Russian journalist Masha Gessen
eloquently summed up critics' concerns:

> What would fall under the definition of this law? Any book or periodical that
> contains, say, a mention of same-sex marriage or a same-sex relationship—unless
> the book or periodical is sold at an adults-only bookstore. Public displays of
> affection among same-sex couples would also be an offense. For gay or lesbian
> parents, simply living with their children might be a breach.[7]

One unprecedented consequence of the law is that lesbianism has, for the first
time in the history of the Russian legal system, fallen under the umbrella of
criminalized activities: until then, no aspect of lesbianism or any act in relation to it has ever been categorized as illegal in Russia. For the first time,
homosexuality in Russia has literally become the love that dare not speak its
name.

The law may be viewed as a reaction against demands for civil rights for the
Russian LGBTQ community. Over the last twenty-five years, the Russian Federation has gone through something of an initiation by fire in terms of having
to respond to the demands of this increasingly vocal group. Several critics of
the law immediately noted its wide range of applicability. Since 2005 LGBTQ
supporters have unsuccessfully applied for demonstration permits for Gay
Pride parades in both Moscow and St. Petersburg. In 2007 Yuri Luzhkov, the
mayor of the Russian capital, replied with a refusal that was as homophobic as
it was categorical: "We don't need liberal candy, but a societal whip." He went
on to equate the "unconcealed propaganda of this so-called single-sex love"
with vices such as "drug addiction, xenophobia, and interethnic strife." Given
Luzhkov's homophobia and the highly autocratic structure of the Moscow
municipality, it was hardly surprising that permission was denied. He explained
that a gay parade (*gei-parad*) "cannot be called anything other than a satanic
rite."[8] Luzhkov's statements reflect an effort to give same-sex desire other names
or at least divest it of the (more positive) terms that some people use, such as
"love." Luzhkov was in large part reacting to the acceptance of more neutral and
nonhomophobic language. In March 2005 a press conference in the office of
St. Petersburg's mayor reflected a new comfort with using gay-friendly terms in
a public context, as a representative of an LGBTQ group asked Mayor Valen-

tina Matvienko about "the future of rights for gays [*geev*], lesbians, bisexuals, and transgendered people in the northern capital."[9]

It would seem that the label for same-sex desire in Russia causes as much anxiety as the desire itself, and that Luzhkov and others glibly associate a love of spectacle and performance with the LGBTQ community. As we saw in chapter 1, that perception of queer culture as eminently suited to capitalism is at the center of many alt-right and religiously conservative critiques of LGBTQ advocacy in the United States. As a member of the Soviet petrochemical intelligentsia, to the end of his life (in 2019) Luzhkov harbored a distrust of both Western-style capitalism and social unorthodoxy that comes through clearly in this public statement, and that brings his views into an unexpected confluence with those of the global alt-right. As the conservative populist academic Darel E. Paul wrote in 2020 in the online magazine *First Things*, the moral obligation of coming out "finds its highest liturgical enactment in the Pride parade, a ritualized demand for and reception of recognition," which also feeds into the marketing of the individual self and into the larger capitalist markets selling to newly liberated selves.[10] Talia Lavin, in *Culture Warlords: My Journey into the Dark Web of White Supremacy* (2020), draws attention to the peculiar fusion within the American alt-right of antiglobalism with homophobia, which has led to the formulation of the concept of "Globohomo."[11] Russian conservative activists have for at least a decade have been engaged in protest against the "foreign" menace of homosexuality, anticipating the American fusillades against it, albeit without the ennobling vocabulary of anticapitalism that the US alt-right sometimes foregrounds in their attacks on sexual non-normativity.

The revealing 2013 survey conducted by the Levada Center in Moscow demonstrated that attitudes in Russia toward same-sex love remained strongly negative and in some matters had become even more so. The number of homophobic protests has significantly increased since 2005, when LGBTQ groups first submitted requests to hold Gay Pride parades in Moscow and St. Petersburg, intensifying since the ratification on 29 June 2013 in the Russian Duma of the ambiguously worded law against "homosexual propaganda." The Levada Center reports that at the beginning of 2013, 87 percent of the respondent pool was opposed to Gay Pride parades in the major cities, whereas in 2010 the figure was 82 percent and in 2005, 74 percent. The survey's conductors note that even the more politically liberal demographic of respondents between the ages of 25 and 40 tended to have homophobic views that outweighed their otherwise socially tolerant attitudes.[12] Judging by the numerous videos posted on YouTube and VKontakte of demonstrations against LGBTQ rights, the majority of the anti-gay demonstrators fall within that younger demographic.

The 2013 law is largely modeled on the one that had passed in St. Petersburg, Ryazan, Arkhangelsk, and Nizhny Novgorod the year before. Although it is vague about what kind of speech is prohibited, making no distinction between statements mentioning homosexuality and those that express a tolerance of it, its object of concern is quite clear. The law prohibits the "propaganda of nontraditional sexual relations in the presence of minors [*sredi nesovershennoletnikh*]." In theory, any statement in support of LGBTQ rights can be understood as breaking the prohibition against "homosexual and anti-family propaganda," resulting in a fine that is assessed in a civil, rather than criminal, court.

Tomas Mielke, who has researched the Russian gay subculture, points out that the association "between gay men and child abuse" is so strong in contemporary Russian culture that one common term for homosexuality is *pederastiia*, which etymologically "denotes an erotic relationship between an adult male and a pubescent or adolescent male," even as the term is "used in modern colloquial Russian for consensual sexual relations between adult males."[13] Crucial here is the shift in the law's wording, from its earliest draft in 2006 in the municipal court of the city of Ryazan to its ratified version as federal law. The text from the Ryazan court stipulates that "in this article, by public actions directed at propaganda of *muzhelozhstvo* [buggery], lesbianism, bisexuality, and transgenderism to minors, the following is understood: intentional activity that involves uncontrolled dissemination of information in open sources that can harm the health, morals and spiritual development of minors," which would also include the potential formation of "deviant ideas about the social equality of traditional and nontraditional marital relationships."[14] Six years later, the law ratified in a few Russian cities would leave out the list of specific orientations—including the peculiar, and archaically biblical, term for male homosexuality—focusing instead on "information directed to the development of nontraditional sexual dispositions, attractiveness of nontraditional sexual relations, perverted understanding of social equality between traditional and nontraditional sexual relations, or imposition of information about nontraditional sexual relations."[15]

Crucial here, as the researcher Alexander Kondakov points out, is the final draft's focus on information rather than individuals.[16] Who has the right to speak about homosexuality, and how? What is the proper way to educate the young? In chapters 1 and 3, we took note of conservative populist attempts to bring about a fusion of moral and scholastic forms of instruction. In a culture where enlightenment (*prosveshchenie*) was, during the nineteenth and twentieth centuries, understood to be synonymous with education, this represented an important component of the intelligentsia's belief system. In the third decade of the twenty-first century, we see something new, an inflection point in Russian attitudes that converges with the negative view of educators that has always been prominent in US culture. The intelligentsia is now regarded in Russia as the corrupter of moral judgment. Yet, as we shall see, such demonization does not exclude a fascination among Russian traditionalists with the nonnormative modalities of the intelligentsia.

New Strategies for Medieval Conflicts: Modernity on Digital Trial

This fascination with sexual non-normativity takes an incandescently expressive form in the public presentation of the militant religious group that calls itself the Union of Orthodox Banner Bearers. As many prominent Russian Orthodox commentators have remarked with chagrin (most notably the cleric Father Vsevolod Chaplin), the Union's internet footprint is considerably larger than either its membership or its role in serious discussions about the church's direction.[17] The group's protests are carefully structured enactments of *épatage*. Their eclectic "uniform" (black t-shirts emblazoned with fanciful pastiches of Orthodox crosses, with elements of Celtic runes, skulls, and Iron Crosses) is itself an indication that all protest for them is first and foremost about provocation. After interviewing members of the group during the first trial of the punk feminist collective Pussy Riot in 2012, the Russian American journalist Sophia Kishkovsky and her colleague David Herzhenhorn wrote: "While the Banner Bearers and their allies may appear cartoonish—visually they seem to conflate the Grateful Dead and the Ku Klux Klan—they say they are fighting for the survival of Russia against a liberal onslaught from within the country and from outside it, especially from the West," with a campaign against gay rights being "one of their biggest battles."[18] Through its website, video blogs, and VKontakte page, the Union has served as something of a midwife, facilitating the new-media birth of exhibitionistic performances of xenophobic absolutism. Like many religiously affiliated hate groups, the Union is much more eloquent in talking about what members loathe than about the creed or principles that they love.

One member, an artist named Igor Miroshnichenko, designed a T-shirt with Russian and Greek versions of the phrase "Orthodoxy or Death," surrounding what is a clearly the SS-Totenkopf skull and crossbones image.[19] Writing about the commercialization of far-right subcultures in Germany, Cynthia Miller-Idriss notes that "the fact that consumers don't always understand the coded symbols" on a piece of extremist merchandise only enhances their appeal as "gateways to the broader far-right scene."[20] Groups like the Union employ categories of sexuality as a stratagem for redefining the concept of "foreignness" as more a matter of sensibility or orientation than actual ethnicity or race.

From this perspective, their homophobia is for them a positive statement of faith.

A curious feature of the group is their eclectic theatricality. Whilst their heraldry and costumes are largely derivative of Tolkien's *The Hobbit* and *The Lord of the Rings*, their blog posts allude to pop-historical accounts of the court of Vlad the Impaler, and idealized legends about the Oprichnina (Ivan the Terrible's elite security force) and the Order of the Teutonic Knights. The self-conscious archaizing tendency of the Union of Orthodox Banner Bearers is particularly evident in its performance of collective prophylaxes against the "foreign threat" of homosexuality. The reflexive Germanophilia of many skinhead and neo-Nazi groups has been a significant obstacle to their wider appeal among a population generally mindful of the tragic legacy of the Second World War.

This archaizing tendency has a distinct logic. As inspired by their founder, the priest-cosplaying activist Leonid Simonovich-Nikshich—who died on 19 March 2022, and who was never ordained in the Orthodox Church—the Union seeks to bring about a firmer ideological coalition between neo-Nazi movements and the Russian Orthodox Church through ritualized public performances that seek to hybridize different symbolic codes among the Russian far right. The Union's high-profile campaign against homosexuality seeks to appeal to the anxieties of skinhead groups about the weakening of solidarity among Russian men by speaking a xenophobic language that identifies the threat of collective emasculation as originating not only in ethnic minorities, but also (and perhaps more dangerously) among European and American supporters of the LGBTQ movement and their Russian quislings. Finessing a striking reversal of ideological values, the Union presents the enemy as the same Europe that the skinheads regard as the nominal carrier of the Aryan legacy. The relations between the younger and older participants that we see in their protest actions (which are widely available on their website and YouTube) seem to underscore the virtue of obedience: that is, that youth should heed the lessons and traditions of their ancestors as a safeguard against their susceptibility to the "foreign" influences of polymorphous sexuality and Western culture. In a country where skinhead groups have a largely hostile attitude to the Russian Orthodox Church and conspicuously lack older mentors, yet fetishize the concept of authority,[21] the Union positions itself as a brotherhood of hirsute elders who are able to instruct rightist youths on the appropriately intimate yet nonsexual relations among males, serving as a bridge for them to engage with institutions of state power.

On the most basic level, the Union's penchant for theatricality and parades is meant to serve as a counterweight to LGBTQ Pride parades planned for St. Petersburg and Moscow. Their political differences notwithstanding, the

Union and anti-Putin performance-art groups such as Voina ("War") act up for the cameras in ways that suggest an understanding of political performance as a digitally recorded act. The Union has consistently demonstrated a conception of nationalist and conservative protest as a religious procession that gains traction only when it is captured in a series of images. Their protests are a form of performance art in search of a videographer.

Spiritual Prophylaxis and the Foreign Threat of Homosexuality

For the media-savvy Russian viewer (a person in their twenties or thirties, on average), the discursive, incomplete, and highly eccentric home page of the Order of the Vanquished Dragon is a prompt and goad to search elsewhere on the site for more information about its goals and activities. A cursory walk through the site brings them to the name of another organization: the Union of Orthodox Banner Bearers. An entire page is devoted to full online versions of its journal *Sviashchennaia khorugv'* (Sacred Banner). Not much in the way of specific information about the organization is available on the Vanquished Dragon site. The site's highly involuted structure is evocative of what the medievalist Dmitri Likhachev identifies as the stylistic hallmarks of old Russian literature: a love of redundancy, sententiousness, and incantatory list making.[22] An exploration of the site eventually leads to the bewildering conclusion that neither the Order of the Vanquished Dragon nor the Order of the Dragon "Dracula" is an actual organization: they are merely different avatars for the Union of Orthodox Banner Bearers. With no call for membership on the website—or even a list of officers—the viewer comes to the realization that the two orders are entirely fictional.

The site is distinctive in evoking a gaming format, but with the peculiarity that it is not individuals who take on multiple identities, but organizations and collectives. Here the Union seems to be addressing an audience of Russian gamers. Writing about the emerging configuration of the Russian gaming community in 2010 and 2011, Catherine Goodfellow notes that the construction of identities among Russian gamers reflects a highly idiosyncratic willingness to scuttle the unitary self, expressed through the serial experiencing of corporate as well as individual identities: "Young Russian gamers . . . have the opportunity to enter Russian, American, Pacific Asian and European virtual worlds and in so doing, try on different aspects of cultural identity and simultaneously reflect on their own Russian national identity."[23] In their design for the Order of the Vanquished Dragon site, the Union places particular emphasis on merging the individual gamer with the group. The instructional point of treating the group as an agent or player would seem to be that a person can never be a viable moral or even ontological category, whereas an organization is. This design feature carries a distinct traditionalist message: a rebuttal of the "Western" glorification of the individual person as the most important category for moral agency.

The conservative essayist and songwriter Vitaly Averianov—Dugin's colleague at the Moscow think tank the Izborsk Club—has written about a "new" theory of dynamic individualism. For Averianov, what is most important for any given person is to be "the fully embodied carrier of their faith, their [governmental] state, and their genealogical [or ancestral] self [*rodovogo litsa*]."[24] The visitor to the site is made to embark on a quest for information, which (in keeping with the configuration of gaming platforms) is never completely satisfied. The Order of the Vanquished Dragon is nestled within the Order of the Dragon "Dracula," and the latter is a subset of the Union of Orthodox Banner Bearers, and yet the link for the Union's official site (http://www.pycckie.org/) is listed nowhere on the site for the Order of the Dragon "Dracula." With its involuted configuration and proliferation of overlapping names, each carrying its own whimsical characterization, the entire website for the group seems to deliberately evoke the aesthetic of "word weaving" (*pletenie sloves*) that was pioneered by the fifteenth-century Russian scribe Epiphanius the Most Wise (*Epifanii premudryi*). Epiphanius's "word weaving" was what we now might call a Borgesian laboratory for experimenting with synonyms, exaggerated rhetorical statements, and set expressions repeated with slight variations, all of which take on a powerful cumulative significance as the reader comes closer to the end of the text. By seeking to complement in literary expression the illustrations in the margins of the manuscript, Epiphanius's style also had a significant ekphrastic component.[25] We see this interplay between different forms of naming and visual images everywhere on the Union's website, which also frames each of its pages with manuscript filigrees suggestive of Medieval Slavic illuminated manuscripts. As someone who did graduate work at the Institute of Slavic and Balkan Studies in Moscow and who himself was an amateur artist, the group's founder Leonid Simonovich-Nikshich would have been well-aware of this artistic convention.[26]

Such highly stylized circumlocution about origins, affiliations, and actual professions of faith encourages a perception of the Union's activities as sprawling, open-ended, and highly attuned to the possibilities of reader response and participation. With its congeries of anti-Semitism, homophobia, anti-Bolshevism, antimodernity, and monarchism, leavened with an accommodating attitude toward Putin's policies, the Union positions itself as an unruly yet welcoming roundtable for different elements of the Russian conservative mainstream, creating a united front against the disease of liberal individualism. As is highly characteristic of what might be termed a Russian form of rightist eclecticism, it manifests a rather charitable attitude toward the Stalin era and its political legacy. Its criticisms of that period have a mildness that is distinctly absent from its blistering condemnation of Lenin. Amid this tyranny of small differences, the Union casts the fear of homosexuality as a core value among the silent majority of Russians.

What we see and experience on the Order of the Dragon "Dracula" page entitled "The Spiritual Oprichnina, or DEATH TO FAGGOTS!" is a vivid reminder that the internet is a hybridized medium that owes its structure to cinema, the personal diary, and the historical chronicle. This homophobic web page is formatted in ways that are expressive of traditional visual and literary diegetic conventions. By asserting the primacy of the act itself over the medium of its representation—defining the page as a portal for joining an event rather than a site that *becomes* a happening—the Union of Orthodox Banner Bearers underscores the distinction between homosexual feelings and acts. As we shall see, this distinction plays a key role in understanding (and excusing) the page's seemingly self-aware homoeroticism. These men see themselves as both the elite security force of Ivan the Terrible and (in keeping with the ahistorical, quasi-medievalist mash-up that distinguishes the site as a whole) monks, with the young participants serving as novitiates under the stern guidance of older men. In the group's internet-based self-presentation, we hear once more distinct echoes of statements by influential ideologues on the political scene of the Russian Federation. The Izborsk Club's advocacy of the establishment of a modern-day Oprichnina within the state security apparatus is well known, as is Stalin's fondness for specific features of Ivan's state-building practices, as opposed to those of Peter the Great. As Marlène Laruelle notes, "Several of the Club's authors, such as Maksim Kalashnikov, refer to the creation of a new oprichnina" for a mass "mobilization project," carrying out ambitious public works projects according to following Stalinist precedents such as the building of the Moscow metro system. The pundit and essayist Maksim Kalashnikov whom she mentions envisions drafting an "army of lightning-force implementation *(armiia molnienosnogo razvitiia)* [consisting] of fifty thousand young men and women, unrestrained by either administrative agencies or the law" to lead a "moral revolution."[27] Kalashnikov's publications brim with conspiracy theories about the treachery of Western-collaborating Soviet officials, who were keen to sabotage the "innovative Oprichnina" of the chief of the Soviet secret police Lavrenty Beria, and who with the death of Stalin ordered Beria's execution at the behest of their American masters.[28] Once again, we see how the entertaining self-presentation of a fringe group serves as a fisheye lens for commanding our attention about views that are both mainstream and extreme.

What we see on this page of the website of the Spiritual Oprichnina is an exorcism of hostile foreign influences that is too disturbing and profane to be enacted before a larger public, or the laity. The internet is a useful setting for the act of purification, and not simply because it removes us from the direct contamination that comes with occupying the same physical space. Here, the internet serves (perhaps more importantly) as a prophylactic filter or buffer: it too can do righteous battle, transmuting nemeses into something less harmful by reformatting them into a digital setting. As the media critic Pierre Lévy wrote in one of his early, and characteristically utopian, discussions of cyberspace: "Digitization enables us to create, modify, and even interact with messages, atom of information by atom of information, bit by bit [thereby enabling us to] retain the timbre of a voice or instrument, while using it to play a different melody."[29] Digitization becomes a necessary disruption of ways of life that have become stale or corrupt. For this group, it is a way of hitting a "refresh" button on the souls of users who have been seduced by capitalist modernity.

On the Spiritual Oprichnina webpage, this idea of reformatting as the actual moment of exorcism takes on its most vivid expression in "killing" the spirit of homosexuality, depicted in a series of photographs that demonstrates the group's repeated attempts to cast out demons from a Russian edition of the magazine *Kvir* (Queer).[30] The scroll of still images that follows suggests that this act of exorcism is powerfully erotic in its own right. As a first step in this rite, pages are torn from the magazine and photographs show "naked, buff men" (*golye nakachennye muzhiki*) are nailed to a fence. Mikhail, the young man who had tried to exorcise the magazine by shooting at it with a homemade arrow (fashioned from an aspen branch), has failed. Enough of these desultory attempts! The elder and group leader Leonid Simonovich-Nikshich mutters to another young man, "Yura, bring the spear!" As even Yura fails, Leonid impatiently grabs a knife and stabs at an image of a cross-dressing man. The photograph at first "emits such a howl and squeal!!!" and then groans and falls silent. The instant of the demon's actual silencing is denoted by a color negative image. In a peculiar coda to the histrionics of the exorcism (the demon emits a "horrific roar" [*strashnyi rev*]) when poked with the spear), the narrative concludes with the statement that it was thus that the "everyday symbolic act of the NEW RUSSIAN SPIRITUAL OPRICHNINA took place." We are to understand two things: the entire process, a record of an actual exorcism, is a paradigm so that the viewer can understand and vanquish his own homoeroticism, and we need to read the entire page the way we read the homepage. The act of scrolling down represents a descent into Hell, a harrowing experience that is incrementally relieved with the promise of a provisional redemption.

From the website of the Union of Orthodox Banner Bearers: "Killing" the spirit of homosexuality by the Order of the Dragon "Dracula."

Toward a Philosophy of the Shared Event:
Archaized Homophobia as Desexualized Intimacy

In August 2012 members of Pussy Riot were sentenced for the collective's protest performance in Moscow's Church of Christ the Savior. Russian skinheads and neo-Nazis cheered the group's arrest and incarceration. Since then, certain ideological formulas and terms from those groups have been more clearly mainstreamed into the political language of the state-controlled media. The archaizing tendency among groups like the Union for Orthodox Banner Bearers is particularly evident in their performance of collective prophylaxes against the "foreign threat" of homosexuality. As we have seen, the group stages what can be plausibly understood as their own versions of performance art, with the public square of the internet chosen as the most rhetorically effective venue for attacking the values and—most significantly—the publications of the LGBTQ community. The Spiritual Oprichnina page emphasizes that homosexuality is false (and therefore evil) by virtue of already being a media representation. A young man shoots an arrow, at the behest of an older man, into the photograph of the backside of a transgender person from the magazine *Kvir*—this is not, as we might think, an instance of homosociality tipping over into open

eroticism; rather, as the web page would have us believe, it is a calculated
meta-iconographical moment that references St. Sebastian and the notion of
homosexuality as a sickness of modernity, brought on by the explosion of mass
print media in the post-Soviet space. And how else can we explain the fact that
the relations among the men presented under the headline "The Spiritual Oprichnina, or DEATH TO FAGGOTS!" clearly reference the homosexual orgy from
the novel *Day of the Oprichnik*, written by an author whose work has been
publicly burned by the Union of Orthodox Banner Bearers? On the Union's
website, the elder Leonid's call for a novitiate to spike the back of a gay man
echoes the shout "Don't be scared, greenhorns!" from Vladimir Sorokin's
novel. In the book, the mentor Batya (whose name is an honorific title meaning "esteemed father") says this to his own group of young apprentices as he
and they intimately join together in an "oprichnik *caterpillar*"[31] (emphasis in
the original). As in Sorokin's novel, the novitiates study under harsh but fair
teachers, but the elderly *oprichniki* on the Union's webpage are proudly asex-
ual, and thus able to break the spirit of sodomy.

The elderly leader is able to resist—and therefore exorcise—homoerotism;
younger men might be tempted by the force that they are expelling. In the
videos of the group posted on the internet, only the leader, Simonovich-
Nikshich, and the artist Igor Miroshnichenko (the second oldest member)
shred and burn images of Madonna, Elton John, and Pussy Riot. With surprising openness, the Union of Orthodox Banner Bearers acknowledges not
just the homosociality but also the homoeroticism within their own group.
From the perspective of performance as a ritualized practice, the Union freely
acknowledges the vividly sexualized aspect of their group work. The Spiritual
Oprichnina webpage bristles with what Eve Kosofsky Sedgwick terms the "less
stable and identity-bound understandings of sexual choice," whose multiple
points of overlap and intersection create highly distinctive "performative
effects [within] a self-contradictory discursive field."[32] In effect, the Union
recognizes erotic polymorphousness as the natural state of things, seeing in *all*
forms of sexuality nothing more than a congeries of destructive forces that
need to be purged of their content of disobedience and submerged pride.
In one interview posted on the organization's main website, Simonovich-
Nikshich even compares Madonna to himself, by referring to her as a priest
("Madonna kak sviashchennik"), as if to underscore the performative charisma of the spiritual teacher, the only figure who may come into contact with
natural instincts without being overwhelmed by them.[33]

The fact that the Union of Orthodox Banner Bearers ultimately insists on
the *symbolic* nature of the eroticized rite suggests that the web page serves as a
medium for rendering the quotidian into the sacred. The Russian verb for

scrolling down on a screen (*prokruchivat'*/*prokrutit'*) can, in other contexts, also be used to refer to an apparatus playing an audio or video recording, such as a disk or tape. Here, both senses of the Russian "scrolling" are suggested, with the page becoming both an instance of transposition into another medium and a site for the suggestively erotic conjoining of disparate individuals. All of this is strongly reminiscent of the theories of the Russian literary critic Mikhail Bakhtin (1895–1975), who developed an understanding of the literary work as punctuated by a series of explosive "events" (*sobytiia*). The 1986 publication of Bakhtin's early (and unfinished) manuscript "Toward a Philosophy of the Act" prompted Russian nationalist philosophers like Yuri Davydov (already embold-ened by the beginnings of *glasnost'* under Gorbachev) to articulate a notion of personal responsibility, not as a Kantian imperative, but rather as an unfolding of call-and-response within a national community. Particularly interesting to Davydov and other nativist commentators—most notably Bakhtin's former student Vadim Kozhinov, who, like Davydov and Dugin, joined the anti-Semitic nationalist group Pamiat ("Memory") during the late eighties—was the critic's insistence that "the unitary yet complex event" consists not of its partici-pants "co-experiencing" with particular others, but rather of each occupying a position outside themselves (*vnenakhodimost'*) that is expressed in the totality of their relations with all others.[34]

Bakhtin's conception of the event (*sobytie*: literally, "co-being") as a shared "happening," a totality of interlocking realms of experience that blurs the significance of particular acts of intimacy, is very helpful in explicating the totality of multiple frames of reference on a site like the Order of the Dragon "Dracula," with its plethora of names for a single organization and its assertion that homoeroticism can be neutralized by being reconfigured into a different representational context. In its understanding of internet images as largely defanged representations of sin, the Union also selectively references the Ortho-dox conception of the icon as the only aesthetic realm that is truly participa-tive for the viewer. With their warped proportions and reverse perspective, icons endeavor to bring the viewer into the same space as the "prototypes" of the divine and sanctified holy figures that they portray.[35] To paraphrase Susan Sontag, the medium of the internet here becomes the solvent for immorality. In their project of providing a site for supposed genuine being and intimacy, the Union is also drawing on the ideas of René Guenon, Julius Evola, Hei-degger, and Dugin himself about the moral rot of an anxiously mindful and politically "progressive" modernity. One of Dugin's VKontakte posts from 2014 about the military leader Igor Strelkov in the pro-Russian breakaway re-gion of Donbas in Ukraine even has the Bakhtinian-sounding title of "Strelkov as an Event" (*Strelkov kak sobytie*). Striking an embarrassing note of New-Age esoteric whimsy—whilst echoing his "Hyperborean" theory of Russians as "People of the Sun"—Dugin characterizes the ex-FSB officer as "taking on the function of the Solar Putin."[36]

In his preface to Dugin's book about Heidegger, Paul Gottfried—the coiner of the term "alt-right," and mentor to the neo-Nazi and "Unite the Right" ringleader Richard Spencer—writes that both Heidegger and Dugin "sought alternatives to the materialist and consumerist ethos of later modernity—and to the ideology of universal political sameness that has accompanied it."[37] The activity of a logrolling global network of radical populists—Gottfried, Dugin, Spencer, and Spencer's Russian ex-wife, Nina Kouprianova, who translated Dugin's book on Heidegger into English—shows us that the modernity of mainstream conservatism is indistinguishable from that of liberalism, insofar as it too relies on material artifacts such as a book for the trafficking of its ideas. Gottfried, however, argues that a more radical conservatism calls for making physical texts redundant, by highlighting the experience of disembodied thought and feeling that the internet offers. Making good on the promise of pure experience as the one and only event, the Union represents its virtual world as a gateway for truly safe sex among men.

The Queering of the Post-Soviet Conservative Intelligentsia

Why does the Union of Orthodox Banner Bearers fixate on queer identity as their target and as an instrument for defining their own identity as a fellowship of cultural activists? To answer this question, we need to address the unorthodox or queer standing of the very notion of the intelligentsia within a conservative national culture. How does a new-right elite, or a conservative intelligentsia, legitimate itself in a way that is consistent with its values? We have spoken about how the Union engaged in a process of self-queering, on the assumption that such contamination would make their holy struggle against the LGBTQ community more compelling and personal. The threat is here, they seem to be saying, and we are only marginally more immune to it than you are. Is it even possible to consider an intelligentsia that is not against normativity? Might there be an affinity in Russian culture between intellectualism and sexual otherness? To answer these questions, we need to take an excursion into the history of Soviet prison slang.

Almost a million inmates died between 1948 and 1952 in the Bitches' War in the Soviet prison system. During the thirties and forties, non-political criminals in the GULAG routinely preyed upon inmates who had been convicted for petty crimes under the 49th article of the Soviet Criminal Code, and those indicted under the political crimes statute of the code's 58th article. Inmates convicted of nonpolitical crimes were often given the task of instilling some order among the prison population, to the point of establishing a kind of parallel or underground legal system that was not necessarily harsher than that of the warders, but was rigidly hierarchical and at times deliberately over-looked—if not encouraged—by the prison authorities. The Bitches' War was ignited by the return to the GULAG of career criminals who had served in the Soviet army during the war, who were regarded as traitors and "bitches" (*suki*) by their *blatnye* (organized crime) brethren for cooperating with the authori-ties, and serving as informants and low-level administrators of specific wards.[38]. Although homosexuals convicted under Article 121.2 of the Soviet Criminal Code were technically nonpolitical, some of them were considered by the thieves to be among the caste of untouchable or *opushchennye* prisoners (liter-ally, those who are "cast down"). This group also included those who defied the thieves' code of honor by snitching to the warders or wearing a tattoo that reflected a status higher than the one they actually possessed. In some instances, the untouchable individual was cast more profoundly into an "othered" state by having the name for his particular misdeed or identity forcibly tattooed on his forehead.[39] The GULAG survivor Anatoly Marchenko and others have recorded that men with tattooed foreheads were singled out for abusive treat-ment by both the warders and the hierarchy of the criminal subculture within the prison.[40]

Danzig Baldaev, the Buryat-Russian ethnographer of Soviet prison culture, emphasizes that Russian prison tattoos should be understood as "uniforms with medals," corporeal dossiers that are readily available to the apprehension of strangers.[41] More often than not, tattoos referring to the homosexuality of their wearer consisted of allegorized representations of people and animals that bear no apparent relation to same-sex desire. These tattoos paint a com-plex picture. What we see in them is that the lowly status of gay men within the Soviet prison system (which defined them not by specific acts of disobedi-ence but by the essentializing fact of their desire) rendered them a third class of inmates, in many ways quite distinct from the "politicals" and the thieves. An *opushchennyi* prisoner could not look a thief in the eye or brush up against him without permission; he had to take special care to keep all his possessions, such as eating utensils, separate and completely out of reach of the thieves. As a result of such strictures, certain individuals among the untouchables were needed to serve as intermediaries, almost literally translators, between their caste and the thieves. The untouchables who were formally assigned to fulfill these negotiating functions were often passive homosexuals; like the thieves themselves, they wore tattoos that designated their function, and in keeping with the zoological preoccupation of the thieves' semiotic imaginary, they were assigned an animal. Occasionally, an untouchable who was a passive homosexual was authorized to serve as a go-between within the prison community.[42] In a curious inversion, a passive homosexual with such authority is designated by an animal representing so-called active sexuality, a rooster (*petukh*).

The subculture within the Soviet GULAG during the fifties and sixties reveals a consistent use of avian imagery in reference to inmates incarcerated because of Article 121.2. It may be regarded as astonishing that this imagery avoids pejorative or homophobic connotations; it arguably points to a conception of queer identity as a positive and even socially dominant sexuality that associates eroticism with freedom. Several sources and autobiographical accounts from the sixties list the masculine noun *golub'* ("dove") and its diminutive form *golubets* ("little dove") as terms for male homosexuals. This is the likely origin of the adjective *goluboi*, in the sense of "queer." *Goluboi* has the additional advantage of serving the dual purpose that is beloved by any argot, acting as a lexical and semantic shifter: it is a commonly used word that also serves as a code term. *Goluboi* in the sense of "[male] homosexual" originated in the argot of this prison subculture and the slang of the *blatnye*, and was subsequently absorbed into the larger field of the Russian language.

With the end of the Bitches' War, the prison authorities' toleration of the exploitive treatment of the non-political prisoners by the *blatnye* was significantly curtailed. The black market flourished during the dramatic downturn of the Soviet economy during the seventies and eighties, resulting in an explosion of career criminals throughout the country and swelling the prison population. As a result, nonpolitical inmates returned to some prominence as proxy prison guards, this time largely without the stigma of being collaborators with the authorities. Within the institutional context of this double panopticon—the official prison administration and the thieves' enhanced micromanagement of the inmate population—homosexual identity was, in the post-Stalin era, understood in distinctly politicized terms for the first time in Russian cultural history. Like the political dissident prisoners, incarcerated homosexuals were compelled to identify themselves and vie for status and limited privileges within an inherently unjust power structure—one that, as many researchers have rightly pointed out, mirrored Soviet society as a whole. Some passive homosexual men within the subculture of the *blatnye* were identified by a tattoo of a woman holding male genitalia with dove wings.[43] Interestingly, the columbine imagery also occurs in tattoos that refer to a heterosexual context. A common one shows a woman haunted by dreams of the lover she betrayed.[44]

These heraldic details have persisted in the prisons of the post-Soviet era. Raising pigeons and doves for recreation and postal purposes is especially strong within the Siberian criminal subculture, which anthropomorphizes the birds in some of its folklore. The Russian sociologist Ekaterina Efimova documents a 1998 drawing by a convict who glossed the image of a hovering dove from his notebook as symbol of freedom.[45] On another page of the same notebook, the convict wrote that a torch behind two men holding hands represented "being free, just as fire is." Within the prison culture, the heraldic representation of the dove existed in a network of images that expressed same-sex love or homosocial interaction in close association with a certain psychological autonomy, sometimes crossing over to represent sexuality without reference to specific orientations. While the paradox of finding freedom within confinement has an honorable history in Russian literature (as reflected in the work of Dostoevsky, Solzhenitsyn, and Evgeniia Ginzburg), linking that paradox to avian imagery and homoeroticism is highly idiosyncratic. Yet it is not unique. In his prison novel *Falconer*, John Cheever (whose oeuvre was significantly influenced by Russian literary models, particularly Chekhov's stories and Dostoevsky's novel about prison life, *Notes from a Dead House*) memorably brings all these details into the same close interrelationship. Queer desire is presented within this network of images as being utterly sui generis within a rigidly hierarchical system, a liminal element that is kinetically distinctive for its function as an intermediary.

We can plausibly speculate that the word *golub'* became associated with certain homosexuals in prison because of a perceived analogy to pigeon messenger services, which had been used in Russian state prisons for decades. Crucial here is the unusual status of particular homosexuals within the prison caste system as messengers or "pigeons." Within that repressive environment, they served as information-bearers and mediators, people whose role was defined by language rather than raw hierarchical power. They acted very much in the mode of what Yuri Slezkine's book *The Jewish Century* calls "Mercurians," deft communicators and messengers who make language their home, while being nomads within their environment. While they tend not to be the captains of the state or licensed violent enforcers, their mental capital and communicative role imbue them with a distinctively ambiguous authority. In an analogy to the representation of the highest authority figures in the thieves' hierarchy, these particular *petukhi* ("roosters") can also be called fathers or "papas."

The Soviet-era carceral subtext of the Russian terminology for male sexual alterity helps us to understand the outsized performativity and ambiguous sexuality of the Union of Orthodox Banner Bearers. It also illuminates how even the conservative intelligentsia may be framed, by virtue of its indeterminate relationship to economic class status, as nonnormative, strange, or queer. The ideological eclecticism of the Union's public actions, a mishmash of tsarism, fascism, and religious traditionalism, situates it as a mediator, communicator, and emissary—like the prison carrier pigeons and their human analogues, the homosexual *petukhi*—within the Russian public square of broadly conservative values. The provocative character of the Union's public actions cannot efface its subservient messenger status, particularly within a value system that prizes submission to authority. The independent union activist and political dissident Lev Volokhonsky summarized the code of the Soviet criminals whom he met in prison as rigidly hierarchical, bound by specific concepts, or rules (*zhizn' po poniatiiam*), that formed an internal system of power relations, strict, yet fairer and more humane than that of Soviet law.[46]

As the criminal world saw it, its "life according to the rules" and the Soviet system of "inhuman" law shared two key assumptions: the absolute power of the authority above you, and a contempt for everything outside one's own system. In 2017 and 2018, I conducted interviews with the former Soviet dissidents Vyacheslav Bakhmin, Alexander Ogorodnikov, and Vyacheslav Dolinin.[47] Bakhmin and Dolinin were convicted of "anti-Soviet" activity (*antisovetism*) under Article 190-1 and 70-1 of the Criminal Code, and Ogorodnikov of "parasitism" or living unemployed and at the largesse of the state (Article 209).[48] Unlike dissidents convicted under other articles, all three were occasionally put into carceral spaces where they fraternized with inmates convicted of nonpolitical crimes. Many of these "nonpoliticals" were traffickers in contraband articles (*kontrabandisty*), and as a result were petty criminals who did not belong to the power networks represented by the new breed of collaborationist *blatnye*. This outsider status within the unofficial prison hierarchies afforded them a perspective that was much closer to the *blatnye* of old, with their contempt of political authority. All three interviewees underscored the nonpolitical inmates' lack of antagonism toward them and other dissidents; sometimes (as Dolinin vividly recalls) they even expressed *uvazhukha* ("great respect") for defying the power structure of the "other" system. For the Union of Orthodox Banner Bearers, the culture of "Globohomo" represents the competing system that they loathe. That system is the one that commands the desperate respect of the normies, or (as Russian criminal slang puts it) the "marks" (*fraera*). Yet the obverse of this contempt and the perception of the other system as deeply immoral is that your own side commands complete submission, even to the point of abjection. The Union's homophobia is a tortuous effort to reconcile their own values of self-abnegation with their self-image as rebels against a global order by casting themselves as elite cultural warriors. As Eduard Limonov would have pointed out, such right-wing attempts to "redeem" the intelligentsia are doomed from the start, simply because they cannot escape the environment of unfreedom that brought them into being.

The Contrarianism of Dmitri Tsorionov and Andrei Kuraev

We now move on to two individuals who manifest an intellectual performativity in regard to the place of sexual non-normativity in contemporary Russian society. As in the case of the Banner Bearers, this thespian self-image can be understood as a projection of their own anxiety about membership in an oppositional intelligentsia. Based in Moscow, the far-right activist Dmitri Tsorionov, also known as Enteo, has been a highly visible presence in protests against numerous progressive movements in Russia. Until 2015 he agitated against LGBTQ civil rights and for the proposed criminalization of abortion in the Russian Federation. Yet unlike his religiously inflected traditionalist counterparts in the United States, Enteo has never been ideologically consistent. He has staged disruptive protests against opponents of two controversial laws that were passed within the last decade: the law against "homosexual propaganda" that went into effect in 2013 and the so-called antiblasphemy law. Both laws are open to expansive interpretation and have been enforced capriciously. Attacks on religion may be understood as a form of grievous "insult against the feelings of believers" and are subject to criminal penalties, which explains the prison sentences for the members of Pussy Riot when they were arrested for their 2012 anti-Putin prayer in the Church of Christ the Savior. In 2017 Enteo joined the Pussy Riot activist Maria Alyokhina and others in protesting against the repressive legacy of the KGB by staging shrewdly theatricalized public actions in front of the security service center on Lubyanka Square in Moscow. Such public actions would seem inconsistent for a person who has otherwise openly advocated for a theocracy that has not been seen on Russian soil since 1917. And indeed, Mila Odegova, the head of the traditionalist antigay alliance God's Will, expelled Enteo from the group he helped form, citing his friendship with a member of a leftist protest group.[49] Since then, without commentary or explanation, Enteo has ceased to engage in performative campaigns has ceased to campaign against LGBTQ rights.

What caused this shift? The Yakut-Russian documentary filmmaker Beata Bubenets (also sometimes known by her married name of Bashkiroff) made the film *Bozh'ia volia* (God's Will, 2013) in an attempt to depict Enteo through his own words to her and, if possible, to present a sensationalistic subject in a directly communicative and therefore nonsensational way. With Enteo's full permission, Bubenets shot footage of him and other members of God's Will on their daily rounds in Moscow in December 2012, during the height of their harassment of supporters of LGBTQ rights.[50] In the documentary, Enteo and his followers mount public actions that mimic progressive groups' supposed disruption of the public order, articulating their behavior as a homeopathic remedy for a diseased body politic. Their reasoning is that if you want to support the cause of law and order, you must treat its enemies to the forms of disorder that

Police detain the Orthodox activist Dmitri Tsorionov (Enteo), demonstrating with the group God's Will in Bolotny Square in Moscow, May 2013. Photo by RIA Novosti.

they are visiting upon society. In her hour-long film—calculated to last no longer than one of God's Will's typical shock-troop counterdemonstrations—Bubenets draws our attention to the movement's contradictory impulses. She presents Enteo and his confederates as actors who are uninterested in finessing or reconciling the logical contradictions of their strategies. How can one be an advocate for order (*poriadok*) without embracing the related notion of decency or probity (*poriadochnost*)?

In *God's Will*, Enteo and his friends plan actions, disrupt peaceful gay-rights protests, go about their daily chores, and eat fish and meat while quaffing copious amount of alcohol during Lent. Quite a bit of screen time is devoted to Enteo's relationship with his girlfriend, who seems to share his ideological values but proclaims them with less militancy. Enteo and his confederates engage in demonstrations that may be understood as a fusion of disparate modes of political activism: at times, they mount traditional forms of public protest, moving with picket signs and placards behind barriers placed by law enforcement; at other times, they engage in varieties of performance art that are not radically different from those practiced by groups like Pussy Riot and Voina, which had their roots in performance arts collectives such as the Moscow Conceptualists of the late eighties. In 2013, Enteo and God's Will disrupted a performance of Oscar Wilde's *An Ideal Husband* at the Moscow Art Theatre, jumping up on stage and declaring the play to be a "sacrilege" (for its portrayal of a homosexual cleric) that "insulted the feelings of believers." Although Bubenets does not show this incident, in her closely observant cinematic diary she draws attention to the paradox of the group's breaking the law against disorderly conduct while simultaneously invoking the relevant sections of the legal code that provisionally define it.

In subsequent days Enteo and his friends shadow and menace demonstrators advocating openness and equal protection for members of the LGBTQ community in Moscow. In their actions we see a preoccupation with homosexuality as, in their perception, the original sin. Much of the film is taken up with the triviality and monotony of Enteo's daily routine and the idle garrulousness and casual snarkiness that define both his general speaking style and his worldview. Bubenets is keen to communicate to her audience that this slack and narcissistic manner of thinking and speaking represents the origin of Enteo's performative and activist self-understanding, rather than any particular religious or nationalistic ideology. In an interview that I conducted with her in Moscow during the summer of 2018, Bubenets emphasized that Enteo never became hostile to her during hours of filming, even though he was aware that she did not share his political or religious views.

We turn now to the political activity of Andrei Kuraev, the Russian priest who has become increasingly vocal in his criticism of the Russian Orthodox Church's involvement in affairs of state. After our immersion in Enteo's pettifogging and vanity-driven projects, the change seems like a blast of fresh air. As in Enteo's case, the most accurate and revealing representation of Kuraev is cinematic. In 2016 the St. Petersburg–based artist Viktor Tikhomirov filmed *Andrei Kuraev: Priamaia rech'* (Andrei Kuraev: Direct Speech). In keeping with his title, Tikhomirov's portrait uses Kuraev's spoken words, as opposed to his voluminous written statements on the Russian blog platform LiveJournal. Like Bubenets, Tikhomirov strove for an honest portrait, which is to say that he tried to undercut his subject's overreliance on social media platforms as the delivery system for his message. The film conveys a palpable tension between the filmmaker's friendship with Kuraev and the representation of his subject's occasionally grating self-righteousness. At the time of filming, Kuraev was already under fire for his opposition to the church's support for the 2014 annexation of Crimea, his sympathetic meeting with members of Pussy Riot, and his criticism of Patriarch Kirill's increasingly autocratic policies.

Yet, it would be a mistake to call Kuraev a friend of ecumenism, or of any progressive understanding of the Eastern Orthodox tradition. In 2013 he launched a patently homophobic campaign accusing high-ranking clerics in

Father Andrei Kuraev with Maria Alyokhina and Nadezhda Tolokonnikova of the feminist punk collective Pussy Riot, January 2014. Photo by Julia Mayorova.

Kazan and Tver, whom he accused of being a politically powerful "gay lobby" within the church. Partly in response to those scurrilous statements, Kuraev is currently undergoing a process of re-evaluation by the church that will likely lead to his defrocking, once Patriarch Kirill confirms the decision that had been reached by the Moscow Eparchial Court on 29 December 2020. Speaking with me on the phone on 23 March 2021, Kuraev bitterly pointed out the church's double standards and, referring to scandals that had nothing do with sexual orientation, told me that other clerics who were guilty of far worse infractions against the reputation of the church have remained untouched. Earlier that month, writing on Facebook about the proceedings to defrock Kuraev, the American historian Scott Kenworthy argued that the Russian Orthodox Church is taking "one more step toward down a dark path of embracing a mirror image of Putin's authoritarianism in the state, with its own authoritarianism and silencing of dissent within the Church."[51]

At several points in his conversations with Kuraev, Tikhomirov switches seamlessly from video to audio recordings, playing excerpts to listeners like the writer Vladimir Shinkarev and the rock musician and songwriter Yuri Shevchuk in their own studios. One interview is intercut with scenes from Kuraev's large public lectures about the complex character of human fellowship—and the necessary acceptance of expressions of male vulnerability in a masculinist culture that otherwise does not tolerate them. The priest warns Tikhomirov of the risk of a stifling social isolation that is inherent in an "author's creation of his own world" (*sozdanie avtorskogo mira*).

In many respects Tikhomirov's film is prophetic of what may be plausibly understood as Kuraev's downfall as an opposition figure. In contrast to his modest social media activity from 2009 to 2018, he now posts on his LiveJournal page on an almost daily basis and reposts his blog entries on Facebook. His posts, furthermore, have changed in content and quality, taking on a rambling, discursive, and gossipy character that is radically different from that of the tightly focused statements about theology he shared before the church began proceedings against him. His tone of personal aggrievement has heightened, as in his posting on 23 March 2021 about how violently homophobic comments by the late Archpriest Dmitri Smirnov in 2012 went unpunished, while Kuraev is being taken to task for less militant comments about sexual orientation.[52]

Much of this change may be ascribed to Kuraev's isolation during the Covid pandemic, as well as the considerable free time that he has now that his pastoral duties have been suspended. As he explained to me on the day of his blog post about Smirnov, the decision about his status in the church lies entirely with Kirill; this, he argues, vividly demonstrates the ways in which the Russian church has been influenced by the political culture of Soviet-era cults of personality. Kuraev, like Rod Dreher and Enteo, has come to see himself as a truth-teller who does not need to listen to the nuanced assessments of those who fall outside the stark binary of ecclesiastical authority on the one hand and undecided parishioners on the other.

Conclusion: The Rightist Intelligentsia's Desperate Embrace of the Media

For all their ideological differences, Tsorionov, Kuraev, Pyotr Verzilov of Voina, and Leonid Simonovich-Nikshich of the Union of Orthodox Banner Bearers share an appreciation of videography as an essential format for both performance and the expression of political dissent. The notion of performance as a rite—an act that is equally capable of purifying or polluting—brings greater clarity to the clash between the Union and Voina that took place at the Moscow Municipal Court on 12 July 2010. The art curator Yuri Samodurov was fined 200,000 rubles that day for commissioning an exhibit of archly pseudo-religious paintings titled "Forbidden Art—2006" during his tenure as director of the Sakharov Museum.[53] One photograph of that day shows Simonovich-Nikshich looking on approvingly as a thrashing Verzilov is arrested in the vestibule of the court building.

In an interview that I conducted with her in June 2018, Beata Bubenets took note of Tsorionov's enthusiasm about her creation of a film diary of his

Pyotr Verzilov of the protest collective Voina ("War") is detained after storming into a courtroom in Moscow, 12 July 2010. Holding the cross is Leonid Simonovich-Nikshich, the leader of the Union of Orthodox Banner Bearers. REUTERS/Alamy Stock Photo.

activism, and the ease of the entire filmmaking with him and his group. As she explained, all of them were quite aware that their political views were radically different from her own. Kuraev, working with Viktor Tikhomirov in the filmmaker's workspace apartment, was often content to let his admirers take over the narrative of his life, as if they were making a filmed record of a personality cult. Anathema to both men and the groups they lead is the earlier counterculture notion of the "happening" as something that is only as real as its on-site participants perceive it to be, and something that does not depend on approval from a cultural mainstream. Gone too is the notion, famously advanced by Moscow Conceptualist Andrei Monastyrsky and the Collective Actions group, of the event as something that can never be directly described, recorded, or characterized in any way, but whose *effects* on people are documented with generous bureaucratic punctiliousness in the form of written logs, photographic images of seemingly ineloquent empty panoramas (*pustóty*), and post-factum interviews with "witnesses." Writing about the Collective Actions that Monastyrsky's group staged in the countryside not far from Moscow, the art historian Ekaterina Bobrinskaya observes that the "action in the

CA (Collective Actions) performances [was] [d]evoid of any symbolic meaning, and sometimes border[ed] on the absurd." She argues that the real object of the "representation" was "the process of perception flowing through the consciousness of the spectator," and that the actions were designed "to transport [the spectator] to a state of 'pure contemplation,' free of continuous mental interpretation and contemplation—a state of 'emptiness' beyond the constraints of language."[54]

Although the art group Voina emerged as an offshoot of the Collective Actions groups instigated by Monastyrsky—and arguably preserves some of the features of his particular brand of Moscow Conceptualism, especially in regard to the ancillary nature of the word to both image and action—its recent actions have foregrounded the notion that an event becomes real only when it is recorded in a digitized format. With their keen interest in digital image capturing as a potent materialization of the voyeuristic act, on 29 February 2008 Voina filmed and photographed "Fuck for the Bear Cub Heir!" (*Ebis' za naslednika medvezhonka!*), a simulated orgy in a stodgy natural history museum in Moscow. Among other things, the protest action was meant to draw attention to the charade of a division of power between Putin and then-president Dmitri Medvedev (whose surname is derived from the word "bear") and also to the nationalistic racism of Medvedev's call for a higher birth rate among citizens of the Russian Federation.[55] The action could not have been further from the principles of Moscow Conceptualism. As Boris Groys puts it, the Moscow Conceptualists believed that "art documentation *is* by definition not art; it merely *refers* to art and thereby makes clear that art is no longer present and immediately visible here."[56]

The flamboyance of an all-encompassing performance aesthetic that includes costumed or naked bodies in movement, captured digitally *in medias res*, is central to the public identities of Voina, Enteo, God's Will, the Union of Orthodox Banner Bearers, and Kuraev. For them, there is no art or political identity without its digital artifact, and no public controversy without a suitable counterevent that pushes symbolic meanings fully into the realm of action and literalization. We are in a better position to understand the media logic of the Union's anti-LGBTQ Internet "action" of "Spiritual Oprichnina, or DEATH TO FAGGOTS!" on 1 June 2010 once we take into account this preoccupation with videography as a form of performance art in itself. The Union believes that the non-normative sexual act can only be nullified by a recorded counter-performance. Such idiosyncratic notions about media strategy suggest other possibilities. Might Pussy Riot's "Punk Prayer" in the Church of Christ the Savior two years later have been intended as a rebuttal to the Union? That feminist action, conceived of as resolutely off the internet grid, was both a political and an aesthetic reversal, asserting the primacy of performance body art over the Union's

Baudrillardian obsession with the simulacra that emerge from re-enactments and recordings.

In their obsessively maintained digital journals about their own activities (to which Kuraev has added a Telegram account, uploaded with voluminous content), the Union, Enteo, and Kuraev exemplify the hedonistic spirit of media excess and hegemonic dominance that they have at various times ascribed to the LGBTQ community and its international nerve center, "Globohomo." With his own recent accelerated use of LiveJournal, Telegram, and Facebook, Kuraev is moving increasingly in this direction, expostulating in the form of a disaggregate solipsistic running narrative that makes extravagant claims of being something that it is not. Like the Union and Enteo—and quite likely seeing himself as following the example of uncompromising autobiography set by the seventeenth-century Old Believer Avvakum—Kuraev advocates a return to a simplified, and institutionally minimalist, form of Orthodoxy.

Kuraev's dissociation of Orthodox belief from Russian identity sets him apart from the Union, which in its demonstrations in 2022 has dropped its preoccupation with homosexuality in favor of boilerplate nationalist calls for the return of tsardom.[57] With the removal of its Facebook page, the absence of updates to its web page, and the disappearance of Igor Miroshnichenko's page devoted to swag (mostly T-shirts) that feature the group's Totenkopf emblem, it seems that the Union is gradually shuttering its doors. None of this is surprising, for a group that prizes submission and hierarchy, and which has lost, as Mironoshchenko puts it in his March 2022 VKontakte obituary of their founder and leader Simonovich-Nikshich, a person who "possessed a charisma that made it possible for him to lead an enormous number of people."[58] Enteo's recent activity on behalf of the victims of Stalin's purges brings him closer to Kuraev, insofar as both men shun the Dostoevskian ideal of Russian suffering as a crucible for holiness. On the contrary, in his 2022 VKontakte posts Enteo underscores the contribution of Russian cultural attitudes to the purges and even serfdom, combining his critiques with quotations from Ayn Rand about the unfortunate consequences of worshiping the administrative state.[59] Yet what is striking about the shifts in Enteo's and the Union's choice of targets is the ease with which they have dropped their campaigns against homosexuality in exchange for another conservative cause. In the Union's case, the new cause is a return to religiously validated autocracy; in Enteo's case, an apparent endorsement of libertarianism that goes against the grain of the embrace of the administrative state that has always been the centerpiece of conservative political theory in Russia, and that starkly distinguishes it from the anarcho-libertarianism that remains a prominent thread in American conservative populist discourse.

Looking at the Union, Kuraev, and Enteo has given us a highly representative overview of Russian conservatism, in its personalized religious and nationalistic forms, and even (in a more recent development, embodied by the Libertarian Party and its head, Sergei Boyko) its antigovernment form. The homophobia that they have all voiced at different points of their careers serves as a kind of jumper cable for restarting the mechanisms of stalled or stagnating media personae. In a series of tweets in English on 11 July 2022, the pro-United Russia political scientist Artyom Lukin, who teaches at the Far Eastern Federal University at Vladivostok, wrote: "Old Europe resembles Russian intelligentsia. They are both constantly griping about their sovereigns: the US for Europe and the Czar for Russia. However, they will never rebel to gain freedom." Furthermore, "both Old Europe and Russian intelligentsia have the woman-like [sic] soul," a fact that explains why "they tend to be submissive to domination and even take pleasure from it."[60] As we see in the figures we have examined in this chapter, such meditations about the supposed effeminacy of the Russian liberal intelligentsia—and the largely gestural character of an oppositional activity that masks a fascination with authority—can be equally applied to the conservative intelligentsia's rueful understanding of itself. In its gravitation toward different form of behavioral non-normativity, if not explicit self-queering, the conservative intelligentsia recognizes that it is largely superfluous in Putin's Russia, where a cult of the administrative state and resilient networks of crony capitalism have no particular need for clusters of autonomous intellectuals who can explain and justify political power to itself, or to a larger world.

CHAPTER FIVE

Statuary Performances

Monuments and Neopaganism in the United States and the Russian Federation

For [Pushkin] the power of "immobile thought" has an undeniably pagan association. It is characteristic that the statues in his poems are usually designated as *idols* (*kumiry*), and Tsar Nicholas was particularly shocked by this designation in [the narrative poem] *The Bronze Horseman*.

—ROMAN JAKOBSON, "The Statue in Pushkin's Poetic Mythology"

Nothing is worse than a Yankee telling a Southerner that his monuments don't matter.

—COREY STEWART, Virginia Republican politician, Twitter post
(later deleted), 24 April 2017

Introduction: Statuary as Story

THE FLASH-MOB THEATRICS of conservative Russian activists occupied center stage in the previous chapter: heterodox, public, and autonomous actors eager to reconcile their flamboyant internet-based activities with their advocacy of a monkish personal austerity and premodern traditionalism. We turn now to a more geopolitically minded publicity stunt in Crimea, three years after the territory was annexed by the Russian Federation.

On 3 March 2017, during a broadcast of Konstantin Malofeev's television outlet Tsargrad, the chief prosecutor of Crimea, Natalia Poklonskaya, made a startling announcement. A bust of Nicholas II, standing on a plinth in front of a church built the previous year outside the prosecutor's office complex in Simferopol, had begun to exude fragrant myrrh. "This is a miracle, which experts and scientists have been unable to explain!" she crowed. The royal family "died for us, so that Russia could blossom, and become great."[1] Chief Prosecutor Poklonskaya declared that the statue was responding to the events of the Russian Revolution almost a hundred years ago.

Although claims of icons inexplicably exuding myrrh are not uncommon, the assertion that a statue is doing so is, within the Russian religious context, very rare. Even stranger, for many reasons, is Poklonskaya's claim that the last tsar sacrificed himself for the greater glory of a future Russia. For one thing, it brackets the entire Soviet era as a time when the question of Russia's fate or "world-historical mission" was in a state of suspension. It seems that the Soviet Union was not so much opposed to the Russian empire as it was neutral about the moral character of its values. Second, the statement suggests a link between a statue's coming to life and the nation's future. The bust was installed in front of a newly built chapel, two years after the annexation of Crimea. Poklonskaya herself, officiating at the ceremony for the opening of the chapel in October 2016, stated: "This chapel will undoubtedly become the spiritual heart of the office of the public prosecutor of the Republic of Crimea." The monument to the last tsar came to life only when it was positioned in front of the chapel, for whose construction Polkonskaya had raised funds; moreover, it was "activated" by being positioned in front of a chapel on the grounds of the chief prosecutor's office in the capital city of Crimea. We are made to understand that the bust's power comes from its location within a triple frame represented by the real-estate presence of the church, the judiciary, and the administrative state, with a new national affiliation.

The location of a political monument is as important as the monument itself. The equestrian statue of Robert E. Lee that ignited the "Unite the Right" rally on 12 August 2017 was located in the courthouse district in Charlottesville; the monument to the former NKVD director Felix Dzerzhinsky in Moscow was positioned at the center of the square adjacent to the Lubyanka, the headquarters of the state security organization that he helped shape into its present-day form. As starkly different as they are in every other respect, the traditions of the Russian Orthodox Church, New England Puritanism, and southern evangelical Protestantism (today most vocally represented in the positions of the Southern Baptist Convention) all prohibit the use of religious statuary as objects of worship. In the case of antebellum architecture, this principled hostility toward graven images was carried over into the relatively unadorned style of neoclassical and Georgian building design in the southern states, to say nothing of the austere designs of churches and even wealthy residences in the North. In both the United States and Russia, partial exceptions were made for gravesites and cemeteries as places for contemplation. Bedecked with busts, vases, and angels, they served as the mental equivalent of repositories for testimonies about lives tragically cut short by the Crimean War (1853–56) and the American Civil War. The historian Drew Gilpin Faust observes that the end of the Civil War precipitated the recognition of "a new public importance for the dead," resulting in the creation of the Confederate Magnolia Cemetery in Charleston, South Carolina, and the Gettysburg National Cemetery in Pennsylvania, among others.[2] The same could be said of the impulses animating the designs of mid-nineteenth-century Russian necropolises such as the Fraternal Cemetery in Simferopol and the Sevastopol Cemetery. They too served as sites to contemplate the abattoirs that were already perceived as representing a new kind of warfare. In the Confederate cemeteries that memorialized the "defeated valor" of those who fell in the so-called War between the States, and in those cemeteries that honored the fallen heroes of the diplomatic and political disaster that was the Crimean War, the dead were ennobled by the understanding that they perished for a worthy, if perhaps misunderstood, cause. This perception was not shared by everyone involved in these conflicts.

The majority of Confederate monuments were built shortly after the end of Reconstruction (most famously the columnar monument to Robert E. Lee in New Orleans, unveiled in 1890 and removed in 2017[3]) and in two waves during the twentieth century: between the two world wars and during the Civil Rights era. The monument to General Lee in Charleston—the focus of agitation for the August 2017 "Unity the Right" rally—was unveiled with great pomp and circumstance in 1924 with the Klan in attendance, three months after the Virginia's Racial Integrity Act had been passed into law.[4] Since Dylann Roof's racially motivated massacre at the Emanuel African Methodist Episcopal Church in Charleston on 17 June 2015, 170 monuments to the Confederate cause have been removed.[5] Prior to the Russian Revolution, statues and monuments to monarchs were never objects of quasi-religious reverence in the same way that certain Soviet-era monuments were, even though the Romanov dynastic line was considered to be divinely anointed (*pomazannyi*). The Soviet monuments that inspired the most genuine grassroots reverence memorialized the fallen soldiers of World War II or the "Great Patriotic War," rather than particular political leaders—hardly surprising, given the horrific experiences of the Soviet populace and army during that war. Prior to the collapse of the Soviet Union in 1991, the near-ubiquitous presence of three- and two-dimensional representations of Lenin were the visual equivalent of tinnitus: continual yet largely unnoticed.

In her book about Trump supporters in Louisiana, frequently cited above, Arlie Russell Hochschild argues for recognizing the importance of the "deep story" of each person or community: "Politics, I argue, gathers itself around a deep story," which may be understood as "metaphor in motion." Deep stories are all about transformation; they engage in an alchemy of concretizing or "crystaliz[ing] preexisting feeling." Understood from this perspective, it is easy to see how a monument may be the most powerful expression of deep story-telling. A political monument is a lot like populism, but in the setting of urban planning: to paraphrase Jan-Werner Müller, its design conjures up an image of speaking for "real people," whom it then rules over by virtue of being positioned in front of actual seats of governmental power. Like the deep story that it refers to, a monument is as significant for its silences and gaps as it is for the testimonies that it gestures at through its design. "Every deep story," Hochschild writes, "implies an area of amnesia, non-story, non-self."[6] Like statues, deep stories are static and set, yet kinetic in the officiousness with which they maintain their core myths. They are rigid in their beliefs, which means that they are editors and cancelers (and chancellors) of the larger human experience that surrounds them. In this chapter, we consider how certain monuments serve as catalysts for transforming collectively held deep stories—which, in Hochschild's book, are those whose "least resistant personalities" make them most vulnerable to received wisdom[7]—into more personal stories that shift to block out new cognitive dissonances.

What merits particular attention are the esoteric aspects of groups' understanding of monumental animism. These features include the neo-Confederate interest in the "Celtic" origins of the Old South and Russian patriotic attempts to negotiate between the Russian Orthodox Church's stricture against statuary representation within hallowed grounds and the growing Native Belief (*Rodnoverie*) movement, which seeks to restore the practice of sanctifying totems of Slavic pagan gods. We need to listen closely to adulatory narratives about patriotic statuary while being careful not to take them at face value, or to attach outsized importance to what speakers assert about the meaning of their responses. These tales are myths projected onto monuments. They are sometimes at variance with or go against the grain of the physical characteristics and commissioned histories of the objects themselves. For all their stubborn solidity, monuments turn out to be remarkably pliable in people's minds, and the political narratives they relate may shift or find their emphases altered by being linked to an object of communal attention. As the American art critic and cultural historian Kelly Grovier puts it in an essay about the BLM-inspired removal of statues that commemorate colonialist exploiters in the US and the UK, such objects are "less about the individuals they depict than about how we see ourselves," and take on the function of self-portraits for their creators and advocates.[8]

American Authoritarian Monuments

In his landmark study of the historiographer's craft, *The Idea of History* (1946), R. G. Collingwood mounts a respectful critique of the work of A. J. Toynbee that addresses the impulse to fetishize monuments in the manner that Grovier describes. Collingwood argues that the result of Toynbee's "positivistic conception of individuality" is that the historian is understood as being "cut off from everything else by a sharp boundary" between their interior lives and the subject of their study.[9] As Collingwood sees it, the error in Toynbee's method is that there is no acknowledgement in his work of the experiential reality of the historian's craft, which is that they must "reenact" in themselves the subject that they typically regard as being foreign to them.[10] Toynbee imagines himself to be an "intelligent spectator of history, in the same way in which the scientist is the intelligent spectator of nature," which is to say that he "fails to see that the historian is an integral element in the process of history itself, reviving in himself the experiences of which he achieves historical knowledge." Like a naturalist, such a historian often imagines that they need to dissect their subject in order to understand it, which is to say that they kill it before examining it. "Just as the various parts of the process are misconceived as placed outside one another, so [in this case] the process as a whole and the historian are placed outside one another."[11] Inevitably, this fallacy about the objectivity of the positivist method renders the studied subject into a "kind of individuality possessed by a stone or any other material body."[12] We could say that the worshipers of political statuary operate in the same flawed epistemological mode that Collingwood identifies in the researcher who is unaware of the considerable weight of their own subjectivity. Here, breaching the fourth wall between observer and object privileges the life of the person over the thing, which still carries traces of its own former life.

The point is that people who revere these political monuments are engaging with them in the manner of historians who manifest a solipsism that they mistake for objectivity. In its 2019 report "Whose Heritage? Public Symbols of the Confederacy," the Southern Poverty Law Center argues that the "Confederate monuments and other symbols that dot the South" owe their existence to the "legions of Southerners [who] still cling to the myth of the Lost Cause as a noble endeavor fought to defend the region's honor and its ability to govern itself in the face of Northern aggression." This "false [historiographical] narrative is the result of many decades of revisionism in the lore and even textbooks of the South that sought to create a more acceptable version of the region's past."[13]

On the face of things, the "naturalist" targets of Collingwood's critique would seem to have little in common with neo-Confederate organizations, or with a Russian nationalist politician who attempts to leverage her portentous effusions into a transfer to the position of deputy in the state parliament. Yet here we can take note of a curious affinity among these otherwise highly disparate movements in nationalism and academic scholarship: namely, totemizing history means dismantling it. For American and Russian nationalist groups, monuments are, first and foremost, fragments of history that take on life only when they are inserted into crystallizations of feeling that exist outside the *longue durée* of actual historical processes.

It Lives! A Genealogy of American Far-Right Understandings of Political Statuary

No discussion of authoritarian statuary can proceed without acknowledging its debt to conceptions of the sublime. What the far right in the United States in particular expresses is a love of affective totems, whether material or notional. Furthermore, the US alt-right practice of rejecting epistemic frameworks has paradoxically led to a splintering of understandings about what a monument means. As the researcher Ignas Kalpokas puts it, the concept of "post-truth" that is embraced by the internet-savvy alt-right is "exactly about narratives" as "escapist fictions that allow people to suddenly feel good about themselves and the world in which they live." Kalpokas goes on to explain that post-truth is not "manipulation of some sort—it is collusion."[14] Here, we need to take into consideration the creative possibilities of collusion, stripping the term of its pejorative associations. Without realizing it, Kalpokas broaches the subject of the monumental aesthetics of online far-right selves. "Even the self becomes somewhat 'post-truth' through [its] technological extension" into "an affective digital effigy." A result of this shift into the virtual communicative realms is that "we increasingly exist more through those digital effigies of ourselves than through our physical [ones]," with "mediatised interactions replac[ing] face-to-face ones."[15]

Extending this line of reasoning into the public square, we may think of a political leader as an effective effigy that is monument in motion, a kinetic version of what Kelly Grovier would describe as the the portrait that a system of values makes of itself. Kalpokas discusses the centrality of Trump as a touchstone for the users of 4chan and 8chan. "Of course, Trump cannot be called a *leader* of Alt-Right in the traditional sense of the term." Nonetheless, "during the election campaign [he] became perfectly placed to act as a *figurehead*, an object of affective investment who suddenly helped to materialize and embody at least those features of the collective brand that were electorally relevant" [author's emphases].[16] During the Charlottesville "Unite the Right" rally on Friday night, 11 August 2017, the tiki-torch-carrying demonstrators chanted "Jews will not replace us!" or, according to some accounts, "You will not replace us!" as they marched to the monument to the Confederate general Robert E. Lee, around which they formed a protective cordon. First-hand accounts of the event differ on which of these phrases was shouted or whether both of them could be heard at different points.[17] What is important here is the protestors' identification, in the vein of projection that Grovier and Kalpokas identify, of Robert E. Lee with themselves. The identification, if not interchangeability, of "Jews" and "you" in relation to a contested public monument, protected by people wielding torches that are artifacts of the American colonial legacy in the Pacific after the Spanish-American War, points to an understanding of cultural preservation as an ongoing project of theatrical re-enactment of a cherished history, shared among those within a particular racial and gendered constituency.

The American alt-right has reached a relatively sophisticated understanding of the classic reactionary writings about monuments to white heroes, and the arguments that underpin them. One key author is the New England fantasy and horror writer H. P. Lovecraft, himself an admirer of "sublime" (as in awe-inspiring and terrifying) statuary. Lovecraft was no stranger to the white nationalist fictions about civilizational decline that decades later would populate Pierre Boule's novel *Monkey Planet* (1963) and Jean Raspail's canonically alt-right *Camp of Saints* (1973). Lovecraft's distinctive aesthetic of demonically transfigured "anti-life" is expressed most succinctly in the Edgar Allan Poe–like couplet from his imaginary grimoire, the *Necronomicon*: "That is not dead which can eternal lie / And with strange eons even death may die."[18] Critics have written insightfully about the racialist configuration of the sinister ultra-mundane gods of his often turgid fiction, in which kraken-like alien creatures are summoned forth by worshipers who are scarcely human themselves by virtue of their implied mixed lineage, as described in the short story "The Call of Cthulhu": "Void of clothing, this hybrid spawn were braying, bellowing, and writhing about a monstrous ring-shaped bonfire; in the center of which stood a great granite monolith some eight feet in height; on top of which, incongruous with its diminutiveness, rested the noxious carven statuette."[19] Significantly, the Louisiana bayou is the site of this profane observance; the story demonizes both people of color and idol-worshipping Catholics as objects of the author's graven-image-loathing Protestant rage.

Often unremarked by critics is the curious fact that such scenes also express a deeply Tory understanding of natural-law jurisprudence: a sense of the fundamental rightness of certain people submitting to their betters. Monumental crypto-deities like Cthulhu merit the adoration of their human inferiors; Joyce Carol Oates shrewdly characterizes this as the "ironic inversion of traditional religious faith" that is omnipresent in the work of a man who felt that his impeccable New England Brahmin lineage earned him the right to dominate those not of northern European background.[20] The "horror"—if that is the word—of Lovecraft's fiction is that WASP culture at the beginning of the twentieth century perceives this right to be under siege by the growing demographic of nonwhite communities and recent immigrants from southern and eastern Europe. The overripe glottal-stopped names of the prodigious monsters in Lovecraft's fiction, such as Yog-Soggoth (or Yog-Sothoth), Nyarlathotep, and Tsathoggua, hark back to his upbringing in a militantly Baptist household, where by all accounts he was intoxicated by the inventories of Semitic names in the Old Testament. Lovecraft's fellow New Englander E. P. Ingersoll was the author of the pseudo-scholarly *Lost Israel Found in the Anglo-Saxon Race* (1886), which imagines the "real" Jews as being of northern European background. In a reflex suggestive of Ingersoll's elegaic indignation about the "lost tribe of Israel," Lovecraft has divine monsters visit punishments upon a human race that has largely forgotten the essential practice of worshipping them.

The title monster of "The Call of Cthulhu" is buried on an island monument, which impresses a group of hapless sea explorers with their own puniness: they are filled with "awe at the unbelievable size of the greenish stone blocks, at the dizzying height of the great carven monolith, and at the stupefying identity of the colossal statues and the bas-reliefs" that surround it, while the vast "geometry of the place" seems completely wrong to their limited human eyes.[21] In his book-length essay *H. P. Lovecraft: Against the World, against Life* (1988), a young Michel Houellebecq observes that misanthropy is at the center of Lovecraft's fiction. As Houellebecq—himself no stranger to racialist fictions in novels such as *The Elementary Particles*—puts it, Lovecraft imagined that any intelligence "far superior" to ours would naturally regard us as little more than food, or as prey to hunt "for the sheer pleasure of killing."[22] Monuments to "great men" make great cognitive demands of us; they are intrusive, insisting on taking up our mental space.

American monuments that chime with authoritarian narratives carry with them an understanding of aesthetic appreciation in which the audience is a superfluous free rider in relation to the sublime work on display. Does that make us parasitic consumers of this consummately authoritative object? Or does such rapt aesthetic appreciation of the predator—what Lovecraft describes in a Norwegian sea-captain's actual witnessing of Cthulhu, as being "awed by the cosmic majesty" of the creature in its "monolith-crowned citadel"— facilitate the viewer's transformation into prey?[23] In 1992 bell hooks wrote that "white consumption of the dark Other has served as a catalyst for the resurgence of essentialist based racial and ethnic nationalism."[24] What we see in these monuments is both a signaling about our own insignificance and a warning that the 'otherness' of a person seduced by a monument may at times be more a matter of scale, than of racial and ethnic difference. Here, the threat or possibility of the monument eating its own serves two functions: it impresses upon its own tribe the importance of submission and hierarchy, and performs an act of unfilial ruthlessness to its own kind that also serves as a warning to racial and ethnic Others. No wonder that it is "agonizingly difficult" for those groups, as Kelly Grovier puts it, "to tolerate the persistence of memorials that venerate past masters of pain": they experience a "deep and crushingly real" outrage that comes "with having to share the streets with such hulking ghosts of oppression."

Lost Causes, Brought to Life

The Charlottesville "Unite the Right" rally, whose ostensible purpose was to defend a statue, represented an inflection point for the nativist right in both the United States and the Russian Federation. The visual cultures researcher Nicholas Mirzoeff asks us to "consider the [Charlottesville] statue in itself" as part of a fully engaged effort to de-colonize both our minds and the external spaces in which we sometimes find ourselves. He writes, "Formally, the sculp-ture evokes that of Roman emperor Marcus Aurelius, whose *Meditations* were one of the books Lee took with him to war." Of no less significance is the fact that the 1895 American edition of the *Meditations* carried a dedication to Gen-eral Lee from its British translator George Long, who described Lee as the "noble Virginia soldier, whose talents and virtue place him by the side of the best and wisest man who sat on the throne of the Imperial Caesars."[25] "Trump's defense secretary Mattis also carries the book with him," Mirzoeff notes, and "the violent polemicist Richard Spencer has even imagined Trump's regime as a new Roman Empire." Mirzoeff argues that Neo-Confederacy in particular and white nationalism in general see themselves "as embodying the legacy of Rome."[26] It is surely significant that the phrase "Southern civilization" was coined only during Reconstruction. Nothing burnishes the image of a culture as thoroughly as the valedictory implication that it was, like Gibbon's Rome, a social order that was vanquished by barbarians and weakened from within by treacherous fellow citizens. An age of crisis calls for a spiritually disciplined elite to protect it, be it a detachment of modern-day Confederates or, as mem-bers of the Russian Izborsk Club have suggested, a detachment of shock troops, like Ivan the Terrible's Oprichnina, for institutional cleansing.

Needless to say, Mirzoeff and the activist scholar and the eloquent BLM sup-porter Keeanga-Yamahtta Taylor express a view of authoritarian monumental-ism that has little in common with the reverence and the palpable experiential perspective of the monuments' defenders. The latter advocate a new devotional practice of pilgrimage centered on those graven images of marble, granite, or wood—or three-dimensional symbols smelted from iron or bronze—as living embodiments of legacies that have otherwise been legislated and litigated out of existence. The Sons of Confederate Veterans, in a policy statement portentously titled "New Orleans & Other Tragedies" (released a few months before the Charlottesville demonstration), underscored that its mission was to "protect Southern history" from the campaigns of "anarchists and Marxists."[27] For the Sons and other groups, monuments represent attempts to give the past a place at the table of the living. Reconstruction-era laws are notional or metaphorical monuments in the sense that they too endeavor to grandfather older realities into the present. Thus the so-called Black Laws perpetuated the practices of the antebellum South by stipulating, as Taylor puts it, that "Blacks could be arrested for vaguely worded or innocuous 'crimes' such as vagrancy and sentenced to 'hard labor' in slavery-like conditions for punishment."[28] A publicly displayed Confederate statue is like the legal theory of the Supreme Court Justice Antonin Scalia: a reassertion of inerrant "originalist" jurisprudence by means of city planning rather than hermeneutical casuistry.

The admirers of authoritarian statuary regard it as the inevitable suburban sprawl of ancient and biblically inspired legal codes. Certainly, the so-called Ten Commandments monument commissioned for the state Judicial Building in Montgomery in 2001 by Roy Moore, then-chief justice of the Alabama Supreme Court, serves as a material reminder of the strong metaphorical association of statuary with statutes. Yet notwithstanding these hefty biblical tropes, the aesthetic sources of Confederate public statuary tend to be drawn from cemeteries in the former slave-owning states rather than any local style of church architecture or ornamentation. It is as if the necropolis of the "War between the States" or the "Second American Revolution" (in the parlance of neo-Confederate apologists) must be permitted to occupy the public space, grizzled and mutton-chopped cheek by jowl with the statehouses that legislate in the modern era.

Groups like the Proud Boys and the League of the South navigate between cathecting onto monuments for their perceived animistic qualities and revering them as representations of tragically terminated or moribund cultural orders. They agitate for the preservation, if not restoration, of controversial monuments by underscoring what we can call statuary performativity: an aesthetic mode that foregrounds both the ponderous weightiness and the forward momentum of politicized monuments. For nativists, these monuments are ambassadors from the still-living past to the gray and joyless ghosts and zombified half-people of the present. Nothing could be more distant from this understanding of monuments than Louisiana governor Mitch Landrieu's withering assessment, in 2017, of statues of Lee, Jefferson Davis, and P. G. T.

Beauregard: that they are objects that ignore the past—specifically, the historical record of the terror of enslavement.[29] Yet there is a partial convergence of these ideas from the opposite ends of the political spectrum as well, insofar as the intensified reminder of fallen "civilizations" can take on, as Lovecraft would put it, a life of its own.

This perception of the authoritarian monument as fully alive is evident in many justifications for Confederate statuary. At the unveiling of the monument to Stonewall Jackson's horse, "Little Sorrel," in September 1997, the curator of the Richmond branch of the Virginia Historical Society attempted to communicate what he understood to be the sculpture's emblematic universalism:

> This is one of the best pieces of outdoor sculpture to be introduced to the Richmond landscape since Jean-Antonin Mercié's [Robert E.] Lee was unveiled a hundred years earlier. It's only a horse, but the sculpture can be viewed as more, as a symbol of the suffering inflicted on so many living creatures in Virginia during the Civil War. People from all ways of life were affected.[30]

This observation is peculiar from a number of perspectives. First, there is a rhetorical attempt to use the suffering of the entire animal kingdom as an entry point for understanding the travails of a particular human community: people living within the United States in the middle of the nineteenth century, slaves and white citizenry alike. Does this comparison elevate the animal to human status, or reify the status of unfree laborers as chattel? Surrounded by such politically irreconcilable constituencies as animal-rights activists, neo-Confederates, and centrist southern Democrats, the statement seems to be hedging its bets.

Second, the assertion that "it's only a horse" blurs the distinction between the representation of a creature and the creature itself, as if the public is incapable of recognizing the difference between these two very different material categories. All objects, it would seem, are implicitly alive. Third, the curator makes an implicit distinction between the animate-seeming object and its symbolic status: the statue impresses us as a living thing rather than a chunk of metal or stone while also serving as an emblem for a historical experience rather than as a representation of it. Any reflection of that experience—any attempt to project it to the observer in a way that would communicate the larger environment of exploitation and pain that surrounds the horse—seems to be taboo. Better to have a statue that reminds us of an experience in the manner of a daguerreotype from the era of the Civil War—oxidized, weathered, and compositionally balanced and clearly bordered or framed—than to have it refer to the larger moral theater of the war, and the reasons for which it was fought. The feeling that is crystalized here is one of generalized suffering. In this curator's speech, we hear several voices and note the absence of others: the plea for national and local reconciliation that was intermittently struck during Reconstruction, a passing over in silence of the horrors of slavery (what Hochschild would call the reflex of "blocking out" that is characteristic of any deep story), and a more personal bibliographer's or librarian's zeal to come into contact with the past as it participants experienced it.

It is plausible to see Little Sorrel as closely parallel to the representation of loyal slaves in pro-Confederate monuments, such as the one installed in 1914 by the United Daughters of the Confederacy in the Arlington National Cemetery in Virginia. The historian Alison M. Parker describes that monument as "featuring panels [that depicted] 'loyal' slaves and a 'mammy' figure with two white children in tow," thereby clearly "gloss[ing] over the violence and pain inflicted upon enslaved women who had their families torn apart."[31] The statue of a beast of burden also serves the felicitous purpose of representing hierarchy as innate, natural, and so widely prevalent as to seem almost devoid of political meaning. As Mirzoeff puts it in a 2017 blog post about the Charlottesville demonstration, political statuary "began its work as part of the unseen operations of enforcing consent, what Frantz Fanon called 'the aesthetics of respect for the established order.'"[32] Although Fanon was referring to practices of education and intellectual primogeniture in capitalist societies— what he called "the teaching of moral reflexes handed down from father to son, the exemplary integrity of workers decorated after fifty years of loyal and faithful service, the fostering of love for harmony and wisdom"—elsewhere in his writing he draws our attention to statuary as a expression of intimidation. In *The Wretched of the Earth*, he describes the world of French colonialism as "compartmentalized, Manichaean and petrified, a world of statues": the statue of the general incessantly reminds us of the conquest he achieved, and the one of the engineer, of the bridge he built. This is a world that is "cocksure of itself, crushing with its stoniness the backbones of those scarred by the whip."[33] "Every statue of Faidherbe or Lyautey, Bugeaud or Blandan, every one of these conquistadors ensconced on colonial soil, is a constant reminder of one and the same thing: 'We are here by the force of the bayonet.'"[34]

We will return to this dichotomy between the denial of the mimetic or representational aspect of political statuary and the perception of that same statuary as a placeholder for experience, whether as a conveniently bowdlerizing emblem or as a symbol for a historical event or even as a steppingstone for a more personal kind of reminiscence. For the time being, suffice it to say that the performative or animistic aspect of this particular kind of political statuary—

its ability to represent lost causes, noble defeats, and honorable failures—is precisely what makes its emergence as a symbol possible. Restoring, modifying, or relabeling a monument to a morally problematic cause accomplishes little in terms of any actual and necessary revisionism. If words were sufficient to impress us with the power of institutions and noble yet flawed causes, we would see a proliferation of plaques rather than statues as monuments. In 1992, as the presiding judge of Etowah County in Alabama, Roy Moore installed a wooden plaque of the Ten Commandments inscribed with burnt letters, a prelude to his later attempt to erect a monument version. This gesture, he later claimed, expressed his desire "to establish the moral foundation of our law," as if moral principles are only fully brought into being by a totemic representation of them.[35]

The metaphor of monumentalization in even nominally mainstream discussions of "law and order" has always been a prominent element of the US political vocabulary. It also serves as a prompt for individual perceptions that diverge from the larger narratives about the God-given character of the American republic. Speaking before a receptive audience of New York City police officers in 1964, with many rhetorical shoutouts to both Jim Crow and South African apartheid, William F. Buckley Jr., whose mother came from a slave-owning family in South Carolina, stated: "My friends, we are in a world in which law and order are disintegrating," and in which "the wrath of the unruly falls with special focus on the symbols of authority, of continuity, of tradition."[36] The 1924 dedication ceremony for the equestrian statue of Robert E. Lee in Charlottesville was organized by the local chapters of the KKK and "the Confederate Veterans, Sons of Confederate Veterans, and the United Daughters of the Confederacy." One attendee wondered aloud if the base of the monument was large enough to anchor and stabilize the statue. The main speaker acknowledged that this was a legitimate concern but explained that they "let it stay that way," since "the planet as a pedestal would be too small for Robert Edward Lee."[37] As W. E. B. DuBois wrote in 1926: "Whiteness is ownership of the earth for ever and ever, amen."[38] One might think that this "lost cause" understanding of statuary projects a view of the world as inhabited not so much by people as by essences. The cause that was thought dead still strives to impress skeptical viewers with an understanding of both their puniness and their agentive passivity, whether it be hero-worshippers who identify with the cause that the statue represents, or those whose existence (as racial or ethnic others) are threatened by it. In both cases, however, the status differential between spectator and statue is understood to be utterly asymmetrical.

This constellation of ideas about the living or charismatic impersonality of such monuments, in which they are highly kinetic yet distinctly or transcendently nonhuman, is a theme of much writing among apologists for the far right in both the United States and the Russian Federation. In an interview with the alt-right blogger Lana Lokteff on "Red Ice Radio," Cody Wilson (the creator of the alt-right crowdfunding site Hatreon) opined about the proposed removal of monuments to the Confederacy:

> There's this recriminative view of history that all narratives that are not consistent with modernity, the narrative of progress—both ethical and material popular progress—all narratives that don't align with that narrative must be whitewashed. It's not just enough to say that it's untrue, the Lost Cause narrative of the South. It's important to eradicate its symbolic heritage and its thought because it's a threat to the progress of history. And so when I see the elimination of a symbol, right [sic] the elimination—I'm not just sympathizing with southern white racists—I'm basically recognizing a dangerous mode of post-politics: the need to eradicate a historical narrative. Not just the need to combat it, the need to make sure that its symbols are gone, the way to articulate it is gone.[39]

At the forefront of Wilson's statement is the conceit that symbols are living and expressive entities. It's not just a monument we're talking about here, he seems to be saying: it's a way of thinking and living, if not being, in the world. His sentiment hinges on an unarticulated assumption about the tragic destruction of the southern agrarian way of life by the ascendant industrial capitalism of the northern states. This version of history has been drawn without acknowledgment by alt-right and conservative political theorists like Patrick Deneen from the crypto-Confederate anthology *I'll Take My Stand: The South and the Agrarian Tradition* (1930). In alt-right and alt-light spokespeople like Wilson we see glimmers of a quasi-Luddite critique of capitalism and an animus against neoliberal progress that could, in principle, dovetail with the damning narrative about the commodification of labor that Marx outlines in *Das Kapital.*

None of these paradoxes and droll correspondences were lost on the Russian American Lokteff, whose own political orientation of gender-role traditionalism and blood-and-soil white nationalism notionally opposes alienating and demeaning forms of postindustrial labor. Writing about the experience of interviewing Lokteff for her book *Sisters in Hate: American Women on the Front Lines of White Nationalism* (2020),[40] Seyward Darby reflected about the extent to which "surfaces are everything" in white nationalism, dictating how "how people look, how history seems, how the future might be." Yet those surfaces are also a barrier to understanding, and are undergirded by an enormous assemblage of unspoken or only partly articulated premises. Those premises function like the blocked-out areas, or moral silences, that accompany the deep stories in Hochschild's book. As Darby writes, the ideology of Lokteff and others in the alt-right is a "mosaic"; we need to regard it as a mass of broken tiles, sometimes selected because they fit in easily with the others. "The result is a coherence wrought from chaos, and people see the whole before they see the parts. Sometimes they don't care to see the parts at all."[41]

Political Statuary in Russia as Idolatry of the Administrative State

Standing in direct opposition to the artistic deification of authoritarian figures is the aesthetic of viewing such attempts at material immortalization as evidence of civilizational decline. *Taurus* (2001) is Aleksandr Sokurov's antihagiographic film about Lenin, the second in a trilogy about the moral corruption of authoritarian nation-states. (*Moloch* [1999] is about Hitler; *The Sun* (2005), about Emperor Hirohito.) The iconoclastic Russian filmmaker suggests that political power inevitably kills and petrifies the values it claims to implement and celebrate. The relative immobility of the convalescing Lenin in Sokurov's film evokes the concretization as well as the desiccation of the ideals that his regime purported to express, as if those values had already become mummified in the final weeks of his life. With deliberately arthritic camera movements, Sokurov gives us a fey and addled Lenin (performed with a disarming yet shrewd guilelessness by Leonid Mozgovoi), who seems to wear a frozen grimace of puerile good humor. The director invites the Russian audience into the space of an aging acquaintance, to experience the shocked recognition of the passage of time. The film is a testimony to what the novelist Vladimir Sorokin would characterize, fourteen years later, in a political essay, as the cognitive reality of hundreds of statues of "Lenin, Stalin, and their bloody associates" standing "not only on Russia's squares and plazas, but [also] in the minds of its citizens."[42]

Certainly, in many of the Soviet-era monuments in Moscow, such as the massive one to Lenin that still stands by the October Metro station or the one to Dzerzhinsky that was removed in 1991, we have a vivid sense of bodies protected by the reinforced folds of their voluminous coats, as if they are wearing their tombs like armor. As the art historian Albert Boime puts it, most monuments to Lenin, Stalin, and Dzerzhinsky are "concealed beneath long heavy coats that transform them into heavy columnar objects," producing the impression that the leader is "divested of individual or personal characteristics and [is] transformed and deified."[43] But perhaps what is being deified here is not the person but death itself, as Lovecraft suggests. Unveiled in 1958, two years after the suppression of the Hungarian uprising, the fast-tracking of the monument's design (by Evgeny Vuchetich) and construction was intended as a reminder of the uncompromising character of Soviet hegemony. The fact that it was unveiled during the Thaw only highlighted its function as an expression of a legacy of intimidation and death, that would not die.

Russian nationalists manifest a range of seemingly contradictory attitudes toward monuments to their political heroes or ancestors. Conservative hard-right activists in both countries perceive those monuments as dead bodies that continue to give off a phosphorescent glow. Kathleen Verdery, in *The Political Lives of Dead Bodies: Reburial and Postsocialist Change* (1999), characterizes that glow as a belief in the miraculous durability of dearly held values: "By arresting the process of that person's bodily decay, a statue alters the temporality associated with the person, bringing him into the realm of the timeless or the sacred, like an icon." No wonder, then, that the act of "desecrating a statue partakes of the larger history of iconoclasm."[44] On the other hand, memorialization in metal or stone abets what Elaine Scarry, in *The Body in Pain: The Making and Unmaking of the World* (1985), describes as a decisive practice of anti-mourning that rehabilitates misunderstood, morally ambiguous, or "lost" causes by rhetorically re-enacting them. Scarry argues that a crafted object like a monument is nothing more than an artifact whose purpose is "to enter into and itself elicit social responsiveness," reminding its audience—that is, its consumers—that the process of making it was always "a social act."[45] In this view—which is quite distinct from Verdery's—monuments are embodiments of the dead, rather than the still-living: here, the only hale and hearty life we see comes from the sparks that fly from the collision of the quick with the dead, of the audience with the art. Or, more precisely: life is the jolt of added energy that the living receive from their contact with the dead, who are more alive than they are. The fact that the subjective experience of mourning is invariably personal creates a cleavage between collective acts of mourning that are often ceremonial in nature (such as the Remembrance Day observances that Scarry mentions, which commemorate the Great War) and individuals' meditations about their loved ones or ancestors.

The observations of the Russian fiction author and essayist Vladimir Sorokin help to illuminate this paradoxical notion that history gains meaning only through the encysting or visible extrusion of one of its parts. Sorokin was transfixed by the idea of Soviet-era collective consciousness as an expression of the alienation and atomization of the individual, rather than their transcendence through incorporation in public rituals:

> The collective body ritualized itself in queues. It was taught order and obedi-
> ence, and rendered maximally governable. At mass demonstrations, show trials,
> [Communist] Party congresses, and soccer games the collective body was allowed

to express the orgiastic side of its nature: it applauded stormily and raged, it shuddered with countless orgasms. But on ordinary workdays the line awaited it. Gray and boring, but inescapable, the line dissected the body into pieces, pacified and disciplined it, gave people time to think about the advantages of socialism and about class struggle; and in the end they were rewarded with food and goods.[46]

Sorokin's explication of the lived reality of the queue is interesting for a number of reasons, not least for its underscoring of the fact that corporate identity dissects and diminishes the body of the person who joins it, as if the integrity of the individual body exists in an inverse relation to that of the collective. He explores and clarifies this formula in greater detail in "Let the Past Collapse on Time!" an essay written five years later, shortly after the annexation of Crimea. In a characteristic and revealing euphemism, many Russian political commentators referred to the annexation of the peninsula that was considered a part of Ukraine from 1954 to 2014 as a "joining" (*prisoedinenie*) or "return" (*vozvrashchenie*) of the territory to the Russian Federation, as if the process was more like regrowing a phantom limb than the incorporation of a distinct territory whose borders had been agreed upon by all the countries in the region shortly after the collapse of the Soviet Union.

What particularly interested Sorokin in 2014 was an incident he witnessed during the month of the Soviet collapse:

> In the course of three days in August 1991, during the failed putsch against Gorbachev, the decaying Soviet empire tottered and began to collapse. Some friends and I found ourselves on Lubianskaya Square, across from the headquarters of the fearsome, mighty KGB. A huge crowd was preparing to topple the symbol of that sinister institution—the statue of its founder, Dzerzhinsky, "Iron Felix," as his Bolshevik comrades-in-arms called him. A few daredevils had scaled the monument and wrapped cables around its neck, and a group was pulling on them to ever louder shouts and cries from the assembled throng.
>
> Suddenly, a Yeltsin associate with a megaphone appeared out of the blue and directed everyone to hold off, because, he said, when the bronze statue fell, "its head might crash through the pavement and damage important underground communications." The man said that a crane was already on its way to remove Dzerzhinsky from the pedestal without any damaging side effects. The revolutionary crowd waited for this crane a good two hours, keeping its spirits up with shouts of "Down with the KGB!"[47]

What relevance, we might ask, does this event have to the Russian annexation of Crimea? Sorokin explains:

The swift dismantling of remaining Soviet monuments recently in Ukraine caused me to remember the Dzerzhinsky episode. Dozens of statues of Lenin fell in Ukrainian cities; no one in the opposition asked people to treat them "in a civilized manner," because in this case a "polite" dismantling could mean only one thing—conserving a potent symbol of Soviet power. "Dzhugashvili [Stalin] is there, preserved in a jar," as the poet Joseph Brodsky wrote in 1968. This jar is the people's memory, its collective unconscious.[48]

The detail that is of central importance here is the quaint solicitude of the Yeltsin-led municipal authorities for a widely reviled public monument. This delicacy of feeling was completely absent from the Ukrainians of the Maidan independence movement, which did not hesitate to topple and rip to pieces the numerous Soviet-era statues of Lenin that dotted their own country. Sorokin's point about the reluctance of Russians to let go of their Lenin totems, in contrast with the widespread "Lenin Fall" (*Leninopad*) in Ukraine, is borne out by recent statistics. In 2019, of the 7,000 monuments that had been erected in the Russian Republic of the Soviet Union in 1991, 6,000 remained; out of the 5,500 in Ukraine during the Soviet era, 350 were still standing.[49] "Doubts about the success of the coming anti-Soviet revolution first stirred in me during those two hours," Sorokin writes. "I tried to imagine the Parisian crowd, on May 16, 1871, waiting politely for an architect and workers to remove the Vendôme Column. And I laughed." The eventual arrival of the crane, and the placing of "Dzerzhinsky" on a truck that drove away as "people ran alongside and spat on him," did nothing to dispel Sorokin's uneasy impression that all of this was more expressive of a backtracked revolution than a genuine and decisive rebellion. In a 2008 interview, six years before Maidan, his recalled his impressions on that day as hopeful but frustrated. Waiting for the crane, "doubts began to creep into my mind that this was really a revolution." Yet "all the same, it was all very pleasant."[50]

This account is distinctly Sorokin's, that of someone who uses a literary and globally political frame of reference to understand the events of that day. His awareness of his positionality as a literate witness to the monument's removal is palpable: among other things, he associates the day with the trajectory of his career as a writer and as the subject of scholarly research. The sole photograph of his vigil on Lubyanka Square that day was taken by the renowned specialist on modern Russian literature Catharine Nepomnyashchy, and it shows him standing next to Jamey Gambrell, the American translator of his work. Eight years later, Sorokin would use Lubyanka Square in his dystopian novel, *The Day of the Oprichnik*, as the location for a monument to Maliuta Skuratov, the leader of Ivan the Terrible's state police force.[51] Looking at the removal of

Vladimir Sorokin and Jamey Gambrell at the time of the failed putsch against
Mikhail Gorbachev, Moscow, August 1991. Photo by Catharine Nepomnyashchy.

the statue of Dzerzhinsky, Sorokin sees a history that is not aware that it is
caught up in a process of regression. His description of the departing truck
imparts a vividly pictorial form to his description of the reflex toward revanch-
ism, as if we were witnessing the rewinding of the events of the French Revolution: instead of the tumbrels bringing the condemned to the guillotine, we see
the wagons taking them away, fully resurrected, and with their heads neatly
reattached.

   "We should have toppled the iron idol even if its head did crash through the
pavement and damage 'important underground communications,'" Sorokin
bluntly asserts toward the end of the essay.[52] Among other insights, he shrewdly
hints that a fixation on totems of authority was reawakened during that spec-
tacular time of change, with the stubbornly conservative discursive realm re-
emerging in the form of a new political underground. The removal of the
Dzerzhinsky monument in a manner that was more like a public hanging than
an expression of iconoclastic zeal points to the parodic aspect of the event,
as if the mob were acknowledging its ambivalence toward its own revolutionary desires.[53] If, as Corey Robin once observed, "Conservatism has always
been a wilder and more extravagant movement than many realize—and it is
precisely this wildness and extravagance that has been one of the sources of its
continuing appeal," then we perhaps need to view the removal as expressing a
sheepish but theatricalized show of respect for a public symbol of authority.[54]

Statue-breaking and statue-removal are, after all, very different acts: one opts for demolition; the other, for de facto preservation.[55]

The aesthetics of the political statuary that mourns the Confederate cause are relatively clear, simulating an arresting animacy while reinforcing a symbolic value that gestures to eschatological causes, in ways that were not always evident to the city planners, architects, and sculptors who designed them. This model seems much less applicable to Russian and Soviet-era public monuments. Indeed, we need to be careful about appropriating the American alt-right's solipsistic fascination with certain monuments into the metaphysical paradigm that we detect in Sorokin's essay. Sorokin characterizes political statuary for Russian nationalists as, first and foremost, a symbol that is itself alive. "Russian bureaucrats," he writes, "understand that their beloved *homo sovieticus* crumbled along with Lenin"; they are mortified at the destruction of monuments to him for the simple reason that those artifacts represented a full embodiment of a particular understanding of Russian history, if not of Russia itself. "'They are destroying monuments to Lenin because he personifies Russia!' one politician exclaimed." Sorokin notes: "It is telling that pro-Russian demonstrations in Crimea and eastern parts of Ukraine [in 2014] invariably took place next to statues of Lenin."[56] The heavy columnar sculpture of Dzerzhinsky on Lubyanka Square and the numerous statues of Lenin (arm extended with cap in hand or palm open in an ambiguous gesture of greeting, taunt, or rallying encouragement) that still stand in many public spaces in the Russian Federation suggest obelisks or plinths poised to ascend Sputnik-like to the sky, or perhaps to tumble dramatically, mosh-pit style, into the surrounding crowd. Unlike the Confederate statuary adored by groups like the Proud Boys, these monuments were built with belligerence and provocation already firmly in mind.[57] They themselves are weapons, plowshares that have been beaten into swords.

Political Statuary and the East Slavic Pagan Legacy

Any discussion of the veneration of statuary in Russian culture inevitably bumps up against its seeming prohibition in East Slavic Christian Orthodoxy and against Alexander Pushkin's narrative poem *The Bronze Horseman* (1833), the first work of golden-age Russian literature to confront monuments as religiously sublimated objects of political idolatry. *The Bronze Horseman* has been required reading in Russian secondary schools since the end of the Second World War and has significantly contributed to the political vocabulary of discussions about the relationship between the individual and the untrammeled state.

The historiography that Pushkin drew on for the poem's subtexts is important for our discussion. In the so-called Primary Chronicle, the oldest extant chronicle of Russian history (most likely first compiled in the twelfth century), the Christianization of Kievan Rus is presented as a deliberately histrionic public renunciation of Slavic paganism. After his baptism in the city of Kherson, Prince Vladimir set off for the capital city. Upon arrival, he ordered that "the idols should be overthrown and that some should be cut to pieces and others burned with fire" (Old Russian *drugiia ognevi predati*: literally, "consigned to fire," possibly thrown into a bonfire). But Vladimir had a particularly theatrical punishment in mind for the statue of Perun, the god of lightning, thunder, and the sky. Perun is a Slavic offshoot of the Lithuanian pagan deity Perkunas, and the etymological source for the modern Polish word for thunderbolt (*piorun*); the figure roughly corresponds to Zeus and Odin/Wotan in the Hellenic and Germanic pagan traditions, and to Elijah, the bearer of fire from heaven (1 Kings 18:38), in the Judeo-Christian one. Vladimir ordered that Perun be removed from the hilltop temple that housed the statues of the entire Slavic pantheon, and that it be "bound to a horse's tail" and dragged to the bank of the Dnieper River. There, twelve men were "appointed . . . to beat the idol with sticks, not because [Prince Vladimir] thought that the wood was sensitive, but to affront the demon who had deceived men in this guise, that he might receive chastisement at the hands of men." The chronicler subsequently propels the account forward with a curious sequence of theological exhortations and arrestingly specific and concrete details:

> Great art thou, O Lord, and marvelous are thy works! Yesterday [Perun] was honored of men, but today held in derision. While the idol was being dragged along the stream [of the Borichev] to the Dnieper, the unbelievers wept over it, for they had not yet received Holy Baptism. After they had thus dragged it along, they cast it into the Dnieper. But Vladimir had given his injunction: "If it halts anywhere, then push it out from the bank, until it goes over the falls. Then let it loose." His command was duly obeyed. When the men let the idol go, and it passed through the falls, the wind cast it out on the bank, which since that time has been called Perun's Bank, a name that it bears to this very day.[58]

The account of Christianization ends with Vladimir ordaining that the Church of St. Basil be built on the hill where the idol of Perun and the other images had been set, and where the prince and the people had "offered their sacrifices" during the pre-Christian era (Old Russian: *idezhe stoiashe kumir-Perun i prochii, idezhe tvoriakhu potre by kniaz' i liud'e*: literally, "where the Perun idol and others had formerly stood, and where the prince and his people used to offer sacrifices").[59]

Numerous scholars have taken note of the strong traces of "double belief" (*dvoeverie*) in this account, as if the chronicler was acknowledging Vladimir's political shrewdness in easing the local population's traumatic transition from pagan religious practices into Christianity. The particular tradition of Christianity that the Byzantine missionaries practiced was radically different from Slavic paganism in abjuring any perception of innate animism in objects made of natural substances such as wood or stone. The purported relics of the cross on which Christ died and the stone in Rome on which St. Peter established the original temple of Christendom cannot be said to represent true exceptions to this principled difference between Byzantine Christianity and what we know of Slavic paganism or indigenous faith; those objects were not regarded as animate but were understood to be enhanced or sanctified by the Holy Spirit, and by the Christianized people who had touched them.

Everything in the Primary Chronicle's narrative of the Christianization of Rus'—which, as historians have long argued, reflects national mythmaking more than it does actual events—points to a lingering perception of the wooden idol that represents Perun as somehow still alive: its beating, the wind (an element controlled by the deity) that carries it over the falls, and even the parallel verbs in the coda-like reminiscence about how the idols and the prince and his people stood, in pre-Christian time, in the space that is now occupied by the Church of St. Basil.[60] Furthermore, Vladimir's injunction of collective conversion in Kyiv is preceded by a curious detail about his own baptism in Kherson, where he "found and appropriated two bronze statues and four bronze horses, which now stand behind the Church of the Holy Virgin, and which the ignorant think [*mniat*, 'fancy,' 'imagine'] are made of marble [*mramaiany sut*: literally, 'are marble']." One especially salient point in the Old Russian text is that the chronicler regards the failings of the benighted pagan Slavs as cognitive as well as moral: they are unable to identify the material from which the four bronze horses are made, imagining that the statues are carved rather than smelted and cast. In other words, by emphasizing the significance of pre-existing material over a medium that is the result of a deliberate process of production, they minimize or offset the role of human agency in the shaping of statuary.

The Gaze of Cold Command:
The Pagan Subtext of Pushkin's *The Bronze Horseman*

As Roman Jakobson has shown, the image of the statue or monument in the poetry of Alexander Pushkin (1779–1837) is closely associated with the oppressive power of the Russian state and its surveillance over its citizens. Jakobson argues that one result of the years that he spent as a boy in the royal Lyceum outside St. Petersburg was an inability to shake off a sense of foreboding in the districts of the Russian countryside that were profusely decorated with statues.[61] The tableau of the sculptural monument as a demonic state deity capable of piercing sight or surveillance also appears in *The Bronze Horseman*. Its protagonist, Evgeny, is rendered homeless and traumatized by the catastrophic flooding of the city, built at sea level by a monarch intent on establishing a powerful maritime empire. Down the midnight streets of St. Petersburg, he is chased by Étienne-Maurice Falconet's statue of Peter the Great, who glares relentlessly at his prey. The poem is, among other things, a meditation on the lives of forgotten people, who in nineteenth-century Russian literature came to be known as superfluous or unneeded (*lishnie*) people, living hand to mouth in the capital city of the world's largest country.

The poem's protagonist is a striving and indigent outcast who becomes tragically caught up in the consequences of bad decisions by the state. One of those decisions, it is suggested, is a foundational one: Peter the Great's determination, at the beginning of the eighteenth century, to hastily build a new capital city on the choppy waters of the Gulf of Finland. The poem begins with a prologue in which we gain access to that monarch's portentous musings: "Upon a shore of desolate waves / Stood *he*, with lofty musings grave / And gazed afar" onto the river and the "marshy, moss-grown bank," where only the presence of a "Finn's poor shelter" and a few other huts disturb the view of a pristine environment.[62] Decades later, the low-level government clerk Evgeny is nothing more than a metal shaving caught up in the magnetic field of the power represented by the statue of Peter the Great. Over the course of the poem, Pushkin shrewdly establishes a series of character traits that the protagonist shares with Peter himself, including a keen intelligence, acute observational skills, and a vivid imagination. Peter is a kind of poet who is privileged with prodigious institutional power and can create structures of thought in the air; Evgeny visualizes his borderline poverty and prospects for advancement in an unnamed government office in a "poetlike" manner, as he exhales a sigh and "falls musing on his lot."[63] One of the potent suggestions that emerges in *The Bronze Horsemen* is that the tsar and the clerk are cognitively equal. The "punishment" for the contemplation of such a leveling possibility—namely, that hierarchy is an artificial construct and has little to do with natural law—is, for Evgeny and the reader, witnessing the vengeance wrought by a monument representing the cruel power of the enhanced bureaucratic state that resulted from Peter's reforms.

The confrontation between monument and man in Pushkin's poem is an allegory for rebellion against divinized existing orders. In her book *Pushkin's Historical Imagination*, Svetlana Evdokimova persuasively argues that the parallel between the figure of Peter and the pagan idol, and the identification of the city itself with the monarch who founded it, is quite palpable in the poem: "And

Petropolis waded, like Triton / Up to its waist in water."[64] The reference to a mythological figure from Greco-Roman antiquity has the effect of opening a side door onto the cultural imaginary of Pushkin's educated audience, who would have known the details of the Primary Chronicle's account of the Christianization of Rus' from Nikolai Karamzin's twelve-volume *History of the Russian State* (*Istoriia gosudarstva rossiiskogo*, 1818–26). Tsar Nicholas I was an admirer of Karamzin's *History*, primarily because he understood it as an eloquently written brief for the sanctity of the Russian state from its very founding in Kyiv. The distinctive reference to a Greek variant of the city's name, together with the identification of Petersburg with a god from pre-Christian antiquity, tells us that this narrative will be about the return of a set of repressed values. St. Petersburg was a city teeming with neoclassical statuary on its buildings and bridges. This was not lost on Pushkin's contemporary Nikolai Gogol, whose interest in Eastern Orthodox theology resulted in a keen appreciation of the church's stricture against three-dimensional graven images depicting religious subject matter. In his essay "Skul'ptura, zhivopis, i muzyka" (Sculpture, painting, and music), published two years after Pushkin's poem, Gogol writes about sculpture as a means to experience voluptuous joy without raising moral qualms in a Christian conscience: "It's useless [to illustrate] the great achievements of Christianity" through the medium of sculpture, which has "separated itself" from Christianity, just as the entire world of paganism has.[65]

Evdokimova points out that Pushkin's description of the bronze monument in the poem all but explicitly references the description of the statue of Perun in the Primary Chronicle. Repeated locutions in the text contain etymological derivations of the word for storm (*groza*), a natural element closely identified with the pagan deity. "In the main draft of the poem," she writes, there are any number of expressions "etymologically or semantically" related to "the idea of a storm: 'the idol on the bronze horse' appears 'threatening with his immobile arm (*grozia nedvizhnoiu rukoiu*),'" and in one variant draft Pushkin supplements that phrase with the arresting oxymoronic locution "in the stormy silence (*v groznoi tishine*)."[66]

The Slavic pagan subtext is reinforced by other details in the poem, and by the physical composition of the statue. Evdokimova also draws attention to the significance of the serpent under the bronze horse's hoof as a reference to the perpetual duel between Perun and his nemesis, Veles, the deity of cattle and livestock, who is variously characterized in Slavic native belief as a bear, wolf, or snake.[67] The drowned wife of the poem's protagonist is named Parasha, which is a diminutive form of Paraskeva, a saint's name. Even in Pushkin's time, St. Paraskeva was widely recognized as a Christianized sublimation of the deity Mokosh (literally, "the wet one"), a goddess of fertility who was an embodiment of the animist concept of "Moist Mother Earth" (*mati syra zem-lya*), which Dostoevsky references in *Crime and Punishment* through Sonya's speech about the need for penitence before the sacred soil.[68]

Not extensively commented upon by Evdokimova and other Pushkin scholars is another subtext: the story of Prince Vladimir's appropriation of the four bronze equestrian statues in the city of Kherson, as told in the Primary Chronicle. In his *History of the Russian State*, Karamzin himself seemed at a loss to explain the special attention to this detail in the eleventh-century account, seeing in it nothing more than evidence of what he clearly assumes is the prince's love for the arts (*v znak liubvi svoei k khudozhestvam*).[69] It would seem that the eponymous monument of Pushkin's poem is meant to provoke a reflection about the magical thinking that figures of authority seek to impress upon their subjects, and to remind us that illusions are made by people rather than by gods. For the custodians of state mythologies, contempt for such monuments can be nothing other than, first, an expression of principled rebellion, and, second, a withering aesthetic assessment.

Pushkin wrote the poem in part as a meditation on the abortive Decembrist revolt that took place eight years earlier, in 1825, on Senate Square, where Falconet's statue of Peter the Great is located. Pushkin's friends and acquaintances in the revolt congregated not in front of the Winter Palace but around the already oxidized monument to the city's founder, because they understood that the staging of their rebellion would be, in symbolic terms, more powerful there. In his book about Falconet's fifteen years of labor on the monument, which Catherine the Great commissioned, Alexander Schenker provides a vivid sense of the ways in which the monument served as an operational catalyst for the poem:

> The monument is at its most dramatic when viewed from the left, that is, the Senate side. . . . With the tsar looking away from the viewer and the snake totally out of sight, it is the horse that commands the viewer's attention. As one approaches the monument from the left-front side, the pedestal eclipses the hind legs of the horse and overwhelms the figure of the tsar. With the forelegs thrust ahead, the massive frame of the horse seems to be taking flight.
>
> The closer one is to the front of the pedestal, the more oppressive are the hooves suspended above the viewer and the more immediate is their menacing outline. That is the angle from which the Russian viewer, whose eyes will always be below the hooves of the tsar's horse, senses most clearly the contrast between the ruler's exalted position and his own lowly status.
>
> That also must have been the spot from which Evgeny, humble foil to Peter the Great in Pushkin's *The Bronze Horseman*, looked up at the statue and through

clenched teeth mumbled his deprecations against the "marvel-working builder," towering above him.[70]

Although Schenker does not comment here about the impression that the monument made, from this vantage point, upon the participants in the Decembrist revolt—which was sparked by the prospect of the ascent to the throne of the notoriously reactionary Nicholas I—we see quite clearly how Pushkin used the poem's horrific details about the persecuting equestrian figure's piercing gaze and raised hooves, as a means for contemplating the uses to which political statuary is put. We may think of the poem as a prescient critique of authoritarian sublimations of religiously inflected animism and idolatry—the ones we hear in the defenses of Confederate monuments as crystallizations of a deep story that justifies social control and surveillance in the name of devotional humility and submission.

Post-Soviet Nationalists and Paganists Go to War with Statues

Pushkin's poem is highly relevant in the present context for the way in which it articulates a cynical weariness that, arguably, continues to characterize Russian responses to political statuary. Defenses of the restoration of Soviet-era monuments like the one to Dzerzhinsky rely on the same language and the same invocation of the Crusades that often characterize neo-Confederate arguments: the individuals in question were fighting for a noble if misunderstood cause, they were "knights" (Russian *rytsari*). For the most part, those arguments do not play a central role in Russian nationalist causes and movements, such as the Alexander Dugin–affiliated Izborsk Club, because their members do not regard such monuments as being in any way holy.[71]

The patently mythopoeic analogy between the removal of Dzerzhinsky's statue in front of the Lubyanka and the deposing and destruction of the quasi-animate statue of Perun in the Primary Chronicle elicited surprisingly little acknowledgment in the Russian-language press in 1991. When the parallel was directly named, in a 2015 article in the *Novaya gazeta*, it was in reference to the Maidan demonstrations for full Ukrainian sovereignty, held in Kyiv the previous year, with the October 1917 revolution being called the Maidan of its day.[72] The re-emergence of the pagan Slavic legacy into the discussion of political statuary inevitably raises questions about the raised public profile of contemporary "Native Faith" (*Rodnoverie*) movements within the Russian Federation, Ukraine, and Belarus. *Rodnovery* fought on both sides in the Donbas conflict and have been especially active in the Azov Battalion. The battalion's nationalist sympathies are well known, and in 2016 a detachment of the group defaced the statue of St. Vladimir in Kyiv because they identified it with the "aggressor nation," even though, among Ukrainian nationalists, the figure of Vladimir ("Volodymyr" in Ukraine) generally enjoys the status of the founder or forerunner of the modern Ukrainian state. Members of the battalion are known to have established a pagan temple with a statue of Perun in the Mariupol area in Donetsk, which pagan "wizards" from different parts of Ukraine have visited, bringing provisions for the militia.[73] Syncretic variations are numerous, and unregistered believer communities draw on religious traditions as varied as the shamanistic practices of indigenous peoples, Hinduism, and Nationalist Socialist occultism, so assessing the number of adherents to *Rodnoverie* in the Russian Federation is extraordinarily difficult. Some adherents are nationalistic, while others emphasize an egalitarian flexibility in the practice of their beliefs; some groups are patriotic and support the domestic and foreign policies of the executive branch of the current Russian government, while others are principled environmentalists and, in a few cases, outspoken critics of the outsized political influence of the Russian Orthodox Church. There is one notion, or ethnographic myth, that seems to unify all groups and associations of Slavic Native Faith: they firmly believe in the importance of racial identity and rarely admit into their numbers anyone who is not a native Slav.

In terms of documents and even oral narrative traditions, there is surprisingly little extant information about the cosmology of Slavic paganism. As Andrei Sinyavsky points out, the "Olympus" of Slavic paganism seems remarkably thin, is largely incomprehensible, and appears to have had a dizzying range of regional variations. "The Eastern Slavic [pagan] religion was extremely amorphous," Sinyavsky writes, "picking up deities as it went along."[74] The most thorough researchers of *Rodnoverie*, such as Marlène Laruelle, Kaarina Aitamurto, and Viktor Shnirelman, categorize it as a "new religious movement," which is to say that its uncodified and liturgically open-ended character makes it dynamically responsive to the affective needs of individuals who often don't consider it to be a religion.[75] Aitamurto writes that for *rodnovery*, "nature is considered more enchanting [than buildings]; instead of tourist attractions that follow the tradition of European buildings, the Russian landscape in its most traditional—and peripheral—form is preferred."[76] For most Rodnovers, statuary representations of Perun in particular are considered essential to religious practice, although some priests (or wizards) in the movement consider totems made from wood to be a sacrilege against the natural world and therefore favor stone as the medium for carving. (The self-appointed native magus and open National Socialism sympathizer Aleksei Dobrovolskii [Dobroslav], who died in 2013, held this view.) Equality in *Rodnoverie* stems from the perception of the wizard at the center of the ceremonial circle as primarily a facilitator. There is no equality, however, between the worshiper and the totemic sculpture of the deity. That figure, as a metonym for the natural world, demands complete submission. What is relevant to our discussion here is the sense that the monument does not simply represent authority; it *is* authority.

It is precisely this tendency to fetishize objects as doxologically immanent that has evoked a strongly negative response among Russian nationalist political figures and commentators. In an email response to this author, the writer Valery Averianov of the Izborsk Club called *Rodnoverie* "a shoddy reconstruction" that has no viable claim to authenticity: "From a functional point of view, it's a rather harmful [social] phenomenon, the goal of which is to undermine the Christian foundation of Russian civilization." Averianov goes on to say that the development of *Rodnoverie* was, in part, provoked by Sovietologists and intelligence agencies in the West, that its manifestations prior to the Revolution were sporadic and isolated, and that its practice during the Soviet period was mostly theoretical.[77]

These concerns about the adulteration of Russian religious identity are not shared by Alexander Prokhanov, the founder of the Izborsk Club and controversial originator of the QAnon-like conspiracy theory known as the "Dulles Plan." (This theory claims, among other things, that Stalin was poisoned by American spies in his inner circle.) In an interview with a colleague, Prokhanov argued for a synthesis of paganism and Eastern Orthodoxy to form a new understanding of "Russianness" in which Lenin himself would be seen as a pre-eminently Christian figure. "All of ancient pagan mythology, all of ethical religious Russian mythology" was evident in Lenin himself, Prokhanov gushed. Taking a thoughtful turn, he mused that "it would be interesting to trace how such mythologies could be realized by Leninism in practice."[78] The title of Prokhanov's interview, "Lightning Lenin" ("*Molniia-Lenin*"), reveals how far the militantly conservative intelligentsia in the Russian Federation today is willing to go to court non-Christian nativist constituencies who see Russian religious identity purely in racial terms. The title is both a pun on a make of Soviet-era pocket watches that had Lenin's face engraved on them and the image of Perun, the master of the Slavic pagan pantheon, who was the wielder of thunder and lightning. An overripe cultural chauvinism is audible throughout the interview and, it must be added, highly characteristic of Prokhanov's activity. In this context the earnest caveat of Prokhanov's interviewee, the theater director turned nationalist agitator Sergei Kurginyan, that Russianness is a state of mind rather than a distinct ethnic identity, seems like an afterthought.[79]

Conclusion: The Convergence of the Twain

Even among the most pro-Soviet nationalists, we rarely find the veneration of the monument or plinth as a type of gravestone that appears in neo-Confederate apologetics. And, as we have seen, even in the American context those apologetics leave room for personal variations that create fissures across the deep story without necessarily undermining it or calling it into question. In Charlottesville, on the morning of the murder of Heather Heyer, a politically progressive group that called itself the NYC Metropolitan Anarchist Coordinating Council (MACC) draped a banner at the bottom of the Robert E. Lee monument. It was consummately ambiguous. On the banner, a heraldic circle with the slogan "Good Night, White Pride" surrounds an image, modeled on the iconography of St. George slaying the dragon, which showed a unicorn representing the LGBTQ community running rampant over a semi-recumbent white outline of a figure emblazoned with the white-nationalist Celtic cross symbol.[80] We could be forgiven for thinking that this is a white-nationalist banner decrying yet another vanquishing of the lost cause. Members of MACC clad in black—suggesting, at first glance, a group signaling common cause with "Unite the Right"—played an important role in the counter-protesting that day, carrying posters that used the heraldry of the right in ways that encouraged closer observation and response. It was a gambit of provocation and disorientation.[81] MACC's witty and shrewd banner design tells us that we need to check our responses to monuments of hegemony and power, no matter how progressive we think we are.

Since at least the so-called Mink Revolution of 2011, public monuments in the Russian Federation have often served in street demonstrations as sites for questioning the legacies—or more precisely, as the sociologist Arlie Russell Hochschild argues, "feelings"[82]—that the monuments are purported to crystallize. The most prominent of these is the monument to Pushkin in Moscow, which has periodically been cordoned off by the city authorities. Writing in 1937, the poet Marina Tsvetaeva noted how the Moscow monument, dedicated to a Russian poet whose great-grandfather was African, served as a counterweight and a rebuke to Falconet's statue of Peter the Great, by suggesting the possibility of a more flexible, and ethnically muted, understanding of Russian identity: "Children who grew up under the Petersburg Falconet Bronze Horseman also grew up under a monument against racism—and for genius."[83] The cultural historian Oleg Kharkhordin observes that much of this project of constructing a counter-system of values can be traced to Pushkin himself, who responded to the 1825 uprising at Falconet's monument by "follow[ing] Gramsci's strategy of hegemony."[84] Although he was indeed "a friend of the Decembrists," he was not in a position to "openly support or poeticize their goals or ideals after they had been crushed"; nonetheless, through his poetry he succeeded in "making them part and parcel" of a tradition of Russian secular education that sought to encourage republican, rather than autocratic or

Banner designed by the New York City Metropolitan Anarchist Coordinating Council (MACC). The flag was placed on the Robert E. Lee statue in Charlottesville, VA, during the "Unite the Right" rally on 12 August 2017, a few hours before the murder of Heather Heyer. Photo by Kim Kelly.

authoritarian, political values. In sharp contrast to the Dzerzhinsky monument and the numerous statues of Lenin that are still a common sight throughout the Russian Federation, that particular Pushkin monument in Moscow
has long spoken to the deep story of the liberal Russian intelligentsia, with its
understanding of Russianness as an open system rather than a club based on
bloodlines and territorial conquests.

As Verdery points out, monuments are important to us because they serve
as sites for enacting spectacles. It is not enough to depose communism: we
need to perform deposition in a dramatized setting. Monuments are fixtures
in the popular imagination. In the case of those dedicated to problematic men
like Nicolae Ceausescu, they underscore a continuity between pagan ancestor
worship and putative heroes of the present. Moreover, the material from which
they are made—marble, granite, or iron—evokes a sense of the object as an
intermediary between the blood of the people and the soil on which they
live.[85] Verdery's insights about the vicissitudes of political monuments—their
literal rise and fall—make us more aware of the importance of the popular
imaginary in sculpting meanings and perceptions.

In her 2017 book about James McGill Buchanan, the 1981 laureate for the
Nobel Prize in Economics, the historian Nancy MacLean describes a libertarian theory of the public marketplace that deliberately eschews empirical study
and posits self-interest—the goal of victory over others, in the form of bend-
ing "losers" to one's will—as the prime motivator in human relations. Buchanan
himself paradoxically understood this voluptuous enjoyment of privilege and
advantage as a "rational" value that often necessitated placing democracy
"under lock and bolt," if not in chains.[86] The fact that he developed his economic theory over several decades while teaching at the University of Virginia
in Charlottesville is suggestive in a number of ways. As an articulate opponent
of antitrust legislation, Buchanan was forthright in his efforts to create a
sophisticated justification for the oligarchical form of governance that was an
important aspect of the antebellum slave-owning South in general (as forcefully defended by John C. Calhoun) and of Virginia's own oligarchic political
traditions. That state legacy was embodied in the patronage system maintained by the Democratic governor Harry F. Byrd (1887–1966). Central to
Buchanan's and Byrd's thinking was the harsh dichotomy between the "makers" and the "takers," between the magnates sitting on top of the mountains of
profits they generated and the citizens who were wage-earners and beneficiaries
of taxpayer-funded state services such as welfare. It has not passed unnoticed
that Buchanan's concepts were primarily expressive of mythic battles, of the
forces of light and dark, of white people and black, locked in an uncompromising war with one another. This understanding of the public square as a

contested field among aspiring winners, losers, and parasites should form the background for any reading of those taking part in the "Unite the Right" rally to defend the monument to Robert E. Lee.

Buchanan's economic theory had a significant afterlife. It abetted the policies of both Pinochet's Chile and Yeltsin's administration, and its theoretical framework undergirded the "Washington consensus" of the early nineties, during which "policies predicated on a strong faith in unfettered markets and aimed at reducing, or even minimizing, the role of government" ended up saddling the Russian Federation with a prodigious debt to the International Monetary Fund, as well as an ascendant oligarchy. The cult of what I would call the libertarian state is firmly at the center of Buchanan's theory of justified class privilege. It has influenced the work of the so-called integralist social theorists, such as Adrian Vermeule at Harvard Law School, who argue for a disposition of spiritual submission to the administrative leviathan of the state.

Paradoxically, this encounter with a state-worshiping libertarianism helps us to contemplate what we may call the Russian style of crony capitalism. Certainly, American libertarianism as an economic practice seems to have affinities to the current macroeconomic model of the Russian Federation. As the political scientist Karen Dawisha puts it, in the Russian Federation "there would be no restrictions on the profits that could be realized" for any oligarch who is loyal to Putin.[87] What is key here, as Tomas Matza writes in his book about Russian psychoanalytic practices that push back against the ravages of neoliberalism even as they gamely draw on its austere inspirational discourse, is the decoupling of politics from economics, of liberal democratic values from the practice of an unfettered market.[88] It bears repeating that the most ardent defenders of corporate and racialized neoliberalism in the United States, such as the Koch brothers and Charles Murray, take Ayn Rand, born in St. Petersburg prior to the Russian Revolution, as one of their ideological touchstones. In her recent *Mean Girl: Ayn Rand and the Culture of Greed* (2019), Lisa Duggan identifies Rand's work as a catalyst for a particular kind of neoliberal thinking that caught fire in the eighties and nineties: a view of the relationship between "makers," "takers," and the state. As Duggan explains, Ayn Rand was anything but a "minarchist," a crypto-anarchist advocate of the minimal state: "The neoliberals set out to retool the state in relation to the market values of property rights and corporate hegemony. While their public propaganda efforts emphasized the key word *freedom* and linked so-called free markets with free minds, they set out via activist interventions in state policy to create a decidedly planned version of 'laissez-faire.'" Duggan goes on to take note of the "gap between the public face and the relatively hidden political planning of neoliberals," between the "utopian theory of neoliberal freedom and the practical class project of installing oligarchic elites at the center of economic and state power."[89]

In Charlottesville, both the "Unite the Right" supporters and the counter-protesters understood the squares enclosing the Lee and Jefferson statues as symbolic of political dominion. As the African American political scientist Keeanga-Yamahtta Taylor puts it, "The rejection of racist symbols, including those commemorating the Confederacy, was an acute response to the fact that they had become important tools for the white-supremacist fringe of the Republican Party, full of contemporary as well as historical meaning." Taylor goes on: "From Dylann Roof's display of the Confederate flag before he massacred nine African Americans in Charleston to the Unite the Right rally in defense of a statue of Robert E. Lee in Charlottesville, these were symbols of white supremacy as a feature of American life."[90] Such symbols call forth, in the manner suggested by Hochschild's understanding of deep stories, practices of veneration that are either collective or personalist in character. In the Russian and US instances cited here, the statues evoke these narratives most audibly in locations that aspire to a moral legitimation. Such monuments are also, as the poet Vladislav Khodasevich reminds us, examples of emotive thought that respect neither the historical record, nor the passage of time. Writing in 1922 about the reflexive idolatry of Pushkin—during a year that saw the end of Russia's own bloody civil war—Khodasevich notes with chagrin that many Russian readers would not recognize the world Pushkin lived in, and which thoroughly informed his work. That essence, he asserts, is completely incomprehensible to modern readers who have been weaned on the doctrine about Pushkin's timelessness and universality. Pushkin has come to have the "secret face," like that of a "demi-God." That face, Khodasevich writes, will change in the manner of a bronze statue that alters with time. No one however is willing to recognize that the poet one generation loves, may not be at all visible to the next one.[91] It is that respect for the actual and granular historical record that the many American and Russian advocates for monument removal seek to restore. As Erin L. Thompson puts it in *Smashing Statues: The Rise and Fall of America's Public Monuments*, they fully recognize that monuments are first and foremost "pledges of allegiance" rather than "history lessons."[92]

Conclusion

The Fight against Rightist Elites

W HAT WAS BEHIND the eruptions of radical and at times violent political groups at the beginning of the third decade of the twenty-first century? Social isolation and alienation were frequently cited as explanations in the United States and the Russian Federation. The most recent national census in the Russian Federation, conducted in 2010, found 14,018,754 individuals (26 percent of private residences) living alone. In a 2018 report that touched on the continued drought of nuanced information about a potentially serious social and demographic problem, an analyst for the state-run demographic website TASS Nauka dryly noted that these statistics tell us nothing about either "the emotional state of these people, or the number of [their] social contacts."[1] Surprisingly, almost half of the people in this residence category were too young to be employed (32,692) or of working age (6,378,617); the remainder (7,598,643) were of retirement age.[2] Over the last two decades, in online news outlets that profess to offer a Russian Orthodox perspective on physical and mental health problems, thousands of articles have been devoted to the consequences of growing atomization, social anomie, and isolation, with particular attention to the most vulnerable—that is, people at the extreme ends of the age spectrum. Yet articles in the most popular and influential Christian news outlet in the Russian Federation, *Pravmir*, which is not officially affiliated with the Russian Orthodox Church, often emphasize the need for stoicism, acceptance, and a recognition of the fallen nature of our spiritual state in the present moment, with an almost studied avoidance of cases where those social conditions facilitated the formation of politically extreme groups to compensate for the experience of intense loneliness.[3]

The continuing drought of informed discussion about this problem in Russia has coincided with a flood of often recriminatory speculation in the United

States since the election of Donald Trump. Much of this analysis focuses on Americans who were "left behind" by the supposed global economic uplift that followed the collapse of the Soviet Union in 1991, and by the ballyhooed yet morally hollow "end of history" described by early apologists for neoliberalism, such as Francis Fukuyama, Thomas Friedman, and a claque of centrist, liberal, and conservative American politicians ranging from Bill Clinton to Newt Gingrich.

In her anthropological study of Louisiana voters, *Strangers in Their Own Land*, Arlie Russell Hochschild draws attention to the resentment of disaffected white citizens, many of them with vivid living memories of the sixties and seventies, toward those who look down on them. Delving into the interviewees' resistance to the march of progress, Hochschild's narrative cracks open a treasure trove of paradoxes and seeming contradictions. They live according to an uncompromising work ethic, but describe the corporations that polluted their local environment and downsized their employment rolls with an unexpected and perhaps unmerited forgiveness. Read together with J. D. Vance's *Hillbilly Elegy*, Hochschild's book deepens our understanding of the feelings and responses to hardship that define the experience of being where these abandoned people live and try to work. We see that gallows humor is both a psychological mechanism for self-protection and a manifestation of the social Darwinism that defines what Pierre Bourdieu calls a "habitus," a niche of cultural signifiers and practices that links people to their class and particular forms of labor.[4]

One persistent belief among Hochschild's interviewees is that big business—or more specifically, big oil—is effective in stimulating the local economy. As one man put it, the BP Deepwater Horizon oil spill of 2010 was caused by "*over-regulation*," by too much oversight: "If the government hadn't been looking over BP's shoulder, it would have regulated itself, and the spill wouldn't have happened."[5] At times we hear in the interviews an oddly tenuous relationship between the categories of work, power, and integrity, which would seem to go against their own principles and values about the inviolability of agreements and the importance of keeping your word.[6] Some of these fissures within the deep stories seem to originate in an understanding of big business as a benevolent parental figure who cannot do its job properly because of interference from outsiders, those who don't belong to a familial cohort. Applied to the implementation of large-scale projects, populist stories tend to underscore the ideal of natural hierarchies as embodying values of decency and kindness that no democratically elected institution can reflect or instill.

Hochschild's interactions with her subjects, together with the careful conclusions she draws from her experience of scaling the "empathy wall" of culture and class that separates her from them, clarify for us the loaded poetic term "elegy" that Vance uses in his title. In both books the elegiac element is fundamentally about the passing of parts of a culture that is already steeped in fatalism. Vance and Hochschild give us a glimpse of a world that is imbued with a compounded sense of mortality—one's own, that of loved ones, and that of a larger community and culture (in Vance's book, the culture of the Scots Irish of Appalachia). In the domain of religious belief—from which so many of the Russian and American subjects of this book take their cues—we are struck by the resourceful and vividly intelligent syncretism of people who turn to forms of political reaction. Hochschild's interviewees take notions about the gift of grace that are distinctly Catholic and blend, fuse, and cross-pollinate them with notions about the United States as the City on a Hill and a sense of the imminence of the end times that are starkly evangelical Protestant, while also adhering to a borderline animist understanding of their local natural environment that some might argue is not recognizably Christian at all.[7] Shifts in religious beliefs reflect a certain dynamism, showing how the deep story can be made to accommodate other systems of value in order to survive. In chapter 2 of this book, we took note of Steve Bannon's particular engagement with Roman Catholic teaching as an appropriation and a creative and syncretic tinkering with religious values that might call into question his commitment to the ideals of tradition and submission that he proclaims. In chapter 4, we observed how far-right religious groups and figures in the Russian Federation, such as the Union of Orthodox Banner Bearers and Dmitri Tsorionov (Enteo), freely draw on the transnational and often distinctly non-Russian heraldry of openly fascistic groups. Finally, in chapter 5's discussion of the veneration of monuments by conservatives and radical traditionalists in both countries, we considered practices that run against the grain of the religious beliefs that they otherwise claim to uphold.

At this juncture, we may take things one step further. The people of Hochschild's and Vance's books exemplify how a thinking class may be coaxed into a robust existence by liberating it from the strict limitations of economic class categories. Gramsci understood this moment as an inflection point or catalyst for the creation of a new and "organic" class of intellectuals. Writing about reading habits in Italy during the 1920s, Gramsci observed that "the entire educated class, with its intellectual activity, is detached from the people, from the nation" because "in relation to this people-nation the indigenous intellectual element is more foreign" than the foreign authors whose publications the working and middle classes typically enjoy.[8] In the Russophilia or concessive attitude toward the current foreign-policy positions of the Russian Federation that we see in the statements of political figures like Trump, Rand

Paul, and Josh Hawley, bloggers and writers like Lana Lokteff, Henrik Palmgren, Rod Dreher, and Helen Andrews, and far-right groups like the Proud Boys and America First, we often witness genuine attempts to formulate new ways of thinking by reaching out to a foreign culture.[9]

Examining the simultaneously pro-Putin and monarchist views of converts to Russian Orthodoxy within one deeply conservative community in West Virginia, the anthropologist Sarah Riccardi-Swartz characterizes this tightly focused flight from American belief-driven localism as a trajectory of transformation, resulting in the sketching out of "dichotomous boundary-making boundaries—us versus them, conservative versus liberal, Christian versus secular, traditional versus progressive."[10] Dreams about the Russian Federation as an agrarian and patriarchal idyll—often pointedly identified as "Putin's Russia," in deference to the power of the absolute sovereign—are pervasive in alt-right writings. As one openly pro-Confederate blogger puts it: "Dixie (like Russia) is an enclave of *civilization itself*" (emphasis in the original). The blogger, a personal friend and supporter of many of the alt-right demonstrators who took part in the "Unite the Right" rally in Charlottesville, asserts that while both "Dixie and Russia cling to the bedrocks of faith and family, in spite of government-coerced progress," we in the South "are quickly losing our grip, whereas Russians are holding on tight."[11] Once more, we see that the possibility of political intimacy suggestive of family relationships—here, that of siblings—is a powerful element of a populism that articulates "real people" as an elite that is as much cognitive as it is spiritual. The world-building of any "political theology" calls for the dynamic creative and intellectual effort of an entire community, or family. As Riccardi-Swartz notes, by drawing on fields of knowledge as diverse as "continental philosophy, political science, anthropology," as well as theology itself, the imaginary of political theology "provides frameworks for thinking through larger issues, such as liberalism, capitalism, and globalism in ways that are sensitive to the subjectivities of individuals."[12] Hochschild herself takes note of the collage-like character of the "deep story" that her Louisianan interviewees verbalize, in which the idealized details of antebellum life among poor whites are often transposed into present.[13] A few of her subjects recognize the cobbled-together and artificial character of that grand narrative. One, a participant in a Civil War re-enactment dressed as a Confederate soldier, ruefully observes that present-day bayou communities are mistaken in perceiving their experiences through the lens of the "War between the States." "You can't secede from oil," and "you can't secede from a mentality." He goes on to say that "you have to think your way into and out of that mentality." He added that "they should get me into a different costume to talk about that."[14]

We need to take heed of the sharp observation of this man from Hochschild's book, reminding ourselves that deep stories and nationalist mythologies are artificial constructs, elaborate networks of aspirational conceits rather than the products of a close engagement with the materiality of the present. Such conservative narratives about idyllic ages of comity among classes paradoxically echo the idealized visions that nineteenth-century Russian progressive intelligentsia had about the peasantry, discussed in chapter 1. As of 2019, only 5.83 percent of the workforce of the Russian Federation was employed in the agricultural sector, which in 2016 accounted for only 4.5 percent of the gross domestic product.[15] Nor has Putin proved to be the persistent burr under the saddle of globalist neoliberalism that many bloggers in the United States and the Russian Federation claimed or hoped that he would be. As the political scientist Peter Rutland points out, we often forget that the Putin administration in the 2000s made a point of bringing the Russian Federation fully into global markets by maintaining a convertible currency, allowing cross-border currency flows, and not raising tariff barriers. While this approach worked well enough during a decade when world oil prices were robust, they were calamitous during the next one, when the disadvantages of the country's "resource curse," its overreliance on energy resources, became vividly clear.[16] Much of the economic policy of the dominant United Russia Party has arguably been a continuation of the "Washington consensus" that marked the Yeltsin administration, a series of free-market strategies that a wide range of both conservative nationalists and progressives in Russia have justifiably assailed. Those policies have resulted in the cratering of people's life savings and a casualization of the workforce, the latter grounded in what Bourdieu calls a "*mode of domination* of a new kind, based on the creation of a generalized and permanent state of insecurity aimed at forcing workers into the acceptance of submission" and "the acceptance of exploitation" (emphasis in the original).[17]

In both countries, much ink has been spilled on behalf of a campaign against the creative class or cognitive elite that has immiserated the world. In modern-day Russian, the adjective *kreativnyi* has taken on an ambiguous meaning. It refers to resourceful—if at times morally sketchy—jet-setting urban types who work in advertising or other branches of private business, and whose jobs call for a keen entrepreneurial zeal combined with a highly developed appreciation for aesthetics. To be creative is to be a master of hegemonic practices, or Gramscian consent-building. As we have demonstrated here, new-right elites in both countries openly embrace this role and have ceased to worry about their extensive borrowing from the practices and even some of the beliefs of the liberal and global elites whom they decry. In her book *In Search of the True Russia: The Provinces in Contemporary Nationalist Discourse* (2018), Lyudmila Parts insightfully examines the toggling within the contemporary Russian cultural sphere between the idealization and the patronizing objectification of the Russia that exists outside the three major cities of Moscow, St. Petersburg, and Novosibirsk. Within the associations and impressions that reverberate within the taut net of the wider national culture, Parts describes how those who live in the urban hubs perceive their compatriots. In this respect they are scarcely different from Joan C. Williams's characterization of privileged, class-clueless American liberals, who "commit to equality for many different groups but arrogantly dismiss 'the dark rigidity of fundamentalist rural America'"—and whose patronizing treatment sparks a understandable fury in working-class white Americans.[18] Parts strikes a similar note, drawing attention to the "Russian Europeans" or "global Russians" who belong to "the other side of the political spectrum." This is the demographic that "the liberal media project *Snob*"—an affluent liberal equivalent of *Vanity Fair* that also publishes cerebral long-form essays and reviews suggestive of the *New York Review of Books*—"designates [as] its target audience."[19]

Yet Parts cautions against the glib assumption that this paternalistic view of the Russian version of "fly-over" country is exclusively the domain of liberals or progressives. "Directed outward," the gaze from the Russian "center" of the capital city perceives the larger territory of post-imperial and post-Soviet Russia as an "object of colonizing practices, interpreted as interference in political and cultural matters" that ultimately undercut local autonomy; that same gaze, "directed inward," imagines itself as enjoying a fellowship with the Russian provinces, as "objects of a sympathetic, though nonetheless objectifying, gaze." We should not be surprised that the provinces "constitute ideal objects for the exercise of hegemonic power and, in fact [are] the only entity available for subjugation by Russian nationalists following the disintegration of the Empire." The "Russian elite" on the right feels justifiably "wronged by the West" in light of its use of the country as a laboratory for free-market "shock treatment" after the collapse of the Soviet Union; but this in no way justifies its treatment of the same territory as "an object for their [own] hegemonic posture."[20] Parts powerfully critiques the rhetoric of the Russian Federation's anti-liberal intelligentsia for using media representations about the "real people" to stand in for actual testimony from them, a flawed reflex that is all too evident in the sudden concern for the US white working class that we hear in Joan C. Williams's book, and in the writing of "classical liberal" commentators such as David Brooks.[21]

Russia has served as a beacon of correct political practice and lifestyle for US alt-right, radical traditionalist, and even mainstream conservative political opinion. As is noted in the introduction to this volume, this attraction has a particular salience because of what they understand to be a half-millennium of autocratic, antidemocratic, and illiberal traditions there. The US right has shown stronger and more expedient sympathy for the top-down governing practices and social conservatism of Jarosław Kaczyński's Law and Justice Party in Poland and Viktor Orbán's Fidesz in Hungary, and yet neither party can be understood as a capstone for a vigorous and age-old tradition of illiberalism combined with an uncompromising national sovereignty, especially in light of the subjugation and fitful attempts at autonomy that those countries experienced at the hands of the Hapsburg and Russian empires during the nineteenth century. If nothing else, the global right appreciates Darwinist stories of political supremacy and territorial domination, which the history of neither country embodies in any way that could be understood as uninterrupted in the modern era.

The platforms of the ruling parties in Poland and Hungary are more important to the US right-wing intelligentsia than that of the United Russia Party in terms of concrete policies that could be implemented in the short term, such as zero tolerance for refugees, impermeable border control, and defiant noncompliance with European Union cultural policies such as LGBTQ rights; some would like to see a parallel American flouting of United Nations human rights policies. Russia is interesting to the American right primarily because of a perceived history of Caesarism. Some among the alt-right, such as the racialist VDare commentator Steven Sailer, even idiosyncratically link the model of ruthlessly decisive yet pragmatic leadership to the Soviet era. In Sailer's view, Lenin developed a theory of history that was far more realistic than Francis Fukuyama's blithe triumphalism about Western values at the end of the Cold War. Sailer argues that the first Soviet leader understood that history is not about "ideology," but rather about the questions "'Who? Whom?' (You can insert your own transitive verb between the two words)." History continues, rather than ending in the way that Fukuyama and other free-market progressives argue, "because the struggle to determine who will be the *who* rather than the *whom* will never end."[22] Not surprisingly, Sailer does not interpret this quotation in the context in which Bolshevism immediately understood it in the mid-twenties, during the heyday of the pragmatically mixed economic practices of the New Economic Policy, which were designed to replenish a state budget exhausted by the ravages of the Russian Civil War (1919–22) and the sanctions of Western nations against the new Soviet Union. For Sailer, this pithy phrase is not so much about who will nonlethally outstrip or outperform whom—the original meaning of the Russian phrase—but rather who will destroy or obliterate whom. As Thomas J. Main points out in *The Rise of the Alt-Right* (2018), "Sailer's proposed alternative to liberal democracy is Leninism without the Marxism," embodying a political reality that is best expressed "by the advertising slogan for a recent Hollywood movie: 'It's not a crime if you're doing it for the good guys.'"[23]

Many citizens of the Russian Federation condemn the idealization of Stalin, both within the state-run media and among the three-quarters of the national population who—according to several surveys over the last ten years—consider the Soviet leader to have been a "hero" or "great man." Nonetheless, we can understand or empathize with aspects of pro-Stalinism in a population that still lives in the shadow of the brutality of the Nazi invasion and the demographic implosion and family tragedies that it caused. While some of this political nostalgia was recently given a boost as a result of the "memory laws" that Putin had ratified in the Duma, we should not forget that the first significant wave of Stalinism after 1991 occurred as a backlash against the Washington consensus policies that sent the national economy into a tailspin. On the numerous and elaborately multimedia pages of the patriotic National Liberation Movement (Narodnoe osvoboditel'noe dvizhenie, or NOD) on VKontakte, earnest and interesting discussions of the bravery of Soviet soldiers during the Great Patriotic War share, to an unsettling degree, narrative space on the same page with allegations that President Biden planned to topple the Russian government on 19 September 2021.[24] But whereas this admiration for Stalin is fathomable, the American alt-right's admiration for Soviet leaders is much more difficult to make sense of. As we saw in chapters 2 and 3, Steve Bannon is a keen appropriator of early Soviet history, with no qualms about throwing overboard any Russophobia that American conservatism may still harbor. In a similar adaptive vein, the anti-Semitic retired academic Kevin MacDonald admires prerevolutionary Russia for the restrictions on travel, employment, and educational opportunities that it placed on its Jewish population, even as he expresses a high regard for Ayn Rand, whose family was actually subjected to those restrictions. Like all beacons, Russia is enticing for the American alt-right because it stands at a distance; in the manner of a lighthouse whose lamp oscillates between dark and light, it points in the general direction of the right course. It is easy to idealize something when it is unfamiliar and strange, and the temptation to imagine a particular world within its notional outlines is very strong. Supporters of populism tend to make assumptions about the benevolence of authoritarian leaders and trust that those strongmen speak for them—a habit that periodically rotates their camera lens into the unfocused setting.

The alt-right and Russian conservative intellectuals have shown themselves to be adept students of Gramsci, who defined Caesarism as a dynamic of pragmatic authoritarianism, "a polemical-ideological formula" rather than "a canon of historical interpretation."[25] We have frequently noted the ideological flexibility and flamboyant syncretism of the American alt-right and radical traditionalist groups in the Russian Federation, which have both absorbed certain lessons from the intellectual legacy of the left. Prominent among these is Gramsci's understanding of the manufacturing of consent through a relentless occupation and dominance of the cultural sphere. For Gramsci, this is a role that organic intellectuals are especially well positioned to undertake, with possible assistance from a traditional intelligentsia that may, uncharacteristically, be sympathetic to their ideals. The French alt-right thinkers Guillaume Faye and Alain de Benoist—both highly influential on figures as varied as Curtis Yarvin ("Mencius Moldbug" on the internet), Richard Spencer, Alexander Dugin, and Valery Korovin—underscore this practice in their strategic thinking about the future of their movements. What remains unexamined is the relationship between their embrace of Gramsci's conception of organic intellectuals' role in manufacturing consent and the category of Caesarism that he discusses elsewhere in his *Prison Notebooks*:

> Caesarism can be said to express a situation in which the forces in conflict balance each other in a catastrophic manner; that is to say, they balance each other in such a way that a continuation of the conflict can only terminate in their reciprocal destruction. When the progressive force A struggles with the reactionary force B, not only may A defeat B or B defeat A, but it may happen that neither A nor B defeats the other—that they bleed each other mutually and then a third force C intervenes from outside, subjugating what is left of both A and B.[26]

As a mechanism for authoritarian restoration, Gramsci's conception of Caesarism has a clear antecedent in the realignment of the political voices of the social estates that Marx describes in *The Eighteenth Brumaire of Louis Napoleon* (1852) as providing the foundation for justifying the suppression of working-class voices in state affairs. Furthermore, Caesarism has striking similarities with Carl Schmitt's conception of the "state of emergency" that may be invoked to suspend democratic mechanisms.

In explaining the dynamically unsystematic character of Gramsci's thought, researchers who have access to the original of his writing often point to the diary-like discursive mode of the *Prison Notebooks*. Joseph A. Buttigieg, Gramsci's most authoritative translator in English, describes the *Prison Notebooks* as "patently decentered, open, tentative, provisional, exploratory."[27] Nonetheless, some strong patterns do emerge from the weave of those texts. In *Caesarism and Bonapartism in Gramsci: Hegemony and the Crisis of Modernity* (2020), Francesca Antonini emphasizes the ideological ambiguity of Caesarism, arguing that its practices are not defined by the association with fascism, or at least not overdetermined by it, in the way that many progressive thinkers have assumed.[28] In the passage above from the *Prison Notebooks*, state practitioners of Caesarism claim to be operating in the name of the common good, when in fact they are engaged in strengthening their political class. Flirting with authoritarianism in the trappings of both ultramontane conservatism (monarchy) and notional leftism (the Soviet legacy), Putin and the United Russia Party have positioned themselves as agents of an autonomous and Caesarist state in which leadership is placed in the role of negotiating and adjudicating between the disparate demands of various constituencies, in a pantomime of acting on behalf of the common good. Here, those constituencies are the business community or oligarchs, the political class (*siloviki*), the Russian Orthodox Church, and the Duma, that assembly of imperfect democratic representation within the Russian Federation. Let us not forget that the title *tsar* comes from a tradition of nomenclature begun by Ivan the Terrible in an attempt to evoke associations with the emperors of Byzantium, who referred to themselves as "Caesar."

Now that autocracy or absolute executive power has disappeared from its political stage, Russia has entered into a phase in the evolution of a hybrid form of governing that is broadly consistent with the details of the Caesarism that Gramsci describes. In an interview from 2020, Putin provided a jokey answer to a question about some Russians' demand that he be named tsar of the Russian Federation. A tsar "sits and looks from above, issues a decree which people then fulfill, after which he straightens his hat and looks in the mirror," he said. "I, on the other hand, work every day."[29] With their selective appropriation of Gramsci close at hand—which ignores Gramsci's emphasis on the organic intellectual's humbling, during the task of listening, and their careful avoidance of ideological tendentiousness—the new-right intellectuals in both countries would say that issuing orders and decrees with the sartorial trappings of authority is precisely what defines the work of the sovereign leader.[30] Roman Titov—a prominent Slavic pagan priest and supporter of United Russia—declared in 2018 that Putin is the tsar of his nation in the same way that Titov is the tsar of his family, and of his "warriors" (*bortsy*), the extreme sport boxers that Titov trains. In a statement that would have been completely at home in a sermon by the Oregon Calvinist minister Mark Driscoll about the spiritual and moral importance of class and gender complementarianism, Titov went on to say in the same interview that "each person is great in their place within the order of things," each one being a "cog in the mechanism of [the nation's] history."[31]

Titov's comment about Putin and tsarism, and Putin's own jocular description of himself as a modernized autocrat, are highly representative of the social vision of Russian political traditionalism. In chapter 5 totem-worship, a part of the pagan Slavic legacy, was discussed as a key to understanding the resistance to the removal of monuments to figures of illiberalism and political repression from the Soviet era. Yet that particular residue of paganism in certain aspects of Russian Orthodoxy is one of the very few things that we know for certain about the religious culture of the pre-Christian East Slavic lands. Historical data about the social organization of those communities in connection with their ritualistic practices is scant; some researchers argue that evidence for the patriarchal hierarchies that many assume to be characteristic of those village settlements is equivocal at best. Other historians go further, arguing that pre-Christian Slavic practices manifest stronger indications of matriarchal social structures. The conservative cultural nationalist Valery Averianov called religions like *Rodnoverie* or Native Faith in Russia and Ukraine crude and mendacious reconstructions.[32] Titov's comments reflect a palimpsest of doxologies, rather than a meaningful fusion or convergence of them. In contrast to the significant body of texts documenting the belief systems of the Norse religion, the Slavic pagan context exists only in fragments and has been largely hollowed out by the victorious accounts left by the Byzantine missionaries and their subalterns in Rus. In Titov's statements, the echoes of prerevolutionary endorsements of autocratic rule are more distinct than the echoes of Slavic paganism. In all likelihood, those practices were primarily dictated by the details of the agricultural calendar, which Andrei Tarkovsky shrewdly reconstructs in the sybaritic "St. John's Eve" celebration scene of his film *Andrei Rublev* (1966).

Like their counterpart critiques in the Russian Federation, strongly conservative assessments of social malaise in the United States fail to see that the actual sources of their views are thoroughly visible to others. Shortly after the publication of his autobiography *Hillbilly Elegy*, J. D. Vance stated in an interview: "If you look at the statistics and see some of the things I've seen, you recognize that these people, despite being very religious and having their Christian faith as something important to them, aren't attending church that much. They don't have that much of a connection to a traditional religious institution." So, while we "tend to think of these areas as the Bible Belt, where everyone is going to church and everyone is actively involved in religious community," what we actually find is a completely different picture. "Religion is important. That conception is right. But religion is quirky, and it's not traditionally practiced in religious institutions."[33] We might draw the conclusion that Vance is directing our attention to the importance of grassroots religious belief ("religion is quirky"). So much discussion about ecumenism and faith in the American blogosphere and cable news platforms seems arid, and seldom makes reference to the customs that are crucial to many believers' self-images. Yet if we are not able to bear witness to any actual practice of "quirky" religion—if people do nothing to practice the religion they are supposedly deeply engaged with—how can we assess their commitment to a particular faith? Vance submits the matter of nonattendance at church as a culture-war talking point and a straw-man argument, with no acknowledgment that many charismatic religious communities in Appalachia observe religious rites such as revival meetings outside the walls of a church.

The only way to make sense of Vance's statement is to acknowledge its subtext, which is Calvinist doctrine. One way of understanding Calvinism is to define it as the belief that certain people are the elect, chosen by God to be saved, and that their "works"—actions and behavioral choices, including church attendance—are largely irrelevant. If Vance were identifying important elements of Calvinism in the beliefs of the people he is referring to, that would certainly be a worthwhile project in view of the complex religious prehistory of the Scots Irish, who espoused strongly Protestant values even as they joined nominally Catholic causes such as the Jacobite rebellion, standing in solidarity against British imperialism. This group still represents the majority ethnic demographic of many counties within Appalachia. But Vance is clearly not doing that, and furthermore no Calvinist denomination in the United States would ever suggest that nonattendance at church services could be evidence of spiritual authenticity. What we see in this statement is a racialized version of Calvinism, with the white working class presented as a populist elite modeled on the notion of God's elect, in dramatic contrast with the decadent and pharisaical churchgoers from the white upper class. This is something we often see in statements about religious values from the traditionalist intelligentsia in the United States and the Russian Federation: more a casually association-driven collaging of statements about traditional values than the probing insight or magisterial synthesis of disparate traditional practices that they claim to be offering.

We would probably be mistaken in categorizing Vance's bundling of memes as a strategy for deflection or mystification of actual rhetorical goals. It is possible that he is completely unaware of the theologically ambiguous mélange that his statements from the 2016 interview represent, and is not cognizant of the residual racism that is present in his statements about white Americans whose behavior and choices stand at a distance from their innate godliness. Three years after the interview in which he discussed the religious culture in which his family was steeped, Vance underwent a change of mind. As the culmination of a growing sense that works and cognitive choices are in fact important, he decided to convert to Catholicism. More significant than the fact of this conversion are the reasons he gave for it: "One of the most attractive things about Catholicism, is that the concept of grace is not couched in terms of epiphany. It's not like you receive grace and suddenly you go from being a bad person to being a good person. You're constantly being worked on. I like that."[34] Yet more recently, running for the US Senate seat in Ohio, Vance returned to excoriating progressive elites—those churchgoers of a "woke" religion—even as his campaign was being financed by Peter Thiel, a prominent figure of the business elite that Vance has elsewhere said "control[s] what we're allowed to say in our own country."[35] Twitter, because it monumentalizes the present moment, is especially effective in overshadowing and concealing the prehistories and arcs of transformation that Vance pointed to as pivotal for his decision to convert to Catholicism. For new-right elites, social media platforms represent the ideal sites for purging cultural and even personal memory.

With this consideration in mind, we can move on to a conclusion about the syncretic and eclectic character of the right wing in the United States and the Russian Federation. Throughout this book, I have argued that it is precisely their resourcefulness in aggregating and hybridizing cultural memes that makes it possible to speak of new-right elites and of a right-wing or radical intelligentsia that regards itself as engaged in a legitimate category of labor, even though the form of its implementation is mental rather than manual. To understand the self-images of the new-right elites, we need to take them at their word when they describe themselves in the meritocratic terms of intellectual acumen, rather than class; we need to believe them when they tell us that they see no contradiction in being both populist and elitist. American traditionalist commentators see a genuinely populist intelligentsia as both the engine for informational insurgency against an expert class and as a lightning-rod for "broader social forces" that, on their own, might be unable to restrain ill-advised globalist ventures such as the second Iraq War (2003–11).[36]

The Russian American blogger Katya Kazbek and the late Eduard Limonov have no problem voicing opinions that are mishmashes of prerevolutionary imperial Russian patriotism, ardent Stalinism, vaguely LGBTQ-friendly views, and quasi-Nazism, garnished with generous helpings of profanity. Profound contradictions permeate these American and Russian justifications for a palace guard defending both humility and "natural" hierarchies, and that is precisely the point. Kazbek, a fiction author, has a closed Twitter account with over twelve thousand followers along with a closed account on VKontakte. In one LiveJournal entry, written in Russian and carrying the English title

"Against the Farts," she describes her enemies as rank pretenders to cultural authority, as "shit" and "drunken William Tells" who aim at her forehead and miss, and who "will never become [like the American writer] William Burroughs" no matter how hard they try.[37] (The last remark is an apparent reference to Burroughs's disastrous attempt to shoot an apple from his wife's head.) Writing about Limonov's quirky personal affect and principled refusal to have views that make sense, Fabrizio Fenghi, in *It Will Be Fun and Terrifying*, takes note of the fact that "this search [in the 1990s] for sexual and political emancipation translated into the quasi-sectarian vision" of the ideologically red-brown—that is, simultaneously communist and fascist—National Bolshevik Party (NBP). It was a vision, Fenghi convincingly argues, that fundamentally "challenged [the] traditional gender roles and family values" that dominated mainstream Russian society—and, as Valerie Sperling demonstrates in *Sex, Politics, and Putin: Political Legitimacy in Russia* (2014), continue to dominate it.[38] Basing his observations about the attractions of red-brown authoritarianism in post-Soviet Russia on interviews with Limonov and others in the ideological orbit of the NBP, Fenghi observes that "closely connected with these ideas was the idealization of childhood and youth as times of uncompromising rebelliousness and untainted promiscuity, and this also became an important component of the *natsboly*'s [NBP members'] ethos." And why not? As Fenghi notes, for Limonov and his cohort, "all children are extremists."[39]

The Russian social networking site VKontakte is especially revealing about the ways in which American and Russian new-right elites think of themselves. VKontakte is distinctive in foregrounding the initial posts of any given thread, which explains why many Russians prefer Facebook, Telegram, and Instagram over VKontakte if they want to interact more dynamically with friends and new acquaintances. Postings and discussion threads are confined to a central ribbon of the screen, which cannot be horizontally expanded in the easy manner that Facebook and Twitter allow. Overall, the platform has the feel of a multimedia roundhouse, allowing users to easily upload sound files and image galleries in a way that Facebook largely disallows, out of copyright considerations. If Facebook is a bulletin board for personal and community notices, VKontakte is an archive or local library of donated materials. Each post lists on its lower right-hand corner how many times it has been viewed, and a visitor to the site is consistently struck by the enormous disparity between the number of viewings and the number of responses. People come here to read often-lengthy posts, and to look and to gasp in wonder at the vivid images, foregrounded even more prominently than on a Facebook post, with accompanying text that seems minuscule compared with the images; users are less interested in reading threads, responding, and conversing.

When many neo-Nazi and other far-right sites and users were banned from Facebook and Twitter in 2018, followed by the termination of the pages and accounts of Donald Trump and many of his followers shortly after the January 6 insurrection, numerous American alt-right figures and groups—including many of the active participants in the Charlottesville "Unite the Right" rally—migrated to VKontakte. There they share space with radical traditionalist and far-right entities in the Russian Federation, who use the platform as their primary home on the internet. Dmitri Tsorionov's sole "official" media space is on VKontakte, as is that of the neo-Confederate organization called the League of the South, which had a prominent part in the "Unite the Right" rally and has been permanently banned from Twitter. The childish intransigence and often-creative vituperation of authoritarian intellectuals like Kazbek and Limonov are on full display here. On the page for the League of the South, puerile stubbornness and resistance to norms blend almost seamlessly with the rhetoric of the Confederacy as a noble lost cause. The personal page of its chairman Michael Hill contains a link to both the League's VKontakte page and its still-operational Google website. Hill pleads: "On this fourth anniversary of Charlottesville, I ask for your prayers and support to help us overcome the great odds against us in this suit."[40] (The League of the South is one of the defendants in a federal lawsuit, *Sines v. Kessler*, in which the organization Integrity First for America is seeking evidentiary sanction against the National Socialist Movement and other groups and individuals for suppressing or destroying documents related to the violent events of 12 August 2017.[41]) Hill claims that "the Judeo-Bolshevik narrative over the past four years has been that we were the villains," but that "nothing could be further from the truth." According to Hill, the "Bolshevik left is well funded and has much influence in the legal system," while "we have little, except the truth."[42]

VKontakte's platform is suggestive of a continuous letterhead scroll, with the flagship picture of each page positioned in the margin of the window like a heraldic seal. The important thing, we are made to understand, is the shingled storefront of information, with a message board from management that speaks passionately about the "eternal truths" that can be found within, whether the page espouses QAnon (migrated from Facebook and Twitter) or Henrik Palmgren's and Lana Lokteff's "Red Ice TV" (banned from YouTube), or a hodgepodge of red-brown views that lovingly advocate for the return of a Russian monarchy that is imbued with Soviet collectivist values.

Web design and curation go only so far in sanitizing inflammatory content, or rendering it more palatable. The advocacy of a strong social order would not seem to easily coexist with the fervent endorsements of irrationality and rage. Certainly, a love of mulish contrarianism runs deep in authoritarian theorizing about its tactics and values. In his "Futurist Manifesto" (1909), F. T. Marinetti famously wrote, "We wish to glorify war, the only healthy giver of the world," and to sing the praises of "militarism, patriotism, the destructive arm of the Anarchist, the beautiful Ideas that kill, [and] the contempt for woman."[43] The alt-right "Dark Enlightenment" propagandist Jack Donovan, who for a time was associated with Richard Spencer's alt-right National Policy Institute, extended this line of thinking about the legitimacy of disruptive violence into a formulation of "anarcho-fascism" as a political ideal.[44] Yet, for the most part, simple irrationality or rationalization of anarchism is not what new-right elites and the alt-right are interested in defending. In *How Propaganda Works* (2015), the political philosopher Jason Stanley argues that "demagoguery is discourse that appears to make a rational contribution to the debate at hand, but instead serves to cut off rational debate by enlisting the forces of passion to make an impartial reasoned stance impossible."[45] He elaborates:

> The capacity to be reasonable requires, as we have seen, a disposition to take the perspective of others in the community in proposing reasons, to be empathetic to them, and to respect their dignity. A contribution to public reason is reasonable only if it takes into account the reasonable perspectives of all those citizens subject to the policy under debate. On this conception, demagoguery is discourse that appears to take every perspective into account but has the goal of rendering some reasonable perspectives invisible.[46]

It is here, at this moment of recognizing the importance of this obdurate and childish intransigence, that we come to a better understanding of the self-image that new-right elites cultivate. The public square of civic virtue leaves them cold. They recall the figure of Odysseus in Nikos Kazantzakis's politically resonant *The Odyssey: A Modern Sequel* (1938), written at the height of the Spanish Civil War and the rapid militarization of Nazi Germany: they find the revisited niceties and pieties of domestic life and political peace to be uninteresting and cloying. A rage against diversity, against a cheek-by-jowl togetherness of different communities and constituencies inhabiting the same space, instead of a rigorously segmented castelike social order, occupies center stage in their public presentations. Here they play the role of an illiberal, and invariably self-appointed, vanguard. In both the United States and the Russian Federation, it is fair to say that those groups embrace, as one researcher puts it, "oligarchy and authoritarianism as normalcy."[47]

The values of a militaristic chain of command, as discussed in chapter 3, are central to the efforts of Alexander Dugin and Kevin MacDonald to give the category of intellectual labor a proper conservative gravitas. As the blogger Alexander Khaldei put it at a meeting of the Izborsk Club that I was allowed to attend, held at its headquarters on 30 May 2018: "We are waging a struggle for interpretation."[48] The Club's advocacy for a literal war in Eastern Ukraine is the larger context in which comments like this should be read. Averianov explained in an email to me that the Izborsk Club seeks to bring together different perspectives—"right and left, conservative and socialist"—into a patriotic coalition that renders it elite "in the eyes of power, and of the society" as a whole.[49] For him and for people like MacDonald, Richard Spencer, and Paul Gottfried, the formulation "populist elitism" contains no contradiction.

Hochschild reminds us of the importance of "scaling the empathy wall" when entering into principled dialogues with political others, without condescension and in a humble effort to understand their deep stories. Others have spoken about the importance of meeting your political opponents "where they are," as if the mental equivalent of a day trip could break the prison of one's own ego. It is true that religious notions about the need to purge or empty oneself, in a manner suggestive of the Eastern Orthodox notion of *kenosis*, are emphasized by many members of the American alt-right who have converted to Russian Orthodoxy and by extremist religious groups in Russia such as the Union of Orthodox Banner Bearers. Yet calls for empathy from the moderate or liberal side often hinge on a self-shaming and a listening process that uneasily blends the religious emptying described above with a call to submit to an interlocutor who, strangely, does not need to adhere to the same discipline. The path that demagoguery takes on its journey to excise opposing opinions has a great deal to do with a deliberate inflation of irrational affect. We will get nowhere in the fight against the intellectual right if we engage in this asymmetric practice of communication, which resembles more a ritualistic self-flagellation than a genuine conversation.

Above all, we need to understand what the new right means when they talk about human history. That new-right elites do not believe in progress—which Patrick Deneen invidiously characterizes as a "modern project of seeing politics as the means of mastering nature" and "liberating the individual from interpersonal bonds and obligations"—should surprise no one.[50] Deneen's hostility toward the idea of progress is but a milder variant of the right's general dislike for the idea of time as a linear progression of any kind. This oppositional stance takes two forms. In one version of this rage against modernity, we often encounter an endorsement of human history as a loop or an eternal return rather than a progression. Often, this antimodernist reflex takes the simplified form of advocating a return to the past. The motto of Palmgren and Lokteff's racialist Red Ice TV page on VKontakte is "The Future is the Past";

the Russian media conglomerate "Tsargrad" routinely posts on all the major internet platforms about the desirability of returning to the monarchist past.

The other version of this rage against modernity is eschatological, rather than cyclical or proudly regressive, and is far more characteristic of the US context than the Russian.[51] A belief in "end times" is never wholly absent from traditionalist populism among white Americans. As the religious historian Anthea Butler explains, the prospect of a divinely ordered global catastrophe is "useful in promoting the evangelical idea that individual salvation, rather than collective action such as socialism or civil rights, would [be able to] stem social and political ills."[52]

What both anti-historiographic ways of thinking have in common is a contempt for quotidian or bread-and-butter issues and an indifference toward reforming institutional practices that reflects a contempt for civil society and democratic participation. When Corey Robin interviewed Irving Kristol and William F. Buckley in 2000, the neoconservative Kristol unapologetically appealed to a mythic approach to history: "There's the Republican Party tying itself into knots. Over what? Prescriptions for elderly people? Who gives a damn? I think it's disgusting that . . . presidential politics of the most important country in the world should revolve around prescriptions for elderly people. Future historians will find this very hard to believe. It's not Athens. It's not Rome. It's not anything."[53] While many have argued that the "old" right that Kristol represents is out of touch with Trumpist populism and the alt-right, it is important to understand that the two converge precisely in their contempt for the granular character of the present and their disgust at the seemingly cumbersome nature of parliamentary governance. Both types of American conservatism would feel perfectly at home with the derisive assessments of representative (as opposed to direct) democracy voiced by Carl Schmitt and by Konstantin Pobedonostsev, the advisor to Tsar Alexander III. Pobedonostsev saw representative democracy as a "mechanism" that the "liberal intelligentsia" praises to the sky, and which the common folk correctly recognize as an instrument of torture. Using language that was strikingly similar, Schmitt described the institution of parliamentary democracy as an "artificial machinery, produced by liberal reasoning," that compares pitifully with the dynamos of "dictatorial and Caesaristic methods."[54]

As we have seen, the intelligentsia of the right often thinks in highly metaphorical, if not mythic and militantly ahistorical, turns. We could say of new-right reasoning what the Russian literary critic Viktor Shklovsky said of poetry: it is a way of thinking in images, which has the signal virtue of giving its speaker the sense—or perhaps the illusion—that thoughtful reflection is most authentic when it is easy.[55] We need to call out new-right elites and expose the tissue-thin degrees that separate them from past and present advocates for authoritarianism and autocracy, while also encouraging them to explain their arguments as fully as possible. Perhaps verbalization will shift their perspectives by allowing them to recognize the strangeness or artificiality of their own arguments, which both Hochschild's Civil War-re-enactor and even Averianov, in his description of the political elite as a constructed category, seem to recognize. Such a step would also force us to listen more closely to what they have to say.

Finally, we need to consider the ramifications of Jason Stanley's insight about demagoguery's practice of rendering other perspectives invisible. Recognizing the banality of some of the right's formulations, in that same 2000 interview with Robin, Buckley quipped that "the trouble with the emphasis in conservatism on the [free] market . . . is that it becomes rather boring. You hear it once, you master the idea. The notion of devoting your life to it is horrifying if only because it's so repetitious. It's like sex."[56] Learning from their elders, new-right elites fully understand that their practices within democracies are defined more by erasure than by engagement with—or vigorous rebuttal against—the ideas and political views that they oppose.

We need to question the language of elitist populists, drawing attention to the absurdity of their political vocabulary about the supposed wisdom of "eternal truths." We must resist the pull of sonorous if arid generalizations about "tradition," "common good," the need for absolute authority, and the assumption of paternalistic benevolence from authority figures with whom we imagine an affinity. Shoutouts to buzzwords have a self-reinforcing character, which a fuller explanation may serve to demystify and decisively shatter. In his acidly bitter poem "Comrade Stalin" (1959), the Russian Jewish writer Yuz Aleshkovsky wrote: "Comrade Stalin, we thought you knew best / We didn't trust ourselves—we trusted you."[57] Rebutting distorted understandings of the historical record that reinforce authoritarian interpretations of culture is a process, and as chapter 5 shows, even the act of removing a monument can be a matter of stages or degrees. The Russian structuralist critic Yuri Lotman, in a book devoted to the dynamics of interpreting a literary text, writes: "Thrown onto the grass, a statue may create a new artistic effect, through the emergence of a [perceived] *relationship* between marble and grass"; the fact that it would not produce the same effect if cast onto a garbage dump doesn't mean that a similar relationship can't be found there as well.[58] The removal of a politically problematic monument ought to take place through a series of deliberative actions that terminate a legacy with the goal of opening up the possibilities for truth and reconciliation. Until its shuttering by the Russian government late in 2021, the human rights organization Memorial International was dedicated to that endeavor of opening the door to granular examinations of the historical record. Fortunately, some of its work has been continued in other venues, most notably by its sister organization in St. Petersburg.[59]

What the Russian context can teach Americans is the importance of skepticism about 'deep stories,' whether they be the defense of the Confederacy as a noble 'lost cause' or apologetics for domestic policies under Stalin and territorial expansion into the countries of the former Soviet sphere. The civic lessons provoked into existence by the Russian experience may also remind us to value what the Moscow-based anticorruption activist Lyubov Sobol identifies as the principles for a life that is "grounded in reason."[60] As a corollary effort, the expatriate Russian scholar Mark Lipovetsky asks us to be attentive to illusion that a "melodramatic form [of expression] creates from the debris and fragments of old values," resulting in an "aura of moral righteousness" around patently imperialistic endeavors such as the invasion of Ukraine.[61] In responding to the right and its new and highly articulate advocates, we need to take their arguments seriously, which means that we call them out when they are unserious: when they bowdlerize histories, when they refuse to listen, when they place too much trust in totems of power even as they attempt to creatively and individualistically engage with them, and when they are silent at moments when they should speak.

Acknowledgments

A LTHOUGH THE EVENTS that unfolded in the United States and the Russian Federation from 2016 to 2022 form the backbone of this book, my earlier research on evolving self-images of nationalism contributed to my discussion about traditionalist elites in both countries. First and foremost, I would like to thank my editor, Amber Rose Cederstrom, for her insightful suggestions and unflagging support at every stage of this complex undertaking. This book would truly not have seen the light of day without her wise counsel, or without the support of Nathan MacBrien, the editor in chief at the press. I am deeply grateful to Jane Barry for her insightful questions and intelligent suggestions at the copyedit stage of the manuscript. I would also like to thank Krista Andrews and my colleagues at the Oakley Center for Humanities and Social Sciences at Williams College for providing frank and encouraging commentary on my work about outlaw sensibilities in contemporary Russian culture. During my time at the center in 2016, Francis Oakley, Marden Nichols, Olga Shevchenko, Jessica M. Fisher, and Jana Sawicki were especially helpful, advising me on how to think more rigorously about the human subjects of my work. In St. Petersburg, Vyacheslav Dolinin, Konstantin Azadovsky, and Alexander Skobov provided invaluable information about the incarceration of dissidents in the Soviet prison system during the eighties, as did Vyacheslav Bakhmin and Alexander Ogorodnikov in Moscow. The staff of the St. Petersburg and Moscow branches of the human rights organization Memorial provided a welcoming atmosphere for my consultation of GULAG memoirs. In particular, I thank Irina Flige and Aleks Gagarinova in St. Petersburg and Tatiana Bakhmina in Moscow. Valery Averianov at the Izborsk Club in Moscow was generous with his time and extremely gracious in providing detailed responses to my questions. Natalya Skrounditaki, the chief administrator at the Izborsk Club, helped me with logistical and technical issues. I am very grateful to Father Andrei Kuraev for answering my questions about his recent activities.

The responses of Svetlana Evdokimova, Tom Nichols, Patricia Anne Simpson, Denis Crnković, Edith W. Clowes, and Neil Roberts to chapter drafts were crucial for the forward momentum of this project. I would like to thank Ronald Radosh for meeting with me to discuss in detail his encounter with Steve Bannon in 2013. Irina Manta from the Law School at Hofstra University took time out from her busy schedule to speak with me extensively about her dealings with Josh Hawley during their student days at Yale Law School. I am indebted to Kim Kelly, Julia Mayorova, and Viktor Nemtinov for giving permission to reproduce images from their work as activists, photographers, and journalists. Carol Ueland helped me secure permission to use Catharine Nepomnyashchy's photograph of Vladimir Sorokin and Jamey Gambrell in front of the Dzerzhinsky monument during the attempted August 1991 putsch in Moscow. I would also like to thank Mika Hirai for enhancing the resolution of a few of the images printed in this book.

As always, my wife, Helga Druxes, provided deeply intelligent assessments of what I wrote at different stages. Through their personal examples and active encouragement, both she and our son, Nicholas, continually reminded me of this project's value and necessity.

This book is dedicated to my mother, Olivera Mihailović, and her brother, Miloš Kontić, both of whom passed away during my work on it. As I wrote, I always bore in mind their experiences as children who were forced to go on a hunger march during the Second World War, and who were homeless during much of the war because of the operations of the Axis powers. It is my hope that this book will contribute, in some small way, to the study of authoritarian modes of thought and their human consequences.

Notes

Preface

1. Vladimir Putin, "Address by the President of the Russian Federation" (21 February 2022): http://kremlin.ru/events/president/news/67828. The official English translation softens the sarcasm of the Russian original, which I have restored. All unattributed translations in this book are mine.

2. Kirill Gundiaev, "Patriarshaia propoved' v nedeliu syropustnuiu posle Liturgii v khrame Khrista Spasitelia," official site of the Russian Orthodox Church (6 March 2022): http://www.patriarchia.ru/db/text/5906442.html.

3. Kirill Gundiaev, "Patriarshaia propoved' v nedeliu syropustnuiu posle Liturgii v khrame Khrista Spasitelia," official site of the Russian Orthodox Church (13 March 2022): http://www.patriarchia.ru/db/text/5908325.html.

4. Helen Andrews (@herandrews), Twitter, 28 April 2022: https://twitter.com/herandrews/status/1519644367056691200.

5. Patrick Deneen, "Russia, America, and the Danger of Political Gnosticism," (2 March 2022).

6. The phrase is from Candida R. Moss and Joel S. Baden, *Bible Nation: The United States of Hobby Lobby* (2017), 20.

7. Interview from documentary "Rebranding White Nationalism: Inside the Alt-Right," *The Atlantic* (15 December 2016), at 00:18.

Introduction

1. Mogelson, "Among the Insurrectionists," 38.

2. Cusset, *How the World Swung to the Right*, 114–15.

3. "'We Just Want Russia to Be Better': Meduza Looks Back on the January 31 Opposition Protests in a Dispatch from St. Petersburg," *Meduza* (2 February 2021).

4. Dilimbetov and Kobyzev, "'Ty dostal tut begat': Na aktsii v podderzhku Alekseiia Naval'nogo zaderzhali pochti tysiachu chelovek i izbili zhurnalista," *Kommersant* (31 January 2021).

5. "V Peterburge na mitinge proizoshli stolknoveniia protestuiushchikh s OMON-om," RBC [RosBiznesConsulting] Daily (31 January 2021).

6. Khavin et al., "Day of Rage: How Trump Supporters Took the U.S. Capitol," *New York Times* (30 June 2021).

7. Land and Jamieson, "Rioters Breached the Capitol as They Waved Pro-Police Flags: Police Support on the Right May Be Eroding, Experts Warn," *Washington Post* (8 January 2021).

8. Broadwater and Fandos, "Beaten, Tased and Crushed by Rioters at Capitol: Four Officers Testify—'I Have Kids,' One Begged Mob," *New York Times* (27 July 2021).

9. For a discussion of the conceit "We [Americans] live in a republic, not a democracy," which has become widespread in both Republican and alt-right circles, see Thomas, "'America Is a Republic, Not a Democracy' Is a Dangerous—and Wrong—Argument."

10. Hobsbawm, *Bandits*, 20, 38.

11. Cooper, "How a Right-Wing Network Mobilized Sheriffs' Departments."

12. Ben-Ghiat, *Strongmen: Mussolini to the Present*, 147.

13. See Lur'e, *Azbuka protesta: Narodnyi plakat*.

14. Limbaugh, "My Bipartisan Stimulus," *Wall Street Journal* (29 January 2009).

15. Fenghi, *It Will Be Fun and Terrifying*, 117.

16. Bernal et al., *Cognitive Warfare*, 30.

17. Lombroso, *White Noise* (film), at 55:00.

18. Quoted in Carrère, *Limonov*, 244.

19. Robin, *The Reactionary Mind*, 41.

20. Robin, *The Reactionary Mind*, 40.

21. De Maistre, *The Executioner*, 83.

22. "L'homme nouveau qui peut parvenir à tout, en vivant et en obtenant des grades, n'a aucun intérêt à troubler l'État. L'esclavage a beaucoup de compensations et n'exclut point l'enthousiasme national." ("The New Man who can reach [or: achieve] everything by living and obtaining promotions has no interest in upsetting the State. Slavery has many compensations and does not at all exclude national enthusiasm.") Quoted in Adamovsky, "Russia as a Space of Hope," 418.

23. Alana Abramson, "White Nationalists Carrying Torches Descend on Charlottesville Again," *Time* (8 October 2017). A longer recording of the October demonstration, posted by Spencer himself, can be found at "Back in Charlottesville" (https://www.pscp.tv/w/1yoKMpodMMexQ).

24. Steve Bannon, with Erik Prince, "War Room 1,660: Scarborough Fear Porn Fails; Putin's 100 Years Humiliation Speech" (podcast), 23 February 2022 (especially 49:00–51:00).

25. Tocqueville, *Democracy in America*, 484–85.

26. Quoted in Hirshson, *General Patton*, 650.

27. For a discussion of Patton's intellectual links to the Confederate cause, and his Spenglerian understanding of war as a crucible for forging and testing Western values, see Prioli, "King Arthur in Khaki," especially 43–44, 47–49.

28. Dissident Mama, episode 19: "Tim Kirby" (podcast).

29. Quoted in Polyakova, "Strange Bedfellows," 39.

30. Titorenko, "Zhirinovskii predlozhil 'vykupat' detei u zhenshchin, planiruiushchikh abort," *Gazeta.ru* (21 June 2021).

31. Azhgikhina, "Russian Women against Militarism: Act II," *The Nation* (8 March 2019).

32. Wodak, *The Politics of Fear*, 126–27.

33. Stanley, *How Fascism Works*, 183.

34. Sokolov, "Baiden vstupilsia za Naval'nogo," *Radio Svoboda* (27 January 2021).

35. Andrews, "2020 Is Tumbling toward 1917" (blog post).

36. Mogelson, "Among the Insurrectionists," 36.

37. Gramsci, "Selections from the *Prison Notebooks*," tr. Joseph A. Buttigieg, *Boundary* 131:3 (Summer 2002), 82. This is the sole translation in English of "Scattered Notes and Jottings for a Group of Essays on the History of the Intellectuals," which comes from Notebook 12, of the *Prison Notebooks*.

38. Gramsci, *Prison Notebooks*, 1:214. (Emphases in the original.)

39. Gramsci, *Prison Notebooks*, 2:203.

40. Mogelson, "Among the Insurrectionists," 35.

41. Goldman, "The Comet Ping Pong Gunman Answers Our Reporter's Questions," *New York Times* (7 December 2016).

42. Mayakovsky, "Razgovor s fininspektorom," 120.

43. Hofstadter, "The Paranoid Style in American Politics," in *Anti-Intellectualism in American Life, The Paranoid Style in American Politics, Uncollected Essays 1956–1965*, 531.

44. Mogelson, "Among the Insurrectionists," 38.

45. Hofstadter, "The Paranoid Style in American Politics," in *Anti-Intellectualism in American Life, The Paranoid Style in American Politics, Uncollected Essays 1956–1965*, 532–33.

46. Bayoumy and Gilsinan, "A Reformed White Nationalist Says the Worst Is Yet to Come."

47. "The balancing-boy ethos courted many hazardous ironies, as the Kennedy White House's disastrous military errand in Vietnam—infamously a project of the nation's best and brightest—was poised to demonstrate at the time Hofstadter's book appeared." Lehmann, "What Richard Hofstadter Got Wrong."

48. Heer, "At Liberalism's Crossroads."

49. Hofstadter, "The Paranoid Style in American Politics," in *Anti-Intellectualism in American Life, The Paranoid Style in American Politics, Uncollected Essays 1956–1965*, 533.

50. Hofstadter, "The Paranoid Style in American Politics," in *Anti-Intellectualism in American Life, The Paranoid Style in American Politics, Uncollected Essays 1956–1965*, 533.

51. Hofstadter, *Anti-Intellectualism in American Life, The Paranoid Style in American Politics, Uncollected Essays 1956–1965*, 451.

52. Hawley, "The Age of Pelagius."

53. Itkowitz, "GOP Sen. Hawley Says He Does Not Regret Raising Fist to Pro-Trump Mob at Capitol on Jan. 6," *Washington Post* (4 May 2021).

54. Phone conversation, 7 August 2021.

55. Hawley, "The Age of Pelagius."

56. MacLean, *Democracy in Chains*, 161.

57. MacLean, *Democracy in Chains*, 163.

58. Quoted in MacLean, *Democracy in Chains*, 79.

59. Slezkine, *The Jewish Century*, 28.

60. Slezkine, *The Jewish Century*, 20.

61. Slezkine, *The Jewish Century*, 24.

62. Quoted in Frankel, "A Majority of the People Arrested for Capitol Riot Had a History of Financial Trouble," *Washington Post* (10 February 2021).

63. Vance, *Hillbilly Elegy*, 57; Deneen, "What I Saw in America" (blog post).

64. Ryan (@dotjenna), Twitter, 6 January 2021, https://twitter.com/dotjenna/status/1346965308041433090.

65. Chryssagvis, "Alfeyev and Lavrov."

66. Shishkov, "The Navalny Protests and Orthodoxy's Apolitical Theology."

67. "Tserkov' i mir: Efir ot 30.01.2021" (video).

68. Frey, "The US Will Become Minority White in 2045, Census Projects."

69. Quoted in Du Mez, *Jesus and John Wayne*, 262–63.

70. Hochschild, *Strangers in Their Own Land*, 61.

71. Gessen, "The Dying Russians."

72. Kondakov, "Regulating Desire in Russia," 404.

73. Polyakova, "Strange Bedfellows," 39.

74. Lenin, *The State and Revolution*, 38.

75. Wodak, *The Politics of Fear*, 12.

76. Kennedy, "The 'Virtual Machine' and New Becomings in Pre-Millennial Culture," 14, 19.

77. Taylor, "No More Charlottesvilles."

78. Sorokin, "Let the Past Collapse on Time!"

79. Laruelle, "Russian and American Far Right Connections," 2–3.

80. "277 iazykov i dialektowe ispol'zuiut narody Rossii."

81. Tocqueville, *Democracy in America*, 276.

82. Caldwell, "Hungary and the Future of Europe."

83. Quoted in Riccardi-Swartz, "Seeking a Sovereign for the End of Democracy."

84. Quoted in Robin, *The Reactionary Mind*, 202.

85. A succinct summary of Burnham's thought is offered in Kelly, *James Burnham and the Struggle for the World*, 174.

86. For a summary of the "Dulles Plan" conspiracy, see Borenstein, *Plots against Russia*, 89–92.

Chapter 1. A Place at the High Table

Epigraph: Blok's essay is translated in *The Spirit of Music*, 19. I have modified the translation with an eye to the specificity of his statement in Russian.

1. Latynina, "Velikaia zapadnaia kul'turnaia revoliutsiia."

2. Barton, "Violent Protest and the Intelligentsia."

3. Morson, "Suicide of the Liberals."

4. Chernyshevsky, *What Is to Be Done*, 369.

5. Tucker, *The Marx-Engels Reader*, 134.

6. Lenin, "Pamiati Gertsena," 261.

7. Chaadaev, "First Philosophical Letter," in *The Major Works of Peter Chaadaev*, 32.

8. Poliakov and Kotov, eds. *N. V. Gogol' v russkoi kritike*, 251.

9. For a discussion of how Stowe and her allies overstated the significance of the novel in precipitating the Civil War, see Vollaro, "Lincoln, Stowe, and the 'Little Woman/Great War' Story."

10. The policies of Nicholas I, in establishing schools such as the Practical Technological Institute in Moscow in 1828, proved especially significant in creating a non-government class of literate citizens. The graduates of that institute were prohibited

from entering government service, "reverting to their class of origin upon graduation" (Walter Mackenzie Pintner, *Russian Economic Policy Under Nicholas I*, 50–51).

11. Chernyshevsky, *What Is to Be Done?* 286–87.

12. Chernyshevsky, *What Is to Be Done?* 287.

13. Chernyshevsky, *What Is to Be Done?* 284.

14. Odoevsky, "Dnevnik V F Odoevskogo, 1859–1869 gg," 211.

15. Jakobson, "Two Aspects of Language," in Jakobson and Halle, *Fundamentals of Language*, 80.

16. Dostoevsky, *Great Short Works*, 208–9. The translation is by Nora Gottlieb.

17. Dostoevsky, *Great Short Works*, 208.

18. Tolstoy, *The Death of Ivan Ilyich and Confession*, 126, 175.

19. Tolstoy, *The Death of Ivan Ilyich and Confession*, 57, 41.

20. Tolstoy, *The Death of Ivan Ilyich and Confession*, 41.

21. Robin, *The Reactionary Mind*, 61.

22. MacLean, *Democracy in Chains*, 97–98; Tomisov, "Fedor Petrovich Pobedonostsev 1827–1909," in *Russkie pravovedy XVIII–XX vekov*, 1:382.

23. Shchepkina-Kupernik, "Peterburgskii noktiurn," 41.

24. Butler, *Undoing Gender*, 207.

25. Dreher, *Live Not by Lies*, 129.

26. See Duberman's *Has the Gay Movement Failed*, especially pages 106–10.

27. Robin, *The Reactionary Mind*, 50.

28. "Russian Political Ad Bashes Gay Marriage."

29. Paul, *From Tolerance to Equality*, 21.

30. Paul, *From Tolerance to Equality*, 19, 21.

31. Deneen, *Why Liberalism Failed*, xvii.

32. Deneen, *Why Liberalism Failed*, xix.

33. Paul, "Under the Rainbow Banner."

34. Deneen, *Why Liberalism Failed*, 145.

35. Deneen, *Why Liberalism Failed*, 147.

36. Deneen, *Why Liberalism Failed*, 147.

37. Faust, *The Creation of Confederate Nationalism*, 29.

38. Deneen, *Why Liberalism Failed*, 146.

39. Crews, "Dialectical Immaterialism," 450, 458, 463.

40. In Shragin and Todd, *Landmarks: A Collection of Essays on the Russian Intelligentsia, 1909*, 14.

41. Morson, "Prosaics Evolving," 70–71.

42. Dreher, "Ukraine: Once More, into the Breach."

43. Dreher, *The Benedict Option*, 9–10, 17, 45.

44. Dreher, *The Benedict Option*, 44.

45. Dreher, *The Benedict Option*, 137.

46. Dreher, *The Benedict Option*, 237.

47. Dreher, *Live Not by Lies*, 155.

48. Dreher, *The Benedict Option*, 67.

49. Dreher, "How (Not) to Think about the Caravan."

50. Dreher (@roddreher), Twitter, 25 July 2020: https://twitter.com/roddreher/status/1287065050692366337.

51. Dreher, *The Benedict Option*, 114.

52. Dreher, *The Benedict Option*, 124.

53. Dreher, *The Benedict Option*, 40.

54. Dreher, *The Benedict Option*, 55.

55. Dreher, *The Benedict Option*, 70–71.

56. Dreher, *The Benedict Option*, 41.

57. Dreher, *The Benedict Option*, 70.

58. Dreher, "Of Sh*tholes and Second Thoughts."

59. Dreher, "It's Jean Raspail's World Now."

60. Jones, "Rod Dreher's Race Problem."

61. Riccardi-Swartz, "American Conversions to Russian Orthodoxy amid the Global Culture Wars," symposium, "The Culture Wars Today."

62. Dreher, "It's Jean Raspail's World Now."

63. Deneen, *Why Liberalism Failed*, 192.

64. Paul, "The Future Is Mixed."

65. Deneen, *Why Liberalism Failed*, 192.

66. Paul, "The Future Is Mixed."

67. This tweet (https://twitter.com/darelmass/status/1385605470925230081) was subsequently taken down.

68. Solzhenitsyn, "Live Not by Lies" (tr. Yermolai Solzhenitsyn).

69. Dreher, *Live Not by Lies*, 213.

70. Morrison, "The Dancing Mind."

71. Kundera, "Die Weltliteratur," 30.

72. Dreher, *Live Not by Lies*, 79.

73. Billington, *The Icon and the Axe*, 504, 767.

74. Dreher, *Live Not by Lies*, 47–48.

75. Dreher, "Save the West, Move to . . . *Europe?*" (blog post).

76. Dreher, *Live Not by Lies*, 66.

77. Dreher, *Live Not by Lies*, 184–85.

78. Dreher, *Live Not by Lies*, 152.

79. Dreher, *Live Not by Lies*, 142.

80. Dreher, *Live Not by Lies*, 196–97. In his 2013 book *Dissident for Life: Alexander Ogorodnikov and the Struggle for Religious Freedom in Russia*, Koenraad de Wolf describes similar moments, including his baptism of fellow prisoners (114, 146). In the interview I conducted with him in February 2017, Ogorodnikov indicated that there were no tensions between him as a dissident and the non-political inmates, many of whom were fascinated by his oppositional activity.

81. Dreher, *Live Not by Lies*, 145. See also page 176.

82. Dreher, *Live Not by Lies*, 54.

83. Dreher, *Live Not by Lies*, 61.

84. Dreher, *Live Not by Lies*, 205.

85. Dreher, "Why George Floyd Died,"

86. Stern, *Proud Boys and the White Ethnostate*, 125.

87. Schmemann, "Forgiveness: A Homily Delivered to the Community at St. Vladimir's Orthodox Seminary on Forgiveness Sunday of 1983."

88. Schmemann, "Forgiveness."

89. Andrews, "2020 Is Tumbling toward 1917."

90. Andrews, "2020 Is Tumbling toward 1917."

91. Anton, "The Regime's Failing Jan. 6 Lie."

92. Andrews (@herandrews), Twitter, 28 January 2021: https://twitter.com/her andrews/status/1354787468004925443.

93. Dreher, "The Tragedy of Franco's Spain."

94. Quoted in Faludy, "The Philosophy of Orbán's Misguided Christian Friends."

95. Du Mez, *Jesus and John Wayne*, 79.

96. Vermeule, "Beyond Originalism."

97. See especially Koni, *M. M. Kovalev'skii v zakonodatel'noi deiatel'nosti*, 10–12.

98. The full extent of Deneen's reference to unions is a now-deleted tweet from 8 September 2020, in which he applauded them for their cultural conservatism. In the same thread, he claimed that Ronald Reagan was a staunch ally of unions, ignoring Reagan's precedent-setting mass firing of striking air-traffic controllers in 1981. What remains of that tweet thread includes some of my responses to him: https://twitter .com/amihailo/status/1303343766586224641

99. "Transcript: Ezra Klein interviews Patrick Deneen," The Ezra Klein Show, *New York Times* (13 May 2022).

100. Eliot, *After Strange Gods*, 15–16.

101. Quoted in Mogelson, "Among the Insurrectionists," 39.

102. Morson, "Suicide of the Liberals."

103. Chekhov, "Tapior," *Sobranie sochinenii 3*, 273. The translation is mine.

104. Baldwin, "The Discovery of What It Means to Be an American," in *Collected Essays*, 141–42.

105. In Baldwin, *The Cross of Redemption*, 5–6.

106. Eliot, *The Sacred Wood*, 51–52.

107. "Transcript: Ezra Klein interviews Patrick Deneen," The Ezra Klein Show, *New York Times* (13 May 2022).

Chapter 2. Whither the State?

Epigraph: The translation is mine.

1. Pagliery, "Trump Adviser Peter Navarro Lays Out How He and Bannon Planned to Overturn Biden Electoral Win."

2. Hochschild, *Strangers in Their Own Land*, 135.

3. The information about Bannon's $30,000 honorarium at the Hudson Institute comes from an interview I conducted with Ronald Radosh on 29 June 2019.

4. Radosh, "D.C. Elites Suck up to Steve Bannon Like He's the Next Henry Kissinger"; Bannon, "Hudson Institute Violent Extremism Conference, Steve Bannon Remarks" (video).

5. Quoted in Robin, *The Reactionary Mind*, 47.

6. Robin, *The Reactionary Mind*, 51, 56.

7. Robin, *The Reactionary Mind*, 223, 226.

8. O'Toole, *Heroic Failure*, 127, 134.

9. Green, *Devil's Bargain*, 159.

10. Collins, "Not a Prophet in His Own Land."

11. Sebestyen, *Lenin: The Man, the Dictator, and the Master of Terror*, 70–71.

12. Ahmed, "Happy Objects," 50.

13. Ahmed, "Happy Objects," 50.

14. Quoted in Robin, *The Reactionary Mind*, 256.

15. Müller, *What Is Populism?* 20.

16. Levada Center, "Vladimir Putin," *Levada Center* (20 November 2017).

17. Müller, *What Is Populism?* 23.

18. Love, speech at the 2012 Republican National Convention (video).

19. Frum, "Is the White Working Class Coming Apart?"

20. For a fuller expression of the grudging admiration for Putin among the American conservative intelligentsia, see Hanson, "The Value of Putin."

21. Müller, *What Is Populism?* 35–36.

22. Müller, *What Is Populism?* 25.

23. Müller, *What Is Populism?* 30.

24. Quoted in Alex Morris, "Donald Trump: The End-Times President," *Rolling Stone* (30 October 2020).

25. Meeting of the Valdai International Discussion Club (video and transcript, 9 September 2013).

26. Graham, "Putin's Olympic Controversy."

27. Müller, *What Is Populism?* 35.

28. Quoted in Redden, "Trump's Powers Will Not Be Questioned, Says Senior Official."

29. Benda, *Treason of the Intellectuals*, 135.

30. Hell and Steinmetz, "A Period of 'Wild and Fierce Fanaticism,'" 374.

31. Quoted in Robin, *The Reactionary Mind*, 69.

32. Müller, *What Is Populism?* 18.

33. "Leading Advocate of a Revival of the Old Confederacy Resigns a Tenured Professorship at a Black College," *The Journal of Blacks in Higher Education* (Autumn 1999), 46.

34. Hill, "To Our Russian Friends."

35. Steiner, "Russia and Red China."

36. Vidal, "Requiem for the American Empire."

37. Vidal, "The Empire Lovers Strike Back."

38. Hill, "Our Russia Outreach Has Struck a Nerve!" (23 July 2018).

39. Lieven, "Against Russophobia."

40. For discussions of Aloise Buckley and her influence on the formation of her son's political views, see Buccola, *The Fire Is upon Us: James Baldwin, William F. Buckley, and the Debate over Race in America*, 14–16.

41. See Tarsaidze's *Czars and Presidents: The Story of a Forgotten Friendship*, 192–210. While Tarsaidze's heroic treatment of political figures and anecdotal style of history writing have not aged well, his account of the political ripples from the 1863 docking of the Russian war ships in New York is both thorough and convincing.

42. Andre M. Fleche, *The Revolution of 1861: The American Civil War in the Age of Nationalist Conflict*, 97, 100–101.

43. John Marquardt, "Russia vs. the Confederacy," *The Abbeville Institute* (17 October 2017).

44. Green, *Devil's Bargain*, 51.

45. Green, *Devil's Bargain*, 206.

46. Green, *Devil's Bargain*, 145.

47. Lenin, *Polnoe sobranie sochinenii*, 36:78–79.

48. Robin, *The Reactionary Mind*, 186.

49. Solzhenitsyn, *Lenin in Zürich*, 116.

50. Wolff, *Fire and Fury*, 60.

51. Radosh, "Steve Bannon, Trump's Top Guy, Told Me He Was a Leninist."

52. Lenin, *The State and Revolution*, 107. Emphasis in the original.

53. "Without the personal experience, if one is looking in from the outside, [the performative demeanor of the sixties radicals] does look messy and almost pointless." Sontag, "What's Happening in America" (1966), in *Essays of the Sixties and Seventies*, 458.

54. Judt, *Reappraisals*, 109.

55. Sante, "Invisible Man."

56. "Conservative Advocate" (National Public Radio interview, 25 May 2001).

57. Phone interview with Ronald Radosh (29 June 2019).

58. Brock, *Blinded by the Right*, 361.

59. Shaw, "The Iago Problem."

60. Avrich, *Kronstadt 1921*, 229, 241; Lenin, *The State and Revolution*, 75.

61. Feder, "This Is How Steve Bannon Sees the Entire World"; Bannon, "Module 3—Should Christians Impose Limits on Wealth Creation?" (video).

62. Koffler, *Bannon: Always the Rebel*, 95–96.

63. Lenin, *The State and Revolution*, 80.

64. Feder, "This Is How Steve Bannon Sees the Entire World"; Bannon, "Module 3—Should Christians Impose Limits on Wealth Creation?" (video).

65. Robin, *The Reactionary Mind*, 202.

66. Lenin, *Selected Works*, 1:764.

67. Benner, *Really Existing Nationalisms*, 106–7.

68. This tweet has been taken down (https://twitter.com/PatrickDeneen/status/133 6700221200461828).

69. Field, "Meet the Reocons."

70. Sebestyen, *Lenin: The Man, the Dictator, and the Master of Terror*, 73.

71. See Read, *Lenin: A Revolutionary Life*, 166–67, 171, 214; White, *Lenin: The Practice and Theory of Revolution*, 156–57.

72. Lenin, *The State and Revolution*, 17.

73. Lenin, *The State and Revolution*, 57, 81.

74. Lenin, *The State and Revolution*, 73, 81.

75. Lenin, *The State and Revolution*, 93.

76. Lenin, *The State and Revolution*, 111.

77. Hell and Steinmetz, "A Period of 'Wild and Fierce Fanaticism,'" 387.

78. Lenin, *The State and Revolution*, 38.

79. Lenin, *The State and Revolution*, 48.

80. Ahmed, "Happy Objects," 41.

81. Quoted in Hsu, "The Feeling When," 62.

82. Solzhenitsyn, *Lenin in Zürich*, 44; Russian text: *Lenin v Tsiurikhe*, 37.

83. Quoted in Robin, *The Reactionary Mind*, 240.

84. Here, the translation is mine because of an inaccuracy in the Willetts translation. Solzhenitsyn, *Lenin v Tsiurikhe*, 153.

85. Quoted in Sebestyen, *Lenin: The Man, the Dictator, and the Master of Terror*, 83.

86. Green, "Inside the Secret, Strange Origins of Steve Bannon's Nationalist Fantasia" (17 July 2017).

87. Hell and Steinmetz, "A Period of 'Wild and Fierce Fanaticism,'" 388.

88. Lenin, *The State and Revolution*, 111.

89. Service, Introduction to Lenin, *The State and Revolution*, xxi.

90. Service, Introduction to Lenin, *The State and Revolution*, xxiv.

91. Tuğal, "The Rise of the Leninist Right."

92. Green, *Devil's Bargain*, 90, 219.

93. Lenin, *The State and Revolution*, 83.

94. Müller, *What Is Populism?* 35–36.

95. Wodak, *The Politics of Fear*, 12.

96. Berlant and Edelman, *Sex, or the Unbearable*, 95.

97. Berlant and Edelman, *Sex, or the Unbearable*, 14.

98. Althusser, *Lenin and Philosophy and Other Essays*, 82.

99. Berlant, *Cruel Optimism*, 16.

100. Berlant, *Cruel Optimism*, 81.

101. Sebestyen, *Lenin: The Man, the Dictator, and the Master of Terror*, 381.

102. Sebestyen, *Lenin: The Man, the Dictator, and the Master of Terror*, 382.

103. Lenin, "Speech on the Dissolution of the Constituent Assembly"; Lenin, *Polnoe sobranie sochinenii*, 35:273–74.

104. Sebestyen, *Lenin: The Man, the Dictator, and the Master of Terror*, 384.

105. Müller, *What Is Populism?* 49.

106. Müller, *What Is Populism?* 102.

107. Hosking, *Russia and the Russians*, 400.

108. Müller, *Democracy Rules*, 59–60.

109. Stern, *Proud Boys and the White Ethnostate*, 32.

110. Said, "On Defiance and Taking Positions," 501.

111. Said, "On Defiance and Taking Positions," 506.

112. Robin, *The Reactionary Mind*, 19.

113. Hosking, *Russia and the Russians*, 402.

Chapter 3. Hijacking Academic Authority

Epigraph: The translation is mine.

1. Slezkine, *The Jewish Century*, 20.

2. Stern, *Proud Boys and the White Ethnostate*, 126.

3. MacDonald, "Alexander Dugin's 4 Political Theory Is for the Russian Empire, Not for European Ethno-Nationalists."

4. Miller, "The Theory behind That Charlottesville Slogan."

5. Cofnas, "Judaism as a Group Evolutionary Strategy."

6. MacDonald, "The 'Default Hypothesis' Fails to Explain Jewish Influence."

7. The incompatibility of "sociobiology" with historiography is a heated topic. Recently the *American Historical Review* assigned a review of Ansley Erickson's *Making the Unequal Metropolis* (2017), a book about education policy during the Civil Rights era,

to an emeritus professor at the University of Delaware who was a known white supremacist. For an account of the scandal, and letters objecting to the review assignment,
see "Communications," *American Historical Review* 122 (April 2017): 637–39; Hesse, "A
Journal's Apology Prompts Soul-Searching about Racial Gatekeeping in the Academy."

8. Cofnas, *Reptiles with a Conscience*, 132, 141, 143–44.

9. Cofnas (@nathancofnas), Twitter, 5 November 2018: https://twitter.com/nathan
cofnas/status/1059453302495166464.

10. Cofnas, "Judaism as a Group Evolutionary Strategy," 156. For similar statements, see Cofnas, "The Anti-Jewish Narrative," 1342.

11. MacDonald, "Reply to Nathan Cofnas."

12. Hofstadter, "The Paranoid Style in American Politics," in *Anti-Intellectualism in
American Life, The Paranoid Style in American Politics, Uncollected Essays 1956–1965*, 531–32.

13. Schoenfeld, review of Kevin MacDonald's *A People That Shall Dwell Alone*, 409.

14. Quoted in MacDonald, *The Culture of Critique*, 241–42. All page references will
refer to the first edition of this book, published in 1998.

15. MacDonald, *The Culture of Critique*, 245.

16. MacDonald, "Memories of Madison—My Life in the New Left."

17. Mosse, *The Crisis of German Ideology*, 142.

18. MacDonald, *A People That Shall Dwell Alone*, 35, 50–51, 80.

19. MacDonald, *Separation and Its Discontents*, 147–50.

20. For the unqualified respect for Lenz's work among American racialists such as
Berkeley's Arthur Jensen, see Tucker, *The Funding of Scientific Racism*, 155–56.

21. Hofstadter, "The Paranoid Style in American Politics," in *Anti-Intellectualism in
American Life, The Paranoid Style in American Politics, Uncollected Essays 1956–1965*, 532.

22. See Stephens-Davidowitz, "The Data of Hate," *New York Times* (13 August 2014).

23. "Sticky: Jewish Crime Report," posted by Elena Haskins; posts to thread, 2,229;
views, 1,405,005: https://www.stormfront.org/forum/t451546/. "Is Dr. William Pierce
Dead Forever?" posted by PolishPride; posts to thread, 1,196; views, 571,593: https://
www.stormfront.org/forum/t443513/. Information about view statistics: https://www
.stormfront.org/forum/search.php?searchid=25836948&pp=25&page=3. Pages last viewed
on 21 July 2022.

24. Posted on 12 July 2014, by TCA, on the thread "Dr. Carl Jung's Diagnosis of
Adolf Hitler": https://www.stormfront.org/forum/t1046318/#post12223800, accessed
12 August 2014.

25. Unfortunately, all of the threads and posts from 2014 were scrubbed and lost
after the temporary shutdown of Stormfront in 2017. For more information about the
shutdown in August 2017, and its connection to the Charlottesville "Unite the Right"
rally, see Hern, "Stormfront: 'Murder Capital of Internet' Pulled Offline after Civil
Rights Action."

26. MacDonald, "Stalin's Willing Executioners," 70.

27. MacDonald, "Stalin's Willing Executioners," 67.

28. See the League of the South page for "Speech at the 2019 LS national conference."

29. MacDonald, "Stalin's Willing Executioners," 89.

30. MacDonald's cross-referenced web pages and social-media sites: Kevin MacDonald, @TOOEdit (on Twitter); http://www.kevinMacDonald.net/; http://www.kevin
MacDonald.net/Blog.htm; http://www.theoccidentalobserver.net/author/kmac/; his

California State University (Long Beach) page, now defunct: http://www.csulb.edu/~kmacd
/index.html; http://www.vdare.com/users/kevin-MacDonald. His columns at the *Occidental Observer* are also automatically linked at the Daily Stormer website (http://
www.dailystormer.com), and MacDonald regularly links his Facebook page to them
(https://www.facebook.com/kevin.MacDonald.77770?fref=ts).

31. Quoted in Tuchman, "Cal. State University Professor Endorses, Fund-Raises for
David Duke" (blog post, 1 July 2012).

32. See MacDonald's essay "What Makes Western Culture Unique?" in *Cultural
Insurrections: Essays on Western Civilization, Jewish Influence and Anti-Semitism*, especially 275–78.

33. Umland, "Kulturhegemoniale Strategien der russischen extremen Rechten,"
442, discusses Dugin's "double strategy" of courting both the extreme right and the
mainstream Russian conservative audience.

34. Dugin, "Evraziiskaia ekonomika," 636.

35. For an overview of Dugin's academic appointment, see Umland, "Dugin i
MGU," 482–87.

36. Laruelle, *Russian Eurasianism*, 116–17.

37. See Glebov, *From Empire to Eurasia*, 89.

38. Dugin's *Giperboreiskaia teoriia* was written in 1989, and first published in 1990.

39. Dugin, *Giperboreiskaia teoriia*, 73, 97–98; *Filosofiia traditsii*, 195; *Misteriia Evrazii*, 125.

40. Dugin, *Russkaia veshch'*, 1:482.

41. Dugin, *Russkaia veshch'*, 1:483.

42. Dugin, *Tseli i zadachi nashei revoliutsii*, 20.

43. Laruelle, *Russian Eurasianism*, 114.

44. Dugin, "Tretii put' i tret'ia sila (analiticheskii doklad)," 45.

45. For a discussion of these ideas, as developed by Dugin, see Laruelle, "The Izborskii Club, or the New Conservative Avant-Garde in Russia," 641; Dugin, "Tretii put' i
tret'ia sila (analiticheskii doklad)," 45–46.

46. Dugin, "Tretii put' i tret'ia sila (analiticheskii doklad)," 46.

47. Gessen, *The Future Is History*, 20–21.

48. Dostoevsky, "Pushkin: A Sketch," 1294. The translator of this speech renders the
phrase "great Aryan family [*rod*]." into "great Aryan race." The Russian original does
not carry quite as strong a suggestion of racialism as the translation suggests. Russian
text: Dostoevsky, "Pushkin. Ocherk," 457–58.

49. Dugin, *Evoliutsiia paradgimal'nykh osnovanii nauki*, 8–9.

50. Laruelle, *Russian Eurasianism*, 121–24.

51. Walker, Ragozin, and Weaver, "Putin Likens Ukraine's Forces to Nazis and
Threatens Standoff in the Arctic." For the Russian text of Putin's statement see Latukhina, "Rossiia prodolzhit' ukrepliat' svoi pozitsii v Arktike"; and the RT segment "Vladimir Putin: Arktika—vazhneishii region Rossii" (video).

52. Dugin, *Osnovy geopolitiki*, 309–10, 311–13.

53. Remnick, "Letter from Moscow: Watching the Eclipse," 62.

54. Laruelle, *Russian Eurasianism*, 109.

55. "Tainoe stanet iavnym: Dugin i Kurekhin, 1995 god.: Efir pered vyborami v Gos.
Dumu" (video of program aired during the Fall of 1995).

56. Quoted in Yurchak, "A Parasite from Outer Space," 330.

57. Dugin, *Tamplery proletariata*, 278.

58. Dugin, *Tamplery proletariata*, 274–75.

59. Clowes, *Russia on the Edge*, 48.

60. Stern, *Proud Boys and the White Ethnostate*, 25.

61. Stern, *Proud Boys and the White Ethnostate*, 23.

62. Laruelle, "The Izborskii Club, or the New Conservative Avant-Garde in Russia," 644.

63. For information about this milieu, and its formative influence on Dugin, see Gessen, *The Future Is History*, 19–21; Umland, "Aleksandr Dugin's Transformation from a Lunatic Fringe Figure into a Mainstream Political Publicist, 1990–1998," 145–47.

64. Quoted in Teitelbaum, *War for Eternity*, 159.

65. For a representative sampling of Prilepin's views about the war in Ukraine and the Donbass region's irredentist aspirations, see the following interview, which took place one month after the beginning of the full-scale invasion: Tel'manov, "'Za poslednie tri nedeli ia ni razu vspominl, chto ia pisatel'. Interv'iu Zakhar Prilepina o sobytiiakh na Ukraine" (27 March 2022). Most recently, Jordan Peterson's flamboyant self-presentation as a genuine academic authority is evident in his droll and meandering YouTube lecture about Russia and Ukraine, in which he delivers "realist" talking points in a smart three-piece suit (Peterson, "Russia vs. Ukraine or Civil War in the United States").

66. Rand, *The Fountainhead*, 679.

67. Finchelstein, "Populism without Borders," 420.

68. For the importance of self-categorization in the far right as a means for creating a strong "in-group" identity, see Kutner, "Swiping Right," 10.

69. Dugin, *Chetvertaia politicheskaia teoriia*, 278.

70. Eurasian Artists Association, Facebook: https://www.facebook.com/Eurasian ArtistsAssociation/timeline.

71. "Ot rektora MGU potrebovali uvolit' profesora Aleksandra Dugina za prizyvy 'ubivat' ukraintsev."

72. Dugin, *Filosofiia traditsionalizma*, 11.

Chapter 4. The Spectacle of God's Will

First epigraph: Jack Donovan, "Positions & FAQ": https://www.jack-donovan.com/sowilo /bio/positions/. For more about Jack Donovan's negotiation of queer identity with alt-right ideology, see Lyons, "Jack Donovan and Male Tribalism," especially 248–53.

1. Lotman, "Dinamicheskaia model' semioticheskoi sistemy," 87.

2. Samuels, "American Racist."

3. Stern, *Proud Boys and the White Ethnostate*, 60–65.

4. Kirillova, "Kremlin Refocuses Its Propaganda in Preparation for War."

5. Hochschild, *Strangers in Their Own Land*, 207.

6. For the exact text of the law, see "Stat'ia 1."

7. Gessen, "Boycott St. Petersburg," *New York Times* (19 March 2012).

8. "Iurii Luzhkov: Gei-parads my ne dopustili i ne dopustim vpred'."

9. "Orgkomitet gei—praida zadal video—voprosy Valentine Matvienko."

10. Paul, "Under the Rainbow Banner."

11. Lavin, *Culture Warlords*, 61–62.

12. Plotko, "Strakh drugogo: Problema gomofobii v Rossii."

13. Mielke, *The Russian Homosexual Lexicon*, 7.

14. Quoted in Kondakov, "Regulating Desire in Russia," 403.

15. Quoted in Kondakov, "Regulating Desire in Russia," 404.

16. Kondakov, "Regulating Desire in Russia," 403–4.

17. Kislina, "Kto takie pravoslavnye khorugvenostsy?"

18. Kishkovsky and Herszenhorn, "Punk Band's Moscow Trial Offers Platform for Orthodox Protesters," *New York Times* (8 August 2012).

19. Kishkovsky, "Artist's 'Orthodoxy or Death' T-shirt Is Extremist, Says Russian Court," *Art Newspaper* (22 March 2012).

20. Miller-Idriss, *The Extreme Gone Mainstream*, 187, 185.

21. "Skinkhedy: Otkuda nogi rastut?"

22. Likhachev, *Istoricheskaia poetika russkoi literature*, 262.

23. Goodfellow, "Videogames.ru."

24. Averianov, *Nash dukh ne slomlen*, 228.

25. One of the most thorough explanations of the ekphrastic aesthetic of "word weaving" can be found in O. F. Konovalova's article "Pletenie sloves i pletennyi ornament kontsa XIV veka," 103–5.

26. For details about Simonovich-Nikshich's biography, see the LiveJournal obituary for him: philologist, "Umer glava Soiuza pravoslavnyh khorugvenostsev Leonid Simonovich-Nikshich" (20 March 2022).

27. Laruelle, "The Izborskii Club, or the New Conservative Avant-Garde in Russia," 630.

28. Kalashnikov, "Innovatsionnaia oprichnina Lavrentiia Berii," 309–26.

29. Lévy, *Collective Intelligence*, 48.

30. "Dukhovnaya oprichnina, ili SMERT' PIDORASAM!"

31. "Ne robei, zelen'!" Sorokin, *Den' oprichnika*, 201; *The Day of the Oprichnik*, 170.

32. Sedgwick, *The Epistemology of the Closet*, 9.

33. "Staruskha Ciccone—ved'ma! 11 avgusta 2012 goda" (video).

34. Bakhtin, *Raboty 20-x godov*, 139; Bakhtin, *Art and Answerability*, 65; Yuri Davydov, "U istokov sotsial'noi filosofii M. M. Bakhtina." See also Davydov and Aleksandr Arkhangel'skii, "Vse vzyvaet k postupku."

35. For an incisive discussion of the evocation of the theology of the icon in contemporary Russian controversies about performance art, see Bernstein, "*Caution, Religion!*" 434–35. For an analysis of the significance of "reverse perspective" of Russian icon art, see Uspenskii, "K sisteme peredachi izobrazheniia v russkoi ikonopisi."

36. Dugin, "Strelkov kak sobytie" (11 September 2014).

37. Gottfried, "Preface to the English Edition," in Dugin, *Martin Heidegger: The Philosophy of Another Beginning*, 3.

38. For a description of the Bitches' War and the dominance of the career criminals over the petty criminals and the political prisoners, see Galeotti's *The Vory: Russia's Super Mafia*, 51–60.

39. Baldaev, *Russian Criminal Tattoo Encyclopedia*, 3:237.

40. "And that is the reason why cons always have to be without their caps during inspection and to uncover their foreheads, so that they can be checked for tattoos" (93): from Marchenko, *My Testimony* (originally published in Russian in 1967), his

account of men who endured such treatment, including one named Shcherbakov, who was put in a cell with "Mazai and the homosexual Misha, both with tattooed faces" (92).

41. Plutser-Sarno, "Yazyk tela i politika: Simvolika vorovskikh tatuirovok," 7.

42. Baldaev, *Russian Criminal Tattoo Encyclopedia*, 2:190, 191, 254.

43. Baldaev, *Russian Criminal Tattoo Encyclopedia*, 2:162.

44. Baldaev, *Russian Criminal Tattoo Encyclopedia*, 1:165.

45. Efimova, *Sovremennaia tiur'ma*, 382–83. Efimova also describes the highly formalized dealings between the thieves and homosexuals (113–14).

46. Volokhonsky, *Zhizn' po poniatiiam*, 7–10, 93–97.

47. Conducted in February 2017 and June 2018.

48. For a detailed account of the circumstances and Ogorodnikov's arrest, see Koenraad de Wolf, *Dissident for Life: Alexander Ogorodnikov and the Struggle for Religious Freedom in Russia*, 101–3.

49. "Dmitriia Enteo iskliuchili iz 'Bozh'ei voli.'"

50. "Beata Bubenets o geroiakh svoego fil'ma 'Bozh'ei voli,' pravoslavnoi art-gruppy."

51. Scott Kenworthy, Facebook, 8 March 2021 (https://www.facebook.com/search/top?q=kenworthy%20kuraev).

52. Kuraev, "Pominaite nastavnikov vashikh. . . .," blog post.

53. For a detailed account of Voina's protest at this legal proceeding, see Bernstein, "*Caution, Religion!*" 419–21. In her article, Bernstein reproduces a striking photograph of Verzilov and Simonovich-Nikshich in the vestibule of the building, both engaged in their signature gestures of political protest (420).

54. Bobrinskaya, "Moscow Conceptual Performance Art," 168–69.

55. Desiaterik, "Moskovskaya art-gruppa 'Voina' kak iskusstvo protestov v chistom vide."

56. Groys, *History Becomes Form*, 149–50.

57. Videos of these demonstrations can be seen on the group's YouTube channel: https://www.youtube.com/channel/UCxIylh7RkJLGz0NYDvyXiPw.

58. Igor Miroshnichenko, "Proshchai, velikii slavianin!" VKontakte post (22 March 2022).

59. See, for example, Enteo's posts on VKontakte 24 and 25 January 2022: https://vk.com/enteo?w=wall152509857_268379; https://vk.com/enteo?w=wall152509857_268380. About Enteo's recent flirtation with libertarianism, see also Boyko, "O pravykh koservatorakh i Enteo."

60. Atryom Lukin, tweets on a thread (11 July 2022): https://twitter.com/ArtyomLukin/status/1546468247914029059; https://twitter.com/ArtyomLukin/status/1546677531180691456

Chapter 5. Statuary Performances

Second epigraph: Stewart subsequently deleted the tweet in the epigraph. That and other deleted tweets by Stewart can be found in Jones, "Corey Stewart Doesn't Get That You Can Be a Southerner without Being Racist."

1. "Natal'ia Poklonskaia soobshchila, chto biust Nikolaia II mirotochit: Vy ne poverite, chto proizoshlo potom" (Natalia Poklonskaia reported that the bust of Nicholas II trickled with myrrh. You have no idea, what happened then).

2. Faust, *This Republic of Suffering*, 100–101 (quotation), 146.

3. See Cox, *No Common Ground*, 42–44, for a history of the Robert E. Lee monument in New Orleans.

4. The law prohibited interracial marriage and mandated segregation. See Erin L. Thompson, *Smashing Statues*, 134.

5. Southern Poverty Law Center, "Six Years Later."

6. Hochschild, *Strangers in Their Own Land*, 297.

7. Hochschild, *Strangers in Their Own Land*, 81.

8. Kelly Grovier, "Black Lives Matters Protests: Why are Statues So Powerful?" *BBC* (12 June 2020).

9. Collingwood, *The Idea of History*, 162.

10. Collingwood, *The Idea of History*, 163.

11. Collingwood, *The Idea of History*, 164.

12. Collingwood, *The Idea of History*, 162.

13. Southern Poverty Law Center, "Whose Heritage? Public Symbols of the Confederacy" (1 February 2019).

14. Kalpokas, *A Political Theory of Post-Truth*, 16, 18.

15. Kalpokas, *A Political Theory of Post-Truth*, 52, 56.

16. Kalpokas, *A Political Theory of Post-Truth*, 63.

17. "Torch-Wielding White Nationalists Clash with Counterprotestors at UVA"; Anti-Defamation League (ADL), "You Will Not Replace Us."

18. Lovecraft, *The New Annotated H. P. Lovecraft*, 92.

19. Lovecraft, *The New Annotated H. P. Lovecraft*, 139. For an overview of Lovecraft's racism as being central to his fiction, see Charles E. Baxter, "The Hideous Unknown of H. P. Lovecraft," *New York Review of Books* (18 December 2014).

20. Joyce Carol Oates, "The King of Weird," *New York Review of Books* (31 October 2014).

21. Lovecraft, *The New Annotated H. P. Lovecraft*, 153–54.

22. Houellebecq, *H. P. Lovecraft: Against the World, against Life*, 42.

23. Lovecraft, *The New Annotated H. P. Lovecraft*, 153.

24. hooks, *Black Looks*, 30.

25. "A Suppressed Tribute to General Lee," *The Confederate Veteran* 4 (April 1895), 102. Mirzoeff, "All the Monuments Must Fall #Charlottesville," *Face Forward* (14 August 2017).

26. Mirzoeff, "All the Monuments Must Fall #Charlottesville." *Face Forward* (14 August 2017).

27. Sons of Confederate Veterans, "New Orleans & Other Tragedies," letter (12 May 2017).

28. Taylor, *From #BlackLivesMatter to Black Liberation*, 109–10.

29. Landrieu, "Speech upon the Removal of Confederate Statues from New Orleans, May 19, 2017," 167.

30. Quoted in Maurantonio, *Confederate Exceptionalism*, 65.

31. Parker, "The Almost-Monument to Black 'Mammie,'" *New York Times, Sunday Review* (6 February 2020), 10.

32. Mirzoeff, "All the Monuments Must Fall #Charlottesville."

33. Fanon, *The Wretched of the Earth*, 15.

34. Fanon, *The Wretched of the Earth*, 42–43.

35. Green, "Roy and His Rock."

36. Quoted in Buccola, *The Fire Is upon Us*, 323.

37. Quoted in Mirzoeff, "All the Monuments Must Fall #Charlottesville."

38. Mirzoeff, "All the Monuments Must Fall #Charlottesville."

39. Quoted in Southern Poverty Law Center, "Neo-Confederate."

40. Darby, *Sisters in Hate*, 187.

41. Darby, *Sisters in Hate*, 187–88.

42. Sorokin, "Let the Past Collapse on Time!"

43. Boime, "Perestroika and the Destabilization of the Soviet Monuments," 218.

44. Verdery, *The Political Lives of Dead Bodies*, 5.

45. Scarry, *The Body in Pain*, 175.

46. Sorokin, "Farewell to the Queue," 257.

47. Sorokin, "Let the Past Collapse on Time!"

48. Sorokin, "Let the Past Collapse on Time!" The quotation comes from Brodsky's poem "A Speech About Spilled Milk," 14.

49. "Skol'ko pamiatnikov Leninu ostalos' v Rossii?"

50. Interview: Sokolov, "'Den' oprichnika i 'Sakharniyi kreml'": Vozvrashchatsia li v Rossiiu traditsiia politicheskoi literatury."

51. Sorokin, *Den' oprichnika*, 43.

52. Sorokin, "Let the Past Collapse on Time!"

53. The similarity of the statue's removal to a public hanging was not lost on the American journalist David Remnick, who was also present at the event: Dzerzhinsky "dangled from a crane, as if from a noose" (quoted in Verdery, *The Political Lives of Dead Bodies*, 12).

54. Robin, *The Reactionary Mind*, 40–41.

55. See Boime, "Perestroika and the Destabilization of the Soviet Monuments," 212.

56. Sorokin, "Let the Past Collapse on Time!"

57. Sorokin, "Let the Past Collapse on Time!"

58. From Zenkovsky, *Medieval Russia's Epics, Chronicles, and Tales*, 40. The Russian text of the Primary Chronicle: http://expositions.nlr.ru/LaurentianCodex/_Project/page_Show.php.

59. Zenkovsky, *Medieval Russia's Epics, Chronicles, and Tales*, 71. Old Russian text, from Laurentian Codex (1377), page 40: http://expositions.nlr.ru/LaurentianCodex/_Project/page_Show.php.

60. Sinyavsky comments about this odd persistent animism of the pagan totem in his study of Russian folk culture (*Ivan-Durak*, 105).

61. "I see myself at any moment on the eve of a misfortune that I can neither foresee nor avoid." Quoted in Jakobson, *Pushkin and His Sculptural Myth*, 22.

62. Pushkin, "The Bronze Horseman," 8–9.

63. Pushkin, "The Bronze Horseman," 12.

64. Pushkin, "The Bronze Horseman," 13. Evdokimova, *Pushkin's Historical Imagination*, 212.

65. Gogol, "Skul'ptura, zhivopis, i muzyka," 9–10.

66. Evdokimova, *Pushkin's Historical Imagination*, 214.

67. For Christian interpretations of the snake, which Falconet included as an allegorical detail that would also serve as a structural stabilizer, see Schenker, *The Bronze Horseman*, 277–78. As Schenker writes, in its final execution, the snake and the horse's tail played no significant role in stabilizing the bronze statue (247).

68. Evdokimova, *Pushkin's Historical Imagination*, 216.

69. Karamzin, *Istoriia gosudarstva rossiiskogo*, vol. 1:153.

70. Schenker, *The Bronze Horseman*, 273.

71. See, for example, Cherniakhovskii's opinion piece for the web page of the Izborsk Club, "Vozvrashchenie rytsaria."

72. Polian, "Gde zhe byt' zheleznomu Feliksu—v muzeone ili v muzee?"

73. "Pamiatnik krestiteliu Rusi v Kieve mogli oskvernit' neonatstisty iz 'Azova.'"

74. Sinyavsky, *Ivan-Durak*, 111.

75. Laruelle, "The *Rodnoverie* Movement: The Search for Pre-Christian Ancestry and the Occult," 298–302; Aitamurto, "Gender in Russian *Rodnoverie*," 184–6; Shnirelman, *Russkoe rodnoverie*, 1–24, 127–40.

76. Aitamurto, *Paganism, Traditionalism, Nationalism*, 93.

77. Valery Averianov to Alexandar Mihailovic, email (9 February 2021).

78. Prokhanov, "Molniia-Lenin," 8–9.

79. Prokhanov, "Molniia-Lenin," 16–17.

80. The identification of the banner's creators comes from the journalist Kim Kelly, who was a member of MACC, DM correspondence, Twitter (18 August 2021).

81. For articles that show the banners and signs carried by the group in Charlottesville in 2018, see "Anti-fascist Groups March in Charlottesville," and "Anti-fascist Demonstrators March in Charlottesville."

82. Hochschild, *Strangers in Their Own Land*, 135. See also page 197.

83. Tsvetaeva, "Excerpt from 'My Pushkin,'" 389.

84. Kharkhordin, *Republicanism in Russia*, 138.

85. Verdery, *The Political Lives of Dead Bodies*, 52, 104.

86. MacLean, *Democracy in Chains*, 150–52.

87. Dawisha, *Putin's Kleptocracy*, 277.

88. Matza, *Shock Therapy: Psychology, Precarity, and Wellbeing in Post-Socialist Russia*, 70–74.

89. Duggan, *Mean Girl*, 79, 81.

90. Taylor, "Did Last Summer's Black Lives Matter Protests Change Anything?"

91. Khodasevich, "Koleblemyi trenozhnik," 84–5.

92. Thompson, *Smashing Statues*, xviii.

Conclusion

1. Shcherbina, "Chelovek odinochestva i vokryg nego."

2. *Itogi Vserossiiskoi perepisi naseleniia 2010 goda.*

3. Highly representative of this pattern of interpretation is Ivanova's "Kogda odinochestvo nakryvaet s golovoi."

4. Hochschild, *Strangers in Their Own Land*, 136.

5. Hochschild, *Strangers in Their Own Land*, 66.

6. Hochschild, *Strangers in Their Own Land*, 59.

7. Hochschild, *Strangers in Their Own Land*, 33, 52–54.

8. Gramsci, *Prison Notebooks*, 2:64.

9. "For decades, at conferences such as CPAC [the Conservative Political Action Committee] international exchanges were mostly assumed to flow in one direction: Americans exporting their largesse, and their ideology, to the rest of the world. [. . .] In recent years, as the future of the Republican Party has seemed increasingly up for grabs, American conservatives have shown more willingness to look abroad for ideas that they might want to try out back home" (Marantz, "The Illiberal Order: Does Hungary Offer a Glimpse of Our Authoritarian Future?" 36–38).

10. Riccardi-Swartz, *Between Heaven and Russia: Religious Conversion and Political Apostasy in Appalachia*, 127.

11. Dillingham, "Russian Lessons for Dixie" (1 January 2020).

12. Riccardi-Swartz, *Between Heaven and Russia*, 84.

13. Hochschild, *Strangers in their Own Land*, 209.

14. Hochschild, *Strangers in their Own Land*, 211.

15. "Employment in agriculture (% of total employment) (modeled ILO estimate): Russian Federation," *World Bank* (29 January 2021); "Mesto sel'skogo khoziastva v ekonomike Rossii."

16. Rutland, "Neoliberalism and the Russian Transition," 352, 356.

17. Bourdieu, "Job Insecurity Is Everywhere Now," in *Acts of Resistance*, 85.

18. Williams, *White Working Class*, 129.

19. Parts, *In Search of the True Russia*, 33.

20. Parts, *In Search of the True Russia*, 33.

21. Williams, *White Working Class*, 122, 129, 159, 160.

22. Sailer, "Will U.S. Retain Its 'Market-Dominant Majority.'"

23. Main, *The Rise of the Alt-Right*, 236.

24. NOD SPB LO [National Liberation Movement, Saint-Petersburg and Leningrad Region]: "Amerika planiruet sverzhenie vlasti v Rossii 19.09.21." NOD has numerous pages on VKontakte for regional branches of its organization, and the page of the Russian member of parliament who is most closely associated with NOD (Natsional'noe osvoboditel'noe dvizhenie, the National Liberation Movement)—Evgeny Federov, a member of the United Russia Party—has over seventy-six thousand followers.

25. Gramsci, *Selections from the Prison Notebooks*, 220.

26. Gramsci, *Selections from the Prison Notebooks*, 219.

27. Buttigieg, "The *Prison Notebooks*: Antonio Gramsci's Work in Progress," 302

28. Antonini, *Caesarism and Bonapartism in Gramsci*, xiii.

29. "Putin ne soglasen s temi, kto nazyvaiut ego tsarem."

30. See especially Buttigieg, "Philology and Politics: Returning to the Text of Antonio Gramsci's *Prison Notebooks*," 104.

31. Nekhezin, "Ognemir, Bogumil, i Tsar Putin."

32. Email to author (9 February 2021).

33. Dallas, "Author J. D. Vance: Faith Made Me Believe in a Hopeful Future," *Washington Post* (9 September 2016).

34. Dreher, "J. D. Vance Becomes Catholic."

35. Vance (@JDVance1), Twitter, 9 July 2021: https://twitter.com/JDVance1/status /1413555392563527683.

36. Paul, "The Siren Song of Geopolitics," 69.

37. Kazbek, "Against the Farts" (blog post, n.d.).

38. Sperling, *Sex, Politics, and Putin*, 34, 37–79, 77. Fenghi, *It Will Be Fun and Terrifying*, 36.

39. Fenghi, *It Will Be Fun and Terrifying*, 36. The statement is from Limonov's novel *It's Me, Eddie*.

40. Hill, post on VKontakte, 12 August 2021: https://vk.com/id388233418?w=wall 388233418_1749

41. "Federal Court Grants Evidentiary Sanctions against Neo-Nazi Hate Group National Socialist Movement in IFA's Charlottesville Suit."

42. Hill, post on VKontakte, 12 August 2021: https://vk.com/id388233418?w=wall 388233418_1749.

43. Marinetti, "Initial Manifesto of Futurism," 4.

44. Lyons, "Jack Donovan and Male Tribalism," 248.

45. Stanley, *How Propaganda Works*, 120–21.

46. Stanley, *How Propaganda Works*, 121.

47. Boggs, *Fascism Old and New*, 4.

48. "My vedem bor'bu za traktovku," Izborsk Club meeting, 30 May 2018.

49. Email response to author (29 July 2018).

50. Deneen, *Why Liberalism Failed*, 172.

51. Interview with Philip Gorski, "The Roots of White Christian Nationalism."

52. Butler, *White Evangelical Racism*, 42.

53. Robin, *The Reactionary Mind*, 202–3.

54. Pobedonostsev, *Velikaia lozh' nashego vremeni*, 45; Schmitt, *The Crisis of Parliamentary Democracy*, quoted in Müller, *What Is Populism?* 52.

55. Shklovsky, "Iskusstvo kak priem," 131.

56. Robin, *The Reactionary Mind*, 202.

57. Boris Dralyuk, "Yuz Aleshkovsky's 'Song about Stalin'" (https://bdralyuk.word press.com/2019/03/21/yuz-aleshkovskys-song-about-stalin/).

58. Lotman, *Struktura khudozhestvennogo teksta*, 99–100.

59. Anna Chernova and Joshua Berlinger, "Russian court shuts down human rights group Memorial International," *CNN* (28 December 2021). The library of the St. Petersburg "Memorial" organization is still operational, and includes a large collection of unpublished memoirs from Soviet citizens incarcerated in the GULAG: https:// memorial-nic.org/library.

60. Gessen, "Lyubov Sobol's Hope for Russia."

61. Mark Lipovetsky, "*Brother 2* as a Political Melodrama. Twenty Years Later, Balabanov's Film Serves to Justify War with Ukraine," *RussiaPost* (11 July 2022).

Works Cited

Abramson, Alana. "White Nationalists Carrying Torches Descend on Charlotteville Again." *Time* (8 October 2017): https://time.com/4973738/white-supremacists-charlottesville-rally-richard-spencer/.

Adamovsky, Ezquiel. "Russia as a Space of Hope: Nineteenth-Century French Challenges to the Liberal Image of Russia." *European History Quarterly* 33, no. 4 (October 2003): 411–49.

Ahmed, Sara. "Happy Objects." In *The Affect Theory Reader*, edited by Melissa Gregg and Gregory J. Seigworth, 29–51. Durham, NC: Duke University Press, 2010.

Aitamurto, Kaarina. "Gender in Russian *Rodnoverie*." *The Pomegranate* 15, nos. 1–2 (2014): 12–30.

———. *Paganism, Traditionalism, Nationalism: Narratives of Russian Rodnoverie*. London: Routledge, 2016.

Allison, David B., ed. *Controversial Monuments and Memorials: A Guide for Community Leaders*. Lanham, PA: Rowman & Littlefield, 2018.

Althusser, Louis. *Lenin and Philosophy and Other Essays*. New York: New York University Press, 2011.

Andrews, Helen. "2020 Is Tumbling toward 1917." *American Conservative* (2 October 2020): https://www.theamericanconservative.com/articles/2020-is-tumbling-toward-1917/.

Anti-Defamation League (ADL). "You Will Not Replace Us." https://www.adl.org/education/references/hate-symbols/you-will-not-replace-us.

"Anti-fascist Demonstrators March in Charlottesville." *WHVS3* (11 August 2018): https://www.whsv.com/content/news/Anti-fascist-demonstrators-march-in-Charlottesville-490637541.html.

"Anti-fascist Groups March in Charlottesville." *AP* (11 August 2018): https://apnews.com/article/bd2607ffec074e06bf4ff984af907473.

Anton, Michael. "The Regime's Failing Jan. 6 Lie." *Compact* (20 June 2022): https://compactmag.com/article/the-regime-s-failing-jan-6-lie.

Antonini, Francesca. *Caesarism and Bonapartism in Gramsci: Hegemony and the Crisis of Modernity*. London: Brill, 2020.

Averianov, Vitaly. *Nash dukh ne slomlen*. Moscow: Institut russkoi tsivilizatsii, 2015.

Avrich, Paul. *Kronstadt, 1921*. New York: W. W. Norton, 1970.

Azhgikhina, Nadezhda. "Russian Women against Militarism: Act II." *The Nation* (8 March 2019): https://www.thenation.com/article/archive/russia-putin-war-women/.

Bakhtin, Mikhail. *Art and Answerability: Early Philosophical Essays*. Translated by Vadim Liapunov. Austin: University of Texas Press, 1990.

———. *Raboty 20-x godov*. Kiev: "NEXT," 1994.

Baldaev, Danzig, ed. *Russian Criminal Tattoo Encyclopedia*. 3 vols. London: Murray and Sorrell, 2003, 2006, 2008.

Baldwin, James. *Collected Essays*. New York: Library of America, 1998.

———. *The Cross of Redemption: Uncollected Writings*. Edited by Randall Kenan. New York: Pantheon, 2010.

Bannon, Steve. "Hudson Institute Violent Extremism Conference, Steve Bannon Remarks." Video. 23 October 2017: https://www.c-span.org/video/?436107-5/hudson-institute-violent-extremism-conference-steve-bannon-remarks.

Bannon, Steve, and Erik Prince. "Episode 1,660: Scarborough Fear Porn Fails; Putin's 100 Years Humiliation Speech." *War Room* (23 February 2022). Podcast: https://warroom.org/2022/02/23/episode-1660-scarborough-fear-porn-fails-putins-100-years-humiliation-speech/.

———. "Module 3—Should Christians Impose Limits on Wealth Creation?" Video. 29 July 2014: https://www.youtube.com/watch?time_continue=159&v=FWXScQaZ2uI.

Barton, Swaim. "Violent Protest and the Intelligentsia: Scholar Gary Saul Morson Sees Disturbing Parallels between Russia before the Revolution and Contemporary America." *Wall Street Journal* (5 June 2020): https://www.wsj.com/articles/violent-protest-and-the-intelligentsia-11591400422.

Bausman, Charles. "It's Time to Drop the Jew Taboo." *Russia Insider* (15 January 2018): https://russia-insider.com/en/politics/its-time-drop-jew-taboo/ri22186.

Bayoumy, Yara, and Kathy Gilsinan. "A Reformed White Nationalist Says the Worst Is Yet to Come." *The Atlantic* (August 2019): https://www.theatlantic.com/politics/archive/2019/08/conversation-christian-picciolini/595543/.

Baxter, Charles E. "The Hideous Unknown of H. P. Lovecraft." *New York Review of Books* 61, no. 20 (18 December 2014): https://www.nybooks.com/articles/2014/12/18/hideous-unknown-hp-lovecraft/.

"Beata Bubenets o geroiakh svoego fil'ma 'Bozh'ei voli,' pravoslavnoi art-gruppy." Video. *Hromadske*: https://hromadske.ua/ru/posts/eti-lyudi-iskrenni-v-svoej-nenavisti-k-lgbt.

Ben-Ghiat, Ruth. *Strongmen: Mussolini to the Present*. New York: W. W. Norton, 2020.

Benda, Julien. *Treason of the Intellectuals*. Translated by Richard Aldington. New York: Norton, 1969.

Benner, Erica. *Really Existing Nationalisms: A Post-Communist View from Marx and Engels*. Oxford: Clarendon Press, 1995.

Berlant, Lauren. *Cruel Optimism*. Durham, NC: Duke University Press, 2011.

Berlant, Lauren, and Lee Edelman. *Sex, or the Unbearable*. Durham, NC: Duke University Press, 2014.

Bernal, Alonso, et al., *Cognitive Warfare: An Attack on Truth and Thought*. Baltimore, MD: Johns Hopkins University, 2020.

Bernstein, Anya. "*Caution, Religion!* Iconoclasm, Secularism, and Ways of Seeing in Post-Soviet Art Wars." *Public Culture* 26, no. 3 (Fall 2014): 419–48.

Billington, James H. *The Icon and the Axe: An Interpretive History of Russian Culture.* New York: Alfred A. Knopf, 1966.

Blok, Alexander. *The Spirit of Music.* Translated by I. Freimon. Westport, CT: Hyperion Press, 1973.

Bobrinskaya, Ekaterina. "Moscow Conceptual Performance Art." In *Moscow Conceptualism in Context,* edited by Alla Rosenfeld, 154–77. Munich: Prestel, 2011.

Boggs, Carl. *Fascism Old and New: American Politics at the Crossroads.* London: Routledge, 2018.

Boime, Albert. "Perestroika and the Destabilization of the Soviet Monuments." *ARS: Journal of the Institute for the History of Art (Slovak Academy of Sciences)* 2–3 (1995): 211–26.

Borenstein, Eliot. *Plots against Russia: Conspiracy and Fantasy after Socialism.* Ithaca, NY: Cornell University Press, 2019.

Bourdieu, Pierre. *Acts of Resistance: Against the Tyranny of the Market.* Translated by Richard Nice. New York: New Press, 1998.

Boyko, Sergei. "O pravykh koservatorakh i Enteo." *Libertarianskaia partiia Rossii,* n.d: https://archive.libertarian-party.ru/blog/o-pravyh-konservatorah-i-enteo.

Broadwater, Luke, and Nicholas Fandos. "Beaten, Tased and Crushed by Rioters at Capitol: Four Officers Testify—'I Have Kids,' One Begged Mob." *New York Times* (27 July 2021).

Brock, David. *Blinded by the Right: The Conscience of an Ex-Conservative.* New York: Broadway Books, 2003.

Brodsky, Joseph. "A Speech Over Spilled Milk." In *Nativity Poems,* 10–37. [Bilingual edition.] Translated by Glynn Maxwell. New York: Farrar, Straus & Giroux, 2002.

Buccola, Nicholas. *The Fire Is upon Us: James Baldwin, William F. Buckley Jr., and the Debate over Race in America.* Princeton, NJ: Princeton University Press, 2019.

Butler, Anthea. *White Evangelical Racism: The Politics of Morality in America.* Chapel Hill: University of North Carolina Press, 2021.

Butler, Judith. *Undoing Gender.* London: Routledge, 2004.

Buttigieg, Joseph A. "Philology and Politics: Returning to the Text of Antonio Gramsci's *Prison Notebooks.*" *Boundary* 21, no. 2 (Summer 1994): 98–138.

———. "The *Prison Notebooks*: Antonio Gramsci's Work in Progress." In *Rethinking Grasmci,* edited by Marcus E. Greene, 301–5. London: Routledge, 2011.

Caldwell, Christopher. "Hungary and the Future of Europe: Viktor Orbán's Escalating Conflict with Liberalism." *Claremont Review of Books* (Spring 2019): https://claremontreviewofbooks.com/hungary-and-the-future-of-europe/.

Carrère, Emanuel. *Limonov.* Translated by John Lambert. New York: Farrar, Straus and Giroux, 2014.

Chaadaev, Peter. *The Major Works of Peter Chaadaev.* Edited and translated by Raymond T. MacNally. South Bend, IN: University of Notre Dame Press, 1989.

Chekhov, A. O. "Tapior." *Sobranie sochinenii v vosmi tomakh,* vol. 3:270–74. Moscow: RIPOL klassik, 2005.

Cherniakhovskii, Sergei. "Vozvrashchenie rytsaria." (25 February 2021): https://izborsk-club.ru/20712.

Chernova, Anna, and Joshua Berlinger. "Russian court shuts down human rights group Memorial International." *CNN* (28 December 2021): https://www.cnn.com/2021/12/28/europe/memorial-international-russia-intl/index.html.

Chernyshevsky, Nikolai. *What Is to Be Done*. Translated by Michael Katz. Ithaca, NY: Cornell University Press, 1989.

Chryssagvis, John. "Alfeyev and Lavrov: A Glimpse into Church-State Relations in Russia." *Commonweal Magazine* (25 July 2021): https://www.commonwealmagazine .org/alfeyev-lavrov.

Clowes, Edith W. *Russia on the Edge: Imagined Geographies and Post-Soviet Identity*. Ithaca, NY: Cornell University Press, 2011.

Cofnas, Nathan. "The Anti-Jewish Narrative." *Philosophia* 49 (2021): 1329–44.

———. "Judaism as a Group Evolutionary Strategy: A Critical Analysis of Kevin MacDonald's Theory." *Human Nature* 29 (2018): 134–56.

———. *Reptiles with a Conscience: The Coevolution of Religious and Moral Doctrine*. London: Ulster Institute for Social Research Press, 2012.

Collingwood, R. G. *The Idea of History. Revised Edition, with Lectures 1926–1928*. Oxford: Clarendon Press, 1993.

Collins, Hubert. "Not a Prophet in His Own Land." Interview with Paul Gottfried. *American Renaissance* (27 April 2018): https://www.amren.com/features/2018/04 /not-a-prophet-in-his-own-land/.

"Conservative Advocate." Interview with Grover Norquist (25 May 2001): https:// www.npr.org/templates/story/story.php?storyId=1123439.

Cooper, Cloee. "How a Right-Wing Network Mobilized Sheriffs' Departments." *Political Research Associates* (10 June 2019): https://politicalresearch.org/2019/06/10 /how-a-right-wing-network-mobilized-sheriffs-departments.

Cox, Karen L. *No Common Ground: Confederate Monuments and the Ongoing Fight for Social Justice*. Chapel Hill: University of North Carolina Press, 2021.

Crews, Frederick. "Dialectical Immaterialism." *American Scholar* 54, no. 4 (Autumn 1985): 449–65.

"The Culture Wars Today." *Georgetown University, Berkley Center for Religion, Peace and World Affairs* (18 December 2019): https://berkleycenter.georgetown.edu/posts /the-culture-wars-today.

Cusset, François. *How the World Swung to the Right: Fifty Years of Counterrevolutions*. Translated by Noura Wedell. London: Semiotext(e), 2018.

Dallas, Kelsey. "Author J. D. Vance: Faith Made Me Believe in a Hopeful Future." *Washington Post* (9 September 2016): https://www.washingtonpost.com/local/social -issues/author-jd-vance-faith-made-me-believe-in-a-hopeful-future/2016/09/09/3c d46d6a-7604-11e6-be4f-3f42f2e5a49e_story.html.

Darby, Seyward. *Sisters in Hate: American Women on the Front Lines of White Nationalism*. New York: Little, Brown, 2020.

Davydov, Yuri. "U istokov sotsial'noi filosofii M. M. Bakhtina." *Sotsiologicheskie issledovaniia* 2 (1986): 170–81.

Davydov, Yuri, and Aleksandr Arkhangel'skii. "Vse vzyvaet k postupku." *Literaturnoe obozrenie* 2 (1987): 102–7.

Dawisha, Karen. *Putin's Kleptocracy: Who Owns Russia?* New York: Simon & Schuster, 2014.

De Maistre, Joseph. *The Executioner*. New York: Penguin, 2013.

Deneen, Patrick J. "What I Saw in America: The Political Theory of Daily Life." (4 September 2008): https://patrickdeneen.blogspot.com/2008/09/small-town-barra cudas.html.

————. "Russia, America, and the Danger of Political Gnosticism." (2 March 2022): https://postliberalorder.substack.com/p/russia-america-and-the-danger-of?s=r.

————. *Why Liberalism Failed*. Rev. ed. New Haven: Yale University Press, 2018.

Desiaterik, Dmitrii. "Moskovskaya art-gruppa 'Voina' kak iskusstvo protestov v chistom vide." *Den'* [Ukraine] 132 (2009): https://m.day.kyiv.ua/ru/article/kultura/moskovskaya-art-gruppa-voyna-kak-iskusstvo-protestov-v-chistom-vide.

Dilimbetov, Oleg, and Egor Kobyzev. "'Ty dostal tut begat': Na aktsii v podderzhku Alekseiia Naval'nogo zaderzhali pochti tysiachu chelovek i izbili zhurnalista." *Kommersant* (31 January 2021): https://www.kommersant.ru/doc/4671359.

Dillingham, Rebecca. "Russian Lessons for Dixie." (1 January 2020): https://www.dissidentmama.net/russian-lessons-for-dixie/.

Dissident Mama. "Episode 19: Tim Kirby." (6 October 2020) Podcast: https://www.dissidentmama.net/dissident-mama-episode-19-tim-kirby/.

"Dmitriia Enteo iskliuchili iz 'Bozh'ei voli.'" *Rbc.ru* (3 October 2017): https://www.rbc.ru/rbcfreenews/59d375319a79471a0cbc1b8d.

Dostoevsky, Fyodor. *Great Short Works*. New York: Perennial Classics, 2004.

————. "Pushkin (A Sketch)." In *A Writer's Diary. Volume 2: 1877–1881*, translated by Kenneth Lantz, 1281–94. Evanston, IL: Northwestern University Press, 1997.

————. "Pushkin. Ocherk." In *Dnevnik pisatelia. Izbrannye glavy*, 442–59. St. Petersburg: Azbuka, 2014.

Dralyuk, Boris. "Yuz Aleshkovsky's 'Song about Stalin'": https://bdralyuk.wordpress.com/2019/03/21/yuz-aleshkovskys-song-about-stalin/.

Dreher, Rod. *The Benedict Option: A Strategy for Christians in a Post-Christian Age*. New York: Sentinel, 2017.

————. "How (Not) to Think About the Caravan." *American Conservative* (25 October 2018): https://www.theamericanconservative.com/dreher/how-not-to-think-about-the-caravan/.

————. "It's Jean Raspail's World Now." *American Conservative* (7 September 2015): https://www.theamericanconservative.com/dreher/its-jean-raspails-world-now/.

————. "J. D. Vance Becomes Catholic." *American Conservative* (11 August 2019): https://www.theamericanconservative.com/dreher/j-d-vance-becomes-catholic/.

————. *Live Not by Lies: A Manual for Christian Dissidents*. New York: Sentinel Books, 2020.

————. "Of Sh*tholes and Second Thoughts." *American Conservative* (19 January 2018): https://www.theamericanconservative.com/dreher/of-shitholes-and-second-thoughts/.

————. "Save the West, Move to . . . *Europe*?" *American Conservative* (8 November 2017): https://www.theamericanconservative.com/dreher/save-the-west-move-to-europe/.

————. "The Tragedy of Franco's Spain." *American Conservative* (9 January 2019): https://www.theamericanconservative.com/dreher/tragedy-franco-spain/.

————. "Ukraine: Once More, into the Breach." *American Conservative* (19 January 2022): https://www.theamericanconservative.com/dreher/ukraine-russia-usa-into-the-breach-orthodoxy/#comment-5700011764.

————. "Why George Floyd Died." *American Conservative* (4 August 2020): https://www.theamericanconservative.com/why-george-floyd-died-bodycam/.

Duberman, Martin. *Has the Gay Movement Failed?* Berkeley: University of California Press, 2018.

Duggan, Lisa. *Mean Girl: Ayn Rand and the Culture of Greed.* Berkeley: University of California Press, 2019.

Dugin, Alexander. *Chetvertaia politicheskaia teoriia.* Moscow: Amfora, 2009.

———. *Evoliutsiia paragdimal'nykh osnovanii nauki.* Moscow: Arktogeia, 2002.

———. "Evraziiskaia ekonomika." In *Osnovy evraziistva*, 626–37. Moscow: Arktogeia-tsentr, 2002.

———. *Filosofiia traditsii.* Moscow: Arktogeia-tsentr, 2002.

———. *Filosofiia traditsionalizma.* Moscow: Arktogeia, 2004.

———. *Giperboreiskaia teoriia.* Moscow: Arktogeia, 1993.

———. *Misteriia Evrazii.* Moscow: Arktogeia, 1996.

———. *Osnovy geopolitiki.* Moscow: Arktogeia, 1997.

———. *Russkaia veshch'. Ocherki natsional'noi filosofii.* 2 vols. Moscow: Arktogeia, 2001.

———. "Strelkov kak sobytie." Post on VKontakte (11 September 2014): https://vk.com/wall18631635_4032.

———. *Tamplery proletariata.* Moscow: Arktogeia, 1997.

———. "Tretii put' i tret'ia sila (analiticheskii doklad)." *Izborksii klub: Russkie strategii* 4 (2013): 40–59.

———. *Tseli i zadachi nashei revoliutsii.* Moscow: Fravarti, 1995.

"Dukhovnaya oprichnina, ili SMERT' PIDORASAM!" http://drakula.org/sv_horugv/7/29.shtml.

Du Mez, Kristin Kobes. *Jesus and John Wayne: How White Evangelicals Corrupted a Faith and Fractured a Nation.* New York: Liveright, 2020.

Efimova, Ekaterina. *Sovremennaia tiur'ma: Byt, traditsii, i fol'klor.* Moscow: OGI, 2004.

Eliot, T. S. *After Strange Gods: A Primer of Modern Heresy.* London: Faber and Faber, 1933.

———. *The Sacred Wood: Essays on Poetry and Criticism.* 7th ed. London: Methuen, 1950.

"Employment in agriculture (% of total employment) (modeled ILO estimate): Russian Federation." *World Bank* (29 January 2021): https://data.worldbank.org/indicator/SL.AGR.EMPL.ZS?locations=RU&year_high_desc=true.

Evdokimova, Svetlana. *Pushkin's Historical Imagination.* New Haven: Yale University Press, 1999.

Faludy, Alexander. "The Philosophy of Orbán's Misguided Christian Friends." *Open Democracy* (16 September 2020): https://www.opendemocracy.net/en/can-europe-make-it/the-philosophy-of-orb%C3%A1ns-misguided-christian-friends/.

Fanon, Frantz. *The Wretched of the Earth.* Translated by Richard Philcox. New York: Grove Press, 2004.

Faust, Drew Gilpin. *The Creation of Confederate Nationalism: Ideology and Identity in the Civil War South.* Baton Rouge: University of Louisiana Press, 1988.

———. *This Republic of Suffering: Death and the American Civil War.* New York: Alfred A. Knopf, 2008.

Feder, J. Lester. "This Is How Steve Bannon Sees the Entire World." *Buzzfeed News* (16 November 2016): https://www.buzzfeednews.com/article/lesterfeder/this-is-how-steve-bannon-sees-the-entire-world#.ylO3kAedo.

"Federal Court Grants Evidentiary Sanctions against Neo-Nazi Hate Group National Socialist Movement in IFA's Charlottesville Suit." *Integrity First for America* (23 June 2021): https://www.integrityfirstforamerica.org/newsroom/federal-court-grants-evidentiary-sanctions-against-neo-nazi-hate-group-national-s.

Fenghi, Fabrizio. *It Will Be Fun and Terrifying: Nationalism and Protest in Post-Soviet Russia* Madison: University of Wisconsin Press, 2020.

Field, Laura K. "Meet the Reocons." (20 February 2020): https://www.niskanencenter.org/meet-the-reocons/.

Finchelstein, Federico. "Populism without Borders: Notes on a Global History." *Constellations* 26 (2019): 418–29.

Fleche, Andre M. *The Revolution of 1861: The American Civil War in the Age of Nationalist Conflict.* Chapel Hill: University of North Carolina Press, 2012.

Frankel, Todd C. "A Majority of the People Arrested for Capitol Riot Had a History of Financial Trouble." *Washington Post* (10 February 2021): https://www.washingtonpost.com/business/2021/02/10/capitol-insurrectionists-jenna-ryan-financial-problems/.

Frey, William H. "The US Will Become Minority White in 2045, Census Projects." https://www.brookings.edu/blog/the-avenue/2018/03/14/the-us-will-become-minority-white-in-2045-census-projects/.

Frum, David. "Is the White Working Class Coming Apart?" *Daily Beast* (6 February 2012): https://www.thedailybeast.com/is-the-white-working-class-coming-apartdavid-frum.

Galeotti, Mark. *The Vory: Russia's Super Mafia.* New Haven: Yale University Press, 2018.

Gessen, Masha. "Boycott St. Petersburg." *New York Times* (19 March 2012): http://latitude.blogs.nytimes.com/2012/03/19/protest-st-petersburgs-homosexual-propaganda-law-by-boycotting-the-city/.

———. "The Dying Russians." *New York Review of Books* (2 September 2014): https://www.nybooks.com/daily/2014/09/02/dying-russians/.

———. *The Future Is History: How Totalitarianism Reclaimed Russia.* New York: Riverhead Books, 2017.

———. "Lyubov Sobol's Hope for Russia." *New Yorker* (26 July 2021): https://www.newyorker.com/magazine/2021/07/26/lyubov-sobols-hope-for-russia?fbclid=IwAR0R8EKaodftiTXDlwU2RtbItBUwdI21G8c1k8klJKf46AJ3CfqiyDVjIYQ.

Glebov, Sergey. *From Empire to Eurasia: Politics, Scholarship, and Ideology in Russian Eurasianism, 1920s–1930s.* DeKalb: Northern Illinois University Press, 2017.

Gogol, N. V. "Skul'ptura, zhivopis, i muzyka." In *Polnoe sobranie sochinenii v 14 tomakh.* Vol. 8:9–13. Moscow: AN SSSR, 1952.

Goldman, Adam. "The Comet Ping Pong Gunman Answers Our Reporter's Questions." *New York Times* (7 December 2016): https://www.nytimes.com/2016/12/07/us/edgar-welch-comet-pizza-fake-news.html.

Goodfellow, Catherine. "Videogames.ru: Constructing New Russian Identities in Virtual Worlds." In *Exploring Videogames: Culture, Design, and Identity*, edited by Nick Webber and Daniel Riha, 115–22. London: Brill, 2013.

Gorski, Philip. "The Roots of White Christian Nationalism." Interview. *Vital Interests*, Center on National Security (25 February 2021): https://www.centeronnationalsecurity.org/vital-interests-issue-65-philip-gorski.

Gottfried, Paul E. "America in 2034." *American Renaissance* (10 June 2014): https:// www.amren.com/news/2014/06/america-in-2034-2/.

———. "Preface to the English Edition." In Alexander Dugin, *Martin Heidegger: The Philosophy of Another Beginning*, 3–9. Translated by Nina Kouprianova. Alexandria, VA: Radix, 2014.

Graham, Franklin. "Putin's Olympic Controversy." *Decision Magazine* (March 2014): https://billygraham.org/decision-magazine/march-2014/putins-olympic-contro versy/.

Gramsci, Antonio. *Prison Notebooks*. 3 vols. Edited by Joseph Buttigieg, translated by Joseph Buttigieg and Antonio Callari. New York: Columbia University Press, 1992.

———. "From the Prison Notebooks." Translated by Joseph A. Buttigieg. *Boundary* 131, no. 3 (Summer 2002): 71–83.

———. "Selections from the *Prison Notebooks*." In *An Anthology of Western Marxism: From Lukács and Gramsci to Socialist-Feminism*, edited by Roger S. Gottlieb, 112–19. Oxford: Oxford University Press, 1989.

———. *Selections from the Prison Notebooks*. Edited and translated by Quentin Hoare and Geoffrey Nowell Smith. New York: International Publishers, 1971.

Green, Joshua. *Devil's Bargain: Steve Bannon, Donald Trump, and the Storming of the American Presidency*. New York: Penguin, 2017.

———. "Inside the Secret, Strange Origins of Steve Bannon's Nationalist Fantasia." *Vanity Fair* (17 July 2017): https://www.vanityfair.com/news/2017/07/the-strange -origins-of-steve-bannons-nationalist-fantasia.

———. "Roy and His Rock." *The Atlantic* (October 2005): https://www.theatlantic .com/magazine/archive/2005/10/roy-and-his-rock/304264/.

Groys, Boris. *History Becomes Form: Moscow Conceptualism*. Cambridge, MA: MIT Press, 2010.

Grovier, Kelly. "Black Lives Matters Protests: Why Are Statues So Powerful?" *BBC* (12 June 2020): https://www.bbc.com/culture/article/20200612-black-lives-matter -protests-why-are-statues-so-powerful.

Gundiaev, Kirill. "Patriarshaia propoved' v nedeliu syropustnuiu posle Liturgii v khrame Khrista Spasitelia." Official site of the Russian Orthodox Church (6 March 2022): http://www.patriarchia.ru/db/text/5906442.html.

———. "Patriarshaia propoved' v nedeliu syropustnuiu posle Liturgii v khrame Khrista Spasitelia." official site of the Russian Orthodox Church (13 March 2022): http://www.patriarchia.ru/db/text/5908325.html.

Hanson, Victor Davis. "The Value of Putin." *National Review* (11 February 2014): https://www.nationalreview.com/2014/02/value-putin-victor-davis-hanson/.

Hawley, Josh. "The Age of Pelagius." *Christianity Today* (9 June 2019): https://www .christianitytoday.com/ct/2019/june-web-only/age-of-pelagius-joshua-hawley.html.

Heer, Jeet. "At Liberalism's Crossroads: The Vexed Legacy of Richard Hofstadter." *The Nation* (6 October 2020): https://www.thenation.com/article/culture/richard-hof stadter-library-america-review/.

Hell, Julia, and George Steinmetz. "A Period of 'Wild and Fierce Fanaticism': Theo-Political Militarism, and the Crisis of US Hegemony." *American Journal of Cultural Sociology* 5, no. 3 (October 2017): 373–91.

Hern, Alex. "Stormfront: 'Murder Capital of Internet' Pulled Offline after Civil Rights Action." *Guardian* (29 August 2017): https://www.theguardian.com/technology/2017/aug/29/stormfront-neo-nazi-hate-site-murder-internet-pulled-offline-web-com-civil-rights-action.

Hesse, Tom. "A Journal's Apology Prompts Soul-Searching about Racial Gatekeeping in the Academy." *Chronicle of Higher Education* (21 April 2017): https://www.chronicle.com/article/a-journals-apology-prompts-soul-searching-over-racial-gatekeeping-in-academe/?cid=gen_sign_in.

Hill, Michael. "Our Russia Outreach Has Struck a Nerve!" (23 July 2018): https://leagueofthesouth.com/our-russia-outreach-has-struck-a-nerve/.

———. "To Our Russian Friends." (17 July 2018): https://leagueofthesouth.com/to-our-russian-friends/.

Hirshson, Stanley P. *General Patton: A Soldier's Life.* New York: Harper Perennial, 2003.

Hobsbawm, Eric. *Bandits.* New York: Delacorte Press, 1969.

Hochschild, Arlie Russell. *Strangers in Their Own Land: Anger and Mourning on the American Right.* New York: New Press, 2016.

Hofstadter, Richard. *Anti-Intellectualism in American Life, The Paranoid Style in American Politics, Uncollected Essays 1956–1965.* New York: Library of America, 2020.

hooks, bell. *Black Looks: Race and Representation.* South Bend, IN: South End Press, 1992.

Hosking, Geoffrey. *Russia and the Russians.* 2nd ed. Cambridge, MA: Harvard University Press, 2011.

Houellebecq, Michel. *H. P. Lovecraft: Against the World, against Life.* Translated by Dorna Khazeni. Paris: Cernunnos, 2019.

Hsu, Hua. "The Feeling When: What Affect Theory Teaches about the New Age of Anxiety." *New Yorker* (25 March 2019): 56–65.

Itkowitz, Colby. "GOP Sen. Hawley Says He Does Not Regret Raising Fist to Pro-Trump Mob at Capitol on Jan. 6." *Washington Post* (4 May 2021): https://www.washingtonpost.com/powerpost/republicans-trump-hawley-jan-6-riot/2021/05/04/9f757304-aced-11eb-acd3-24b44a57093a_story.html.

Itogi Vserossiiskoi perepisi naseleniia 2010 goda: http://www.gks.ru/free_doc/new_site/perepis2010/croc/Documents/Vol6/pub-06-09.pdf.

"Iurii Luzhkov: Gei-parads my ne dopustili i ne dopustim vpred'." *Regions.ru* (21 January 2010): http://www.regions.ru/news/2266605/.

Ivanova, Miroslava. "Kogda odinochestvo nakryvaet s golovoi." *Pravmir* (13 July 2015): https://www.pravmir.ru/blizost-boga-ili-kak-ne-ostatsya-na-svete-odnomu/.

Jakobson, Roman. *Pushkin and His Sculptural Myth.* Translated and edited by John Burbank. The Hague and Paris: Mouton, 1975.

Jakobson, Roman, and Morris Halle. *Fundamentals of Language.* 2nd ed. The Hague: Mouton, 1956.

Jameson, Fredric. *Fables of Aggression: Wyndham Lewis, the Modernist as Fascist.* Berkeley: University of California Press, 1981.

Jones, Sarah. "Corey Stewart Doesn't Get That You Can Be a Southerner without Being Racist." *New Republic* (25 April 2017): https://newrepublic.com/article/142254/corey-stewart-doesnt-get-can-southerner-without-racist.

———. "Rod Dreher's Race Problem." *New Republic* (25 January 2016): https://newrepublic.com/article/146758/rod-drehers-race-problem.

Judt, Tony. *Reappraisals: Reflections on the Forgotten Twentieth Century*. New York: Penguin, 2008.

Kalashnikov, Maksim. "Innovatsionnaia oprichnina Lavrentiia Berii: K voprosu o modeli parallel'nogo 'pravitel'stva razvitiia,' razrushennaia v 1953-om godu." In *Na prostranstvakh imperii: Traditsiia, istoriia, kul'tura*, edited by V. V. Averianov et al., 309–26. Moscow: Institut dinamicheskogo konservatizma, 2012.

Kalpokas, Ignas. *A Political Theory of Post-Truth*. Cham, Switzerland: Palgrave, 2019.

Karamzin, N. M. *Istoriia gosudarstva rossiiskogo v dvenadstati tomakh*. Vol. 1. Edited by Andrei Sakharov. Moscow: Nauka, 1989.

Kazbek, Katya. "Against the Farts." https://ljsear.ch/savedcopy?post=568478764.

Kelly, James. *James Burnham and the Struggle for the World*. Wilmington, DE: ISI Books, 2002.

Kennedy, Barbara M. "The 'Virtual Machine' and New Becomings in Pre-Millennial Culture." In *The Cybercultures Reader*, edited by Barbara M. Kennedy and David Bell, 14–21. London: Routledge, 2002.

Kharkhordin, Oleg. *Republicanism in Russia: Community before and after Communism*. Cambridge, MA: Harvard University Press, 2018.

Khavin, Dmitri, et al. "Days of Rage: How Trump Supporters Took the U.S. Capitol." *New York Times* (30 June 2021): https://www.nytimes.com/video/us/politics/100000007606996/capitol-riot-trump-supporters.html.

Khodasevich, Vladislav. "Koleblemyi trenozhnik." In *Sobranie sochinenii v chetyrekh tomax*. Vol. 2, edited by V. P. Kochetov, 77–85. Moscow: Soglasie, 1996.

Kirillova, Kseniya. "Kremlin Refocuses Its Propaganda in Preparation for War." *Eurasian Daily Monitor* (21 January 2022): https://jamestown.org/program/kremlin-refocuses-its-propaganda-in-preparation-for-war/?fbclid=IwAR0qs9r0bq8°vJLGMvNWtuI5iBY61°plUhSz92iVSBAOi4_9-C4AXKHLyoY.

Kishkovsky, Sophia. "Artist's 'Orthodox or Death' T-shirt Is Extremist, Says Russian Court." *Art Newspaper* (22 March 2012): https://www.johnsanidopoulos.com/2012/03/artists-orthodoxy-or-death-t-shirt-is.html.

Kishkovsky, Sophia, and David M. Herszenhorn. "Punk Band's Moscow Trial Offers Platform for Orthodox Protesters." *New York Times* (8 August 2012): https://www.nytimes.com/2012/08/09/world/europe/punk-bands-moscow-trial-offers-platform-for-orthodox-protesters.html.

Kislina, Irina. "Kto takie pravoslavnye khorugvenostsy?" *Pravoslavie i mir* (11 August 2011): http://www.pravmir.ru/kto-takie-pravoslavnye-xorugvenoscy/.

Klayman, Alison, dir. *The Brink*. Los Angeles: Magnolia Home Entertainment, 2019. DVD.

Koffler, Keith. *Bannon: Always the Rebel*. Washington, DC: Regnery, 2017.

Kondakov, Alexander. "Regulating Desire in Russia." In *Research Handbook on Gender, Sexuality, and the Law*, 397–408. Cheltenham, UK: Edward Elgar, 2020.

Koni, A. F. *M. M. Kovalev'skii v zakonodatel-noi deiatel'nosti*. St. Petersburg: n.p., 1916.

Konovalova, O. F. "Pletenie sloves i pletennyi ornament kontsa XIV veka. K voprosu sootnosheniia." In *Trudy otdeneniia drevnerusskoi literatury*. Vol. 22:101–11. Moscow/Leningrad: Nauka, 1966.

Kundera, Milan. "Die Weltliteratur." *New Yorker* (1 January 2007): 28–35.

Kuraev, Andrei. "Pominaite nastavnikov vashikh. . . ." *Zhivoi zhurnal* (23 March 2021): https://diak-kuraev.livejournal.com/2021/03/23/.

Kutner, Samantha. "Swiping Right: The Allure of Hyper Masculinity and Cryptofascism for Men Who Join the Proud Boys." *ICCT Research Paper* (May 2020).

Land, Marisa L., and Peter Jamieson. "Rioters Breached the Capitol as They Waved Pro-Police Flags: Police Support on the Right May Be Eroding, Experts Warn." *Washington Post* (8 January 2021): https://www.washingtonpost.com/local/capitol -police-officers-support/2021/01/08/a16e07a2-51da-11eb-83e3-322644d82356_story .html.

Landrieu, Mitch. "Speech upon the Removal of Confederate Statues from New Orleans, May 19, 2017." In *Controversial Monuments and Memorials: A Guide for Community Leaders*, edited by David B. Allison, 165–72. Lanham, MD: Rowman & Littlefield, 2018.

Laruelle, Marlène. "The Izborskii Club, or the New Conservative Avant-Garde in Russia." *Russian Review* 75 (October 2016): 626–44.

———. "The *Rodnoverie* Movement: The Search for Pre-Christian Ancestry and the Occult." In *The New Age of Russia: Occult and Esoteric Dimensions*, edited by Birgit Menzel, Michael Hagemeister, and Bernice Glatzer Rosenthal, 293–310. Munich-Berlin: Verlag Otto Sagner, 2012.

———. "Russian and American Far Right Connections: Confluence, Not Influence." *PONARS Eurasia Policy Memo*, no. 516 (March 2018): http://www.ponarseurasia.org /node/9641.

———. *Russian Eurasianism: An Ideology of Empire*. Translated by Mischa Gabowitsch. Baltimore, MD: Johns Hopkins University Press, 2008.

Latukhina, Kira. "Rossiia prodolzhit' ukrepliat' svoi pozitsii v Arktike." *Rossiiskaia gazeta* (29 August 2014): https://rg.ru/2014/08/29/arktika-site-anons.html.

Latynina, Yulia. "Velikaia zapadnaia kul'turnaia revoliutsiia." *Novaya gazeta* (30 June 2020): https://novayagazeta.ru/articles/2020/06/30/86074-velikaya-zapadnaya-kul turnaya-revolyutsiya.

Lavin, Talia. *Culture Warlords: My Journey into the Dark Web of White Supremacy*. New York: Hachette Books, 2020.

"Leading Advocate of a Revival of the Old Confederacy Resigns a Tenured Professorship at a Black College." *The Journal of Blacks in Higher Education* 25 (Autumn, 1999): 46.

Lehmann, Chris. "What Richard Hofstadter Got Wrong." *New Republic* (16 April 2020): https://newrepublic.com/article/157190/richard-hofstadter-got-wrong-para noid-style-reissue-review.

Lenin, Vladimir. "Pamiati Gertsena." *Polnoe sobranie sochinenii*. Vol. 21: *Gosudarstvo i revoliutsiia*, 255–62. 5th ed. Moscow: Izd. Politicheskoi literatury, 1974.

———. *Polnoe sobranie sochinenii*. Vol. 33: *Gosudarstvo i revoliutsiia*. 5th ed. Moscow: Izd. Politicheskoi literatury, 1969.

———. *Polnoe sobranie sochinenii*. Vol. 35: *Oktiabr' 1917—mart 1918*. 5th ed. Moscow: Izd. Politicheskoi literatury, 1974.

———. *Polnoe sobranie sochinenii*. Vol. 36: *Mar—iiul' 1918*. 5th ed. Moscow: Izd. Politicheskoi literatury, 1974.

———. *Selected Works*. Vol. 1. Moscow: Progress Publishers, 1963.

———. "Speech on the Dissolution of the Constituent Assembly: Delivered to the All-Russian Central Executive Committee." (January 6 [19], 1918): https://www.marxists.org/archive/lenin/works/1918/jan/06b.htm.

———. *The State and Revolution*. Translated by Robert Service. New York: Penguin, 1993.

Levada Center. "Vladimir Putin." (20 November 2017): https://www.levada.ru/2017/11/20/vladimir-putin-5/.

Lévy, Pierre. *Collective Intelligence: Mankind's Emerging World in Cyberspace*. Translated by Robert Bononno. Cambridge, MA: Perseus Books, 1997.

Lieven, Anatol. "Against Russophobia." *World Policy Journal* 17, no. 4 (Winter 2000/2001): 25–32.

Likhachev, D. S. *Istoricheskaia poetika russkoi literature: Smekh kak mirovozzrenie*. St. Petersburg: "Aleteia," 1997.

Limbaugh, Rush. "My Bipartisan Stimulus." *Wall Street Journal* (29 January 2009): https://www.wsj.com/articles/SB123318906638926749.

Limonov, Eduard. *Kontrol'nyi vystrel*. Moscow: Ul'tra.Kul'tura, 2003.

———. *Moia politicheskaia biografiia*. Moscow: Amfora, 2002.

Lipovetsky, Mark. "*Brother 2* as a Political Melodrama. Twenty Years Later, Balabanov's Film Serves to Justify War with Ukraine." *RussiaPost* (11 July 2022): https://russiapost.net/society/brother2?fbclid=IwAR2Wn_m5zc1__xl9mrxeJrxlZBez8zf-0LNTW4B7mtbkZqMKasuHdQ417KA.

Lombroso, Daniel, dir. *White Noise*. Film. 2020: http://www.daniellombroso.com/white-noise.

Lotman, Yuri. "Dinamicheskaia model' semioticheskoi sistemy." In *Readings in Soviet Semiotics (Russian Texts)*, edited by L. Maetjka et al., 76–93. Ann Arbor: Michigan Slavic Texts, 1981.

———. *Struktura khudozhestvennogo teksta*. Providence, RI: Brown University Press, 1971.

Love, Mia. "Mia Love's 2012 Republican National Convention Speech." Video. *Washington Post* (5 November 2014): https://www.washingtonpost.com/video/politics/mia-loves-2012-republican-national-convention-speech/2014/11/05/3bdaafc4-64f8-11e4-ab86-46000e1d0035_video.html?utm_term=.1acf2dc71ac5.

Lovecraft, H. P. *The New Annotated H. P. Lovecraft*. Edited by Leslie S. Klinger. New York: Liveright, 2014.

Lur'e, Vadim, ed. *Azbuka protesta: Narodnyi plakat*. Moscow: O. G. I. Polit.ru, 2012.

Lyons, Matthew N. "Jack Donovan and Male Tribalism." In *Key Thinkers of the Radical Right: Behind the New Threat to Liberal Democracy*, edited by Mark Sedgwick, 242–59. New York: Oxford University Press, 2019.

MacDonald, Kevin. "Alexander Dugin's 4 Political Theory Is for the Russian Empire, Not for European Ethno-Nationalists." *Occidental Observer* (18 May 2014): https://www.theoccidentalobserver.net/2014/05/18/alexander-dugins-4-political-theory-is-for-the-russian-empire-not-for-european-ethno-nationalists/.

———. *The Culture of Critique: An Evolutionary Analysis of Jewish Involvement in Twentieth-Century Intellectual and Political Movements*. Westport, CT: Praeger, 1998.

————. "The 'Default Hypothesis' Fails to Explain Jewish Influence." Retracted article, *Philosophia* 22 (2022): https://link.springer.com/article/10.1007/s11406-021-00439-y.

————. "Memories of Madison—My Life in the New Left." *VDare* (18 March 2009): https://www.vdare.com/articles/memories-of-madison-my-life-in-the-new-left.

————. *A People That Shall Dwell Alone: Judaism as a Group Evolutionary Strategy.* Westport, CT: Praeger, 1994; 2nd ed., Bloomington, IN: 1st Books Library, 2002.

————. "Reply to Nathan Cofnas: Debating *The Culture of Critique.*" *Unz Review* (20 March 2018): https://www.unz.com/article/reply-to-nathan-cofnas/.

————. *Separation and Its Discontents: Toward an Evolutionary Theory of Anti-Semitism.* Westport, CT: Praeger, 1998; 2nd ed., Bloomington, IN: 1st Books Library, 2003.

————. "Speech at the 2019 LS National Conference." https://leagueofthesouth.com/dr-kevin-macdonalds-speech-at-the-2019-ls-national-conference/.

————. "Stalin's Willing Executioners: Jews as a Hostile Elite in the USSR." *Occidental Quarterly* 5, no. 3 (Fall 2005): 65–100.

————. "What Makes Western Culture Unique?" In *Cultural Insurrections: Essays on Western Civilization, Jewish Influence and Anti-Semitism*, 271–99. Atlanta, GA: Occidental Press, 2007.

Maclean, Nancy. *Democracy in Chains: The Deep History of the Radical Right's Stealth Plan for America.* New York: Viking, 2017.

Main, Thomas J. *The Rise of the Alt-Right.* Washington, DC: Brookings Institution Press, 2018.

Marantz, Andrew. "The Illiberal Order: Does Hungary Offer a Glimpse of Our Authoritarian Future?" *New Yorker* (4 July 2022): 36–47.

Marchenko, Anatoly. *My Testimony.* Translated by Michael Scammell. New York: E. F. Dutton, 1969.

Marinetti, F. T. "Initial Manifesto of Futurism." In *Exhibition of Works by the Italian Futurist Painters*, 3–8. London: Sackville Gallery, 1912.

Marquardt, John. "Russia vs. the Confederacy." *The Abbeville Institute* (17 October 2017): https://www.abbevilleinstitute.org/russia-vs-the-confederacy/.

Matza, Tomas. *Shock Therapy: Psychology, Precarity, and Wellbeing in Post-Socialist Russia.* Durham, NC: Duke University Press, 2018.

Maurantonio, Nicole. *Confederate Exceptionalism: Civil War Myth and Memory in the Twenty-First Century.* Lawrence: University Press of Kansas, 2019.

Mayakovsky, Vladimir. "Razgovor s fininspektorom." In *Polnoe sobranie sochinenii.* Vol. 7:119–27. Moscow: Gosudarstvennoe izdatel'stvo khudozehstvennoi literatury, 1958.

Meeting of the Valdai International Discussion Club. 9 September 2013. Video and transcript. http://en.kremlin.ru/events/president/news/19243.

"Mesto sel'skogo khoziastva v ekonomikę Rossii." *Agrovestnik* (30 July 2018): https://agrovesti.net/lib/industries/mesto-selskogo-khozyajstva-v-ekonomike-rossii.html.

Mielke, Tomas M. *The Russian Homosexual Lexicon: Consensual and Prison Camp Sexuality among Men.* Charleston, SC: CreateSpace, 2017.

Miller, Abraham. "The Theory behind That Charlottesville Slogan." *Wall Street Journal* (2 April 2018): https://www.wsj.com/articles/the-theory-behind-that-charlottesville-slogan-1522708318.

Miller-Idriss, Cynthia. *The Extreme Gone Mainstream: Commercialization and Far-Right Youth Culture in Germany.* Princeton, NJ: Princeton University Press, 2017.

Miroshnichenko, Igor. "Proshchai, velikii slavianin!" VKontakte post (24 March 2022): https://vk.com/miroig?w=wall55950642_4309%2Fall.

Mirzoeff, Nicholas. "All the Monuments Must Fall #Charlottesville." *Face Forward* (14 August 2017): http://www.nicholasmirzoeff.com/bio/all-the-monuments-must-fall -charlottesville/.

Mogelson, Luke. "Among the Insurrectionists." *New Yorker* (25 January 2021): 33–53.

Morris, Alex. "Donald Trump: The End-Times President." *Rolling Stone* (30 October 2020): https://www.rollingstone.com/politics/politics-features/donald-trump-christians -fundamentalists-end-times-rapture-1083131/.

Morrison, Toni. "The Dancing Mind." *National Book Foundation* (6 November 1996): https://www.nationalbook.org/tag/the-dancing-mind/.

Morson, Gary Saul. "Prosaics Evolving." *Slavic and East European Journal* 41, no. 1 (Spring 1997): 57–73.

———. "Suicide of the Liberals." *First Things* (October 2020): https://www.firstthings .com/article/2020/10/suicide-of-the-liberals.

Moss, Candida R., and Joel S. Baden. *Bible Nation: The United States of Hobby Lobby.* Princeton, NJ: Princeton University Press, 2017.

Mosse, George L. *The Crisis of German Ideology: Intellectual Origins of the Third Reich.* Madison: University of Wisconsin Press, 2021.

Müller, Jan-Werner. *Democracy Rules.* New York: Farrar, Straus and Giroux, 2021.

———. *What Is Populism?* Philadelphia: University of Pennsylvania Press, 2016.

"Natal'ia Poklonskaia soobshchila, chto biust Nikolaia II mirotochit: Vy ne poverite, chto proizoshlo potom." *Meduza* (6 March 2017): https://meduza.io/feature/2017 /03/06/natalya-poklonskaya-soobschila-chto-byust-nikolaya-ii-mirotochit-vy-ne -poverite-chto-proizoshlo-potom.

Nekhezin, Viktor. "Ognemir, Bogumil, I Tsar Putin: Kak zhivut neoiazychniki v Rossii." *BBC News, Russkaia sluzhba* (20 September 2018): https://www.bbc.com/rus sian/features-45502454.

NOD SPB LO [National Liberation Movement, Saint-Petersburg and Leningrad Region]. "Amerika planiruet sverzhenie vlasti v Rossii 19.09.21." (14 August 2021): https://vk.com/nod_spblo?w=wall-64024736_108253.

Oates, Joyce Carol. "The King of Weird." *New York Review of Books* 42, no. 17 (31 October 2014): https://www.nybooks.com/articles/1996/10/31/the-king-of-weird/.

Odoevsky, V. F. "Dnevnik V. F. Odoevskogo, 1859–1869 gg." *Literaturnoe Nasledstvo* 22–24 (1935): 79–308.

"Orgkomitet gei—praida zadal video—voprosy Valentine Matvienko." (19 February 2010): https://gazeta.spb.ru/269016-0/.

"Ot rektora MGU potrebovali uvolit' profesora Aleksandra Dugina za prizyvy 'ubivat' ukraintsev." *News.ru* (16 June 2014): https://www.newsru.com/russia/16jun2014 /dugin.html.

O'Toole, Fintan. *Heroic Failure: Brexit and the Politics of Pain.* London: Apollo Books, 2018.

Pagliery, Jose. "Trump Adviser Peter Navarro Lays Out How He and Bannon Planned to Overturn Biden Electoral Win." *Daily Beast* (21 December 2021): https://www

.thedailybeast.com/trump-advisor-peter-navarro-lays-out-how-he-and-steve-ban non-planned-to-overturn-bidens-electoral-win?fbclid=IwAR1u609TzFYekjQ4O5j C7ktoX0-E8ChpCTo2_uJqsYXr-YrMRu3TX860UxE.

"Pamiatnik krestiteliu Rusi v Kieve mogli oskvernit' neonatsisty iz 'Azova.'" *Life* (2 October 2016): https://life.ru/p/911270.

Parker, Alison M. "The Almost-Monument to Black 'Mammie.'" *New York Times, Sunday Review* (6 February 2020), 10.

Parts, Lyudmila. *In Search of the True Russia: The Provinces in Contemporary Nationalist Discourse.* Madison: University of Wisconsin Press, 2018.

Paul, Darel E. *From Tolerance to Equality: How Elites Brought America to Same-Sex Marriage.* Waco, TX: Baylor University Press, 2018.

———. "The Future Is Mixed." *First Things* (November 2019): https://www.firstthings .com/article/2019/11/the-future-is-mixed.

———. "The Siren Song of Geopolitics: Towards a Gramscian Account of the Iraq War." *Millennium: A Journal of International Studies* 36, no. 1 (December 2007): 51–76.

———. "Under the Rainbow Banner." *First Things* (June 2020): https://www.first things.com/article/2020/06/under-the-rainbow-banner.

Philologist. "Umer glava Soiuza pravoslavnykh khorugvenostsev Leonid Simonovich-Nikshich." LiveJournal (20 March 2022): https://philologist.livejournal.com/12312420 .html.

Pintner, Walter Mackenzie. *Russian Economic Policy under Nicholas I.* Ithaca, NY: Cornell University Press, 1967.

Peterson, Jordan. "Russia vs. Ukraine or Civil War in the United States." Video (10 July 2022): https://www.youtube.com/watch?v=JxdHm2dmvKE.

Plotko, Masha. "Strakh drugogo: Problema gomofobii v Rossii." https://www.levada .ru/2013/03/12/strah-drugogo-problema-gomofobii-v-rossii/.

Plutser-Sarno, Aleksei. "Yazyk tela I politika: Simvolika vorovskikh tatuirovok" [Politics and the language of the body: the symbolism of thieves' tattoos]. In *Tatuirovki zakliuchennykh, Skopirovannye i sobrannye veteranom MVD SSSR Baldavevym D. S. s 1948 po 2000 g. Iz lichnogo sobraniia avtora.* Edited by Danzig Baldaev, 3–24. St. Petersburg: Limbus Press, 2001.

Pobedonostsev, K. P. *Velikaia lozh' nashego vremeni.* Moscow: "Russkaia kniga," 1993.

Poliakov, Mark Iakovlevich, and A K Kotov, eds. *N. V. Gogol' v russkoi kritike.* Moscow: Gosudarstvennoe izdatel'stvo khudozhestvennoi literatury, 1953.

Polian, Pavel. "Gde zhe byt' zheleznomu Feliksu—v muzeone ili v muzee?" *Novaya gazeta* (30 June 2015): https://novayagazeta.ru/articles/2015/07/31/65084-krasnyy -terrorist-8470-1.

Polyakova, Alina. "Strange Bedfellows: Putin and Europe's Far Right." *World Affairs* 177, no. 3 (September/October 2014): 36–40.

Prioli, Carmine A. "King Arthur in Khaki: The Medievalism of General George S. Patton, Jr." *Studies in Popular Culture* 10, no. 1 (1987): 42–50.

Prokhanov, Aleksandr. "Molniia-Lenin: Beseda s Sergeem Kurginianom." *Izborskii klub* 4 (2017): 8–9.

Pushkin, Alexander. "The Bronze Horseman." Translated by Walter Arndt. In *The Portable Nineteenth-Century Russian Reader*, edited by George Gibian, 8–21. New York: Penguin, 1993.

Putin, Vladimir. "Address by the President of the Russian Federation." (21 February 2022): http://kremlin.ru/events/president/news/67828.

"Putin ne soglasen s temi, kto nazyvaiut ego tsarem." *Tass* (19 March 2020): https://tass.ru/obschestvo/8022941.

Radosh, Ronald. "D.C. Elites Suck up to Steve Bannon Like He's the Next Henry Kissinger." *Daily Beast* (25 October 2017): https://www.thedailybeast.com/dc-elites-suck-up-to-steve-bannon-like-hes-the-next-henry-kissinger.

———. "Steve Bannon, Trump's Top Guy, Told Me He Was a Leninist." *Daily Beast* (22 August 2016): https://www.thedailybeast.com/steve-bannon-trumps-top-guy-told-me-he-was-a-leninist.

Rand, Ayn. *The Fountainhead*. New York: Signet, 1993.

Read, Christopher. *Lenin: A Revolutionary Life*. London: Routledge, 2005.

"Rebranding White Nationalism: Inside the Alt-Right." *The Atlantic* (15 December 2016): https://www.theatlantic.com/video/index/510533/rebranding-white-nationalism-inside-the-alt-right/.

Redden, Molly. "Trump's Powers Will Not Be Questioned, Says Senior Official." *The Guardian*, (12 February 2017): https://www.theguardian.com/us-news/2017/feb/12/trump-administration-considering-narrower-travel-ban.

Remnick, David. "Letter from Moscow: Watching the Eclipse." *New Yorker* (11 & 18 August 2014): 52–65.

Riccardi-Swartz, Sarah. *Between Heaven and Russia: Religious Conversion and Political Apostasy in Appalachia*. New York: Fordham University Press, 2022.

———. "American Conversions to Russian Orthodoxy amid the Global Culture Wars." Symposium." *The Culture Wars Today* (18 December 2019): https://berkley center.georgetown.edu/responses/american-conversions-to-russian-orthodoxy-amid-the-global-culture-wars.

———. "Seeking a Sovereign for the End of Democracy: Monarchism and the Far Right." *Canopy Forum on the Interactions of Law and Religion* (10 August 2021): https://canopyforum.org/2021/08/10/seeking-a-sovereign-for-the-end-of-democracy-monarchism-and-the-far-right/.

Robin, Corey. *The Reactionary Mind: Conservatism from Edmund Burke to Donald Trump*. 2nd ed. Oxford University Press, 2018.

"Russian Political Ad Bashes Gay Marriage." *Moscow Times* (3 June 2020): https://www.themoscowtimes.com/2020/06/02/russian-political-ad-bashes-gay-marriage-a70459.

Rutland, Peter. "Neoliberalism and the Russian Transition." *Review of International Political Economy* 20, no. 2 (2013): 332–62.

Ryan, Jenna (@dotjenna). "We just stormed the Capital. It was one of the best days of my life." Twitter, 6 January 2021: https://twitter.com/dotjenna/status/1346965308041433090.

Said, Edward. "On Defiance and Taking Positions." In *Reflections on Exile and Other Essays*, 500–506. Cambridge, MA: Harvard University Press, 2000.

Sailer, Steven. "Will U.S. Retain Its 'Market-Dominant Majority.'" *VDare* (2 Feb 2003): https://vdare.com/articles/will-u-s-retain-its-market-dominant-majority.

Samuels, David. "American Racist: A Q&A with Kevin MacDonald, the Country's Most Influential White Identitarian Ideologue." *Tablet* (11 June 2020): https://www.tabletmag.com/sections/news/articles/kevin-macdonald-american-anti-semitism.

Sante, Lucy. "Invisible Man." *New York Review of Books*, 10 May 1984: https://www
.nybooks.com/articles/1984/05/10/the-invisible-man/.

Scarry, Elaine. *The Body in Pain: The Making and Unmaking of the World.* Oxford
University Press, 1985.

Schenker, Alexander M. *The Bronze Horseman: Falconet's Monument to Peter the Great.*
New Haven: Yale University Press, 2003.

Schmemann, Alexander. "Forgiveness: A Homily Delivered to the Community at
St. Vladimir's Orthodox Seminary on Forgiveness Sunday of 1983": https://www
.schmemann.org/byhim/forgiveness-1983.03.20.html.

Schoenfeld, Eugen. Review of Kevin MacDonald's *A People That Shall Dwell Alone:
Judaism as a Group Evolutionary Strategy. Journal for the Scientific Study of Religion*
34, no. 3 (September 1995): 408–10.

Sebestyen, Victor. *Lenin: The Man, the Dictator, and the Master of Terror.* New York:
Pantheon Books, 2017.

Sedgwick, Eve Kosofsky. *The Epistemology of the Closet.* Updated with a new preface.
Berkeley: University of California Press, 2008.

Shaw, Tamsin. "The Iago Problem." *NYR Daily* (14 December 2016): https://www
.nybooks.com/daily/2016/12/14/iago-problem-choosing-evil-othello/.

Shchepkina-Kupernik, Tatiana. "Peterburgskii noktiurn." In *Russkie poetess XIX veka*,
by N.V. Bannikov, 231. Moscow: Sovetskaia Rossiia, 1979.

Shcherbina, Evgeniia. "Chelovek odinochestva i vokryg nego." *Tass-Nauka* (22 February 2018): https://nauka.tass.ru/sci/6820547.

Shishkov, Andrei. "The Navalny Protests and Orthodoxy's Apolitical Theology: Mum-
blings of the Sacred." *Public Orthodoxy* (9 February 2021): https://publicorthodoxy.
org/2021/02/09/the-navalny-protests-and-orthodoxys-a-political-theology/#more-8365.

Shklovsky, Viktor. "Iskusstvo kak priem." In *Formal'nyi metod: Antologiia russkogo
modernizma.* Vol. 1: *Sistemy*, edited by Sergei Oushakine, 131–46. Moscow: Kabinet-
nyi uchenyi, 2016.

Shnirelman, Viktor. *Russkoe rodnoverie: Neoiazychestvo i natsionalizm v sovremennoi
Rossii.* Moscow: Izdatel'stvo BBI, 2012.

Shragin, Boris, and Albert Todd, eds. *Landmarks: A Collection of Essays on the Russian
Intelligentsia, 1909.* Translated by Marian Schwartz. New York: Kartz Howard, 1977.

Sinyavsky, Andrei. *Ivan-Durak. Ocherk russkoi narodnoi very.* Fontenay-aux-Roses,
France: Sintaksis, 1991.

"Skinkhedy: Otkuda nogi rastut?" *Pravmir* (24 August 2011): https://www.pravmir.ru
/skinxedy-otkuda-nogi-rastut/.

"Skol'ko pamiatnikov Leninu ostalos' v Rossii?" *Aif* (29 January 2020): https://aif.ru
/dontknows/file/skolko_pamyatnikov_leninu_ostalos_v_rossii.

Slezkine, Yuri. *The Jewish Century.* Princeton, NJ: Princeton University Press, 2004.

Sokolov, Mikhail. "Baiden vstupilsia za Naval'nogo." *Radio Svoboda* (27 January 2021):
https://www.svoboda.org/a/31071547.html.

———. "'Den' oprichnika' i 'Sakharniyi kreml': Vozvrashchatsia li v Rossiiu traditsiia
politicheskoi literatury." Interview. *Radio Svoboda* (22 August 2008): https://www
.svoboda.org/a/462097.html.

Solzhenitsyn, Alexander. *Lenin in Zürich.* Translated by H. T. Willetts. New York: Farrar, Straus and Giroux, 1976.

———. *Lenin v Tsiurikhe*. Paris: YMCA Press, 1975.

———. "Live Not by Lies." Translated by Yermolai Solzhenitsyn: https://www.sol zhenitsyncenter.org/live-not-by-lies.

Sons of Confederate Veterans. "New Orleans & Other Tragedies." Letter (12 May 2017): https://www.facebook.com/LouisianaSCV.

Sontag, Susan. *Essays of the Sixties and Seventies*. New York: Library of America, 2013.

Sorokin, Vladimir. *The Day of the Oprichnik*. Translated by Jamie Gambrell. New York: Farrar, Straus and Giroux, 2011.

———. *Den' oprichnika*. Moscow: Zakharov, 2009.

———. "Farewell to the Queue." In *The Queue*, 253–63. Translated by Sally Laird. New York: New York Review of Books, 2008.

———. "Let the Past Collapse on Time!" *New York Review of Books* (8 May 2014): https://www.nybooks.com/articles/2014/05/08/let-the-past-collapse-on-time/.

Southern Poverty Law Center. "Neo-Confederate." https://www.splcenter.org/fighting -hate/extremist-files/ideology/neo-confederate.

———. "Six Years Later: 170 Confederate Monuments Removed since Charleston Church Massacre." (17 June 2021): https://www.splcenter.org/news/2021/06/17/six -years-later-170-confederate-monuments-removed-charleston-church-massacre.

———. "Whose Heritage? Public Symbols of the Confederacy." (1 February 2019): https://www.splcenter.org/20190201/whose-heritage-public-symbols-confederacy ?gclid=CjoKCQjw2_OWBhDqARIsAAUNTTFwLqLQ94pMeci19NM3fyghOZZ qXMO9LzfoUaM-b_DTA7doejLgMSsaAmjJEALw_wcB.

Sperling, Valerie. *Sex, Politics, and Putin: Political Legitimacy in Russia*. Oxford Studies in Culture and Politics. New York: Oxford University Press, 2014.

Stanley, Jason. *How Fascism Works: The Politics of Us and Them*. New York: Random House, 2020.

———. *How Propaganda Works*. Princeton, NJ: Princeton University Press, 2019.

"Staruskha Ciccone—ved'ma! 11 avgusta 2012 goda: Interv'iu Glavy Soiuza Pravo- slavnykh Khorugvenostsev dla 'Den' TV." Video: http://www.pycckie.org/video /video-11082012.shtml.

"Stat'ia 1." (7 March 2012): http://base.garant.ru/35365308/1cafb24d049dcd1e7707a22 d98e9858f/#block_11.

Steiner, George. "Russia and Red China." *Harper's* (February 2019): 67.

Stephens-Dawidowitz, Seth. "The Data of Hate." *New York Times, Week in Review* (13 August 2014), 4.

Stern, Alexandra Minna. *Proud Boys and the White Ethnostate: How the Alt-Right Is Warping the American Imagination*. Boston: Beacon Press, 2019.

"A Suppressed Tribute to Gen. Lee." *The Confederate Veteran* 4 (April 1895): 102.

"Tainoe stanet iavnym: Dugin i Kurekhin, 1995 god.: Efir pered vyborami v Gos. Dumu." Video (Fall 1995): https://www.youtube.com/watch?v=tqGjyMGhdqU.

Tarsaidze, Alexandre. *Czars and Presidents: The Story of a Forgotten Friendship*. New York: McDowell, Obolensky, 1958.

Taylor, Keeanga-Yamahtta. "Did Last Summer's Black Lives Matter Protests Change Anything?" *New Yorker* (6 August 2021): https://www.newyorker.com/news/our -columnists/did-last-summers-protests-change-anything.

————. *From #BlackLivesMatter to Black Liberation.* Chicago: Haymarket Books, 2016.

————. "No More Charlottesvilles." (14 August 2017): https://www.jacobinmag.com /2017/08/charlottesville-racist-march-heather-heyer.

Teitelbaum, Benjamin R. *War for Eternity: Inside Bannon's Far-Right Circle of Global Power Brokers.* New York: Harper Collins, 2020.

Tel'manov, Denis. "'Za poslednie tri nedeli anii razu vspominl, chto ia pisatel'. Interv'iu Zakhar Prilepina o sobytiiakh na Ukraine." *Gazeta.ru* (27 March 2022): https:// www.gazeta.ru/politics/2022/03/27/14671219.shtml.

Thomas, George. "'America Is a Republic, Not a Democracy' Is a Dangerous—and Wrong—Argument." *The Atlantic* (2 November 2020): https://www.theatlantic.com /ideas/archive/2020/11/yes-constitution-democracy/616949/.

Thompson, Erin L. *Smashing Statues: The Rise and Fall of America's Public Monuments.* New York: W. W. Norton & Co., 2022.

Tikhomirov, Viktor, dir. *Andrei Kuraev: Priamaia rech'.* Video (2016): https://www .youtube.com/watch?v=0NY2eDno2Mo&t=248s.

Titorenko, Danila. "Zhirinovskii predlozhil vykupat' detei u zhenshchin, planiruiush-chikh abort." *Gazeta.ru* (21 June 2021): https://www.gazeta.ru/social/news/2021/06 /21/n_16136780.shtml.

Tocqueville, Alexis de. *Democracy in America.* Translated by Gerald E. Bevan. New York: Penguin, 2003.

Tolstoy, Leo. *The Death of Ivan Ilyich and Confession.* Translated by Peter Carson. New York: Liveright, 2014.

Tomisov, V. A. *Russkie pravovedy XVIII–XX vekov: Ocherki zhizni i tvorchestva.* Vol. 1. Moscow: Zertsalo, 2007.

"Torch-Wielding White Nationalists Clash with Counterprotestors at UVA." *Daily Beast* (12 August 2017): https://www.thedailybeast.com/torch-wielding-white-na tionalists-clash-with-counter-protestors-at-uva.

"Transcript: Ezra Klein interviews Patrick Deneen." The Ezra Klein Show, *New York Times,* (13 May 2022). Podcast: https://www.nytimes.com/2022/05/13/podcasts /transcript-ezra-klein-interviews-patrick-deneen.html.

"Tserkov' i mir: Efir ot 30.01.2021." Video: https://smotrim.ru/video/2263996.

Tsvetaeva, Marina. "Excerpt from 'My Pushkin.'" Translated by Ellen Niddy. In *Under the Sky of My Africa: Aleksandr Pushkin and Blackness,* edited by Cathy Theimer Nepomnyashchy, Nicole Svobodny, and Ludmilla A. Trigos, 384–92. Evanston, IL: Northwestern University Press, 2006.

Tuchman, Aryeh, "Cal. State University Professor Endorses, Fund-Raises for David Duke." Blog post on JHate: A Blog about Anti-Semitism (1 July 2012): http://jhate .wordpress.com/2012/07/01/cal-state-university-professor-endorses-fund-raises -for-david-duke/.

Tucker, Robert C., ed. *The Marx-Engels Reader.* New York: W. W. Norton, 1978.

Tucker, William H. *The Funding of Scientific Racism: Wickliffe Draper and the Pioneer Fund.* Urbana: University of Illinois Press, 2002.

Tuğal, Cihan. "The Rise of the Leninist Right." Blog post on Verso Books website (20 January 2018): https://www.versobooks.com/blogs/3577-the-rise-of-the-leninist -right.

"277 iazykov i dialektowe ispol'zuiut narody Rossii." *Ministerstvo nauki i vsshego obrazovaniia rossiiskoi federatsii* (27 February 2021): https://www.minobrnauki.gov.ru/press-center/news/?ELEMENT_ID=29672#:~:text=Наша%20страна%20может%20похвастаться%20разнообразием,языков%2С%20на%20которых%20они%20г.

Umland, Andreas. "Aleksandr Dugin's Transformation from a Lunatic Fringe Figure into a Mainstream Political Publicist, 1990–1998: A Case Study in the Rise of Late and Post-Soviet Russian Fascism." *Journal of Eurasian Studies* 1 (2010): 144–52.

———. "Dugin i MGU: Pravoradikal'nyi ideolog kak professor vedushschego VUZa Rossii." *Forum vostochnoevropeiskoi istorii i kul'tury* 1 (2013): 482–87: http://www1.ku-eichstaett.de/ZIMOS/forum/inhaltruss19.html.

———. "Kulturhegemoniale Strategien der russischen extremen Rechten: Die Verbindung mit faschistischer Ideologie und metapolitischer Taktik im 'Neoeurasismus' des Alexander Dugin." *Österreichische Zeitschrift für Politikwissenschaft* 33, no. 4 (2004): 437–54.

Uspenskii, B. A. "K sisteme peredachi izobrazheniia v russkoi ikonopisi." *Trudy po znakovym sistemam* 2 (1965): 248–57.

Vance, J. D. *Hillbilly Elegy: A Memoir of a Family and Culture in Crisis.* New York: Harper, 2016.

Verdery, Kathleen. *The Political Lives of Dead Bodies: Reburial and Postsocialist Change.* New York: Columbia University Press, 1999.

Vermuele, Adrian. "Beyond Originalism." *The Atlantic* (30 March 2020): https://www.theatlantic.com/ideas/archive/2020/03/common-good-constitutionalism/609037/.

Vidal, Gore. "The Empire Lovers Strike Back." *The Nation* (22 March 1986): http://spikethenews.blogspot.com/2013/11/the-empire-lovers-strike-back-by-gore.html.

———. "Requiem for the American Empire." *The Nation* (11 January 1986): https://www.thenation.com/article/requiem-american-empire/.

"Vladimir Putin: Arktika—vazhneishii region Rossii." Video. *RT* (29 August 2014): https://www.youtube.com/watch?v=ksg5×6kD_d8.

Vollaro, Daniel R. "Lincoln, Stowe, and the 'Little Woman/Great War' Story: The Making, and Breaking, of a Great American Anecdote." *Journal of the Abraham Lincoln Association* 30, no. 1 (Winter 2009): https://quod.lib.umich.edu/j/jala/2629860.0030.104/—lincoln-stowe-and-the-little-womangreat-war-story-the-making?rgn=main;view=fulltext.

Volokhonsky, Lev. *Zhizn' po poniatiiam: Proiskhozhdenie sovremennoi obshchestvnnoi morali.* Moscow: OLMA, 2011.

"V Peterburge na mitinge proizoshli stolknoveniia protestuiushchikh s OMON-om." RBC [RosBiznesConsulting] Daily (31 January 2021): https://www.rbc.ru/politics/31/01/2021/60167a1c9a7947614306c1a4.

Walker, Shaun, Leonid Ragozin, and Matthew Weaver. "Putin Likens Ukraine's Forces to Nazis and Threatens Standoff in the Arctic." *Guardian* (29 August 2014): http://www.theguardian.com/world/2014/aug/29/putin-ukraine-forces-nazis-arctic.

"'We Just Want Russia to Be Better': Meduza Looks Back on the January 31 Opposition Protests in a Dispatch from St. Petersburg." *Meduza* (2 February 2021): https://meduza.io/en/feature/2021/02/02/we-just-want-russia-to-be-better.

White, James D. *Lenin: The Practice and Theory of Revolution.* New York: Palgrave, 2001.

Williams, Joan C. *White Working Class: Overcoming Class Consciousness in America.* Boston, MA: Harvard Business Review Press, 2017.

Wodak, Ruth. *The Politics of Fear: What Right-Wing Populist Discourses Mean.* London: SAGE Publications, 2015.

Wolf, Koenraad de. *Dissident for Life: Alexander Ogorodnikov and the Struggle for Religious Freedom in Russia.* Translated by Nancy Forest-Flier. Grand Rapids, MI: William B. Eerdsmann Publishing, 2013.

Wolff, Michael. *Fire and Fury: Inside the Trump White House.* New York: Henry Holt, 2018.

Yurchak, Aleksei. "A Parasite from Outer Space: How Sergei Kurekhin Proved That Lenin Was a Mushroom." *Slavic Review* 70, no. 2 (Summer 2011): 307–33.

Zenkovsky, Serge A. *Medieval Russia's Epics, Chronicles, and Tales.* Revised and enlarged edition. New York: E. P. Dutton, 1974.

Index

abolition of Russian serfdom and American slavery: assassination of the tsar following, 34; effects on the landed gentry, 41–42; granting "quasi-freedom," 12; literary catalysis and development of the intelligentsia, 37–44

action, cult of, 78–79

administrative state: the authority and idolatry of political statuary, 165–66, 178–83; Bannon's appropriation of Leninist antistatism, 89–95; Enteo and Kuraev's political positions, 162–63; rightist elites' veneration of, 31–32; Vermeule anchoring American constitutional law, 67. *See also* state, the

affect theory, 100

African Americans: January 6 insurrection, 6–7

agrarian way of life, American, 68, 177

Ahmed, Sara, 76, 100

Aitamurto, Kaarina, 190

Aleshkovsky, Yuz, 215

Alfeyev, 24–25, 29, 51

Althusser, Louis, 104

Alyokhina, Maria, 155, *158*

American Civil War: Confederate statuary, 165–69, 173–75; ideology of southern religion, 48–49; origins of neo-Confederate Russophilia, 83–86; role of imaginative literature, 38–39.

See also Confederacy, American; neo-Confederates

American Conservative journal, 15, 52, 64–65

American Freedom Party, 111–12, 121

American Renaissance journal, 75

Americans for Tax Reform, 93

American traditional intellectuals. *See* intellectuals, American traditional

Amis, Martin, 15

anarcho-fascism, 211–12

Andrei Kuraev: Priamaia rech' (Andre Kuraev: Direct Speech) documentary, 157–59

Andrews, Helen, xii–xiii, 15, 27, 50, 64–65, 105, 110, 200

animal imagery: queer subculture in the GULAG, 151–53

Anna Karenina (Tolstoy), 40, 70

anti-blasphemy law (Russia), 155

Anti-Intellectualism in American Life (Hofstadter), 19–20

antinormativity, 33, 45, 66

antipolitics, 78–79. *See also* libertarianism

anti-Semitism: American League of the South, 85–86; Dugin's posited Arktogaya civilization, 125; Eliot's anti-immigrant views, 68; MacDonald equating Jewish identity with anti-white hatred, 121–22; MacDonald's